The Nordic Economic, Social and Political Model

The Nordic model is the 20th-century Scandinavian recipe for combining stable democracies, individual freedom, economic growth and comprehensive systems for social security. But what happens when Sweden and Finland – two countries topping global indexes for competitiveness, productivity, growth, quality of life, prosperity and equality – start doubting themselves and their future? Is the Nordic model at a crossroads?

Historically, consensus, continuity, social cohesion and broad social trust have been hailed as key components for the success and for the self-images of Sweden and Finland. In the contemporary, however, political debates in both countries are increasingly focused on risks, threats and worry. Social disintegration, political polarization, geopolitical anxieties and threat of terrorism are often dominant themes. This book focuses on what appears to be a paradox: countries with low-income differences, high faith in social institutions and relatively high cultural homogeneity becoming fixated on the fear of polarization, disintegration and diminished social trust. Unpacking the presentist discourse of "worry" and a sense of interregnum at the face of geopolitical tensions, digitalization and globalization, as well as challenges to democracy, the chapters take steps back in time and explore the current conjecture through the eyes of historians and social scientists, addressing key aspects of and challenges to both the contemporary and the future Nordic model. In addition, the functioning and efficacy of the participatory democracy and current protocols of decision-making are debated.

This work is essential reading for students and scholars of the welfare state, social reforms and populism, as well as Nordic and Scandinavian studies.

Anu Koivunen is Professor of Gender Studies at the Faculty of Social Science at Tampere University, Finland, and is on a leave of absence from professorship in the Department of Media Studies at Stockholm University, Sweden.

Jari Ojala is Professor of Comparative Business History at the University of Jyväskylä, Finland. He is also Vice Dean at the Faculty of Humanities and Social Sciences, responsible for research and innovations.

Janne Holmén is Associate Professor of History of Education at Uppsala University, Sweden, and researcher at the Institute of Contemporary History, Södertörn University, Sweden.

Perspectives in Economic and Social History

Series Editors: Andrew August and Jari Eloranta

A History of States and Economic Policies in Early Modern Europe
Silvia A. Conca Messina

Fiscal Policy in Early Modern Europe
Portugal in Comparative Context
Rodrigo da Costa Dominguez

Workers, Unions and Truck Wages in British Society
The Fight for Real Wages, 1820–1986
Christopher Frank

Early Modern Overseas Trade and Entrepreneurship
Nordic Trading Companies in the Seventeenth Century
Kaarle Wirta

Credit and Debt in Eighteenth-Century England
An Economic History of Debtors' Prisons
Alexander Wakelam

Luxury, Fashion and the Early Modern Idea of Credit
Edited by Klas Nyberg and Håkan Jakobsson

The Nordic Economic, Social and Political Model
Challenges in the 21st Century
Edited by Anu Koivunen, Jari Ojala and Janne Holmén

North Eurasian Trade in World History, 1660–1860
The Economic and Political Importance of the Baltic Sea
Werner Scheltjens

For more information about this series, please visit www.routledge.com/series/PESH

The Nordic Economic, Social and Political Model

Challenges in the 21st Century

Edited by Anu Koivunen, Jari Ojala and Janne Holmén

Routledge
Taylor & Francis Group

LONDON AND NEW YORK

First published 2021
by Routledge
2 Park Square, Milton Park, Abingdon, Oxon OX14 4RN

and by Routledge
605 Third Avenue, New York, NY 10158

Routledge is an imprint of the Taylor & Francis Group, an informa business

British Library Cataloguing-in-Publication Data
A catalogue record for this book is available from the British Library

Library of Congress Cataloging-in-Publication Data
A catalog record for this book has been requested

ISBN: 978-0-367-13475-4 (hbk)
ISBN: 978-0-367-72440-5 (pbk)
ISBN: 978-0-429-02669-0 (ebk)

Typeset in Bembo
by Apex CoVantage, LLC

Contents

Contributors

Ainur Elmgren is docent in Nordic History. She is currently teaching the didactics of history and social studies at the University of Oulu, Finland. Her fields of expertise include conceptual history, political history and history of identities and nationalism. She defended her doctoral thesis on stereotypes of Swedishness in the Finnish press (1918–1939) at Lund University in 2008.

Jari Eloranta is Professor of Economic History at the University of Helsinki, Finland. He completed his PhD at the European University Institute in Florence, Italy, and he has held academic positions outside of Finland prior to 2018. He has produced over 100 peer-reviewed publications, focusing mostly on the fiscal development of states, crises and Nordic development paths.

Heikki Hiilamo is Professor of Social Policy at the University of Helsinki and Research Professor at the National Institute for Health and Welfare, Finland. His research interests include family policy, poverty, inequality, welfare state research and tobacco control. His articles have appeared in leading journals.

Janne Holmén is Associate Professor of History of Education at Uppsala University, Sweden, and researcher at the Institute of Contemporary History, Södertörn University, Sweden. His research focuses on comparative studies in educational history, with an emphasis on the Nordic countries. He has published studies on Cold War textbooks, reforms of teacher education, as well as mental maps and historical consciousness.

Antero Holmila is an associate professor at the Department of History and Ethnology, University of Jyväskylä, Finland. He received his PhD from Royal Holloway, University of London, in 2008. His fields of expertise include media history, the history and politics of the United States, the Holocaust and Finnish political history, and post-war studies.

Johanna Kantola is Professor of Gender Studies at the Faculty of Social Sciences, Tampere University, Finland. She is the director of the European Research Council (ERC) Consolidator Grant project EUGenDem (2018–2023), which studies European parliament's political groups.

Anu Koivunen is Professor of Gender Studies at the Faculty of Social Science at Tampere University, Finland, and is on a leave of absence from professorship in the Department of Media Studies at Stockholm University, Sweden. She is the PI of the Academy of Finland consortium Flows of power – media as site and agent of politics (2019–2022) and work package leader of "Politicized Intimacies" in *Intimacy in Data-Driven Culture* (Academy of Finland, Division of Strategic Research, 2019–2022).

Henrik Meinander is Professor of History at the University of Helsinki, Finland. He acted as the leader of "Driving forces of democracy. Context and characteristics in the democratization of Finland and Sweden 1890–2020" research programme (Jane and Aatos Erkko Foundation, 2015–2018). He has published numerous monographs and articles on Finnish and Nordic 20th- century history. While earlier focusing on sport, education, biographies and new war history, he has recently published articles on memory culture, security politics and democracy. He is currently writing a biography of the fourfold Finnish Prime Minister Kalevi Sorsa.

Torbjörn Nilsson is Professor of History at Södertörn University, Sweden. His field of expertise is political and ideological history, mainly in the Nordic context, and his publications include books and articles on civil servants in 19th-century Sweden, the Swedish-Norwegian Union, 1814–1905, local politics in Stockholm, state and bureaucracy. He is currently studying Nordic and British conservatism and the democratic breakthrough in Sweden, 1918–1921.

Jari Ojala is Professor of Comparative Business History at the University of Jyväskylä, Finland. He is also Vice Dean at the Faculty of Humanities and Social Sciences, responsible for research and innovations. His areas of expertise include economic, business and maritime history. Currently, he is leading a research project which creates aggregate time series on Finnish early modern economic growth. He has published in major journals in economic and business history and has served as editor-in-chief in *Scandinavian Economic History Review* and in *Scandinavian Journal of History*.

Emilia Palonen is Senior Lecturer at the Department of Political and Economic Studies, University of Helsinki, Finland. Her research focuses on populism, political identities and politics of memory and nationalism in Hungary and Finland. She is currently the PI of Whirl of Knowledge in European Polarised Societies and Politics (WhiKnow, 2019–2022), funded by the Academy of Finland, as well as Now-Time Us-Space: Hegemonic Mobilisations in Central Eastern Europe (2020–2023), funded by Kone Foundation.

Petri Roikonen is a doctoral candidate in economic and social history at the Faculty of Social Sciences, University of Helsinki, Finland. His dissertation is entitled "Dimensions of Inequality: Income Inequality, Social Mobility and Heterogamy in Finland, 1700–2017".

Matti Roitto is a postdoctoral fellow at the Department of History and Ethnology, University of Jyväskylä, Finland. He received his PhD from the
University of Jyväskylä in 2015, with a dissertation on Anglo-American
atomic politics in the immediate post-war era. His other interests include
Finnish-Swedish security policy and relations during the 20th century, parliamentary history, Finnish Cold War political economy, Nordic geopolitics
and history of education.

Pasi Saukkonen is a political scientist working at the City of Helsinki Executive Office, Urban Research and Statistics unit on immigration and immigrants in Finland. He has also been a senior researcher and the director
of the Finnish Foundation for Cultural Policy Research (Cupore) and in
different positions at the University of Helsinki. He holds an adjunct professorship at the University of Helsinki (political science) and at the University
of Jyväskylä (cultural policy). He has published widely on nationalism and
national identity, on local and national integration policies and on politics in
a multicultural society.

Liv Sunnercrantz has been a postdoctoral fellow in sociology at the Department of Media and Social Sciences, University of Stavanger, Norway,
since 2019. Her work falls mainly in the areas of post-foundational discourse theory, studies of populism, sociology of knowledge and sociology
of intellectuals.

Kjell Östberg is Professor Emeritus of History at Södertörn University, Sweden. His areas of expertise include processes of democratization, old and
new social movements, social democracy and party cultures in Europe.

1 Always in crisis, always a solution?

The Nordic model as a political and scholarly concept

Anu Koivunen, Jari Ojala and Janne Holmén

While campaigning for the 2016 US Democratic Party presidential nomination, Senator Bernie Sanders invoked the Nordic countries as a model for future politics. In a debate, he declared, 'I think we should look to countries like Denmark, like Sweden and Norway, and learn from what they have accomplished for their working people.'[1] Hailing the Nordic countries, especially Denmark, as an example of 'democratic socialism',[2] Sanders's vision engendered a heated debate, with political opponents critiquing the implied political agenda, the prime minister of Denmark protesting the idea of Denmark as a socialist country, and journalists and pundits presenting corrective views of the economic and social policies of the Nordic countries.[3] The critiques notwithstanding, the notion of the Nordic model has continued to circulate in US political imaginary, invoked by both left and centre Democratic politicians. For example, Alexandria Ocasio-Cortez, a Democratic representative from New York, promotes her Green New Deal agenda with references to Nordic countries: 'My policies most closely resemble what we see in the U.K., in Norway, in Finland, in Sweden.'[4] In the polarised US political debate of the 21st century, the Nordic countries serve as an imaginary horizon for both a new kind of socialism and a reformed capitalism in the age of accelerated climate change.

However, the idea of the Nordic model as fuel for political imagination and a trope for global comparison and competition is an old one. The Nordic countries – especially Sweden and Denmark – have been invoked by Nordic and foreign actors as a social and economic model for the rest of the world in times of crisis dating back to the Great Depression of the 1930s.[5] In particular, the interplay between the Nordic Social Democrats and the forces on the left and the centre of the US political spectrum has been a driving force behind establishing the idea that there is a Nordic recipe for how to alleviate the ills of capitalism while avoiding the pitfalls of socialism.[6] In the Nordic countries, this discourse about a third way has been adopted by both right- and left-wing governments, and the Nordic model has come to serve as a tool in the global competition and regional and national branding of the 21st century. Both policymakers and economists have rebranded the Nordic model as a benchmark for constant renewal and for 'embracing globalization by sharing risks'.[7] At the World Economic Forum in Davos, 2011, 'the Nordic way' was

DOI: 10.4324/9780429026690-1

touted as a recipe for 'the new reality' – that is, the world in the wake of the 2008 financial crisis and the Eurocrisis.[8] A report, released by a think tank and endorsed by the five Nordic governments, paraded the virtues of countries that top global indexes for competitiveness, productivity, growth, quality of life, prosperity and equality. Rejecting the notion of the Nordic countries as a compromise between capitalism and socialism, it defined the Nordic model as a 'combination of extreme individualism and a strong state that has shaped the fertile ground for an efficient market economy'. The report highlighted social cohesion and broad social trust as key for the Nordic way, enabling resilience through constant renewal.[9] In 2013, *The Economist* termed the Nordic countries 'the next supermodel' for 'reinventing their model of capitalism' and 'a blueprint' for politicians from both the right and the left of 'how to reform the public sector, making the state more efficient and responsive'.[10]

In these framings, the Nordic model appears to have two sides. On the one hand, it is a set of crisis narratives; the model is perpetually called into question and seen as facing daunting challenges. Furthermore, its economic foundation is threatened by globalisation, an ageing population and the digital revolution. On the other hand, the Nordic model is invoked as a recipe for dealing with these future challenges.[11] Both as a set of policies and as self-branding, the Nordic model has had an institutional footing in official parliamentary and governmental cooperation since the 1950s. While the political relevance of Nordic cooperation waned after the Cold War and European integration, the actors involved in the many layers of transnational cooperation – parliaments, governments, academia and civil society – continue to invest in Nordicness.[12]

This book joins in this tradition by asking whether the 21st-century Scandinavian recipe for combining stable democracies, individual freedom, economic growth and comprehensive systems for social security is at a crossroads in the current conjuncture of the global digital economy, geopolitical tensions and changes in political culture, as well as challenges to democracy. The chapters were written in the aftermath of the global financial crisis and the Eurocrisis and amid a sense of accelerating global unrest (war in Syria, the Russian annexation of Ukrainian Crimea in 2014, the continuing war in Eastern Ukraine), threats of European disintegration (Brexit, European Union member states breaching the rule of law) and the intensifying political polarisation and disruption of party structures in many countries, but before the COVID-19 pandemic. In this framework, this book asks how the Nordic economic, social and political model is currently challenged as both an idea and a practice. The underlying question, following German sociologist Wolfgang Streeck's invocation of Antonio Gramsci, is whether we are living in an age of *interregnum*, an era between systemic changes. In other words, we examine whether we are in 'a period of tremendous insecurity in which the accustomed chains of cause and effect are no longer in force, and unexpected, dangerous and grotesquely abnormal events may occur at any moment'.[13] For Streeck and many other commentators of a 'democratic decline' in the 21st century, the present reads as a period of dramatic, foundational changes in the global economy and political systems.[14] According to Streeck, *interregnum* is characterised by a sense of inability to predict the future as 'disparate lines of development run unreconciled, parallel to one another, resulting in unstable configurations of many kinds, and chains of surprising events take the place of predictable structures'.[15] This book asks how this age affects the Nordic model as a trope of political imagination and a vocabulary for futurity.

This book analyses the Nordic model as an empirical, policy-based phenomenon and as a political idea and a trope for the imagination through the lenses of social scientists and historians. While exploring contemporary economic, social and political challenges, the emphasis is, however, on historicising the presentist narratives of crisis and tracing longer and diverse developments.

The emergence of the Nordic model

Although fluid as a geographical referent, *Norden*, as the Nordic region is called in Scandinavian, primarily refers to the five nation-states of Denmark, Iceland, Finland, Norway and Sweden, as well as the autonomous territories of the Faroe Islands, Greenland and the Åland islands. However, the Nordic identity has an appeal outside of this traditional core. For example, Estonian youths are more likely to identify as Nordic than as Baltic, and voices emphasising the Nordic identity of Scotland, as well as tangible Nordic-Scottish political cooperation, have been increasing in the last decade.[16] Although the Nordic countries are often regarded as fairly homogeneous from the outside, from within, the notion of a single economic and social model can be called into question. Is there one model? Are there many models, but is the Swedish model the most well known? What is Nordic about the model? What does it entail? And are these national models simple, unique and – moreover – only associated with positive connotations?[17]

Nevertheless, the concept of the Nordic model circulates and has political currency internationally, as well as in the Nordic countries, where it operates as a signifier and vehicle for various political goals, a tool of transnational comparison – that is, to examine the policies of neighbouring countries – and a shared resource for regional and national self-branding.[18] The model is a productive and performative concept; it is mediated by histories and imaginaries and mobilised to engender policies.[19]

The emergence and development of the Nordic model as a concept in international discussion can be roughly outlined by a quantitative bibliometric analysis using Google Books Ngrams.[20] As illustrated in Figure 1.1, there has been a gradual increase in the use of the term, Nordic model, in international discussions over the 1990s and the early 2000s.

Apparently, the Nordic model concept first surfaced in Google Books' English corpus in the late 1970s. Although Google Books Ngrams presents many challenges, these results are in line with previous research, showing an increase in discussions over the Nordic and Swedish model.[21] Several hype-cycles can be traced in these discussions; after a first hype during the late 1970s

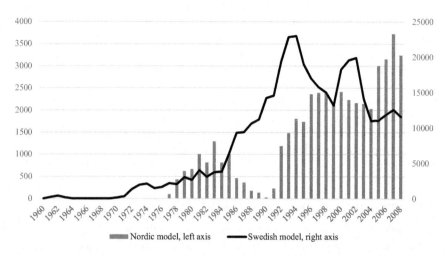

Figure 1.1 Appearance of 'Nordic model' (left axis) and 'Swedish model' (right axis) in Google Books Ngrams from 1960 to 2008 (Index: Nordic Model 1977 = 100).

Source: Google Books Ngrams (https://books.google.com/ngrams). Cited 15 September 2019.

Note: Google Books Ngrams traces the relative share of the concept used in the whole corpus. As these shares are relatively small (0.000000145% in 1977), we used an index series (Nordic model 1977=100) instead to show the changes in time. Google Ngrams taps all the texts using the phrases 'Nordic Model' or 'Swedish model'; thus, they include ones that do not have a societal content. Nevertheless, the figures mostly relate to texts that are interesting from the perspective of this book. Furthermore, Ngrams refers in this case only to books published in English; thus, the widespread discussion in the Nordic languages is omitted.

and the early 1980s, the Nordic model faded in discussions, but it rapidly rose again during the early 1990s. These hype-cycles correlate with periods of economic crisis, strengthening the argument that the Nordic model is primarily referenced when there is a perceived need to find alternative ways of organising society and the economy. According to Google Books (Figure 1.1), the Nordic model concept was mentioned over 30 times more frequently in texts in the 2000s than in the late 1970s. As these are relative shares from the whole corpus, the absolute increase in the use of the concept was even more dramatic.

Discussions of the Nordic model have had different emphases during different decades. The earliest books found by Google Books Ngrams used the term while discussing, for example, environmental education in the Nordic countries[22] and macroeconomic policies on inflation, whereas afterwards the topic was discussed more in relation with the welfare state.[23] Furthermore, the Nordic model has its roots in the older Swedish model concept; as can also be clearly seen in Figure 1.1, this concept appeared in international discussions in the early 1960s. The Swedish model was far more frequently discussed in the literature than the Nordic model throughout the 1970s, 1980s, 1990s and the 2000s. Even though there was a clear declining trend in the use of the term

'Swedish model' and an increase in the use of the term 'Nordic model' in the early 2000s, Google Ngrams found six times more mentions of the Swedish model than the Nordic model.

Although the Nordic model concept is only a few decades old, the common traits it describes from the social models of the Nordic countries have much older roots. Klaus Petersen has shown that the Nordic countries began to synchronise their social policies in the early 1900s through regular meetings of public servants, covering topics such as workers' accident insurance (from 1907), the protection of children (from 1919), general social insurance (from 1935) and unemployment insurance (from 1947). In the 1920s and the 1930s, Denmark was the leader and reference point for the other Nordic countries, a position that was taken over by Sweden after 1945. From 1953, Nordic social policy cooperation was subordinated to the newly founded Nordic Council. From at least the late 1940s, the Nordic countries began to describe their welfare societies as a model for Western Europe. For example, Pauli Kettunen has shown how Nordic delegates to the International Labour Organization during the 1950s depicted their countries as a homogeneous area for social and economic policies.[24]

Thus, the Nordic model, regardless of how it is defined, has to be seen as the outcome of a century-long process of voluntary cooperation.[25] The Nordic countries have influenced each other's policies and have learned from each other's experiences but have been free to apply bespoke national solutions when it suited them. This explains why it is almost always possible to find at least one exception among the Nordic countries that defies any attempt to strictly define the Nordic model. Such a genetic view of the Nordic model is articulated by historians, such as Mary Hilson. She uses the Nordic model as a central concept in her attempt to write the history of the Nordic countries as a *Geschichtsregion* while trying to avoid a traditional national historiographical framework.[26]

The notion of a distinctive Nordic social model began to attract international attention during the Great Depression of the 1930s. For several decades, it was most commonly referred to as the 'middle way', a term coined by Marquis Childs in 1936.[27] As Carl Marklund describes, Sweden was particularly well positioned to benefit from the goodwill bestowed upon the Nordic countries since it had created the American-Swedish News Exchange (ASNE), which actively promoted the country in the United States. High-level Swedish politicians used their country's celebrated position as a middle way in social policies in order to gain acceptance for their less popular middle way in foreign policy after the Second World War, namely their neutrality between the North Atlantic Treaty Organization (NATO) and the Soviet bloc. In 1949, ASNE published a book called *Sweden – Model for a World*, but, as noted earlier, the Swedish model concept did not come into broader use until the late 1960s and the early 1970s (Figure 1.1).[28] A decade later, when the Nordic vision of social organisation was perceived to be under threat, as Bo Stråth has confirmed, the Nordic model concept started to spread.[29] In addition, several other concepts have been used to describe the Nordic countries and the particularity of their societies, most commonly the welfare state and the *folkhem* (literally people's home).

It seems that the Nordic model concept had its breakthrough as a political battle cry at the 29th meeting of the Nordic Council in 1981. There, leading figures in the Nordic Social Democratic parties rallied around the Nordic model in the general debate. The president of the Norwegian Storting, Guttorm Hansen, initiated the debate by urging the Nordic Council to cooperate in order to protect the Nordic social model, which, for the first time, was under threat from unemployment. The prime minister of Denmark, Anker Jørgensen, answered by defining the common core of the Nordic model as democracy, welfare state, peace, solidarity with the Third World and, despite the differences between the Nordic countries, a strong cultural affiliation. The leader of the Swedish Social Democrats, Olof Palme, then described how the Nordic model was under threat from war, economic crisis and conservatism. According to him, the model played an important role in a wider international context. To the list of threats, Finland's Ulf Sundqvist added that the Nordic economies were especially vulnerable to international developments and needed to cooperate in order to adapt to the energy crisis, increasing automation and the rise of the information society.[30] Thus, leading figures of the Social Democratic parties in each country not only were active in proliferating the Nordic model concept but also detected threats that would materialise on scale decades later, when they would return in reinvigorated discussions about the crisis of the Nordic model.

Thus, the Nordic model concept was born during a period when the Nordic societies saw their model threatened by an economic recession, the rising tensions in the Cold War and the conservative or neoliberal offensive from Reaganism and Thatcherism. Most of the challenges to the Nordic model identified by leading Social Democrats in 1981 are strikingly familiar to the concerns of today. However, there are also differences. In 1981, inflation was considered a serious threat, while immigration was not mentioned, except indirectly as a question of solidarity. In contrast, inflation was not considered a major threat to the Nordic model in the 2010s, but the impact of immigration was discussed as both an economic and a cultural issue.

Swedish Social Democrats began to use the Nordic model concept more widely during the centre-right government of 1976–1982, which was the first time the Social Democrats slipped into opposition since the 1930s. As the prime minister of Sweden in 1969–1976, Palme actively used the Swedish model as a tool in his foreign policy and as an example of a middle way between Soviet socialism and capitalism. Being in opposition in 1981, he was in no position to conduct official Swedish foreign policy. However, as the head of the Swedish delegation to the Nordic Council, he could advocate for joint Nordic policies. In the process, he used the Nordic model concept as he had used the Swedish model concept as a minister. Therefore, the transition from the Swedish to the Nordic model might be interpreted as having been driven by a need to join forces to combat strong challenges, as well as a pragmatic adaptation of the political vocabulary from the Swedish to the Nordic arena.

As the political hegemony of the Swedish Social Democrats was challenged by forces from the centre-right in the early 2000s, Sweden's conservative prime minister in 2006–2014, Fredrik Reinfeldt, appropriated the Nordic model in his political rhetoric. The Social Democratic Party countered by registering *den nordiska modellen* as a commercial trademark in Sweden. Objections from the Nordic Council, among others, were rejected by the Swedish Patent and Registration Office. However, the trademark protection does not extend to political use.[31] It can be claimed that, although Social Democratic parties have generally been on the retreat in the 21st century – even while leading governments in Sweden, Finland and Denmark in 2019 – their championed welfare state model has gained wide acceptance across the political spectrum. In fact, parties on the far right have embraced the basic tenets of the Nordic model. In their opposition to immigration and humanitarian asylum policies, right-wing populist parties employ the rhetoric of welfare nationalism, claiming that immigration is the main threat against the Nordic model.[32]

The Nordic model in research

As evident from the Google Books Ngrams data in Figure 1.1, over the decades since the early 1990s, the Nordic model has gained ample attention in social scientific research. An analysis of the appearance of the Nordic and Swedish models in the Web of Science database, as depicted in Table 1.1 and Figure 1.2, further refines this picture, capturing the evolution of the concept in different disciplines.[33]

As shown in Table 1.1, the two concepts are favoured by different disciplines. The notion of the Swedish model is most common in business and economics

Table 1.1 Appearance of the Nordic and Swedish models in journal articles.

Research area	Total number of articles	Number of articles on the Nordic model	Number of articles on the Swedish model	Per mil Nordic model	Per mil Swedish model
Business & Economics	961,506	265	1,206	0.28	1.25
Education & Educational Research	492,224	62	204	0.13	0.41
International Relations	119,202	24	34	0.20	0.29
Public Administration	114,571	61	125	0.53	1.09
Social Issues	166,900	37	52	0.22	0.31
Social Work	110,268	37	82	0.34	0.74
Sociology	172,384	45	134	0.26	0.78
History	306,358	29	62	0.09	0.20
Total	2,443,413	493	1,807	0.20	0.74

Source: Web of Science. Cited 15 September 2019.

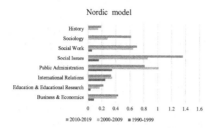

Figure 1.2 Share of articles using the Nordic and Swedish models as concepts in certain research areas from 1990 to 2019 (per mil from all articles in different time cohorts).

Source: Web of Science. Cited 15 September 2019.

and in public administration. In these fields, the Swedish model is mentioned more than once per every thousand articles published in the Web of Science. The Nordic model concept, in turn, is most frequently used in articles dealing with public administration, education and sociology. Figure 1.2 shows how the use of these concepts in different research areas changed over time. Only in public administration research do both concepts seem to have declined during the 2010s, while the use of these concepts increased in the 2010s in many disciplines, especially in research dealing with social work and social issues.

Most articles analysing the Nordic model in our sample ($N = 493$) deal with voluntary associations, donors interests and globalisation affecting European social models,[34] whereas most of the cited articles analysing the Swedish model ($N = 1,807$) analyse customer behaviour in Sweden and Swedish multinational enterprises.[35] Thus, the Swedish model is more widely used in terms of corporate strategies; this has also been noted by Michael Porter in his famous book on the competitive advantage of nations.[36] Over time, interestingly, we can also see a shift wherein the Nordic model is less associated with international relations and increasingly associated with social policies. In any case, the Web of Science (Figure 1.2) indicates the wide and diversified currency of the concepts across a range of disciplines.

In the Nordic context, scholarship on the Nordic model is a vast and lively field – impossible to subsume in a way that accurately mirrors its diversity and complexity. Scholars across disciplines have investigated the histories and futures of the Nordic welfare state visions and policies, participating in an ongoing discursive construction, de- and reconstruction of the model.

In his book of 1990, *The Three Worlds of Welfare Capitalism*, Gösta Esping-Andersen identified what he termed 'Scandinavian' welfare system as a distinct model, which he characterised as social democratic.[37] Also, in a more recent 2013 account by Nikolai Brandal, Øivind Bratberg and Dag Einar Thorsen, the history of the Nordic welfare state reads as a narrative of Swedish, Danish and Norwegian social democracy. Although there are differences between the policies of the different Nordic countries, Brandal, Bratberg and Thorsen argue, they are united by a common social democratic ambition to eradicate the evils of industrial capitalist society – namely, 'want, disease, ignorance, squalor, and idleness'.[38] The authors emphasise that centre- and right-wing parties, when in power after 1970, have maintained most of the social democratic policies.

According to Johannes Kananen, summarising an extensive field of welfare and social policy research, the history of the Nordic welfare state developed in three phases. Until the 1960s, increased emancipation and equality were achieved with the help of collectivist means. However, by then, collectivism had begun to be perceived as a constraint, and policies of individual emancipation were conducted in the 1970s and the 1980s. Since the 1990s, the Nordic welfare states have come under pressure from the international competition state paradigm, which places economic goals, such as competitiveness, before social goals, such as equality.[39]

In *Changing Social Equality. The Nordic Welfare Model in the 21st Century* (2012), Jon Kvist, Johan Fritzell, Bjørn Hvinden and Olli Kangas conclude that support for equality and welfare policies is still high in the Nordic countries, although it is even higher in Southern Europe. While the Nordic countries are still good at mitigating old social risks, such as large families and advanced age, they are less good at managing new risk factors for poverty, such as immigration. Overall, the Nordic countries are still more economically egalitarian than most other countries, except the Netherlands, which is even better in this regard.[40]

Besides economic equality, gender equality has been frequently discussed as an important dimension of the Nordic model. However, this narrative has been problematised as feminist and, more recently, postcolonial scholarship has shown that the self-image of being equal has been a hindrance to addressing gender inequalities and discriminatory practices.[41] As Kari Melby, Anna-Birte Ravn and Christina Carlsson Wetterberg conclude in *Gender Equality and Welfare Politics in Scandinavia: The Limits of Political Ambition?* (2008), gender equality in the Scandinavian welfare model has historically often entailed equality based on gender difference.[42] At the same time, equality politics has meant 'empowerment and inclusion of some women, and marginalisation and exclusion of others' as Nordic welfare states supported gender hierarchies among ethnic 'others'.[43] Diana Mulinari, Suvi Keskinen and other postcolonial feminist scholars in *Complying with Colonialism: Gender, Race and Ethnicity in the Nordic Region* (2009) and *Undoing Homogeneity in the Nordic Region: Migration, Difference, and the Politics of Solidarity* (2019) have questioned complacent monolithic accounts of gender equality as well as narratives of exceptional homogeneity characterising much scholarship on the Nordic model.[44]

The criticisms notwithstanding, the Nordic model continues to be discussed among scholars as a recipe for the future, such as for how to become best in class in the globalised knowledge economy. In their *Learning Factories: The Nordic Model of Manufacturing* (2018), Halvor Holtskog, Elias G. Carayannis, Aris Kaloudis and Geir Ringen promote the Nordic model of the labour market and work organisation as a system of wage negotiations between trade unions and employer federations, safety nets of health insurance, welfare benefits, pensions, job mobility and career experimentation combined with job safety, democratic decision-making processes and high employee participation in the organisation of work. This model is depicted as fostering innovation and creativity, allowing high-cost countries to compete on the international market and providing key to the re-industrialisation of the Western world.[45] As another example, *Sustainable Modernity. The Nordic Model and Beyond* (2018), a volume by scholars from the humanities, the social sciences and evolutionary science, rebrands the narrative of the Nordic model for the age of the climate crisis, presenting it as a recipe for a well-being society. In this account, Norway, Sweden and Denmark stand as icons of 'socially sustainable Nordic modernity', combining competition and cooperation – the familiar elements of economists' accounts – with their resilience in the age of globalisation, cultural collisions, the digital economy, the fragmentation of the work/life division and often intrusive EU regulation.[46]

'If the strict criteria of social research are applied, it is impossible to say that a Nordic Model has ever existed', Norwegian sociologist Lars Mjøset contended in a 1992 seminar *The Nordic Model – Does It Have a Future? Has It Ever Existed?* held in Helsinki. However, he continued, 'the Nordic model has and does exist as a pan-nationalistic idea, and in the context of a regional identity movement, it may gain strength in the future'.[47] Indeed, the 1990s saw an emergence of a rich, comparative literature on the development of the Nordic welfare state, in both intra-Nordic and European perspectives. As Pauli Kettunen has concluded, discourse of competitive state and 'the making of a globally competitive "us"' increased the use of the concept of the model.[48] In the context of European integration, the Nordic Council of Ministers and the many Nordic research-funding bodies launched networks and research programmes examining the distinctiveness and the new challenges for the Nordic model.[49] At the same time, historians became interested in historicising the welfare state, and Øystein Sørensen and Bo Stråth discussed the notion of 'Nordic model' in the context of culture and identity work.[50] A special issue of *Scandinavian Journal of History* entitled *Nordic Welfare States 1900–2000* (2001) as well as the 2005 anthology *Nordic Model of Welfare: A Historical Reappraisal* marked a turn to welfare history in studies of the Nordic model as long-term Nordic research networks introduced conceptual history, social movements, religion as well as gender history as interpretive frameworks.[51]

The broad and intense scholarly interest in the Nordic model was epitomised in the multidisciplinary, cross-national research project 'The Nordic Welfare State – Historical Foundations and Future Challenges (NordWel)', a NordForsk-funded Nordic Centre of Excellence (2007–2012), which studied the social security and service systems, societal patterns and normative value systems of Denmark, Finland, Iceland, Norway and Sweden. The Centre published a range of anthologies on workfare, education, bureaucracy, migration, welfare nationalism and social policies.[52] In *Beyond Welfare State Models: Transnational Historical Perspectives on Social Policy* (2011), Pauli Kettunen and Klaus Petersen, the directors of the centre, described the comparative welfare state research as 'a veritable industry' obsessed with models.[53] Questioning the use of models as an analytical framework for research, Kettunen and Petersen discuss the Nordic model as 'a good case for discussing the analytical limits and political meanings of model comparisons' and a case for studying how transnational processes influence national policies.

Combining perspectives from the aforementioned strands of research, this volume continues to interrogate the Nordic model as Nordic identity work while making a historically rooted attempt to charter the possible futures of the Nordic model that might be the outcome of the present crisis.

The structure of the book

In this book, we address the Nordic model as political imagination and as policy practice by bringing together three topical debates: the past and future of the Nordic model as a social, economic and political model; the force and effects of populist politics on the political system; and contemporary concern over political instability. Although these debates are usually distinct, the key idea of this volume is to investigate the Nordic model at their intersection. Drawing from the rich interdisciplinary literature on the Nordic model and on the Scandinavian welfare state, we go beyond discussing its economic and financial foundations and detailed policies to focus instead on its democratic legitimacy and questions of political efficacy and social cohesion.

In Chapters 1–5 of the book, the Nordic model is discussed in terms of democratisation and forms of governance.[54] Henrik Meinander analyses the challenges to the Nordic model posed by the globalised economy, geopolitical tensions and national political cultures. Next, in her investigation of how the *land of bliss* concept has been used in visions and nostalgic memories of the welfare state, Ainur Elmgren approaches the Nordic model as a foundational yet changing social narrative. What used to be a progressive project of the future has become the lost golden age of the past. Then, while worry over the future of the welfare state dominates the public sphere, the question of whether the Nordic countries have actually experienced a regression from equality does not have a simple and straightforward answer, as illustrated by Petri Roikonen, Jari Ojala and Jari Eloranta, who compare economic data on equality with the debate on equality in academia and major daily newspapers. The geopolitical landscape is discussed in the light of NATO debates by Matti Roitto and Antero Holmila.

Chapters 6–10 of the book focus on the key developments within politics, the party structure and the mediated public sphere. Kjell Östberg discusses the development of social democracy, describing how the Nordic Social Democratic parties have experienced losses in influence and electoral support for decades and how they have fundamentally reformed their old welfare policies. Torbjörn Nilsson analyses how Nordic conservative parties have reacted to the challenge from right-wing populism, comparing the threats and available strategies during two distinct periods in the development of the Nordic welfare state: the 1930s and the first decades of the new millennium. The current wave of populism in the Nordic countries is also analysed by Emilia Palonen and Liv Sunnercrantz, who trace the transformation of populist parties from opposing welfare statism to promoting an anti-immigration agenda, sometimes with welfare chauvinist undertones. Pasi Saukkonen discusses how cultural policies in different Nordic countries address the increasing ethnic and cultural diversity and how neo-nationalist political ideas influence Nordic cultural policies. Anu Koivunen's chapter focuses on the language of politicians and journalists in identifying the public debate and social media in particular as key sites and agents of polarisation, division and extreme opinions.

Chapters 11–13 of the book focuses on policies that envision a renegotiation of the Nordic model. Johanna Kantola analyses gender policies, highlighting the paradoxical gap between progressive gender discourses and policies in the Nordic countries, and, for example, their gender-polarised labour markets and high rates of domestic violence. She also discusses the effects of recent waves of neoliberalism, conservatism and nationalism on Nordic gender policies. Pursuing the question of Nordic distinctiveness, Heikki Hiilamo investigates how the Nordic societies are preparing for unemployment caused by automation, yet another emerging risk factor. In the final chapter, Janne Holmén analyses how government planning in Norway, Sweden and Finland envisions the adaptation of the educational system to the challenges and possibilities posed by rapid technological advances.

At the threshold of the 2020s, the Nordic model is once again perceived to be in crisis, and once again it continues to have political currency as political imagination, surfacing as a reference point both in the Nordic countries and abroad. Beyond connoting something valuable yet threatened or something to be reformed and defended, it is difficult to predict where the Nordic model will be heading in the coming decade. It is also too early to assess the effects and consequences of the COVID-19 pandemic. On the one hand, the Nordic model embodies a political vision of a society in which consensual decision-making engenders policies that are able to alleviate social and economic inequalities. On the other hand, it highlights its inherent adaptability, underlining its ability to accommodate and survive change and crises.

Acknowledgements

This book is a result of 'Driving forces of democracy. Context and characteristics in the democratization of Finland and Sweden 1890–2020', a research programme funded by Jane and Aatos Erkko Foundation and The Foundation for Baltic and East European Studies (Östersjöstiftelse) in 2015–2018. The editors wish to express their gratitude to these foundations for their generous support.

Notes

1 *Washington Post* 13 October 2015.
2 Moody 2016.
3 See e.g. Yglesias 2015, Tassinari 2015, Swanson 2015, Tharoor 2015. On the Nordic response, see Acher 2015.
4 Cooper 2019.
5 Rom-Jensen 2017, Marklund 2010, Marklund & Petersen 2013.
6 Andersson 2009, Andersson & Hilson 2009, Lloyd 2011, Brandal, Bratberg & Thorsen 2013.
7 See the title for Andersen et al. 2007.
8 WEF 2011.
9 Ibid., 3. Similarly, a group of Finnish economists named globalisation and the rapidly ageing population as unprecedented threats to the welfare state but described the virtue of the Nordic model as its 'ability to reconcile risks and uncertainties with openness and the market economy' (Andersen et al. 2007, 156). See also the 2014 report by Nordic economists for the Nordic Council that, while downplaying the distinctiveness and uniformity of the model, hailed its capacity 'to reform and adjust' as the key feature of the Nordic model: 'The Nordics have a strong track record in adjusting to the pressures of structural change' (Valkonen & Vihriälä 2014, 348).
10 Wooldridge 2013, The Economist 2013.
11 Kettunen 2012.
12 Götz & Haggrén 2009, Strang 2016.
13 Streeck 2017, 14.
14 'Is Democracy in Decline?' was the title of the twenty-fifth anniversary issue of *The Journal of Democracy* (Plattner 2015). See also Krastev 2017, Norris 2017, Mounk 2018, Levitsky & Ziblatt 2018, Runciman 2018. For Nordic discussions, see Forsgård (ed.) 2017, Gelin & Åsard 2019.
15 Streeck 2017, 14.
16 Estonian Human Development Report 2016/2017, Widman 2013, Scottish Government 2017.
17 On a 'Finnish model', see Andersson, Kosonen & Vartiainen 1993, Saari 2006, Bergholm 2009.
18 Regarding branding, see Marklund & Petersen 2013, Harvard & Stadius 2013c.
19 Regarding the notion of the Nordic region as 'a mediated region', see Harvard & Stadius 2013a, 2013b.
20 Due to linguistic variety, this method is not suitable for analysing domestic discussions on the Nordic model in the Nordic countries nor does it tap all texts written for an international audience. Furthermore, Google Books Ngrams registers all conceivable uses of the search term, some of which are unrelated to the social and economic Nordic model. Nevertheless, they can be used to track the general trends in the discussions.
21 For example, Stråth 1993.
22 Nordic Council of Ministers 1977.
23 Lundberg 1978, Paunio & Haltunen 1976.
24 Petersen 2006, 67–71, 86, Kettunen 2013.
25 A recent overview of different aspects of this cooperation can be found in Strang 2016.
26 Hilson 2008.
27 Childs 1934, 1936.
28 Marklund 2013a.
29 Stråth 1993.
30 Nordiska rådets svenska delegation 1981, Nordisk råd 1981, 64, 72, 120.
31 Patent och Registreringverket.
32 For Nordic welfare nationalism and its 'others', see e.g. Pyrhönen 2015, Keskinen, Tuori, Irni & Mulinari 2009; Keskinen, Norocel & Jørgensen 2016.

33 The database has its shortages, including linguistic ones since it consists of articles published in established journals in English. Nevertheless, a search identified 2,735 articles using the Nordic model concept and 10,507 articles using the Swedish model concept. Web of Science traces concepts from titles, abstracts and keywords only. The Nordic model concept has become so successful in attracting interdisciplinary attention that it has even been adopted by the sciences, such as through the 'the Nordic model of dairy cow metabolism' (Danfær et al. 2005), which is far removed from its original use in labour market policies. To identify the social, economic and political content we wanted to study, our analysis was limited to eight partly overlapping research areas representing 17%–18% of all articles in the database. A single article can be included in several categories in Web of Science, such as in both history and economics. In the total column in Table 1.1, these overlaps have been removed.
34 Curtis, Baer & Grabb 2001, 783–805, Berthélemy 2006, Sapir 2006.
35 Fornell 1992, Andersson, Forsgren & Holm 2002, Anderson, Fornell & Rust 1997.
36 Porter 2011.
37 Esping-Andersson 1990, 26–29.
38 Brandal, Bratberg & Thorsen 2013, 188.
39 Kananen 2014, 163–164.
40 Kvist, Fritzell, Hvinden & Kangas (eds.) 2012, 61–62, 177, 204.
41 E.g. Allén 1992, Melby, Ravn & Wetterberg 2008, Mulinari, Keskinen, Irni & Tuori 2009.
42 Melby, Ravn & Wetterberg 2008, 1.
43 Ibid., 15, Mulinari 2008.
44 Mulinari, Keskinen, Irni & Tuori 2009, Keskinen, Skaptadóttir & Toivanen 2019.
45 Holtskog, Carayannis, Kaloudis & Ringen 2018, 2–3.
46 Witoszek & Midttun 2018.
47 Mjøset 1992, 652.
48 Kettunen 2011a, 16. See also Kettunen 1998, 2006, 2012.
49 For important anthologies summarising comparative Nordic research projects, see Kautto et al. 1999, 2001.
50 Stråth 1993, Sørensen & Stråt 1997.
51 Christiansen & Petersen 2001, Christiansen, Petersen, Edling & Haave (eds.), 2006. For conceptual history of the welfare state, see Edling 2019.
52 Blomberg & Kildal 2011, Suszycki 2011, Jønsson, Onasch, Pellander & Wickström 2013, Buchardt, Markkola & Valtonen 2013, Marklund 2013b, Jónsson & Stefánsson 2013, Kettunen, Kuhnle & Ren 2014.
53 Kettunen & Petersen 2011, 6. See also NordWel 2007–2012.
54 For context, see Aylott (ed.) 2014.

References

Acher, John, 2015: "Nordic Nirvana: Børnie Sanders 'Speaks Our Language'" in *Politico. eu*, 15 October 2015. www.politico.eu/article/bernie-sanders-denmark-sweden-norway-welfare-state/ [Accessed 2 March 2020].

Allén, Tuovi, 1992: *The Nordic Model of Gender Equality: The Welfare State, Patriarchy and Unfinished Emancipation*. Helsinki: Työväen taloudellinen tutkimuslaitos.

Andersen, Torben M., Holmström, Bengt, Honkapohja, Seppo, Korkman, Sixten, Honkapohja, Söderströmm Hans Tson & Vartiainen, Juhana, 2007: *The Nordic Model: Embracing Globalization and Sharing Risks*. Helsinki: ETLA.

Anderson, Eugene W., Fornell, Claes & Rust, Roland T., 1997: "Customer Satisfaction, Productivity, and Profitability: Differences between Goods and Services" in *Marketing Science*, 16:2, 129–145.

Andersson, Jan-Otto, Kosonen, Pekka & Vartiainen, Juhana, 1993: *The Finnish Model of Economic and Social Policy. From Emulation to Crash.* Meddelanden från Ekonomisk-stats vetenskapliga fakulteten vid Åbo Akademi A:401. Åbo: Åbo Akademi.

Andersson, Jenny, 2009: "Nordic Nostalgia and Nordic Light: The Swedish Model as Utopia 1930–2007" in *Scandinavian Journal of History*, 34:3, 229–245.

Andersson, Jenny & Hilson, Mary, 2009: "Images of Sweden and the Nordic Countries" in *Scandinavian Journal of History*, 34:3, 219–228.

Andersson, Ulf, Forsgren, Mats & Holm, Ulf, 2002: "The Strategic Impact of External Networks: Subsidiary Performance and Competence Development in the Multinational Corporation" in *Strategic Management Journal*, 23:11, 979–996.

Aylott, Nicholas (ed.) 2014: *Models of Democracy in Nordic and Baltic Europe: Political Institutions and Discourse.* Farnham: Ashgate.

Bergholm, Tapio, 2009: "The Making of the Finnish Model" in *Scandinavian Journal of History*, 34:1, 29–48.

Berthélemy, Jean-Claude, 2006: "Bilateral Donors' Interest vs. Recipients' Development Motives in Aid Allocation: Do All Donors Behave the Same?" in *Review of Development Economics*, 10:2, 179–194.

Blomberg, Helena & Kildal, Nanna (eds.) 2011: *Workfare and Welfare State Legitimacy.* Nord-Wel Studies in Historical Welfare State Research 1. Helsinki: NordWel.

Brandal, Nikolai, Bratberg, Øivind & Thorsen, Dag Einar, 2013: *The Nordic Model of Social Democracy.* Basingstoke: Palgrave Macmillan.

Buchardt, Mette, Markkola, Pirjo & Valtonen, Heli (eds.) 2013: *Education, State and Citizenship.* NordWel Studies in Historical Welfare State Research 4. Helsinki: NordWel.

Childs, Marquis, 1934: *Sweden: Where Capitalism Is Controlled.* New York: John Day.

Childs, Marquis, 1936: *Sweden: The Middle Way.* New Haven, CT: Yale University Press.

Christiansen, Niels Finn & Petersen, Klaus, 2001: "Preface. The Nordic Welfare States: A Historical Reappraisal" in *Scandinavian Journal of History*, 26:3, 153–156.

Christiansen, Niels Finn, Petersen, Klaus, Edling, Nils & Haave, Per (eds.) 2006: *The Nordic Model of Welfare: A Historical Reappraisal.* Copenhagen: Museum Tusculanum Press.

Cooper, Anderson, 2019: "Alexandria Ocasio-Cortez: The Rookie Congresswoman Challenging the Democratic Establishment" in *CBSnews.com*, 6 January 2019. www.cbsnews.com/news/alexandria-ocasio-cortez-the-rookie-congresswoman-challenging-the-democratic-establishment-60-minutes-interview-full-transcript-2019-01-06/ [Accessed 2 March 2020].

Curtis, James E., Baer, Douglas E. & Grabb, Edward G., 2001: "Nations of Joiners: Explaining Voluntary Association Membership in Democratic Societies" in *American Sociological Review*, 66:6, 783–805.

Danfær Allan Christian, Huhtanen, Pekka, Uden, Peter, Sveinbjornsson, Johánnes & Volden, Harald, 2005: "The Nordic Dairy Cow Model, Karoline – Description" in Ermian Kebreab, Jan Dijkstra, André Bannink, Walter J. J. Gerrits & James France (eds.) *Nutrient Digestion and Utilization in Farm Animals – Modelling Approaches.* Wallingford: CABI Publishing, 383–407.

Edling, Nils (ed.) 2019: *The Changing Meanings of the Welfare State. Histories of a Key Concept in the Nordic Countries.* London: Berghahn Books.

Esping-Andersson, Gösta, 1990: *The Three Worlds of Welfare Capitalism.* Cambridge: Polity Press.

Estonian Human Development Report, 2016/2017: *Estonia at the Age of Migration. 4.5. Identity in an Open World.* https://2017.inimareng.ee/en/estonia-at-the-age-of-migration/ [Accessed 2 March 2020].

Fornell, Claes, 1992: "A National Customer Satisfaction Barometer: The Swedish Experience" in *Journal of Marketing*, 56:1, 6–21.

Forsgård, Nils-Erik, 2017: *Demokratins öde – Demokratian kohtalo.* Helsingfors: Förlaget.

Gelin, Martin & Åsard, Erik, 2019: *Hotet mot demokratin. Högerpopulismens återkomst i Europa och USA.* Lund: Historiska Media.

Götz, Norbert & Haggrén, Heidi (eds.) 2009: *Regional Cooperation and International Organizations. The Nordic Model in Transnational Alignment.* London and New York: Routledge.

Harvard, Johan & Stadius, Peter (eds.) 2013a: *Communicating the North: Media Structures and Images in the Making of the Nordic Region.* Burlington: Ashgate.

Harvard, Johan & Stadius, Peter, 2013b: "A Communicative Perspective on the Formation of the North: Contexts, Channels and Concepts" in Johan Harvard & Peter Stadius (eds.) *Communicating the North: Media and Marketing in the Making of the Nordic Region.* Burlington: Ashgate.

Harvard, Johan & Stadius, Peter, 2013c: "Conclusion: Mediating the Nordic Brand – History Recycled" in Johan Harvard & Peter Stadius (eds.) *Communicating the North: Media and Marketing in the Making of the Nordic Region.* Burlington: Ashgate.

Hilson, Mary, 2008: *The Nordic Model: Scandinavia Since 1945.* London: Reaktion.

Holtskog, Halvor, Carayannis, Elias G., Kaloudis, Aris & Ringen, Geir, 2018: *Learning Factories: The Nordic Model of Manufacturing.* Cham: Springer International Publishing.

Jónsson, Guðmundur & Stefánsson, Kolbeinn (eds.) 2013: *Retrenchment or Renewal? Welfare States in Times of Economic Crisis.* NordWel Studies in Historical Welfare State Research 6. Helsinki: NordWel.

Jönsson, Heidi Vad, Onasch, Elizabeth, Pellander, Saara & Wickström, Mats (eds.) 2013: *Migrations and Welfare States. Policies, Discourses and Institutions.* NordWel Studies in Historical Welfare State Research 3. Helsinki: NordWel.

Kananen, Johannes, 2014: *The Nordic Welfare State in Three Eras. From Emancipation to Discipline.* Farnham: Ashgate.

Kautto, Mikko, Fritzell, Johan, Hvinden, Bjørn, Kvist, Jon & Uusitalo, Hannu (eds.) 2001: *Nordic Welfare States in the European Context.* London and New York: Routledge.

Kautto, Mikko, Heikkilä, Matti, Hvinden, Bjørn, Marklund, Staffan & Ploug, Niels (eds.) 1999: *Nordic Social Policy. Changing Welfare States.* London and New York: Routledge.

Keskinen, Suvi, Norocel, Ov Christian & Jørgensen, M. B., 2016: "The Politics and Policies of Welfare Chauvinism Under the Economic Crisis" in *Critical Social Policy*, 36:3, 321–329.

Keskinen, Suvi, Skaptadóttir, Unnur Dís & Toivanen, Mari, 2019: "Narrations of Homogeneity, Waning Welfare States, and the Politics of Solidarity" in Suvi Keskinen, Unnur Dís Skaptadóttir & Mari Toivanen (eds.) *Undoing Homogeneity in the Nordic Region: Migration, Difference, and the Politics of Solidarity.* London: Routledge, 1–17.

Keskinen, Suvi, Tuori, Salla, Irni, Kuurna & Mulinari, Diana (eds.) 2009: *Complying with Colonialism: Gender, Race and Ethnicity in the Nordic Region.* Farnham: Ashgate.

Kettunen, Pauli, 1998: "Globalisation and the Criteria of 'Us': A Historical Perspective on the Discussion of the Nordic Model and New Challenges" in Daniel Fleming, Pauli Kettunen, Henrik Søborg & Christer Thörnqvist (eds.) *Global Redefining of Working Life: A New Nordic Agenda for Competence and Participation?* Copenhagen: Nordic Council of Ministers, 33–80.

Kettunen, Pauli, 2006: "The Power of International Comparison: A Perspective on the Making and Challenging of the Nordic Welfare State" in Finn Christiansen Christiansen (ed.) *The Nordic Model of Welfare: A Historical Reappraisal.* Copenhagen: Museum Tusculanum Press.

Kettunen, Pauli, 2011a: "The Transnational Construction of National Challenges: The Ambiguous Nordic Model of Welfare and Competitiveness" in Pauli Kettunen & Klaus Petersen (eds.) *Beyond Welfare State Models: Transnational Historical Perspectives on Social Policy.* Cheltenham and Northampton, MA: Edward Elgar Publishing, 16–40.

Kettunen, Pauli, 2011b: "Welfare Nationalism and Competitive Community" in Andrzej Marcin Suszycki (ed.) *Welfare Citizenship and Welfare Nationalism.* NordWel Studies in Historical Welfare State Research 2. Helsinki: NordWel, 79–117.

Kettunen, Pauli, 2012: "Reinterpreting the Historicity of the Nordic Model" in *Nordic Journal of Working Life Studies,* 2:4, 21–43.

Kettunen, Pauli, 2013: "The ILO as a Forum for Developing and Demonstrating a Nordic Model" in Sandrine Kott & Joelle Droux (eds.) *Globalizing Social Rights. The International Labour Organization and Beyond.* Basingstoke and New York: Palgrave Macmillan, 210–230.

Kettunen, Pauli & Petersen, Klaus (eds.) 2011: *Beyond Welfare State Models: Transnational History Perspectives on Social Policy.* Cheltenham: Edward Elgar Publishing.

Kettunen, Pauli, Kuhnle, Stein & Ren, Yuan (eds.) 2014: *Reshaping Welfare Institutions in China and the Nordic Countries.* NordWel Studies in Historical Welfare State Research 7. Helsinki: NordWel.

Krastev, Ivan, 2017: *After Europe.* Philadelphia: University of Pennsylvania Press.

Kvist, Jon, Fritzell, Johan, Hvinden, Bjørn & Kangas, Olli (eds.) 2012: *Changing Social Equality: The Nordic Welfare Model in the 21st Century.* Bristol: Policy Press.

Levitsky, Steven & Ziblatt, Daniel, 2018: *How Democracies Die.* New York: Crown.

Lloyd, Christopher, 2011: "The History and Future of Social Democratic Welfare Capitalism: From Modernization to the Specters of Ultramodernity" in Pauli Kettunen & Klaus Petersen (eds.) *Beyond Welfare State Models: Transnational Historical Perspectives on Social Policy.* Cheltenham and Northampton, MA: Edward Elgar Publishing, 199–217.

Lundberg, Erik (ed.) 1978: *Inflation Theory and Anti-Inflation Policy.* London: Macmillan.

Marklund, Carl, 2010: "Sharing Values and Shaping Values: Sweden, Nordic Democracy and the American Crisis of Democracy" in Jussi Kurunmäki & Johan Strang (eds.) *Rhetorics of Nordic Democracy.* Helsinki: Finnish Literature Society.

Marklund, Carl, 2013a: "A Swedish Norden or a Nordic Sweden? Image Politics in the West During the Cold War" in Jonas Harvard & Peter Stadius (eds.) *Communicating the North: Media Structures and Images in the Making of the Nordic Region.* Farnham: Ashgate, 263–287.

Marklund, Carl (ed.) 2013b: *All Well in the Welfare State? Welfare, Well-Being and the Politics of Happiness.* NordWel Studies in Historical Welfare State Research 5. Helsinki: NordWel.

Marklund, Carl & Petersen, Klaus, 2013: "Return to Sender: American Images of the Nordic Welfare State Branding" in *European Journal of Scandinavian Studies,* 43:2, 245–257.

Melby, Kari, Ravn, Anna-Birte & Carlsson Wetterberg, Christina, 2008: "A Nordic Model of Gender Equality? Introduction" in Kari Melby, Anna-Birte Ravn & Christina Carlsson Wetterberg (eds.) *Gender Equality and Welfare Politics in Scandinavia: The Limits of Political Ambition?* Bristol: Bristol University Press, 1–24.

Mjøset, Lars, 1992: "The Nordic Model Never Existed, But Does It Have a Future?" in *Scandinavian Studies,* 64:4, 652–671.

Moody, Chris, 2016: "'Bernie Sanders' American Dream is in Denmark" in *CNN.com,* 17 February 2016. https://edition.cnn.com/2016/02/17/politics/bernie-sanders-2016-denmark-democratic-socialism/index.html [Accessed 20 March 2020].

Mounk, Yascha, 2018: *The People vs. Democracy.* Cambridge, MA: Harvard University Press.

Mulinari, Diana, 2008: "Women Friendly? Understanding Gendered Racism in Sweden" in Kari Melby, Kari Melby, Anna-Birte Ravn & Christina Carlsson Wetterberg (eds.) *Gender Equality and Welfare Politics in Scandinavia: The Limits of Political Ambition?* Bristol: Bristol University Press, 167–182.

Mulinari, Diana, Keskinen, Suvi, Irni, Kuurna & Tuori, Salla, 2009: "Postcolonialism and the Nordic Models of Welfare and Gender" in Suvi Keskinen, Salla Tuori, Kuurna Irni & Diana Mulinari (eds.) *Complying with Colonialism: Gender, Race and Ethnicity in the Nordic Region.* Farnham: Ashgate, 1–16.

Nordic Council of Ministers, 1977: *Environmental Education in the Nordic Countries: Denmark, Finland, Iceland, Norway, Sweden.* Copenhagen: Nordic Council of Ministers, Secretariat for Nordic Cultural Cooperation.

Nordisk råd, 1981: *Nordisk råd. 29. Session 1981 København. Del1.* Norstedts: Stockholm.

Nordiska rådets svenska delegation, 1981: *Redogörelse 1981/82:4. Nordiska rådets svenska delegations berättelse angående sin verksamhet, 7.* http://data.riksdagen.se/dokument/G5044 [Accessed 2 March 2020].

NordWel, 2007–2012: *Nordic Centre of Excellence NordWel.* https://blogs.helsinki.fi/nordwel/ [Accessed 20 March 2020].

Norris, Pippa, 2017: "Is Western Democracy Backsliding? Diagnosing the Risks" in *SSRN Electronic Journal.* https://doi.org/10.2139/ssrn.2933655; https://papers.ssrn.com/sol3/papers.cfm?abstract_id=2933655 [Accessed 2 March 2020].

Patent och Registreringsverket [Swedish Trademark Database], *Nordiska modellen, registreringsnummer: 502189.* https://was.prv.se/VarumarkesDb/.

Paunio, J. J. & Haltunen, Hannu, 1976: "The 'Nordic' Approach to Inflation" in Michael Parkin & George Zis (eds.) *Inflation in the World Economy.* Manchester: Manchester University Press, 259–271.

Petersen, Klaus, 2006: "Constructing Nordic Welfare? Nordic Social Political Cooperation 1919–1955" in Niels Finn Christiansen, Klaus Petersen, Nils Edling & Per Haave (eds.) *The Nordic Model of Welfare: A Historical Reappraisal.* Copenhagen: Museum Tusculanum Press, 67–98.

Plattner, Marc F., 2015: "Is Democracy in Decline?" in *Journal of Democracy*, 26:1, 5–10.

Porter, Michael E., 2011: *Competitive Advantage of Nations: Creating and Sustaining Superior Performance.* New York: Simon and Schuster.

Pyrhönen, Niko 2015: *The True Colors of Finnish Welfare Nationalism: Consolidation of Neo-Populist Advocacy as a Resonant Collective Identity through Mobilization of Exclusionary Narratives of Blue-and-White Solidarity.* Helsinki: University of Helsinki, Swedish School of Social Science.

Rom-Jensen, Byron, 2017: "A Model of Social Security? The Political Usage of Scandinavia in Roosevelt's New Deal" in *Scandinavian Journal of History*, 42:4, 363–388.

Runciman, David, 2018: *How Democracy Ends.* London: Profile Books.

Saari, Juho (ed.) 2006: *Suomen malli. Murroksesta menestykseen?* Sosiaalipoliittisen yhdistyksen tutkimuksia 61. Helsinki: Yliopistopaino.

Sapir, André, 2006: "Globalization and the Reform of European Social Models" in *Journal of Common Market Studies*, 44:2, 369–390.

Scottish Government, 2017: *Nordic Baltic Policy Statement.* www.gov.scot/publications/points-north-scottish-governments-nordic-baltic-policy-statement/pages/4/ [Accessed 2 March 2020].

Sørensen, Øystein & Stråth, Bo (eds.) 1997: *The Cultural Construction of Norden.* Oslo: Scandinavian University Press.

Strang, Johan (ed.) 2016: *Nordic Cooperation: A European Region in Transition.* London: Routledge.

Stråth, Bo, 1993: "Den nordiska modellen. Historisk bakgrund och hur talet om hur en nordisk modell uppstod" in *Nordisk tidskrift för vetenskap, konst och industri*, 69:1, 55–61.

Streeck, Wolfgang, 2017: "The Return of the Repressed" in *New Left Review*, 104, 5–18, March–April.

Suszycki, Andrzej Marcin (ed.) 2011: *Welfare Citizenship and Welfare Nationalism*. NordWel Studies in Historical Welfare State Research 2. Helsinki: NordWel, 79–117.

Swanson, Ana, 2015: "Why Denmark isn't the Utopian Fantasy Bernie Sanders Describes" in *Washington Post*, 3 November 2015. www.washingtonpost.com/news/wonk/wp/2015/11/03/why-denmark-isnt-the-utopian-fantasy-bernie-sanders-describes/ [Accessed 20 March 2020].

Tassinari, Fabrizio, 2015: "Scandinavia's Real Lessons. It's not all Welfare and Social Justice" in *Foreignaffairs.com*, 27 October 2015. www.foreignaffairs.com/articles/northern-europe/2015-10-27/scandinavias-real-lessons [Accessed 20 March 2020].

Tharoor, Ishaan, 2015: "Bernie Sanders Loves Denmark. But Here's How It's Letting Down Progressives. Denmark's Government Has Taken a Very Unfriendly Attitude Toward Syrian Refugees" in *Washington Post*, 14 October 2015. www.washingtonpost.com/news/worldviews/wp/2015/10/14/bernie-sanders-loves-denmark-but-heres-how-its-letting-down-progressives/ [Accessed 20 March 2020].

The Economist, 2013: "The Nordic Countries: The Next Supermodel" in *The Economist*, 2 February 2013, 950.

Valkonen, Tarmo & Vihriälä, Vesa (eds.) 2014: *The Nordic Model – Challenged but Capable of Reform*. Copenhagen: Nordisk Ministerråd.

WEF, 2011: *Shared Norms for the New Reality: The Nordic Way*. World Economic Forum, Davos 2011. Stockholm: Global Utmaning.

Widman, Thomas, 2013: "Scotland as a Nordic Country" in *Arc of Prosperity. Scottish Independence within the EU – with a Scandinavian Slant*. www.arcofprosperity.org/scotland-as-a-nordic-country/ [Accessed 20 March 2020].

Witoszek, Nina & Midttun, Atle (eds.) 2018: *Sustainable Modernity: The Nordic Model and Beyond*. London: Routledge.

Wooldridge, Adrian, 2013: "Special Report: The Nordic Countries – Northern Lights" in *The Economist,* 2 February 2013, 950.

Yglesias, Matthre, 2015: "Denmark's Prime Minister Says Bernie Sanders is Wrong to Call His Country Socialist" in *Vox*, 13 October 2015. www.vox.com/2015/10/31/9650030/denmark-prime-minister-bernie-sanders [Accessed 20 March 2020].

2 Three driving forces

Structural challenges for Nordic democracies in the 2010s

Henrik Meinander

'Europa braucht die Nation' (Europe needs the nation) wrote the German sociologist Wolfgang Streeck, joined by his colleagues, in a debate article in the weekly *Die Zeit* in July 2016 after Brexit became a reality. Inspired by the US social scientist Lawrence Summer's recent request for 'responsible nationalism', by which he meant a combination of a sound economic and welfare policy with constructive cooperation with other nations, the German intellectuals urged the European Union (EU) to return to the monetary system that had existed before the introduction of the euro and limit the power of the European Court of Justice.[1]

Similar academic outbursts of frustration were frequently expressed in many European countries in the summer and autumn of 2016. It was not only Brexit and the heavy debt burden of most of the European states that caused their articulated irritation towards the EU. Equally alarming was the massive inflow of refugees from the Middle East and Northern Africa to Europe, which sparked protests from the populist movements in different parts of the continent. It also functioned as a revealing stress test of how liberal and human the Europeans actually were towards people in need. Within a year even the most generous recipient countries, Germany and Sweden, had hardened their immigration regulations and the EU reached an agreement with Turkey in order to stop refugees from entering the EU.

By then, Streeck had also sharpened his critique of the market economy and banking system of the EU with his essay collection *How Will Capitalism End?* (2016), in which he demanded that the nation-states and their democratic governments regain some of the control over their economies they had had before the 1970s.[2] Naturally, this idea of 'de-globalizing capitalism' awoke much criticism. One of the responses to Streeck's general theory was published in the *London Review of Books* by the original British historian Adam Tooze. He characterised Streeck as a nostalgic and Eurocentric nationalist, who rather unconvincingly accused the banks and finance elites of being the cause of most of the structural problems in EU. The future of capitalism will be decided in Asia, not in Europe, claimed Tooze.[3]

The views may differ considerably, but in the centre of this debate is how the EU states and other Western countries can afford to maintain their welfare states and representative democracies amidst the stronger competition in the

DOI: 10.4324/9780429026690-2

global market and the geopolitical scene. Politicians are, for understandable reasons, inclined to argue that these challenges can be solved on a national level. How could they otherwise attract votes and gain power? However, among academic scholars this nationally framed perspective on the development of the European welfare states and their democracies has gradually been replaced by more transnational framings and questions. The nation-states are still important units and actors but are increasingly forced to face the challenges of the ongoing globalisation of a world economy and its ever-faster driver, the digital revolution. Is the answer welfare nationalism or a new international political order?[4]

Contextualisation has been a growing trend in research on the development in Nordic countries. A representative example of this has been Mary Hilson's seminal study *The Nordic Model: Scandinavia since 1945* (2008), in which she especially highlights the economy and security issues in a wider European framework. And during the last decade, a large research programme on the historical foundations and future challenges of the Nordic Welfare State (Nord-Wel) has delivered a number of outstanding anthologies with a systematically European and global angle on the matter.[5]

In the 2010s, the awareness of how intertwined political cultures on the national level are with the world economy and geopolitics has almost exploded due to the digital revolution, which again has uncovered and accentuated the turbulence and inefficiency of liberal democracies. Information technology does not determine the direction of societal development. But it is fundamentally quickening the rhythm of the discourses on the public spheres and thereby revealing how these driving forces interact and form Nordic welfare states and democracies.

The Swedish scholar Lennart Schön has, in his historical synthesis of the world economy, spotted a larger pattern behind this change of societal rhythm. The world economy has, since the mid-19th century, gone through two globalisation waves (1850–1914 and 1970–present), and each time they have reached a turning point, due to technological and financial factors, crucial changes have concurrently taken place also in the political culture of nation-states and geopolitical dynamics in the Western hemisphere.[6]

Schön identified in his *An Economic History of Modern Sweden* (2012) four such turning points in the world economy during the last 130 years: in the 1890s, 1930s, 1970s and 2010s. Having already applied Schön's theory in studies on the patterns of democratisation in Finland and Sweden in the 20th century,[7] I will discuss here how feasible it is for understanding the structural challenges for Nordic democracies in the 2010s. First, I outline the historical development of the Nordic countries, and then I analyse how the world economy, geopolitics, and the traditions and trends in domestic political cultures have formed their democracies in the 2010s.

Patterns of democratisation

The emergence and development of representative democracies in the Nordic countries has predominantly been explained as an outcome of a certain political culture and its deeply rooted institutions, which paved the way for the implementation of a specific Nordic version of the Western European welfare state. There is clear evidence for this claim. Demands of political rights increased in all parts of Europe at the end of the 19th century. The northern periphery of Europe had until then lagged economically, significantly behind the more industrialised countries of the continent, but despite this, democratic reforms and other civic rights were implemented in the Nordic countries to some degree before they were implemented in other wealthier countries. Simultaneously, the Nordic countries had considerably higher economic growth than in the equally rural countries in the Balkan and Iberian regions.[8]

The American historian Mary Nolan has in her fine synthesis *The Transatlantic Century* explained the Nordic leap as a consequence of certain societal structures: 'A different agrarian culture, a better educational system, better transport opportunities, and Protestantism all contributed to Scandinavian success.' The Protestant Church was a guarantee for a strong central administration and the rule of law, whereas the free peasantry would be the same progressive force in political life as the middle classes in Central Europe.[9]

When the democratic breakthrough took place in Europe after the First World War, the Nordic countries were well prepared for parliamentary processes and compromises, which partly explains why they, at the outbreak of the next world war, were among the very few European countries that had maintained their democratic constitutions. Having escaped a Soviet occupation and thereby maintaining their democracies, the Nordic countries were able to construct their own type of welfare system during the post-war period. Social equality was promoted by offering benefits to all citizens, which secured middle-class support for the system and its acceptance of high progressive income taxation until the present day.[10]

However, the success of Nordic democracy and its welfare system has also crucially been dependent on relatively swift economic growth, which transformed the Nordic people between 1890 and 1970 from poor cousins to something of lucky siblings within the European family. Nordic countries have more efficiently implemented recent technological innovations than most other European countries. One reason for this has been their small populations and functional state governance, which has made it easier to adjust their natural and human resources to the new technology.[11]

Equally important has been their favourable geographical position. On the one hand, the Nordic countries have been close enough to large markets in Central Europe and North America. On the other, they have been sheltered by the seas and in their peripheral geopolitical location. The Danish historian Uffe Østergård claims that the geographic site is the major structural explanation to the economic and political success of what has lately become known as the 'Nordic model'.[12]

Both Finland and Denmark have had mighty neighbours invading them for military reasons. But in most cases, Finns and Danes have gained considerably from their geographical closeness to the Russian and German markets. And in contrast to the Baltic States and other Eastern regions of Central Europe,

Finland and Denmark have at the same time been aloof enough to avoid being heavily squeezed between the great powers in major conflicts in Europe. The geographical site is naturally not the destiny, but it definitely plays a part in the story, even though it is easily understood as too simple an explanation.

The Second World War is a case in point. Finland was dragged into the war in autumn 1939 because the Soviet Union wanted to secure its defence of Leningrad. Denmark and Norway were again occupied by Germany in the spring of 1940 as a preventive measure against the plans of the Western powers to cut off the Swedish export of iron ore to the German war industry. Yet none of these three Nordic countries became major battlefields in the horrific war between the Axis and Allies, whereas both Sweden and Iceland avoided an involvement in the war altogether. In other words, the Nordic countries maintained their infrastructures and civilian populations, which put them in a totally different position than most of the other countries in war-torn Europe.[13]

World market

The beginning of the third globalisation wave is usually dated to the 1970s when the ground structures of the free movement of capital were laid and the outsourcing of Western industrial production to other continents began on a larger scale. After the end of the Cold War and together with the simultaneous liberalisation of the digital technology, the world economy grew swiftly between 1995 and 2008. This time it was no longer the Western hemisphere that was the tractor of world economy but, above all, China and India with their huge populations and growth potentials. The negative side of the coin was a rapidly growing inequality of income, whereas the positive was a considerable rise of the standard of living among the poorest populations of our planet.[14]

The Nordic countries coped well in this economic race until 2008 due to the outsourcing of a considerable part of their labour-intensive industry, the ability to adjust to new digital technology and the transformation into service economies. The Norwegian economy went through an even swifter growth thanks to the income from the state-owned energy industry. The worldwide financial crisis of 2008 shook the Nordic economies differently. Iceland was hit by a banking crisis in 2003 and touched bottom in 2006–2008 but has, since 2012, shown bold growth. Norway, Sweden and Denmark maintained their budget surplus and returned to a growth path in 2010. Finland's economy withered for a number of structural reasons until 2016 and the state will therefore struggle with a budget deficit at least until the early 2020s.[15]

As a consequence, the recession in the world economy had different political implications for each Nordic country. Due to its oil resources and income, Norway was much less impacted by the financial crisis. Yet the Social Democratic government that had held power for eight years lost the parliamentary elections in 2013 to a centre-right coalition. However, it was not due to budget cuts, but rather it was a typical wish for changes in domestic politics. The winning populist Fremskrittspartiet (Progress Party) joined the government for the first time and continued in it after the 2017 election, which resulted in a tightened immigration policy, much like the one in Denmark had begun to implement a decade earlier.[16]

As an EU country with its most important trade markets in the Union, Denmark was more directly affected by the turmoil in world finances and the European sovereign debt crisis in 2008–2011. Although Denmark had maintained its own currency, its financial market and banking system were closely intertwined with the euro-zone. Many expected that the victory of a Red-Green Alliance in the parliamentary elections in 2011 would lead to a rollback of some of the austerity measures initiated by the former government led by the Centre Party, Venstre. This did not happen. The Red-Green government loosened up the stricter immigration policy implemented by the former government in exchange of support from the nationalistic populist party Dansk Folkeparti (Danish People's Party).[17]

After the elections four years later (2015), a new centrist minority cabinet took over once again with right-wing support, including from the populist party. Consequently, further restrictions on the immigration and asylum policy were enforced at the same time as the refugee crisis reached its peak within the EU. This anti-immigration policy continued after the 2019 elections. The populist party lost a considerable part of their support to the Social Democrats, who after lengthy negotiations formed a minority government. One reason for this power shift was that the Social Democrats' campaign had backed the stricter immigration requirements. Another was that the climate question got much more attention in election debates and consumed the support of the climate-skeptical populist party.[18]

One thing was obvious; the Danish measures in the immigration policy cannot be seen as a reaction to increasing unemployment or other substantial difficulties in the domestic economics. Quite the contrary, the Danish 'flexicurity' with its flexibility in the labour market combined with a strong social security and activating labour market policy now showed its efficiency. Noticeable also is that this employment policy has continued since the 1990s despite regular shifts between Left and Centre governments.[19]

Denmark's main export markets are in Germany and Sweden, both of which sailed through the financial crisis of 2008–2015 without any substantial problems and were actually growing throughout the 2010s. A closer look at the Danish export profile reveals that a substantial proportion of exports is high-tech products and refined raw materials for niche markets is less sensitive to economic conjunctures.[20] Denmark's economic success in the 2010s is in this sense a good example of what Lennart Schön described as the positive outcome of the 'transformation of development blocks': 'During transformation periods after structural crises, development blocks of major innovations have emerged, particularly in relation to power supply, transport and communications.'[21]

The Swedish reactions to the turmoil in the European financial market in 2008–2015 were also rather moderate. The Swedes, in a 2002 referendum, voted for staying out of the euro-zone, which meant that the Swedish bank-ing system was only indirectly involved in the measures taken to rescue Greece from financial collapse. As in Norway and Denmark, Sweden had during the 2010s both non-socialist (2006–2010, 2010–2014) and Left-Green govern-ments (2014–2018, 2019–present) that, despite some distinctively diverse elec-tion promises, have not made any radical changes in the national economic policy.

One reason for this solidification has been the growing support for the nationalistic populist party Sverigedemokraterna (Swedish Democrats), which has had representation in the Swedish parliament since 2010. Due to its ideo-logical roots in the radical-right movement and strong critique of Sweden's generous immigration policy, the other parties refused to make political deals with Sverigedemokraterna. In spite of this, since the election in 2014, the party has held a balance of power in the parliament. The two Left-Green minority coalitions have therefore since 2014 been forced to rely on passive support from the socialist Vänsterpartiet (Left Party) and some of the other non-socialist par-ties, which hindered the coalitions from carrying out any substantial social or economic reforms.[22]

Yet an equally important reason for this linear policy has been the stable recovery of the Swedish economy after the recession in 2009. As in Denmark, the Swedish export industry has, due to a number of technological rationalisa-tions, efficient attraction of foreign capital, made a substantial move towards more service products and expanded its international markets despite problems in the European economy. An illustrative example of this is the production of Volvo cars. Since a Chinese car manufacturer bought the company in 2010, Volvo has rapidly regained its profitability thanks to the use of robots in pro-duction, improved design and global market planning. A car is no longer a mere instrument for movement; it is increasingly an expression of taste and lifestyle.[23]

These significant improvements in the technological landscape and societal productivity, which, following Schön's macro-thesis, suggest bold growth for Sweden at least into the 2020s and have clearly moderated the interest for radi-cal change in economic policy. Income tax has remained high in comparison with other countries, but as in other Western market economies, Swedish capi-tal tax has been considerably decreased since the 1990s. The two Left-Green coalitions of the 2010s have neither raised the considerably lowered capital tax nor reintroduced the inheritance tax abolished by the non-socialist cabinet of 2004. The most debated economic question is instead the rapid income increase of the wealthiest strata of the Swedish population.[24]

Finland's economic path through the 2010s was much more troublesome. The deep dip in the world market in 2008–2009 and the following financial crisis in the EU impacted Finland and led to a number of other structural prob-lems in its economy and competitiveness. The dramatic fall and sell-out of the giant mobile phone section of the Nokia company took place between 2008 and 2013. At the same time, the economically important forest industry went through a major renewal of its products, leading to a cut in export incomes. In addition to this, the significant export to Russia declined due to both falling oil prices and EU sanctions following the Russian annexation of the Crimean Peninsula in 2014.[25]

This was certainly not the first time the Finnish economy was rocked much harder by economic conjunctures than the other Nordic countries. During the previous economic recession in Europe in the early 1990s, Finland had faced even graver problems with huge unemployment numbers and considerable cuts in welfare services. Such drastic decisions were not required in the 2010s, although unemployment rates would remain high until 2016, when the economy finally began to grow again. But the price for maintaining the welfare services was a substantial increase of state debt, which put Finland in the same category as Iceland.[26]

The first bold reactions to these structural problems in the economy came in the parliamentary election in 2011, when the populist party Perussuomalaiset (True Finns) received substantial support and sharpened its anti-immigration demands with a strong critique of the participation of Finland in the financial rescue of the Greek economy. The Finnish governments had since the 1970s been large coalitions. The Conservatives and Social Democrats were dominant parties in the cabinet in 2011–2015, but they were unable to push through substantial economic reforms.

This paved the way for a new victory for the populist party in the election in 2015 and its participation in a non-socialist cabinet. Two years later, the governmental position caused a split within the True Finns, in which the old party leadership formed a new party that remained in the government, which was able to carry out some reforms that improved Finnish competitiveness in the world market. These austerity measures rather predictably led to a clear loss for the coalition in the 2019 election and a formation of a Left-Center government, which promised improvements in social welfare despite signs of a recession in the world economy.[27]

However, the foremost reason for the Finnish growth numbers since 2016 was the recovery of the European economy. In contrast to the other Nordic countries, Finland has so far not been able to fully transform into an economy that maintains stable growth through an advanced technology and a service export industry with profitable niche markets.[28]

The Finnish economic structures are thus also substantially stiffer than the much smaller Icelandic economy. The financial meltdown in 2003–2007 of the three leading Icelandic banks was a consequence of irresponsible speculation on the global financial markets and awoke large protests against plans of a state-funded rescue programme. The government decided, against all odds, to let the banks fail, which has resulted in an astonishing recovery and a thorough rearrangement of the political map. At the same time, the country has begun paying back its enormous loans early.[29]

Geopolitics

As pointed out earlier, another often neglected external factor in analyses of the development of political cultures in the Nordic countries have been the turning points on the geopolitical scene and their different chain reactions. The end of the Cold War, the emergence of the European Union and the eastward expansion of the Union together with NATO had self-evident far-reaching consequences for the political dynamics for Northern Europe. Finland with its over 1,300 kilometre-long eastern border with the unstable Russia was in the beginning most influenced by these changes. But as new geopolitical tensions turned up in other parts of the world, each Nordic country would get its specific share of the friction they caused.

As NATO members Denmark and Norway took active part in the United States-led warfare in Afghanistan (2001–present) and Iraq (2003–2007), a number of their soldiers got killed and the military involvement sparked protests in the Danish-Muslim communities and among domestic pacifists. However, apart from Left-wing socialists, would the political party elites and leading media continue to support Danish participation in the wars? When in 2005 a Danish cartoonist drew insulting caricatures of Muhammed and caused large demonstrations against the Danes in different parts of the Muslim world, regrets were expressed, but the deed was defended by many of his compatriots in the name of freedom of speech.[30]

These experiences and controversies clearly enforced the nationalistic opinion in the Danish immigration debate. It explains also why the Danish nationalist-populist party Danske Folkparti succeeded earlier than the other Nordic populist parties to get their anti-immigration demands carried out. In exchange for this, the party has supported the two recent centre minority cabinets. Another consequence of the tightening attitudes towards immigration was that Danish scepticism towards the EU, which is essentially a deep-rooted popular attitude against all kinds of top-down administration, lost something of its edge.

Suddenly, Danish society seemed to be not so threatened by the Germans and Brussels but by Muslims and immigrants from the Middle East. This attitude shift was even more bluntly expressed when the big wave of refugees from the Middle East and Africa swept over Europe in 2015. Like many other EU citizens, Danes demanded that the EU Commission do much more to control the borders and distribute the responsibility for humanitarian aid more equally among its member states.[31]

Very few commentators would point out the obvious contradiction in these often nationalist demands. As is so often the case with challenges of global magnitude, the public discourses in the Nordic countries were unable to view the national consequences of the 2015 refugee crisis as chain reactions of changing geopolitical priorities among the great powers. The failures of US forces in the wars in Afghanistan and Iraq had convinced the Obama administration of the necessity of a controlled retreat from the Middle East.[32] This strategy, which Obama's successor Trump would in practice follow, gradually led to a number of unpredicted constellations in many parts of the Arabic world: swiftly rising demands for democratic reforms through social media, large public demonstrations, increasing political chaos, new but unstable regimes, and chaotic civil wars in Libya and Syria, which resulted in large refugee waves to Europe.[33]

The Swedish reaction to the refugee crisis in 2015 was noticeably different and altered more over time. In contrast to the Danish and Norwegian media, which had given diversified attention to anti-immigration opinions since the early 2010s, would the leading media houses in Sweden defend their government's generous refugee policy and either condemn or neglect the protests against it by the populist party Sverigedemokraterna? By the end of 2015, nearly 163,000 refugees had arrived in Sweden, which was many times more than in any other Nordic country or small EU nation.[34]

One reason for these differences in the public attitudes towards immigration was that Sweden had since the 1950s received a great number of labour immigrants and refugees from different parts of the world who had integrated rather well and already contributed much to their new homeland. This established a positive attitude towards immigration and had become a crucial part of the Swedish self-image, which made it truly difficult to question the political elite and media when the inflow of refugees reached its peak. In late autumn 2015, the Swedish government was forced to introduce similar immigration restrictions as the other Nordic countries. While, the Red–Green government gradually began to implement a more restricted immigration policy, the media coverage of anti-immigration opinions became more nuanced.

However, the reason for this transformation of the Swedish immigration policy was not only the challenges it caused for the local authorities but also the considerable growth of the populist party Sverigedemokraterna in the opinion polls from 2015 to 2017. When their popularity neared 20 per cent, the other parties were inclined to somehow recognise their views and even discuss the possibility of forming a government with support from the populist party.[35]

In this sense, the Swedish discourse would slowly turn in the same direction as in Denmark and Norway, although it was still dominated by the old ideal of clear-cut Left or Right governments. Another sign of the existing differences in the Nordic debate climates is that Norwegian and Danish media still often point out social problems and criminality in immigrant-dense Swedish suburbs as a warning example of a too-generous immigration policy.[36]

The Finnish reaction to the refugee crisis of 2015 was also quite different. Although Finland has had a consistently smaller immigrant population than the other Nordic countries (2018: 4.5 per cent), anti-immigration attitudes played a considerable role in Finnish politics and were given more space in the media than in Sweden. As a consequence, the populist party Perussuomalaiset would, after their second election victory in row, join a non-socialist majority coalition in the spring of 2015.[37]

Almost as soon as the government had been formed, the flow of refugees reached Finland, which, following the Swedish example, first accommodated them as well as it could but then gradually enforced new restrictions against immigration. But being itself in the government, the Finnish populist party would, contrary to the Swedish populist party, not gain any new supporters during this process, especially since they at the same time had to accept Finnish participation in new EU loans to the bankrupt Greece. As earlier mentioned, in 2017 the more outspoken anti-immigration faction took over the party, which led to a party split and clear backlash in the polls for the two populist parties.

Taken together, it is hardly possible to distinguish a certain model for how the immigration question has been discussed and solved in the Nordic countries. In contrast to this diversity, there are clear signs that the earlier Nordic security policies have begun to converge and affect Swedish and Finnish political cultures. As EU members since 1995, Sweden and Finland have in most questions followed the foreign policy lines drawn by the leading EU countries, which are all also NATO countries. At the same time, they have step by step synchronised their military defences with US forces. In 2014, both countries signed an agreement with NATO, which allows NATO forces to operate from their territories in case of a conflict in Northern Europe.[38]

This development has also stimulated inter-Nordic defence cooperation and led to concrete consequences after the Russian annexation of the Crimean Peninsula in 2014 and the sharpening security atmosphere in the Baltic region. Nevertheless, lacking popular support, NATO membership is not a realistic option for Sweden or Finland in the near future. Many leading politicians have preferred to describe Swedish-Finnish military cooperation more as an alternative than as an integrated part of the expanding synchronisation with the NATO forces, which undoubtedly has caused much confusion in the defence debates in both countries.[39]

Political cultures

Finally, let us look more closely at how these external factors have interacted with and impacted the political cultures in the five Nordic countries. Even if they belong to the most stable democracies in the world and influenced each other, they have all, over the years, formed their own political cultures distinct from each other.

The American political scientist Pippa Norris, in her broad analyses of how societies and political systems develop, has often pointed out the far-reaching consequences of their institutional foundations and functionality: 'Cultural change is path-dependent.'[40] This explains also the institutional stability of the Nordic democracies in the 2010s. Having their roots in two Lutheran kingdoms, in which the loyalty towards the state remained strong, the rule of law was firmly implemented and their civic societies established a steady basis for democratic constitutions, the five Nordic countries were able to develop into

modern welfare societies, which so far have fought social inequality more efficiently than other Western democracies.[41]

Even if these welfare reforms have predominantly been carried out by governments with a strong social democratic representation, they have, as Mary
Hilson has emphasised, been outcomes of larger compromises with progressive
forces within the non-socialist blocks. Furthermore, these compromises have
also been strongly formed by the specific conflict dimensions that have existed
in domestic politics in each country and which differ quite a bit from each
other.[42]

In a study of current trends in Swedish political life, Johannes Lindvall and
his research group have analysed the locked situation in the national parliament
since 2014, when the balance of power tipped to the populist party Sverigedemokraterna. The dominant conflict dimension in the Swedish representative democracy has, according to them, during the last decades been formed by
a clear-cut competition between the Left and the Right party blocks. Neither
block is therefore especially skilled or motivated to reach compromises with
each other or to embrace support from Sverigedemokraterna.

The established parties and liberal media houses have so far shown the new-
comer the same kind of distrust the Communists faced at the beginning of
the Cold War. Some of its ideological roots are undoubtedly in the Swedish
right-radical movement. But as Lindvall's research group points out, the current party stands in both economic and defence issues closer to the Social
Democrats than to the conservative Moderaterna. The voters are also inclined
to see Sverigedemokraterna as a non-socialist centre party than as a right-wing
or extreme right party.[43]

Ronald Inglehart and Pippa Norris arrive at the same conclusion in a large
comparative survey of the European populist parties in the 2010s. The Swedish populists Sverigedemokraterna are, together with their Danish and Finnish
counterparts, classified as 'Populist-Left' parties primarily on the basis of their
views on social welfare and economic issues. The Norwegian parallel is for
the same reason characterised as a 'Populist-Right' party; its support does not
spring from economic insecurity but from a strong sense of threatened cultural
values. Conservative and ultra-nationalist values are also shared by the other
Nordic populists and, in fact, Inglehart and Norris conclude that European
political populism should fundamentally be understood as a cultural backlash:
populism's 'support can be explained as a retro reaction by once-predominant
sectors of the population to progressive value change'.[44]

This mixture of populist ideas explains much of the uncertainty Sverigedemokraterna caused to the Left-Right conflict dimension that had previously been so manageable in Swedish politics. It is also a key to understanding
why populist parties in the other Nordic countries have been able to communi-
cate, cooperate and even share power with the older parties in their parliaments
and municipalities. In their countries, political cultures have been continuously
formed by at least two or three conflict dimensions, which in shifting variations
have divided and gathered support across the Left and Right axis.

Finland is the most obvious example of this. Four conflict dimensions have formed Finnish politics since organised parties emerged in the beginning of the 20th century: the class struggle, the language feud, the centre-periphery conflict and the complicated relationship to Russia. In none of these issues have the opinions been divided only on a Left-Right axis. Social Democrats demanded social and economic equality, but so did the strong Fennomanic movement supported by the Agrarian League, later a Centre party. Many Social Democrats and Conservatives were also eager Fennomans; others saw language as a minor question, not least because Swedish was an important tongue in their own social classes. Regional interests have always been crucial for the agrarians, later a Centre party, and the Communists, later the Left Alliance, and even for the Swedish People's Party.

And yet, none of these conflict dimensions have cut through the Left-Right axis as much as the attitudes towards Russia. During the Cold War, the Centre party and the Communist were most in favour of a flexibility towards their mighty neighbour, whereas the Social Democrats together with the Liberals and Conservatives favoured a more cautious line. The safest way to balance this existential dispute has therefore been large coalitions over the political centre line, which have hindered political polarisation that would have benefitted above all the Soviet Union and its systematic attempts to influence and direct Finnish domestic politics.

In such a political climate it has not been out of the question for other parties to cooperate with a populist party. In 1983–1987, the predecessor of the current populist party was in the government and in 2015 it got a new chance to get a taste of power. Both times the consequences have been grave for their popularity. In 2017, the party was split apart, and the moderate faction continued in the government despite minimal support in the opinion polls.[45]

Similar overlapping conflict dimensions have formed and still have a strong impact on Danish and Norwegian political cultures. In both countries the regional question has been in the centre of the debate since the 19th century and is the main reason populist parties, despite their nationalistic overtones, have earned credibility in domestic politics. This regionalism explains also why the attitudes towards the EU are more dubious in Denmark and especially Norway, where the citizens have twice voted against membership. In contrast to the officially militarily non-aligned Finns, who despite their regionalism joined the EU originally for security reasons, Danes and Norwegians have never had such expectations concerning the EU due to their NATO membership.

The Swedish populist party fits this pattern quite well and has its strongest support in Scania, the southern-most part of the country neighbouring Denmark. Although having been a part of Sweden since the 17th century, Scania has maintained its distinct identity and intonation.[46] Another obvious reason for the relatively strong support for the populist party in Scania is that some of its urban regions have a large population of immigrants. As such, Sverigedemokraterna can be seen as a regional protest against the rather centralised political culture in Sweden.

Another often forgotten reason for this centralism is the Swedish election system with the so-called long candidate lists. The party organisations decide in which order their election candidates are listed. The members of the Swedish parliament are thus more obedient to their party leaderships than, for example, the Finnish MPs, who are elected on the basis of the votes they have received personally and therefore have a stronger regional legacy to lean on.

Conclusion

All in all, Nordic political cultures have a number of specific national conflict dimensions, which in their own way have been influenced and formed by external driving forces. But if they are viewed from a larger European perspective, these differences look much less substantial. The Social Democrats play an important role in Nordic politics despite their gradual retreat from a dominant position. Other bigger parties with longer traditions are in the same situation, although each election brings surprises in their support.

In contrast to most other European countries where the dialogue between the established and populist parties still is not very rational, Nordic populist parties have shown attempts to mature into more responsible political forces during the 2010s. However, this trend will ultimately depend on how the Nordic economies can adjust to a number of ongoing changes in the world market, which all seem to support Lennart Schön's theory of the 'transformation of development blocks'. If they succeed in this and continue to deliver growth and welfare, the populist parties will have to emphasise their anti-immigration rhetoric and regional demands as well as cultural conservatism to maintain political support.

The impact of mass migration and geopolitics should not be forgotten. It is a safe guess that the Nordic countries will receive a growing number of immigrants in the next few decades and that this could substantially stimulate their domestic economies. An efficient integration of this new population will nevertheless require increasing measures and many political compromises, in which populist opinions will be represented. And yet, each time geopolitical shifts and international crises occur, such agreements are difficult to maintain when the economies suffer and the sudden influx of refugees demand swifter actions.

Notes

1 Höpner, Scharpf & Streeck 2016.
2 Streeck 2016.
3 Tooze 2017.
4 Piketty 2014, Suszycki 2011.
5 Hilson 2008, Nordic Studies in Historical Welfare State Research homepage.
6 Schön 2010.
7 Schön 2012, 10–11, Meinander 2014, 395–410, Meinander 2018, 25–64.
8 Meinander 2018.

9 Nolan 2012, 21, Markkola, Kettunen & Petersen 2011, 102–118.
10 Hilson 2008.
11 Fellman, Iversen, Sjögren & Thue 2008, Jonsson 2008.
12 Østergård 2005, 147–184.
13 Meinander 2012b, 49–91.
14 Kristensen & Lilja 2011, Piketty 2014, 252–261, Bourguignon 2016.
15 Gross national income: Total US dollars/capita 1996–2017, OECD homepage; Net lending/borrowing by sector 2015, *OECD homepage.*
16 Bjerkem 2016, 233–243, Regjeringen Sohlberg 2018.
17 Weinberg 2018.
18 Henley 2019, Nordstrand 2019.
19 Schulze-Cleven, Watson & Zysman 2007, 451–475.
20 *Denmark OEC: Exports, Imports, Trade Balance* 2017.
21 Schön 2012, 10.
22 Valresultat 2018.
23 Gifford, Holgersson, McKeveley & Bagchi-Sen 2015, 231–256.
24 Ohlsson, Roine & Waldenström 2014.
25 Meinander 2017, 286–288.
26 Funke, Schularick & Trebesch 2016, 227–260, Henley 2018.
27 Muhonen 2019.
28 Kaartemo & Kaivo-oja 2010.
29 Matsangou 2015.
30 Henkel 2010.
31 Breznau 2018.
32 Dekhakhena 2013.
33 Diamond 2019, 18–19.
34 *Dagens Nyheter* 3 October 2016.
35 Fratzke 2017, 3–11.
36 Herkman 2016, 147–161.
37 Ulkomaan kansalaiset 2018.
38 Bringeus 2016.
39 For an international perspective, see Etzold & Opitz 2015.
40 Norris 2004, 220.
41 Petersen 2011, 41–64.
42 Hilson 2008.
43 Lindvall et al. 2017.
44 Inglehart & Norris 2016, 1, 30–31.
45 Meinander 2012a, 469, Nurmi 2017.
46 Sannerstedt 2017, 451–471.

References

Bjerkem, Johan, 2016: "The Norwegian Progress Party: An Established Populist Party" in *European View*, 15:2, 233–243.

Bourguignon, Francois, 2016: "Inequality and Globalization: How Rich Get Richer and the Poor Catch Up" in *Foreign Affairs*, 95:1, 11–15.

Breznau, Nate, 2018: "Anti-Immigrant Parties and Western European Society: Analyzing the Role of Immigration and Forecasting Voting" [PDF]. *osf.io*. [Accessed 28 February 2019].

Bringéus, Krister, 2016: *Säkerhet i ny tid*. Stockholm: Regeringskansliet.

Dagens Nyheter, 3 October 2016: "Ett år sedan flyktingkrisen – så ser det ut i dag".

Dekhakhena, Abdelkrim, 2013: How 9/11 Triggered the Arabic Spring. http://dx.doi.org/10.2139/ssrn.2293858 [Accessed 28 February 2019].

Denmark OEC, 2017: *Exports, Imports, Trade Balance*. https://atlas.media.mit.edu/en/profile/country/dnk/#Exports [Accessed 20 February 2019].

Diamond, Larry, 2019: "Democracy Demotion: How the Freedom Agenda Fell Apart" in *Foreign Affairs*, 98:4, 17–25.

Etzold, Tobias & Opitz, Christian, 2015: *Between Military Non-Alignment and Integration: Finland and Sweden in Search of a New Security Strategy* (SWP Comments, 25/2015). Berlin: Stiftung Wissenschaft und Politik SWP- Deutsches Institut für Internationale Politik und Sicherheit. https://nbn-resolving.org/urn:nbn:de:0168-ssoar-431317 [Accessed 28 February 2019].

Fellman, Susanna, Iversen, Martin Jes, Sjögren, Hans & Thue, Lars (eds.) 2008: *Creating Nordic Capitalism – The Development of a Competitive Periphery*. Basingstoke: Palgrave Macmillan.

Fratzke, Susan, 2017: *Weathering Crisis, Forging Ahead: Swedish Asylum and Integration Policy*. Transatlantic Council on Migration. www.migrationpolicy.org [Accessed 28 February 2019].

Funke, Manuel, Schularick, Moritz & Trebesch, Christoph, 2016: "Going to Extremes: Politics After Financial Crises, 1870–2014" in *European Economic Review*, 88, 227–260.

Gifford, Ethan, Holgersson, Marcus, McKevely, Maureen & Bagchi-Sen, Sharmistha, 2015: "Tapping into Western Technologies by Chinese Multinationals: Geely's Purchase of Volvo Car and Huawei's Hiring of Ericsson Employees in Sweden" in Maureen McKevley & Sharmistha Bagchi-Sen (eds.) *Innovation Spaces in Asia: Entrepreneurs, Multinational Enterprises and Policy*. Cheltenham: Edward Elgar Publishing.

Henkel, Heiko, 2010: "Fundamentally Danish? The Muhammad Cartoon Crisis as Transitional Drama" in *Human Architecture: Journal of Sociology of Self-Knowledge*, 8:2, 67–82.

Henley, Jon, 2018: "Iceland's New Leader: 'People don't Trust Our Politicians" in *Guardian*, 9 February 2018. www.theguardian.com/world/2018/feb/09/icelands-new-leader-people-dont-trust-icelandic-politicians [Accessed 20 February 2019].

Henley, Jon, 2019: "Denmark's Centre-Left Set to Win Election with Anti-Immigration Shift" in *Guardian*, 4 June 2019. www.theguardian.com/world/2019/jun/04/denmark-centre-left-predicted-win-election-social-democrats-anti-immigration-policies [Accessed 28 February 2019].

Herkman, Juha Pekka, 2016: "Construction of Populism: Meanings Given to Populism in the Nordic Press" in *NORDICOM Review*, 37, Special Issue. https://doi.org/10.1515/nor-2016-0029 [Accessed 28 February 2019].

Hilson, Mary, 2008: *The Nordic Model: Scandinavia Since 1945*. London: Reaktion.

Höpner, Martin, Scharpf, Fritz & Streeck, Wolgang, 2016: "Europa Braucht Die Nation" in *Die Zeit*, 15 September 2016. https://wolfgangstreeck.files.wordpress.com/2016/09/hc3b6pner-scharpf-streeck2016_zeit_europa-braucht-die-nation.pdf [Accessed 22 February 2019].

Inglehart, Ronald & Norris, Pippa, 2016: *Trump, Brexit, and the Rise of Populism: Economic Have-Nots and Cultural Backlash*. HKS Working Paper No. RWP16-026. SSRN. https://ssrn.com/abstract=2818659 or http://dx.doi.org/10.2139/ssrn.2818659 [Accessed 28 February 2019].

Jonsson, Gudmundur (ed.) 2008: *Nordic Historical National Accounts*. Reykjavík: University of Iceland Press.

Kaartemo, Valtteri & Kaivo-oja, Jari, 2010: "Finland 2050 in the Perspective of Global Change" in Patrycja Jakubowska, Antoni Kukliński & Piotr Zuber (eds.) *The Future of Regions in the Perspective of Global Change. Case Studies. Part Two* (vol. 4, 2nd edition). Warsaw and Wroclaw: Lower Silesian Foundation for Regional Development, 113–122.

Kristensen, Per Hull & Lilja, Kari (eds.) 2011: *Nordic Capitalisms and Globalization: New Forms of Economic Organization and Welfare Institutions*. Oxford: Oxford University Press.

Lindvall, Johannes, Bäck, Hanna, Dahlström, Carl, Naurin, Elin & Teorell, Jan, 2017: *Samverkan och strid i den parlamentariska demokratin*. Stockholm: SNS. www.sns.se/wp-content/uploads/2017/09/samverkan-och-strid-i-den-parlamentariska-demokratin.pdf [Accessed 28 February 2019].

Markkola, Pirjo, Kettunen, Pauli & Petersen, Klaus, 2011: *The Lutheran Nordic Welfare States. Beyond Welfare State Models. Transnational Historical Perspectives on Social Policy*. Cheltenham: Edward Elgar Publishing.

Matsangou, Elizabeth, 2015: "Failing Banks, Winning Economy: The Truth about Iceland's Recovery" in *Word Finance: The Voice of the Market*, 15 September 2015. www.world finance.com/special-reports/failing-banks-winning-economy-the-truth-about-icelands-recovery [Accessed 20 February 2019].

Meinander, Henrik, 2012a: *Republiken Finland i går och i dag*. Helsingfors: Sets.

Meinander, Henrik, 2012b: "Finland and the Great Powers in World War II: Ideologies, Geopolitics, Diplomacy" in Tiina Kinnunen & Ville Kivimäki (eds.) *Finland in World War II: History, Memory, Interpretations*. Leiden: Brill.

Meinander, Henrik, 2014: "Tre drivkrafter: Om finlandssvenska samtidskänslor och framtidshorisonter 1914" in *Historisk tidskrift för Finland*, 99:4.

Meinander, Henrik, 2017: *Finnlands Geschichte: Linien, Strukturen, Wendepunkte*. Regensburg: Scoventa.

Meinander, Henrik, 2018: "Det långa 1900-talet" in Henrik Meinander, Petri Karonen & Kjell Östberg (eds.) *Demokratins drivkrafter: Kontext och särdrag i Finlands och Sveriges demokratier 1890–2020*. Helsingfors: SLS.

Muhonen, Teemu, 2019: "Rinteen hallituksen arvostelu perustuu osin kahteen sitkeään väärinkäsitykseen" in *Helsingin Sanomat*, 13 June 2019. www.hs.fi/politiikka/art-2000006141661.html [Accessed 28 February 2019].

Nolan, Mary, 2012: *The Transatlantic Century: Europe and America, 1890–2010*. Cambridge: Cambridge University Press.

Nordic Studies in Historical Welfare State Research Homepage. https://blogs.helsinki.fi/nord-wel/publications/bookstore/ [Accessed 22 February 2019].

Nordstrand, Marie, 2019: "Det är danskarnas klimatångest som avgjort det här valet" in *SVT Nyheter*, 6 June 2019. www.svt.se/nyheter/utrikes/greta-effekten-avgjorde-det-danska-valet [Accessed 28 February 2019].

Norris, Pippa, 2004: *Sacred and Secular: Religion and Politics Worldwide*. Cambridge: Cambridge University Press.

Nurmi, Lauri, 2017: *Perussuomalaisten hajoamisen historia*. Helsinki: Into.

OECD. *Gross National Income: Total US Dollars/Capita 1996–2017*. https://data.oecd.org/natincome/gross-national-income.htm#indicator-chart [Accessed 20 February 2019].

OECD. *Net Lending/Borrowing by Sector 2015*. https://data.oecd.org/natincome/net-lending-borrowing-by-sector.htm#indicator-chart [Accessed 20 February 2019].

Ohlsson, Henry, Roine, Jesper & Waldenström, Daniel, 2014: *Inherited Wealth Over the Path of Development: Sweden, 1810–2010*. IFN Working Paper No. 1033. https://ssrn.com/abstract=2543475 [Accessed 28 February 2019].

Østergård, Uffe, 2005: "Lutheranismen og den universelle velfærdsstat" in Jens Holger Schiørring (ed.) *Kirken og velfærdsstaten*. København: Anis Forlag.

Petersen, Klaus, 2011: "National, Nordic and Trans-Nordic: Transnational Perspectives on the History of the Nordic Welfare States" in Pauli Kettunen & Klaus Petersen (eds.)

Beyond Welfare State Models Transnational Historical Perspectives on Social Policy. Cheltenham: Edward Elgar Publishing.

Piketty, Thomas, 2014: *Capital in the Twenty-First Century*, Harvard: Belknap.

Regjeringen Sohlberg, 2018: www.regjeringen.no/no/om-regjeringa/solberg/Regjer ingen-Solberg/id753980/ [Accessed 28 February 2019].

Sannerstedt, Anders, 2017: "Sverigedemokraterna: Skånegapet krymper" in Ulrika Andersson, Jonas Ohlsson, Henrik Oscarsson & Maria Oskarson (eds.) *Larmar och gör sig till.* Göteborg: Göteborgs universitet, SOM-institutet.

Schön, Lennart, 2010: *Vår världs ekonomiska historia. Del II: Den industriella tiden.* Stockholm: SNS.

Schön, Lennart, 2012: *An Economic History of Modern Sweden.* London: Routledge.

Schulze-Cleven, Tobias, Watson, Bart & Zysman, John, 2007: "How Wealthy Nations Can Stay Wealthy: Innovation and Adaptability in a Digital Era" in *New Political Economy*, 12:4, 451–475.

Streeck, Wolfgang, 2016: *How Will the Capitalism End? Essays on a Failing System.* London and New York: Verso.

Suszycki, Andrzej Marcin (ed.) 2011: *Welfare Citizenship and Welfare Nationalism.* NordWel Studies in Historical Welfare State Research. Helsinki: NordWel. https://helda.helsinki. fi/bitstream/handle/10138/42137/nordwel2.pdf?sequence=1&isAllowed=y [Accessed 22 February 2019].

Tooze, Adam, 2017: "A General Logic of Crisis" in *London Review of Books.* [Accessed 5 January 2017].

Ulkomaan kansalaiset, 2018: *Tilastokeskus.* www.tilastokeskus.fi/tup/maahanmuutto/maahan muuttajat-vaestossa/ulkomaan-kansalaiset.html [Accessed 28 February 2019].

Valresultat, 2018: *Valmyndigheten.* www.val.se/valresultat/riksdag-landsting-och-kommun/ 2018/valresultat.html [Accessed 28 February 2019].

Weinberg, Christian, 2018: "Denmark's Biggest Party Adopts Anti-Immigrant Views" in *Bloomberg*, 6 June 2018. www.bloomberg.com/news/articles/2018-06-06/anti-immigrant-view-adopted-by-denmark-s-biggest-political-party [Accessed 28 February 2019].

3 Lost land of bliss

Imagined temporalities of the Nordic welfare state

Ainur Elmgren

In the early modern imagination, the golden age of ancient mankind proceeded inevitably towards decadence. At the dawn of the Industrial Revolution, a new way of conceptualizing temporality took form. Progress would lead humanity and the nation towards future perfection.[1] In the second half of the 20th century, the Scandinavian or Nordic welfare states integrated aspects of this faith in progress into their identities. In practice, Sweden came to symbolize this aspiration, both internally and outwardly. Historian Bo Stråth has written about a peculiar "Swedish feeling of chosenness" in his study on the labour unions and the Swedish model.[2] Finnish nationalism viewed Finland as "chosen", too – but the Finnish rhetoric of "chosenness" has been dominated by the experiences of war, suffering, and loss. Historian Jussi Kurunmäki notes that, while Finland has been discussed "as a survivor" in the literature of democratization and interwar crisis, Sweden has appeared as an example of "successful social democratic reformism".[3]

Towards the end of the 20th century, the welfare state project's very existence was questioned. The "end of history" and the victory of liberal democracy were announced during the reception of Francis Fukuyama's famous book – partly simplifying its message. Two of the bastions of Nordic neutrality fell as Finland and Sweden joined the European Union. Today, the political arenas of Sweden and Finland accommodate parties that arguably promote welfare state nationalism. These parties were funded in the 1990s, but they lay claim to the "true" heritage of their respective nation-states. Has nostalgia replaced visions of future glory regarding the Nordic welfare state? It can be argued that protest parties are attempting to take control of the national narrative. The continuity of history is established retroactively. All political actors participate in this "retconning" process. This chapter explores such imagined, constructed temporalities of the Nordic welfare state from the perspective of the original liberal critics of the welfare state project and through their uses of toponyms associated with utopia.

Mythical and literary place names used for the land of bliss, such as *lintukoto* in Finland and the more generic *lyckoland* (land of bliss) in Sweden, are here used as a red thread leading the narrative from the beginnings of the welfare state project to its nostalgic denouement during the last three decades. Such

DOI: 10.4324/9780429026690-3

concepts have an even longer heritage in the former realm of Sweden, which Finland was split off from in 1809. As historian Joachim Östlund states in his study on the legitimization of power in Swedish public rhetoric in the early modern and modern eras, the idyllic portrayal of the country as a "land of bliss" has shown "remarkable continuity" over the centuries, but it was not until the late 19th century that the people as a nation began to be imagined as a unit independent from God or Crown. The utopian "land of bliss" could become immanent as a union of convenience: "the rhetoric from above somewhere has to meet the dreams from below – in a Land of Bliss".[4]

In Finnish public discourse, the folkloristic-literary expression *lintukoto* (lit. bird's abode; figuratively, safe haven) is often used to denote an imagined utopia of peace and harmony. In early modern folk belief, it was an island at the rim of the Earth disc where the sky was low and the people consequently small in stature. The migratory birds would spend the winters there. Paradoxically, the name of this exotic imaginary place is today often used for Finland, specifically a lost idyllic past.

Lintukoto was first mentioned in print in the dictionary of Erik Schroderus of Uppsala in 1637.[5] Folk beliefs about little people that live at the edge of the earth's disc, as well as lands far away where the migratory birds spend the winter, have been recorded around the world. In an ancient Greek version of the myth, mentioned in the Iliad, "pygmies" live on the shore of the world-encircling river Oceanus, where they wage war against the cranes.[6] While the pygmies of ancient Greek myths tended to live in the south or south-east, early modern authors placed them sometimes in the far north – most famously Swedish cosmographer Olaus Magnus in his *Historia de gentibus septentrionalibus* (1555).[7] Finnish folklore was conflated with classical references in the works of 18th-century folklorist Christfrid Ganander and 19th-century poet Aleksis Kivi.[8] *Lintukoto* and its tiny inhabitants achieved literary status through an eponymous poem by Kivi, published in 1866. Kivi infused the folkloric tale with the isle of bliss topos, inherited from German and Scandinavian Romanticism. Unlike the mythical pygmies, Kivi's little people (*kerikansa*) did not fight migratory birds but happily rode on swans around their "isle of peace".[9]

Kivi's idyll influenced successive generations of Finnish writers. Folklorists used Kivi's poem as a testimony of the enduring power of native beliefs in the spirit of late national romanticism. Literary scholar Toni Lahtinen states that Kivi's poem has been seen as historically significant as a reworking of a universal topos "into a Finnish, that is, national, land of bliss".[10] It foreshadowed the imagined ideal welfare state in other ways, as Kivi – in contrast to many other literary depictions of the land of bliss as a land of leisure – showed the inhabitants happily at work, the men ploughing and mowing, the women weaving and cooking. However, *Lintukoto's* pronounced isolation and the small size of its inhabitants also invited pejorative uses. The poet Eino Leino, who often utilized folkloric themes in his works, compared the Finns to Kivi's *kerikansa* in a poem expressing disdain for narrowmindedness. His Finland was not a summery isle of bliss, but another land at the edge of the world, the desolate Ultima Thule.[11]

The Swedish concept *lyckoland* (or *lyckorike*, kingdom of bliss) overlaps the meaning of *lintukoto*, as redefined by Kivi. The land of bliss had been pictured as an island since antiquity. The poem *Lycksalighetens ö* (Isle of Bliss, 1833) by the Swedish Late Romantic Erik Johan Stagnelius, Kivi's "favourite poet", was an important source of inspiration for *Lintukoto*.[12] Stagnelius' island is a timeless paradise where autumn's bountiful harvest can be enjoyed in "eternal May sun", similarly to Kivi's *Lintukoto*. But unlike Kivi's chaste idyll, Stagnelius' fantasy is straightforwardly erotic.[13]

The literary origins of Stagnelius' isle of bliss can be traced to a popular 18th-century novel with the same name, a translation of a 1690 novelization of a traditional French fairy tale by Marie-Catherine d'Aulnoy. The tale inspired an eponymous play by Per Daniel Amadeus Atterbom from 1824. In this version, King Astolf leaves his native Hyperborea – another mythological allusion – for the isle of bliss, where he enjoys opulence and immortality with the appropriately named Felicia. After 300 years, Astolf returns to his northern homeland and finds it transformed: monarchy and nobility have been abolished, and the former subjects have lost their warlike honour. Instead, they waste their time on speeches and newspapers and get burdened with ever-increasing taxes.[14] Atterbom's Hyperborea foreshadows the 20th-century welfare state dystopia, although his targets were the liberals of his time.[15] Neither Stagnelius' poem, nor Atterbom's play, were ever translated to Finnish, but this was no obstacle for the largely Swedish-speaking Finnish intelligentsia of the 19th century.[16]

From these 19th-century exchanges of cultural tropes grew a literary tradition that contrasted the dream of perfect happiness with the nightmare of failure and loss. Throughout the 20th century, *lyckoland* was used in the sense of utopia or fairy-tale land of happiness in the Swedish language. The uses of the trope revealed awareness of its impossibility – Stagnelius' erotic idyll could only be reached through the imagination, and Atterbom's island of eternal beauty was a golden cage. These connotations made *lyckoland* an apt trope of political satire, for example in August Strindberg's Robinsonade *De lycksaliges ö* ("The Isle of the Blissful Ones") from 1882.[17] Until the mid-1930s, *lyckoland* was mainly used in *Dagens Nyheter* as a satirical description of the Soviet Union or, in a milder tone, of the United States as a destination for immigrants. It is as a description of migrants' hopes that the concept returns in the 1980s, but between these decades, it is also increasingly used for Sweden and the progressive project of the Social Democratic Party.

In comparison to the concepts *folkhem* (people's home, originally a conservative metaphor appropriated by the Swedish Social Democrats)[18] or *välfärdsstaten* (the welfare state), usually describing something realized in the present, the land of bliss is a place in the immediate future or the near past. If it is overlapping with the present, it is usually employed with an ironic meaning. The liberal critics of the welfare state began applying the terms ironically and reluctantly to contemporary society and increasingly adopted the terms as national self-definitions, until a turning point in 1989–1992. Around and after those dates, the terms are used in a nostalgic or moralizing sense to denote a lost era, but there have also been attempts to reclaim land of bliss as a cautiously optimistic future vision.[19]

Visions of Nordic progress

The connection between the Nordic countries and the land of bliss, as well as its dark side, preceded the modern welfare state. Hyperborea and Ultima Thule of ancient myth could be imagined as the two sides of the same coin – happy Hyperborea representing the nightless summer in the far north, and miserable Ultima Thule wrapped in endless winter dusk. The name Scandia, originally a Mediterranean toponym, was used for islands in Northern Europe by Greek and Roman geographers. By reinterpreting the works of Jordanes, who created a glorification of Gothic history in the 6th century, Early Modern Swedish scholar Olof Rudbeck the Elder resurrected the idea of Scandza/Scandinavia as an island – literally or metaphorically – for political purposes.[20] Rudbeck's Sweden, the state that was destined to rule Scandinavia, was not just any island, or peninsula – it was the mythical Atlantis that would rise again and relive its glorious past.[21] According to Rudbeck, already the ancient Greeks had "not without reason" testified that Sweden was "the isle of the Gods, the Kings, the High-Born, and the Blissful" (*de Lycksaligas ö*).[22]

Rudbeck's ideas were revived in the early 19th century after the loss of Finland. Although Finnish national romanticists were influenced by this "Neo-Gothicist" movement, they kept their work locally focused. With the rise of Finnish nationalism, the isle of bliss could be found in Finland itself. In a collection of children's stories in 1891, prolific author Zacharias Topelius combined the latest geological findings about post-glacial rebound in the Baltic Sea with folklore and national romantic poetry in his tale of the rise of an isle of bliss from the depths of the sea.[23] In Topelius' version, the isle of bliss consists of both Scandinavia and Finland. Happiness is disrupted by a jealous Arctic sorceress. She sends giants to unite the island with Asia by a land bridge. The isle of bliss transforms into a mundane peninsula "where paths of nations cross, where powers struggle, where hounds hunt, worries wake and sorrows cast their shadows upon glimpses of sunshine. Where, where is the isle of bliss?"[24] Topelius assures the reader that it lives on in the pure hearts of Finnish children.[25] The progress of post-glacial rebound became a metaphor for societal progress as a moral duty. The rising land was a gift from God, a miracle that distinguished Finland among the nations. Hence, the children of Finland have inherited the Christian duty to serve as stewards over God's creation and "grow, like the land, in body and soul, wisdom and mercy . . . to leave [the land] better off than you once received it".[26]

In the Nordic countries, the idea of progress became central to several political movements, including patriotic movements of civil rights and national liberation, the labour movement, the temperance movement, and liberal parties and associations. Christians like Topelius could embrace ideas of societal progress as a service to God. For a long time, the progressive land of bliss was not identified as actually present. Such utopian visions were, on the contrary, often mocked and parodied. All "lands of bliss" were not progressive, but all were somewhat dubious; most of them were clearly fictional, such as the 1924 Ernst Rolf revue *Lyckolandet*, one of the most successful shows of the 20th century in Sweden.[27] Much like Atterbom's isle of bliss, the revue featured orientalist exotism in costumes and scenery.

Transposed on mundane Sweden, the idyll invariably looked ridiculous. In the winning verses of a leap year poetry competition of *Dagens Nyheter's* humour section "Namn och Nytt", everyday nuptial harmony is promised to the presumptive groom in the style of 1936: "We shall dwell in the lands of bliss,/and our fashion shall be à la Myrdal."[28] The vision of modern marital happiness is tempered with mild irony and the mention of the fashionable social scientist couple, whose public example was extended into the private sphere.

Until the 1930s, most *lyckoländer* in *Dagens Nyheter* were either the destination of emigrants, such as the United States or Latin America, or the land of the Bolshevik revolution, the USSR. Even though the liberal newspaper could have been expected to show greater sympathy towards the "land of bliss in the West" (*lyckolandet i väst*), it was relatively cautious. The heyday of Swedish mass emigration was over by the time of the First World War, but the fear of depopulation and the moral doubts left their effect on public discourse.[29]

In independent Finland, the lands of bliss lay elsewhere long into the postwar era. The independence process was a painful disillusionment culminating in a Socialist uprising and a disastrous civil war in 1918. The liberal press, along with the conservatives on the side of the victors, adopted a cautionary line towards utopianism, especially its universalist and cosmopolitan expressions. Literary critics also approached idylls with nationalist caution. In 1922, Aleksis Kivi's poem *Lintukoto* was praised by critic Johannes Vihtori Lehtonen for having put the stamp of Finnishness on the universal topic the isle of bliss, creating an "unbroken *Finnish* [emphasis in the original] poem about this eternal dream of humanity, . . . that nations and social classes have tried to reach by wading through streams of blood".[30] Kivi's idyll was rooted in Finnish nature and tamed with "honest Finnish farmer's work".[31] *Lintukoto's* nature and culture was recognizably local, unlike Atterbom's exotic fantasy land.[32] This localization of utopia meant that the danger of universalism – the upsetting of the existing order – was evaded. Lehtonen backed his national and moral interpretation of *Lintukoto* with the words of philosophers who proved the impossibility of man-made utopias: "they would not last long, humanity being what it is, for suffering and toil is its inevitable lot".[33] For Lehtonen, it was important to promote Kivi's modest, national idyll "especially in current times, when man seems to need more than ever everything that is bright, fair and liberating".[34] Lehtonen even reread Kivi's lullaby *Sydämeni laulu* (The Song of My Heart), where the child is lulled to sleep in the Hades of Finnish folklore, as an idyll of "happy melancholy . . . the intuitive dreaming of the happy dwellers of Lintukoto, "'painless yearning'", that soon fades away".[35]

Lintukoto was rarely used to describe really existing Finland until the 1960s, but it did appear sporadically in descriptions of achievements of the budding welfare state – such as small homes for young families, exhibited at the Social Museum in Helsinki in the war year 1942.[36] The connection between *lintukoto* and the smallness of its inhabitants was not lost, as well as the idea that *lintukoto* was only a temporary haven from the evil of the real world.[37] The name had an appeal for holidaymakers and was used as a name for summer cottages (along with Onnela, literally a place of bliss).[38] This might have been due to the influence of author Joel Lehtonen, who used *Lintukoto* as the name of his countryside retreat in the prose work *Lintukoto* (1929) and the post-humous poetry collection *Hyvästijättö Lintukodolle* ("Farewell to Lintukoto") from 1934.[39]

Joel Lehtonen's private Lintukoto was an island in the lake Vanajavesi in southern Finland. Even though Lehtonen pictured the island as an escape, a "sovereign realm" or a monastery "in splendid isolation", his island was not an abode of indolent bliss. Every living creature on the island participated in the struggle for survival. The blue flower of Romanticism was the humble corn-flower in the rye field, a product of the previous settler's hard work.[40] Lehtonen distanced his island dreams from the pretentious and hedonistic "rascals" of the European Robinsonade and picaresque literature.[41] Finally, he abandoned his island shortly before his own death. Literature scholar Juhani Niemi sees in Lehtonen's two Lintukoto works a pastoral idyll with traits of parody and even apocalyptic elements. The topos Lintukoto turns into an atopos, a bridge to the afterlife, or to oblivion.[42] Did Kivi's extinction of the idyll's Eros inevitably lead to Lehtonen's embrace of its Thanatos?

The adoption of Lintukoto as a Finnish self-description by journalists and authors coincides with the self-identification as a Nordic welfare state. In Swe-den, this process was initiated a few decades earlier. On the pages of the reluctant *Dagens Nyheter*, it started as a satirical self-identification in the 1930s, referenc-ing the progressive projects of *folkhemmet*, the Myrdals and the trend of "New Objectivity" (*nya sakligheten*, from the Weimar era art style *Neue Sachlichkeit*).[43] Conservatives also employed such ironic terminology. The diplomat and writer Rütger Essén, a Nazi sympathizer, entitled one of his popular radio plays on political themes in the late 1930s "Idyllen Sverige" (Sweden the Idyll).[44] Essén let a particular character, a Swedish expatriate, express his discomfort with his old homeland: the Swedes, taking the credit for peace and prosperity that was merely due to luck, "with sensible and self-wise virtuousness observe their own splendidness and distribute warning and advice to a world gone astray".[45] Essén, like other radical conservatives, lamented that democracy hindered indi-vidual talents from leading. In *Dagens Nyheter*, Ivar Harrie reminded Essén about his relative privilege: "In authoritarian states, the police take care of [dis-sidents]. Democratic societies can afford to keep them around, and profit from them. Dr Essén owes the Swedish idyll much gratitude."[46]

In the face of such self-sufficiency, even from the liberal critics of the welfare state, it is not surprising that discomfort with the welfare state project had to be expressed through poetry and fiction. Finnish poet Elmer Diktonius's prose work *Onnela* (1925), "land of bliss", on which the poem's speaker states ambiguously: "Here I am at home – here I am in a foreign land", was still the "meagre earth" of the pre-welfare state.[47] Gunnar Ekelöf's *Non Serviam* (1945), on the other hand, is a frustrated individualist manifesto against *folkhemmet* Sweden: "I am not at home in this land/but this land acts as if it is at home in me!"[48]

But as foreign commentators began to praise Nordic progress, the temptation to repeat their words arose – first with mild irony, then increasingly matter-of-factly. British professor C. E. M. Joad, who visited Sweden in 1946 and identified it as the happiest country in the world, had his words repeated verbatim in *Dagens Nyheter*.[49] However, his explanation for Sweden's happiness was not in superior social planning and "socialism without tears", but in the smallness of the population and the national temperament, or rather lack of it. The image of Nordic progressivism was created in concert with the foreign – mainly Anglo-American – discourse on Nordic particularism. Still, in 1975, when Prime Minister Olof Palme's first government made the country "unbearable politically" for many US businessmen, the magazine *Business Week* presented Sweden as a "land of bliss" (according to *Dagens Nyheter*) for business investment and a model for US lawmakers.[50]

Parallel to the creeping acceptance of the *lyckoland* identity and the breakthrough of the "golden age" of capitalism, the 1950s has been seen as the peak of the *folkhemmet* discourse, while self-identification as a welfare state has been seen as a feature of the 1960s.[51] The notion of the Swedish idyll was losing its satirical connotations, while the original bearers of this myth were facing challenges to it. The liberal and conservative press gladly quoted the chair of the central organization of the labour unions (LO), Axel Strand, beset by the challenges of post-war inflation and the government's demands to lower expectations: "the land of bliss without difficulties and worries only exists in our dreams".[52] Parallel to the land of bliss, the dystopias – "the future as a nightmare" according to writer Olof Lagercrantz in *Dagens Nyheter* – were always present. As Lagercrantz observed, the warnings of Yevgeny Zamyatin, Aldous Huxley, and George Orwell, as well as those of the Swedes Pär Lagerkvist and Karin Boye, were inspired by the real sociopolitical projects of Nazi Germany and the Soviet Union. These authors contributed to a "horror for the future" that Lagercratz predicted would turn many countries in the West towards conservatism. The Soviet Union had killed the old utopia.[53]

Lagercrantz identified very different interpretations of happiness among the dystopian writers. In Orwell, he sees no promise of even artificial happiness. The future is "a boot stamping on a human face forever", an image inherited from Jack London's *Iron Heel* (1908). But Zamyatin's totalitarian collective *We* (1920–1921) lures its inhabitants into simple happiness. Adam and Eve could choose between happiness without freedom and freedom without happiness – they chose freedom and became unhappy. Since then, humanity has longed for fetters. In Zamyatin's dystopia, humanity has been restored to simplicity, innocence, and chains. Similarly, Huxley shows a society where misery has been organized away, at the expense of freedom. Lagercrantz quotes the example of an elevator operator, who has been injected with a drug that makes him feel that the height of bliss is to reach the top floor. He loves his job!

Lagercrantz does not compare the worlds of Zamyatin and Huxley outright to the *folkhem* project, but he asks:

> In the new society that we are approaching . . . we buy a little fortune cookie [*lyckokaka*] for freedom and unlimited personal opportunities. We swap our soul for biological satisfaction. Is such a development . . . the necessary result of the new technology, the centralized state, the new mass communications and the Zamyatinesque bliss-philosophy?

There are echoes of the heritage of Protestant pietism in Lagercrantz's judgement of his contemporaries. The fulfilment of worldly desires meant "the risk of enslavement under happiness".[54] Instead, one should seek the grace of God through the cultivation of virtue, above all contentment with one's lot, and use these "tools of reason" to vanquish worldly desires.

Sixteen years later, psychiatrist and writer Jan Gudmundsson echoed Lagercrantz's concerns for the psychological consequences of "biological satisfaction" in his novel *Löfteslandet* (The Land of Promise, 1976). The main character, Henning, was a worker suffering from a crippling anxiety evidenced by both physical and behavioural symptoms. Despite being both married and unionized, Henning felt like an outsider. According to a review in *Dagens Nyheter*, the utopian "myth of a worker-led welfare society" obscured reality, namely Hemming's alienation. Henning had grown up in an individualistic culture that values wealth and celebrity, in the "blinding light of the Swedish land of bliss . . . the Swedish compromise". The reviewer felt that Gudmundsson gave tangible form to an almost hopeless contradiction in contemporary ideals, and the individual's consequential alienation. In "the solidarity-based 'worker-led' welfare society" all conceivable services were readily available to fulfil Hemming's needs, but availability was not the issue: "The issue is that society, in its chief and decisive normal functions, lacks solidarity."[55]

Even as the contemporary age began to be identified as an age of increased welfare and happiness, the concept of happiness was tainted with the negative connotations of worldly desires. Just as in Atterbom's play, the isle of bliss cannot give the hero the freedom that he craves, and he abandons it for an ultimately fatal quest into a world that has moved on. The virtues of yore, "truth and beauty", seemed to have been dismissed as unmodern just as they were in Huxley's *Brave New World*. This criticism would continue to haunt the Nordic welfare state until its mysterious dislocation into the past.

The perils of progress

The liberal critique of the socialist project – usurping the modern project at least in Sweden – from the very beginning focused on its character as a utopia (*lyckorike, lyckoland*), an impossible dream world of happiness. But as more and more of the promises began to come true, often with practical support of the liberals themselves, the critique changed character.[56] The *folkhem* project began to be criticized as fulfilling every wish and therefore limiting ambition. By making everything possible, it paradoxically limited people's will to explore them. It was dangerously similar to totalitarian systems that also promised heaven on earth.

The sociologist Antti Eskola was an early Finnish critic of the conflict-less land of bliss and an early adopter of the term *lintukoto* for Finland. The self-described "anarchist" and "ultra-democrat" Eskola was the son of a crofter from the same estate that novelist Väinö Linna immortalized in his 1959–1962 trilogy *Under the North Star*. In the 1950s, Eskola became a student of sociologist Erik Allardt and later eulogized this "golden age of bourgeois sociology" that aimed to utilize research in order to make democracy more accessible, increase tolerance, remove ingrained misconceptions, and help individuals and groups adapt to the structural changes in society.[57]

However, in 1968, Eskola painted a satirical image of this brave new society in his polemical book *Suomi sulo Pohjola* ("Finland Sweet North", 1968):

> In this ideal Finland . . . the sun is shining, the tractors buzz in the fields and the merry roar of GDP growth is heard everywhere. The tiny lads and lasses [a reference to the pygmies inhabiting *lintukoto*] walk around beaming with tolerance, enduring difference and regulating conflicts. Nobody asks the fundamental questions, nobody inquires about the legitimacy of the basic rules. // There are no abnormals or antisocials. Everyone has their functional place: the communists have been integrated by receiving responsibilities.[58]

Eskola's lintukoto–Finland was closely inspired by Kivi's 1866 poem and even picked up some of the darker shades that Kivi had included in his description of the fairy-tale island's happy inhabitants:

> In such a utopia, people are not conscious of the foundations of the social order and their own actions. Only occasionally does the hazy shadow of such a thought cross their mind, just like the inhabitants of Kivi's *Lintukoto*, who sometimes sink into a semblance of gloomy contemplation. In reality, they do not contemplate anything, because they cannot articulate their feeling in a question: "They seek no answer, they find none."[59]

Kivi scholars had puzzled over this mysterious shadow of gloom in Kivi's idyll throughout the 20th century. In the interwar era, Johannes Vihtori Lehtonen proposed that it reflected the premonition of death in Atterbom's play, while poet and writer Veikko Antero Koskenniemi interpreted it as an effect of pre-lapsarian innocence.[60] Koskenniemi's interpretation foreshadowed Eskola's, who had found one flaw in the idyll: "To reduce suffering, knowledge has to be reduced." The way out of the land of ignorance-is-bliss was to bite the fruit of knowledge and create a "conscious society", to "make people painfully aware that society is founded on coercion, that we are only free to do what is currently tolerated to be done, and that we have no personality, will, or behaviour of our own independent of society". In outright religious terms, Eskola demanded that everyone become aware of their participation in a system of oppression where they were both exploited and privileged in relation to others: "Man has to comprehend that his every act is a sin; bad conscience must trouble him day and night; and mercy must be almost out of reach."[61] A decent human being, a "child of Marx and Christ", had to be able to defend herself against manipulation and persuasion of the type that Stanley Milgram demonstrated in his famous study in social psychology. In Eskola's words, Milgram had revealed that "our culture did not seem to offer the individual suitable ways of refusing to obey unjust orders".[62] The democratic welfare state seemed to be even more difficult to rebel against than a totalitarian state.

Helsingin Sanomat critic Teuvo Mällinen saw a contradiction in Eskola's fear of a utopia without conflict and his fear of a utopia that regulates conflict.[63] Mällinen pointed out that Eskola himself had modelled democracy according to the ideals of regulation of conflict. Eskola returned to the *lintukoto* topic in an interview almost 30 years later. The old radical re-evaluated his views on post-war Finland, and longed for more harmonious times. "[W]e no longer live safely in a *lintukoto* between Sweden and the Soviet Union", he lamented.[64]

In 1970s literature, the toponym became more frequently associated with contemporary society, perhaps idyllic and swiftly passing, but really existing in youth culture.[65] It became synonymous with the hippie movement, popularized – and perhaps institutionalized – in Finland via cultural imports such as *Hair* the musical. This *lintukoto* of youth was full of "innocent self-sufficiency", much like the Swedish idyll, and Kivi's poem was reinterpreted in light of "ideological escape", "hippie solutions", and "rock poetry".[66] Perhaps the consciousness of the toponym's literary roots and its fictitiousness has been stronger in Finland, and therefore it was not easily applied to the Finnish welfare state project, a product of pragmatic compromise. It could be recognized as such in past projects, such as the research on peasant folklore, reinterpreted as an exercise in national self-sufficiency and utopianism: "In our history, romantic wanderlust did not have to escape to Medievalism or the wonders of India and El Dorado . . ., because in East Karelia was found a living legendary Atlantis, a *lintukoto* of antiquity", claimed historian Matti Klinge.[67]

Parallel to the immanentization of *lintukoto*, the Swedish idyll began to lose some of its ironic connotations. Critics of the welfare state like the leader of the Swedish Moderate party Gösta Bohman were forced to accept its achievements.

These were integrated in the Swedish Moderate party's vision of the past in the book *Kurs mot framtiden* from 1981, where Bohman envisioned a change of tack for Sweden.[68] Bohman argued that Swedish Social Democrats had chosen the way of liberalization – "freedom and change" – in the 1930s and 1950s, but since the late 1960s, socialism and stagnation had been their choice. Bohman connected his critique to conservative values of tradition by describing how "our ancestors" had preferred individual liberation before collectivism. Still, post-war Sweden had been an economic success story, and it was this positive continuity that the Moderate party set out to preserve, not disrupt.[69] The progressive welfare state had reached a level of hegemony that forced even its opponents to work within its historical framework. In the 1930s, Swedish conservatives accepted democracy "because it was historical".[70] Similarly, Bohman's liberal-conservatives accepted, at least temporarily, the reformist welfare state.

Gösta Bohman openly admired Social Democratic leaders like Per Albin Hansson, who had led a coalition government through the war years, and Tage Erlander, the longest-sitting prime minister in the post-war era. Bohman's vision of the happy past was, paradoxically, a national "we" of individuals working together consensually for the common good. In 1981, he criticized the "new" direction of the Social Democrats that was, in contrast to the previously conciliatory path of progress, the road to socialism, collectivism, and conflict. Thirty years later, Bohman's successor Fredrik Reinfeldt described Olof Palme as "radicalizing" the Social Democratic Party, while Erlander was part of a "Swedish tradition of consensus and spirit of concord".[71]

Similar signs of critique appeared in the liberal press in Finland in the early 1980s. Although the Social Democratic Party had never reached a comparable hegemonic position, some of its politicians became targets for liberal critique. For Eero Silvasti in *Helsingin Sanomat*, the social politician and researcher Pekka Kuusi was the architect of the "*lintukoto* of welfare".[72] Acting mainly in the role of an expert and a civil servant, Kuusi had promoted redistribution of wealth and income as an equalizing measure. Although Silvasti admitted that never-before-seen levels of prosperity had been reached thanks to societal reforms in Finland, he also noted that people were experiencing dissatisfaction and unhappiness – the same paradoxical malaise of the welfare state that Swedish authors had identified in the 1960s and the 1970s. Silvasti found that "the slavery of work" had been replaced by "the slavery of consumption": "The well-meaning Pekka Kuusi ended up drawing a cage". Against the optimism of literary scholar Matti Mäkelä, who saw a glimmer of hope in the increased consumption of trainers and bicycles enabling the consumer to move and possibly even think independently from the "global gutenbergian-electromagnetic magical circle of mental stuffing", Silvasti predicted the future menace of "belt-stereos" and "wristwatch-televisions". The interconnected society of the 2010s has made his prediction come true in surprising ways, as methods of consumer manipulation, surveillance, and data processing have become increasingly refined and totalistic.

The turning point: looking back at the lost golden age

The older idea of a golden age in the past and its descent into decadence remained alive, albeit advocated by a vocal minority. The welfare state was contested and depicted as a potential dystopia during its construction in the mid-20th century. When did the progressive "brave new world" of the future become the lost golden age of the past?

Foreign commentators influenced this turn, too. Eleven years after Olof Lagercrantz alluded to the welfare state as a Brave New World in his article series on utopia and dystopia, the British journalist Roland Huntford published the book *The New Totalitarians* in 1971.[73] Eleven years later, Hans Magnus Enzensberger's famously anti-utopian critique of the welfare state and the Swedish model, *Schwedischer Herbst*, was written as an article series for *Dagens Nyheter* in 1982. The series was part of a greater debate under the by-line "Is Sweden Totalitarian?" echoing Huntford's book. Franz Zimmer sees Enzensberger evaluate Sweden as a heterotopia in Foucault's sense, an actually realized utopia. Enzensberger inquires about the price that the individual has had to pay to belong to this egalitarian paradise – the loss of a healthy mistrust of authority.[74] According to Enzensberger, the Swedes remained in a "state of historical innocence". Did the utopia take them out of time, out of the temporal development that all other post-war nations in Western Europe were partaking of, and condemn them to eternal timeless immaturity and a nationwide regression into childhood? Enzensberger's critique was well received in Sweden. It provided an opportunity for defenders of the welfare state to respond to his abstract critique with paeans to the welfare state's actual achievements. Enzensberger's ability to express such severe criticisms was taken as proof of the fact that Sweden was not only safe and prosperous but also an open society.[75]

After Enzensberger, various events were used as emblems for a return to history, a loss of historical innocence: the murder of Olof Palme on 28 February 1986, the Estonia disaster in 1994, or the murder of Anna Lindh on 11 September 2003. However, such imagined turning points had already been publicized before 1986. The destruction of the land of bliss seems to be a recurring event. As early as in 1973, as historians Marie Cronqvist, Sara Kärrholm, and Lina Sturfelt have observed, a creeping suspicion had entered the Swedish public debate that something was rotten in the land of bliss.[76] The year was marked by two dramatic mediatized spectacles: the hostage drama at Norrmalmstorg that would give a name to "Stockholm Syndrome" and the sudden illness and death of King Gustav VI Adolf. In May, the existence of a secret intelligence organization whose purpose was to register internal dissidents had been revealed to the public and endangered the untoppled, 40-year incumbent Social Democratic Party's victory in the coming election. Social Democrats took the opportunity to include the passing king in the rhetoric of a modern welfare state both as a "co-worker" (Erlander) and a symbol of the nation that had accepted change and become integrated harmoniously with the progressive ideals of the welfare state (Palme).[77] In their responses to the king's stoic death-bed struggle, many members of the public expressed fears that a unique era was over, and doubted that the crown prince, more famous as a playboy than a serious worker, could fill his grandfather's shoes.

Meanwhile, the hostage drama that unfolded over several weeks at the bank at Norrmalmstorg twisted the very definitions of good and evil. The socially conscious crime novels of Maj Sjöwall and Per Wahlöö had already handled themes that now became reality as conveyed through the tabloid press. Sjöwall-Wahlöö's crime novels laid the foundations of the genre that is now known internationally as Nordic Noir.[78] Reality and fiction intertwined in a narrative of criticism against the repressive side of the welfare state.[79] In Sjöwall-Wahlöö's works, Sweden was not an exceptional utopia, but a part of the Western capitalist system, sharing its burden of exploitation and guilt. The responsibility for faults in the system fell on those in power. The happy ending of the hostage drama contributed to the re-election of the Social Democratic government, which had promised "security". A few years later, the Swedish prime minister was assassinated in a Sjöwall-Wahlöö novel, eerily foreshadowing the murder of Olof Palme in 1986 that would again shake the fundaments of the Swedish land of bliss.

Interestingly, the dramatic events of 1973 had also been foreshadowed in the Finnish press in a review of an exhibition of Swedish modern art. "The people's home is malfunctioning, but why", the headline asked. The reviewer made the careful generalization that "Swedish art seems to prefer to show the malaise of society, but does not hint at a cure".[80] Among the visual expressions of "the chilliness of the welfare state against the individual", the reviewer noted the skyscrapers of central Stockholm in the miniature works of Lennart Mörk and a Finnish jail cell in the works of Dick Bengtsson. Optimistically, he concluded that "stating the truth and reflecting [reality] is also progress". It is also in the 1970s that critics note how Joel Lehtonen's aforementioned literary *Lintukoto* also contained the destruction of utopia. The narrator follows the life of the ants on his island and sees in the ant colony "the image of an organized human utopian state". He destroys the anthill with fire like a vengeful god.[81]

Historian Jussi Lahtinen has shown how a Janus-faced image of progress took form in Finnish literature in the 1960s and the 1970s, the "golden age" of realist working-class novels.[82] Lahtinen has limited his study to novels written by male authors, which begs the question of the welfare state malaise as a crisis of masculinity. In the novels, Finland appears on the one hand as a welfare state where the individual's standard of living and social security has improved somewhat. On the other hand, the worker protagonists experience the increasingly globally connected economy of Finland as a system that primarily benefits grand capital and the economic elite, while small entrepreneurs, wage earners and single women remain in an inferior, even exploited position. Societal problems are seen as either problems of capitalism or − similar to the liberal critique in Sweden − products of a nanny state collapsing under excessive taxation and bureaucratization.

The new Finland was not a utopia. In the 1980s, *lintukoto* first appeared – if we disregard Antti Eskola's attempt in 1968 – as a denigrating description of Finland. *Helsingin Sanomat*'s Eero Silvasti wrote a pessimistic column on the development of Finnish society entitled "Portent of Storm?" in July 1981. In Silvasti's eyes, the greatest paradox of the present was that "the feared and threatening 1980s . . . had been taken over so securely and assuredly". He saw dreadful portents in the world economy and international politics, while Finland was prospering. Just as before the First World War, Finland was indus-trializing thanks to the growing trade with Russia, but a bloody storm was brewing again. Finland would not be in control of that coming storm, either. For Silvasti, "the harmony of *lintukoto* was the eternal dream of all constructive forces", but now Finland had been "somehow secretly and half-accidentally" surprised by it, and not everyone was satisfied: "The intellectuals are mutter-ing . . . moralism in different forms raises its head and searches irrational forces for allies." The mysterious malaise that Silvasti detected was precisely the suspi-ciously empty consensus bemoaned by the critics of the Swedish welfare state in the 1970s and the early 1980s – the calm before the storm.[83]

Other authors were also now using the term in a negative sense. Finland was a "*lintukoto* of culture", but this did not mean a safe haven or a blissful island, but a state of "exceptional consensus".[84] Scholars and journalists equated con-sensus and homogeneity with social tranquillity and income policy solidarity. Their respective emphasis on correlation versus causation varied, but most of them shared the fear of a future where this package would be lost: a future of increasing inequality and increasing distinction between social groups, leaving behind the blissful years of the 1960s and the 1970s.

Swedish anti-utopian discourse was also reflected in *Helsingin Sanomat*'s reporting on the neighbouring country. During the 1982 elections, "the people's home" was no longer in order, a commentator wrote.[85] The Social Democratic Party had spent six years in opposition, so this malaise could not be personified by the party. Instead, Olof Palme was able to claim that the bourgeois coalition government would endanger the welfare state if they con-tinued to govern. In 1985, after the victory of Palme's party and its economic measures that were not welcomed by the labour unions, the Finnish press could still report that Swedish scholars felt confident in the future of Swedish social democracy and the concept of the egalitarian people's home.[86] The Finnish reviewer, himself a researcher at Stockholm University, still had to question the idyll: "is the people's home truly so democratic and egalitarian"? Scholars, he felt, evaded the debate about "control-Sweden, the Orwellian society, where public power penetrates the private lives of people ever deeper".

The next year was a turning point. The murder of the Swedish Prime Min-ister Olof Palme created a shock on both sides of the Baltic Sea. Sensitive to international reactions, Swedish media reported statements such as Richard Reeves' in the *New York Times*: "The Swedish idyll disappeared".[87] The same year, the Chernobyl disaster, paradoxically, enforced the image of Finland as a safe haven for all the wrong reasons. Previously unspeakable things became articulated, for "even in the Finnish *lintukoto*, the world today demands that a responsible minister be found who supplies information now and not on the fifteenth day".[88] External threats, like ecoterrorism[89] and environmental disasters,[90] not internal harmony, now seemed to determine the identity of *lintukoto*. Even so, a happy *lintukoto*, even in literature, was "disgusting and unrealistic".[91] The Swedish idyll, on the other hand, was sorely missed. In 1989, journalist Mats Nörklit penned the following hopeful verses in *Dagens Nyheter* upon the arrest of a suspect in the Palme murder case: "He has become a symbol for our democracy/For our dream of the Swedish idyll would end/If he wasn't the one."[92]

The frustration with *lintukoto* in Finland reached political levels. In 1987, unexpected radicals, such as Olli Rehn, the leader of the youth organization of the Centre Party, spoke at a "surprisingly fierce" student demonstration against "consensual *lintukoto*-Finland".[93] Even the mild-mannered presidential candidate of the left, Kalevi Kivistö, was opposed to "*lintukoto* thinking".[94] This antipathy seems surprising, considering that lintukoto was generally associated with positive ideals. However, it was also a symbol of smallness and weakness. *Lintukoto*, like Lehtonen's anthill, was doomed to die, and Finns were ready to kill it with fire. In 1988, historian Osmo Jussila described "the house of democracy" in the world itself as "quite a small *lintukoto*" in comparison with the conquests of Leninism and other "ideologies of salvation", echoing J. V. Lehtonen's 1920s juxtaposition between the purely national land of bliss and blood-drenched universalist utopia.[95] The 1980s flood of *lintukoto* rhetoric also covered areas like credit cards – in 1988, 40 per cent of the population were still living without debt of any kind.[96] Finland became *lintukoto* in theatre,[97] but even in the world of fiction, a Finlandized *lintukoto* made certain comparisons and translations impossible: a translation of an Austrian play, with all its references to the violent past and the volatile present in Central Europe, became incongruous to the critic in the context of the "peace of the Finnish *lintukoto*".[98] If Finland's own war-torn and conflicted history seemed irrelevant as a point of comparison, had the country finally reached the point of happy oblivion that J. V. Lehtonen had hoped for, and Antti Eskola had warned against?

In 1989, the great changes in the European political landscape were greeted with surprise and also joy in Finland. Among Social Democrats, optimist and even utopian visions could be found on the rebuilding of Europe with the power of popular movements. The Åland islands, an autonomous region of Finland with a neutralized and demilitarized status, were presented as a model for Finland as a whole. This insular vision was characterized as a *lintukoto* by *Helsingin Sanomat*.[99] The model of the fiercely independent island appeared as naïve in light of the changing present, which inspired re-evaluations of the past and a revival of interest in the nationalist project, although "*lintukoto*-Finland" threatened to dilute "the fury of Finnishness into toothless tolerance".[100] Despite such protests, the concept's insular and protectionist connotations imbued it with positive potential in the national context. For example, although markets were integrating globally, Finnish protectionism enabled a *lintukoto* for the vitally important forestry industry.[101] Finnish nuclear energy production still trusted the bedrock "in our *lintukoto*".[102] Thus, a nostalgic potential could be activated through the use of this concept in the right context.

The end of Finland as a *lintukoto* came as abruptly as the downfall of the Soviet Union. In September 1990, cinematographer Aki Kaurismäki, the great critic and nostalgist of the Finnish post-war era, announced in an interview that "the time of the *lintukoto* is past, unfortunately".[103] Social scientist Eero Ojanen mused on the culture pages in November 1991: "It is especially amusing that the metaphor is usually employed by those debaters who belittle the meaning of national values and traditions." Ojanen pointed out that the usage of *lintukoto* to describe Finland was quite distinct from Kivi's 1866 poem: "a different reality somewhere else, far away where the sky and the earth meet". According to Ojanen, Kivi's escapist "*Lintukoto*-romance" resembled contemporary "Euro-romance" much more than homely Finland. For Ojanen, the newfound fancy for the European Union was not wrong, but "utopias ought to remain utopias . . . the attempt to realize utopias has, however, often left ugly traces".[104] *Pace* J. V. Lehtonen, Kivi's *Lintukoto* now lost its national character and its usefulness as a down-home utopia.

Aleksis Kivi created a related concept in the toponym Impivaara ("Virgin Hill"). This safe haven in the wilderness figured in his novel *Seven Brothers* (1870), the first published novel in the Finnish language. The brothers retreat to Impivaara after failing to adapt to social conventions; they return after adventures in the forest and become esteemed members of the community. In the original novel, Impivaara is a temporary retreat for the brothers, enabling them to grow from boys to men. In contemporary discourse, the place name is used in the same sense as *lintukoto* − a safe but lost haven.[105] In the early 20th century, Impivaara was interpreted almost an ideal Thoreauesque Walden, although the novel is rather an original and almost satirical take on the Bildungsroman. Towards the end of the 20th century, the meaning of Impivaara became increasingly negative.[106] Now Finns were accusing each other of being unable to adapt to the demands of progress, such as internationalization and globalization.[107]

When the splendid isolation of *lintukoto* was breached inevitably "in this present time of rupture", a strengthening of local roots and culture was offered as a protection.[108] But concrete measures were needed − the first special police forces for crowd control were introduced in 1994 as "preparation for internationalization". According to a senior inspector from the Ministry of the Interior, dangerous "extremist elements might come to Finland . . . this country is no longer a *lintukoto*".[109] In 1996, the chief of police emphasized that despite the fact that the prediction of an invasion of extremist elements had not come true, "Finland was still no *lintukoto*".[110] The imagined loss of the idyll was utilized to bolster requests for increased public funding.

The land of bliss and the other

The 1980s and the 1990s also meant a change in the *lyckoland* rhetoric in the Swedish press. Earlier in the 20th century, any destination of emigrants might have been designated a *lyckoland*, a land of bliss, whether it really offered happiness or not: the United States, the Soviet Union, Norway, or Venezuela.[111] Although Sweden had – often reluctantly – received refugees before, it was in the 1960s that Sweden itself became a *lyckoland* or idyll in newspaper reports about migrants and refugees, mainly in contrast to the countries that these refugees were leaving.[112] In Finland, *lintukoto* was employed similarly in the 1980s and early 1990s. The toponym immediately conjured up its counter-concept in the form of the threatening outside world. Whereas the *lintukoto* of the poets, the original isle of bliss, had everyday Finland as its implicit or explicit counter-image, *lintukoto*-Finland expelled its own harshness to the outside world. For example, the reviewer of Günter Wallraff's book *Ganz unten*, translated into Finnish in 1986, where Wallraff reported on his impersonation of a Turkish guest worker, presented different reactions of Finns to the possibility of dealing with the same problems in "the northern *lintukoto*": "Fright: [May we never have] a migrant problem in this country! Relief: What a wise refugee policy we have! Or smugness: It's different here, foreigners are even treated too well here!"[113]

Without distinction between labour migrants or political refugees, the line between push and pull factors was blurred. The word *lycksökare*, seeker of bliss, has a negative tone in Swedish: it can mean opportunist as well as adventurer and fortune hunter, although the meaning is connected to the expression *söka sin lycka*, to look for one's fortune (in the world).[114] In Swedish folk belief, *lycka* was a limited resource that could be lost or stolen.[115] In Finland, the *lintukoto* rhetoric carried connotations of unwillingness to share the bliss with outsiders, although this could be subverted: "I believe that in *lintukoto*, the mythical land of bliss, a much friendlier atmosphere is reigning than in our closed society."[116] *Helsingin Sanomat* returned to the topic as refugees increasingly reached Finland in the early 1990s. Municipal politicians shirking their duties in the settlement of "more than 500 refugees" were still "living in a *lintukoto*", but these were obviously behind the times.[117]

In *Dagens Nyheter* and *Helsingin Sanomat*, the idyllic concepts could be used without an obvious hint of sarcasm in news items describing the hopes and dreams of refugees and migrants.[118] Visitors from Namibia were introduced to the "Swedish idyll", meaning Swedish democracy, represented by election campaigners from parties left, centre and right, in the midst of the summer greenery of the Djurgården district in Stockholm.[119] Visits of international VIPs, such as the UN Secretary General, and the crises that Swedish politicians set out to solve as self-evident mediators, also provided an effective contrast to "the Swedish idyll" in newspaper copy.[120] With the increasing crises in Europe during the dissolution of the Eastern Bloc, the idyllic character of Sweden could be admitted to exist – in the eyes of the Other.

In the context of the "welfare state malaise" rhetoric published by the same newspapers, the connotation of mockery was not entirely possible to ignore. Just as the US land of bliss proved to be a disappointment to many Swedish emigrants, the Swedish *lyckoland* could be a trap to unhappy migrants, for example "Finns stranded in the Swedish land of bliss".[121] In the early 1990s, the most reliable land of bliss was again projected into the exotic past – in the shape of a Danish-Norwegian co-production of the South Seas fantasy musical *Styrman Karlsens flammer*, originally performed in 1929, "a true Nordic myth about Utopia".[122]

Was Utopia something one could buy and consume? In 1980, an Ikea advertisement had invited *Dagens Nyheter* readers to a "paradise" and "land of bliss" of sofas: "not for the rich, but for the smart".[123] "The Swedish idyll" appeared in real estate advertisements in the 1980s.[124] It could even be utilized to attract West German companies.[125] As we have seen, the literary genre of Nordic Noir achieves much of its thrills from the clash between a peaceful society and the horrors that break the illusion. Long before Stieg Larsson's *Millennium* trilogy, *Dagens Nyheter* advertised crime series contrasting the "Swedish idyll" with "the absurd, crazy and rule-breaking reality of crime".[126] However, the paradox of the genre as a marketable product is that the idyll needs to be reinstated in order to be destroyed again and again. The publicity around the events that each seemed to spell the end of the Swedish idyll followed this pattern. Two years after the Palme murder, a museum advertised its exhibits with the lurid promise: "Bring your family on an expedition back in time this summer. The Swedish idyll is full of historical horrors."[127] Bliss and nightmare could coexist and even depend on each other for their continuation.

If "our" land of bliss had retreated to the fantasies of past generations, what about "their" search for bliss here and now? The gaze of the Other could be constructed as deluded or greedy. The gaze on the Other could make viewers aware of their privilege.[128] The Swedish idyll could be constructed as a safe haven worthy of protection, but also a reason to feel shame and guilt: "Swedish idyll as usual. . . . Seventeen-year-old boy deported to the Soviet Union. . . . Prisoners tear-gassed in Kumla".[129] In the 1980s and 1990s, the topic of Swedish guilt towards the victims of the Holocaust repeatedly appeared on the culture pages of *Dagens Nyheter*.[130] There was even something farcical about the contrast, as shown in the comedy film *Leif* (1987), the story of a small town that lives peacefully on the profits of its arms factory.[131] The Swedish idyll had been maintained at the expense of refugees and victims of war in the same dangerous world that it tried to shield itself from.

Conclusion: the cycle of Utopia and Dystopia

With the fall of the Berlin wall, it was expected that the liberal newspapers would join the announcement of victory over disastrous utopias. In *Dagens Nyheter*, the young editor Johannes Åman noted in 1990 that the relatively recent "discovery of the future" gave radical meaning to politics. A dangerous gift, according to Leif Lewin, historian of ideas, for this discovery "led directly – not to the Land of Bliss – but to Gulag and Auschwitz". If the breakdown of the Soviet bloc meant "total victory" for liberalism, future ought to lose its value as a political concept, Åman concluded. But was it really likely? Ever since the discovery of the future "as a source of inspiration for those that are dissatisfied with society", there had been no turning back, Åman wrote. Evidently, the future would continue to be used politically, for good and for evil.[132]

As Susan Buck-Morss notes in her monumental work on the passing of modern mass utopias, there is "real tragedy in the shattering of the dreams of modernity". Even though some goals of progress, equality, and material plenty have been reached, the grand vision remains unfulfilled, and in fact it is revealed to have been built upon immense human suffering. Indeed, she warns the reader not to confuse "the loss of the dream with the loss of the dream's realization". On "political cynicism", Buck-Morss cautions that "in denying possibilities for change it prevents them; anticipating defeat, it brings defeat into being".[133] But if the promise of utopia had been annihilated and the status quo became celebrated as the end of history, what else remained to expect than dystopia?

Resentment, bitterness and lack of hope are real emotions that have been identified as driving causes behind the rise of xenophobic and welfare nationalist parties in the last three decades.[134] These emotions must be taken seriously, not in the sense that scapegoating is accepted uncritically, but in the sense that the feeling of loss is not rationalized away as inevitable. The defenders of the status quo come to the defence of the achievements of the welfare state when they have become realized, or when other dystopias disguised as utopias rise to threaten the status quo, but often they rush to the barricades after the battle against economic rationality has already been lost.

To overcome pessimism about the future, how can promises of progress be formulated in the present? Today, narratives of the decay and decadence of the nation-state, the welfare state, the labour movement, and other past carriers of Progress have taken over public discourse. Concerns over retrograde "populism" inspire political actors to present their ideological projects as the only bearers of dynamic anti-change. If half of the political leaders declare that the welfare state is currently too expensive, the other half will conclude that it could be affordable in the future – if the "undeserving" were excluded.

The idea that the land of bliss was maintained at the expense of excluding others was not new. In the 1930s, in response to the violent upheavals in Europe, the "Swedish idyll" in particular was employed in contrast to the dangers of the outside world that suddenly came uncomfortably close. The cartoonist Jac (pseudonym of Carl Agnar Jacobsson, 1884–1942)[135] illustrated "the Swedish idyll" in 1935 as an island populated by a family peacefully seated around their garden table, dwarfed by their big folkloristic flowers and the even bigger waves towering over their cottage.[136] The similarities to Aleksis Kivi's poem are striking. In the very first verse, Kivi compares the fierce waves falling over the island to armies. In Jac's cartoon, only a small sign, "anchorage prohibited", stands between the isle of bliss and the raging sea.

As the progressive welfare state project became hegemonic in the 1960s and the 1970s, the arguments of its critics also began to emulate its ideals. While the environmentalist movement focused on new challenges to a global humanity, the liberal critique focused on the unfulfilled needs of the individual that collective efforts could not contain. But the malaise that its liberal critics identified in the 1970s and the early 1980s was increasingly abstract: a discomfort in modernity despite – or because of – the fact that all basic needs were provided for, which was reflected in the discomfort of Huxley's protagonist in *Brave New World* at the sight of his fellow human beings living out their base desires encouraged by the state.

Moral arguments and appeals to higher values such as truth and beauty were outdated, but appeals to liberty made a sudden comeback in the 1990s. By the time the welfare state started to be dismantled, welfare state nostalgia returned with a vengeance – dissatisfaction channelled by new parties, some of which had previously been anti-taxation, others of which had defended the welfare state but only for the most deserving.

In Finland, the modern project was never conclusively dominated by the Social Democratic Party. Every party and movement continued to project their own battles onto it. However, from the early 1980s until the very end of the decade, the utopia seemed to have been reached. *Lintukoto* – the safe and blissful haven of Finnish folklore – suddenly became immanent within the nation. Paradoxically, those who admitted that it existed seemed to be most critical of it. *Lintukoto* and related terms carried connotations of innocence that were no longer desirable in the 1980s but became objects of nostalgic longing in the 1990s.

Notes

1 Koselleck 2006, 159–181.
2 Stråth 1998, 12.
3 Kurunmäki 2010, 40–41.
4 Östlund 2007, 287–288.
5 Lahtinen 2017, 76.
6 Ibid., 75. Lahtinen mentions an island as the home of the pygmies, but most ancient sources do not mention it. The island theme seems to be introduced to the myth in European literature in the 16th century; see Toggweiler 2017, 1–3.
7 Toggweiler 2017, 16.
8 Lehtonen 1928, 34–35, Harva 1948, 58–60, Tanner 1954, 177–183, T. E. Uotila, "Sanat puhuvat", *HS* 14 December 1944.
9 Lahtinen 2017, 75–76.
10 Ibid., 76.
11 Tanner 1954, 183.
12 Lehtonen 1922, 80, Lahtinen 2017, 73.
13 Kivi removed a description of the island as a "land of love" in the second version of his poem. Lahtinen 2017, 78, Stagnelius 1833, 452.

14 Atterbom 1827, 228–232.
15 Vetterlund 1920.
16 Lahtinen 2017, 74.
17 On Strindberg's *De lycksaliges ö* as political satire, see Lahtinen, Laakso & Sagulin 2017, 19, and Niemi 2017, 104.
18 Kurunmäki 2010, 70–71.
19 Karvinen 2015.
20 Riikonen 2017, 49.
21 Lahtinen, Laakso & Sagulin 2017, 19.
22 Eriksson 2002, 326.
23 Topelius 1891, 3–8; one influence on Topelius was Atterbom's play. Lehtonen 1928, 57.
24 Topelius 1891, 13–19.
25 Lahtinen, Laakso & Sagulin 2017, 9.
26 Topelius 1891, 19.
27 Lagerroth 1978, 206–207.
28 Margit, "Dagens frieri", *DN* 14 January 1936, 8.
29 Alm 2002.
30 Lehtonen 1922, 74–75.
31 Most of the myths about the pygmies did not feature the "isle of bliss" topos. Lahtinen 2017, 80.
32 On the influence of literary Orientalism in Atterbom, see Santesson 1924.
33 Lehtonen 1922, 74–75.
34 Ibid., 99.
35 Lehtonen 1928, 78.
36 "Tapaturmien vuosittaiset vahingot maassamme", *HS* 15 January 1942, 7, 10.
37 Pekka Tarkka, "Kukkelman – rujo Simson", *HS* 23 July 1961, 10, Pekka Piirto, "Kiinalaiset ymmärsivät". *HS* 15 September 1962, 16.
38 *HS* 23 February 1950, *HS* 22 June 1954, *HS* 1 February 1981.
39 Elmgren 2016, 328.
40 Niemi 2017, 102–103.
41 Ibid., 105.
42 Ibid., 109.
43 On the reception, use, and evolution of the concept *neue Sachlichkeit* in the Nordic countries, see Hjartarson 2019, 31–40.
44 Essén 1941, 9–30.
45 Ibid., 14.
46 I. H., "Den svenska idyllen", *DN* 5 February 1942, 4.
47 Tidigs 2009, 370.
48 Zimmer 2008, 183.
49 "Färgrik engelsk beskrivning över lyckolandet Sverige", *DN* 21 April 1946, 7.
50 "Pressgrannar", *DN* 23 December 1975, 2.
51 Zimmer 2008, 183, Agrell 1993, 141.
52 "Pressgrannar", *DN* 3 May 1952, 2.
53 Olof Lagercrantz, "Framtiden som mardröm", *DN* 5 January 1960, 4.
54 Nilsson Hammar 2012, 229–230.
55 Karl Erik Lagerlöf, "Happy Marmelade eller rapport från Löfteslandet", *DN* 26 March 1976, 4.
56 Wiklund 2006, 334–348.
57 Virtanen 2002, 291–292.
58 Eskola 1968, 122.
59 Ibid., 122.
60 Lahtinen 2017, 80.
61 Eskola 1968, 122–123.
62 Ibid., 128.

63 Teuvo Mällinen, "Anti Eskola", *HS* 18 December 1968, 19.
64 Vesa-Matti Lahti, "Partaradikaalin pitkät jäähyväiset", *HS* 6 July 1997, 49.
65 "Kerran kuulut niihin, jotka elivät kauan sitten", *HS* 26 March 1969, 13.
66 Sole Uexküll, "Hiukset huiskuvat Hämeessä", *HS* 17 August 1969, 16, Pekka Tarkka, "Kansalliskirjallisuuden viikolla", *HS* 22 February 1970, 24.
67 Matti Klinge, "Kalevalan kansaa etsimässä", *HS* 9 December 1969, 19.
68 For a discussion of the book, see Wiklund 2006, 334–337.
69 Wiklund 2006, 335.
70 Kurunmäki 2010, 77.
71 Sjöshult 2011.
72 Eero Silvasti, "Me kuluttajat", *HS* 22 September 1982, 20.
73 For a discussion of the book, see Marklund 2009, 83–101.
74 Zimmer 2008, 184–185.
75 Lars Anell, "Sverige – ett av världens friaste länder", *DN* 5 October 1982.
76 Cronqvist, Kärrholm & Sturfelt 2008, 37–52.
77 Ibid., 41.
78 Stougaard-Nielsen 2017, chapter 2.
79 Cronqvist, Kärrholm & Sturfelt 2008, 48.
80 Markku Valkonen, "Kansankoti reistaa mutta minkä tähden", *HS* 25 February 1973, 30.
81 Pekka Tarkka, "Taskukirjoista apua valikoimien aukkoihin", *HS* 15 September 1974, 28.
82 Lahtinen 2013.
83 Eero Silvasti, "Myrskyn enne?" *HS* 19 July 1981, 11.
84 Heikki Hellman, "Suomi on kulttuurin lintukoto", *HS* 4 January 1986, 3, 21.
85 Olli Kivinen, "Kansankoti sekaisin", *HS* 19 September 1982, 32.
86 Olli Kangas, "Kansankoti vailla ruotsintautia", *HS* 29 March 1985, 27.
87 "Den svenska idyllen försvann", *DN* 1 March 1987, 5.
88 Olli Kivinen, "Muinaisperinteet ohjaavat tiedotusta", *HS* 11 May 1986, 40.
89 Olli Kivinen, "Saako luonnon puolesta tappaa?" *HS* 8 November 1987, 24.
90 Sakari Määttänen, "Lintukodon julkisuus", *HS* 24 June 1988, 11.
91 Jorma Rotko, "Saarelaisen jäähyväiset", *HS* 28 July 1988, 15.
92 Mats Nörklit, "Misstänkt", *DN* 24 May 1989, 24.
93 Martti Heikkinen, "Nuoret viskoivat tomaateilla . . .", *HS* 18 November 1987, 13.
94 "Siisti ja fiksu, mutta . . .", *HS* 30 December 1987, 11.
95 Osmo Jussila, "Puritaani Jumalan kaupungista", *HS* 4 June 1988, 14.
96 Anna Paljakka, "Yhdysvaltain maksukorttien markkinat . . .", *HS* 19 July 1988, 18.
97 Kirsikka Moring, "Lintukodossa kaikki hyvin", *HS* 17 October 1987, 31.
98 Kirsikka Moring, "Kun teatterin vahakabinetissa palaa", *HS* 3 September 1988, 33.
99 Unto Hämäläinen, "Tuomiojan haavekuvat ja Kairamon realismi", *HS* 28 January 1989, 21.
100 Matti Kinnunen, "Mietosuomalaista itsetutkiskelua", *HS* 22 February 1990, 21.
101 Jouko Jokinen, "Metsäteollisuus osaa kilpailun rajoittamisen", *HS* 6 March 1990, 43.
102 Ari Hakahuhta, "Ydinvoimaloiden purkamisesta . . .", *HS* 7 August 1990, 47.
103 Juhani Aromäki, "Aki Kaurismäen yksinäinen maraton", *HS* 23 September 1990, 70.
104 Eero Ojanen, "Lintukotoon Brysseliin", *HS* 26 November 1991, B 5.
105 Lahtinen 2017, 83.
106 Ibid., 94.
107 Knuuttila 2008, 12–21.
108 Irmeli Niemi, "Paikalliskulttuurille väylät Eurooppaan ja maailmaan", *HS* 13 September 1992, 2.
109 Virpi Suutari, "Kaiken varalta", *HS* 5 November 1994, 67.
110 Jarkko Sipilä, "Rikollisuus väkivaltaisempaa ja ammattimaisempaa", HS 14 April 1996, 11.
111 "Pelle Molin och 'Grå jägarn' . . .", *DN* 22 July 1949, 7; "Radio", *DN* 25 October 1957, 19, Ingrid Arvidsson, "Vulkaner i medelåldern", *DN* 17 January 1966, 4; "Amerikadrömmar på Gubbhyllan", *DN* 23 July 1966, 6.

112 "Svensk hjälp räddar liv . . .", *DN* 21 October 1964, 21; "De sålde allt de ägde", *DN* 23 January 1966, 31; Birgitta Edlund, "Svensk idyll bräcklig fristad för albaner", *DN* 3 February 1990, A 6.
113 Hannu Marttila, "Ali-ihmisen via dolorosa", *HS* 13 April 1986, 20.
114 Nilsson Hammar 2012, 167.
115 Ibid., 50.
116 Reijo Härkönen, "Vieras torjutaan tehokkaasti", *HS* 20 August 1988, 26.
117 "Asuntopolitiikka Uudellamaalla", *HS* 8 April 1991, 2.
118 Leif Dahlin, "Människosmugglare mutade tull . . .", *DN* 9 October 1981, 5; Christian Palme, "Väntan på asyl bakom murar . . .", *DN* 13 December 1984, 18; Christian Palme, "Ny flyktingvåg till Danmark", *DN* 13 August 1986.
119 Anders Mellbourn, "Valet en stor upplevelse . . .", *DN* 20 September 1982, 12.
120 Anders Mellbourn, "Iran bannlyser kemiska vapen", *DN* 7 July 1984, 10; Anders Mellbourn, "Redo fara till kriget", *DN* 8/7/1984, 8; Pierre Schori, "Veckan då . . .", *DN* 29 March 1987, 40.
121 Kerstin Fried, "Ivrig väntan på Katarina", *DN* 29 February 1992, 88.
122 Christian Palme, "Styrman på ny seglats", *DN* 30 December 1990, B 6.
123 "Paradis", *DN* 1 February 1980, 7.
124 *DN* 31 May 1984, 54; 17 September 1984, 46; 9 March 1989, 30; 6 July 1990, 37; Jan Källman, "Svensk idyll för européer", 21 May 1990, 5.
125 Mats Holmberg, "Sverige är ett drömland", *DN* 16 November 1984, 12.
126 Ann Helena Rudberg", Rysarserie i svensk idyll", *DN* 21 February 1982, 55.
127 "Titta om du vågar", *DN* 25 May 1988, 68.
128 Peder Alton, "Brutala bilder från Paris", *DN* 5 May 1983, 4; Anders Öhman, "Försvaret är inte så effektivt", *DN* 31 January 1988, 7; Sören Löfvenhaft, "Inte bara Sörgården", *DN* 14 May 1989, 37.
129 Bäckman, "Afrikas blå lilja", *DN* 14 July 1990, 11.
130 Britt-Marie Svedberg, " 'Här är ditt liv' . . .", *DN* 29 March 1982, 57; Jackie Jakubowski, "Dokument om förtvivlans ansikte", *DN* 4 February 1988, 4.
131 Mårten Blomkvist, " 'Leif' är inte som andra", *DN* 26 June 1987, 18.
132 Johannes Åman, "Upptäckten av framtiden . . .", *DN* 22 September 1990, 2.
133 Buck-Morss 2000, 68.
134 Betz 1993, Poutvaara & Steinhardt 2018.
135 Norstedt & Söner 1933, 402.
136 Jac, "Den svenska idyllen", *DN* 31 December 1935, 10.

References

Newspapers

Accessed through the digital archives of *Helsingin Sanomat* (HS) and *Dagens Nyheter* (DN). For *Helsingin Sanomat*, the digital archives of the Finnish National Library were also utilized.

Literature

Agrell, Beata, 1993: *Romanen som forskningsresa, forskningsresan som roman.* Daidalos: Göteborg.
Alm, Martin, 2002: *Americanitis: Amerika som sjukdom eller läkemedel.* Lund: Nordic Academic Press.
Atterbom, Per Daniel Amadeus, 1827: *Lycksalighetens ö. Sagospel i fem äfventyr. Sednare afdelningen.* Uppsala: Palmblad & Co.
Betz, Hans-George, 1993: "The New Politics of Resentment: Radical Right-Wing Populist Parties in Western Europe" in *Comparative Politics*, 7:1, 413–427.

Buck-Morss, Susan, 2000: *Dreamworld and Catastrophe: The Passing of Mass Utopia in East and West*. Cambridge, MA: MIT Press.

Cronqvist, Marie, Kärrholm, Sara & Sturfelt, Lina, 2008: "Oro i lyckolandet – Mellan Sofiero och Norrmalmstorg" in Marie Cronqvist, Lina Sturfelt & Martin Wiklund (eds.) *1973: En träff med tidsandan*. Lund: Nordic Academic Press, 37–55.

Elmgren, Ainur, 2016: "Förfinskandet av Finland: Självexotism i den finländska kulturdebatten under första hälften av 1900-talet" in Mats Wickström & Charlotta Wolff (eds.) *Mångkulturalitet, nation och minoriteter i Finland under tre sekel*. Helsingfors: SLS, 319–354.

Eriksson, Gunnar, 2002: *Rudbeck 1630–1702: Liv, lärdom, dröm i barockens Sverige*. Stockholm: Atlantis.

Eskola, Antti, 1968: *Suomi sulo Pohjola*. Helsinki: Kirjayhtymä.

Essén, Rütger, 1941: *Den svenska idyllen: nio dialoger*. Helsingfors: Söderströms.

Harva, Uno, 1948: *Suomalaisten muinaisusko*. Porvoo: WSOY.

Hjartarson, Benedikt, 2019: "Cosiness and Subversion: From Post-Cubism to Functionalism and 'Scandinavian Surrealism'" in Benedikt Hjartarson et al. (eds.) *A Cultural History of the Avant-Garde in the Nordic Countries 1925–1950*. Leiden: Brill, 1–79.

Karvinen, Matti, 2015: *Lintukodosta Pohjolan onnelaksi: Suomen mahdollisuudet ja tulevaisuus vuonna 2040*. Helsinki: Suomalaiset Oikeusjulkaisut SOJ.

Knuuttila, Seppo, 2008: "Impivaara suomalaisten symbolina" in Seppo Knuuttila et al. (eds.) *Entinen aika, nykyinen mieli*. Suomalaisen Kirjallisuuden Seuran toimituksia 1185. Helsinki: SKS, 12–21.

Koselleck, Reinhart, 2006: "Fortschritt und Niedergang: Nachtrag zur Geschichte zweier Begriffe" in Reinhart Koselleck (ed.) *Begriffsgeschichten: Studien zur Semantik und Pragmatik der politischen und sozialen Sprachen*. Frankfurt a. M.: Suhrkamp, 159–181.

Kurunmäki, Jussi, 2010: "'Nordic Democracy' in 1935: On the Finnish and Swedish Rhetoric of Democracy" in Jussi Kurunmäki & Johan Strang (eds.) *Rhetorics of Nordic Democracy*. Helsinki: Finnish Literature Society, 37–82.

Lagerroth, Ulla-Britta, 1978: *Regi i möte med drama och samhälle: Per Lindberg tolkar Pär Lagerkvist*. Stockholm: Rabén & Sjögren.

Lahtinen, Jussi, 2013: *Duunarin tarinoita murroksen yhteiskunnasta: Romaanihahmojen arkisia käsityksiä ja kokemuksia suomalaisesta palkkatyöyhteiskunnasta 1960–1970-lukujen työläiskirjallisuudessa*. Master's thesis. Tampere: Tampereen yliopisto.

Lahtinen, Toni, 2017: "Keskellä ikäisyyden myrskyjä: Onnen ja nälän saaret Aleksis Kiven tuotannossa" in Maria Laakso et al. (eds.) *Lintukodon rannoilta: Saarikertomukset suomalaisessa kirjallisuudessa*. Helsinki: Suomalaisen Kirjallisuuden Seura, 70–97.

Lahtinen, Toni, Laakso, Maria & Sagulin, Merja, 2017: "Johdatus suomalaisen kirjallisuuden saarille" in Maria Laakso et al. (eds.) *Lintukodon rannoilta: Saarikertomukset suomalaisessa kirjallisuudessa*. Helsinki: Suomalaisen Kirjallisuuden Seura, 9–43.

Lehtonen, J. V., 1922: *Aleksis Kivi taiteilijana: eräitä piirteitä*. Porvoo: WSOY.

Lehtonen, J. V., 1928: *Runon kartanossa: johdatusta Aleksis Kiven runouteen*. Helsinki: Otava.

Marklund, Carl, 2009: "Hot Love and Cold People: Sexual Liberalism as Political Escapism in Radical Sweden" in *NORDEUROPAforum*, 19:1, 83–101.

Niemi, Juhani, 2017: "Lintukodosta Letheen: Onnellisten saaren muunnelmia Joel Lehtosen myöhäistuotannossa" in Maria Laakso et al. (eds.) *Lintukodon rannoilta: Saarikertomukset suomalaisessa kirjallisuudessa*. Helsinki: Suomalaisen Kirjallisuuden Seura, 98–111.

Nilsson Hammar, Anna, 2012: *Lyckans betydelse: sekularisering, sensibilisering och individualisering i svenska skillingtryck 1750–1850*. Lund: Agerings bokförlag.

Norstedt, P. A. & Söner (eds.), 1933: *Vem är det: Svensk biografisk handbok*. Stockholm: P. A. Norstedt & Söner.

Östlund, Joachim, 2007: *Lyckolandet: maktens legitimering i officiell retorik från stormaktistid till demokratins genombrott*. Lund: Sekel.

Poutvaara, Panu & Steinhardt, Max Friedrich, 2018: "Bitterness in Life and Attitudes Towards Immigration" in *European Journal of Political Economy*, 55, 471–490.

Riikonen, H. K., 2017: "Ylitse meren yhdeksän: Saaria Elias Lönnrotin Kalevalassa" in Maria Laakso et al. (eds.) *Lintukodon rannoilta: Saarikertomukset suomalaisessa kirjallisuudessa*. Helsinki: Suomalaisen Kirjallisuuden Seura, 47–69.

Santesson, Carl, 1924: "Exotism och orient i 'Lycksalighetens ö'" in *Samlaren: Tidskrift för svensk litteraturhistorisk forskning. Ny följd. Årgång 4, 1923. Skrifter utgivna av Svenska Litteratursällskapet 1*. Uppsala: Almqvist & Wiksells Boktryckeri AB, 98–171.

Sjöshult, Fredrik, 2011: "Reinfeldt: Palme radikaliserade S" in *Expressen*, 25 February 2011. www.expressen.se/nyheter/reinfeldt-palme-radikaliserade-s/ [Accessed 29 May 2018].

Stagnelius, Erik Johan, 1833: *J. Stagnelii samlade skrifter, utgifne af L. Hammarsköld. Tredje delen*. Stockholm: A. Wiborgs Förlag.

Stougaard-Nielsen, Jakob, 2017: *Scandinavian Crime Fiction*. London: Bloomsbury.

Stråth, Bo, 1998: *Mellan två fonder: LO och den svenska modellen*. Uddevalla: Atlas.

Tanner, Kerttu, 1954: *Myytilliset tarinat suomalaisessa taidelyriikassa*. Turku: Turun yliopisto.

Tidigs, Julia, 2009: "Multilingualism, Modernism and (De)Territorialization in Elmer Diktonius" in Sascha Bru et al. (eds.) *Europa! Europa? The Avant-Garde of Modernism and the Fate of a Continent*. Berlin: Walter de Gruyter, 359–372.

Toggweiler, Michael, 2017: *Die Odyssee der Pygmäen. Eine andere Geschichte der neuzeitlichen Anthropologie*. Bern: Philosophisch-historische Fakultät, Universität Bern.

Topelius, Zacharias, 1891: *Läsning för barn. Sjunde boken. Visor, sagor och lekar*. Helsingfors: G. W. Edlund.

Vetterlund, Fredrik, 1920: "Per Daniel Amadeus Atterbom," in *Svenskt Biografiskt Lexikon*. urn:sbl:18908. https://sok.riksarkivet.se/sbl/artikel/18908 [Accessed 12 February 2021].

Virtanen, Matti, 2002: *Fennomanian perilliset: Poliittiset traditiot ja sukupolvien dynamiikka*. Hämeenlinna: SKS.

Wiklund, Martin, 2006: *I det modernas landskap: Historisk orientering och kritiska berättelser om det moderna Sverige mellan 1960 och 1990*. Stockholm: Symposion.

Zimmer, Frank, 2008: *Engagierte Geschichte/n: dokumentarisches Erzählen im schwedischen und norwegischen Roman 1965–2000*. Frankfurt am Main: Peter Lang.

4 More or less equality?

Facts, debates, and policies related to the Nordic model

Petri Roikonen, Jari Ojala, and Jari Eloranta

The topic of income inequality has become a new nexus of research among historians and social scientists recently.[1] Piketty (2014) has famously argued:

> Inequality is shaped by the way economic, social, and political actors view what is just and what is not, as well as by the relative power of those actors and the collective choices that result. It is the joint product of all relevant actors combined.

Given that redistribution is a core element of the Nordic model and understood as key to the development of social trust and cohesion, all debates about social and cultural polarization are also debates about economic inequalities and the possible policy choices related to those issues. Moreover, in public and political discussion – in Finland especially – income inequality is in many cases conflated with various other forms of inequality in the society. This crucial difference in what is meant by scholarly versus political discourses at large can often lead to inexact policy debates and solutions. In this chapter we concentrate, mainly, on exploring the specific concepts of income inequality that are measurable and definable, especially what they tell us about this form of inequality in Finland and Sweden as our case studies. In addition, we will contextualize these cases through comparisons with the other Nordic countries as well as other polities. However, as we can see from our discussion here, there are striking differences, especially in the public discussions as measured by newspaper articles both in Finland and in Sweden, whether the discussion is focused on societal inequality in broader terms or, more specifically, on income inequality and its ramifications.

In this chapter, we will discuss the period from the late 1960s to the recent years, thus examining *how income inequality has developed in Finland and Sweden, how it has been debated both in research and in public discussions,* and *whether these discussions can be linked to changes in welfare state creation as well as redistribution trends.* This is an interesting period, since welfare states emerged in force during this era, thus offering new policy solutions to various forms of inequality, but it also saw a widespread challenge to welfare states in the policies of Ronald Reagan and Margaret Thatcher, as well as deregulation of many European economies,

DOI: 10.4324/9780429026690-4

including Finland and Sweden. Finally, we also want to touch on the issue of what kind of data should and could be used to examine these issues, especially from the perspective of income inequality. However, we have to clarify one caveat of our chapter in the outset. We will *not* analyze the actual policy debates in the Finnish and Swedish political arenas, since that would require a chapter of its own (and they are, to a certain extent, covered in the other chapters of the book). Instead, we more broadly focus on the potential linkages in the evolution of Nordic welfare and tax policies.

This chapter is organized as follows; we will first introduce data and methods (Data and methods: research, discourses, and policies) and examine the *facts* (Economic inequality: what do we know) – that is, what do socio-economic data tell us about income inequality over time – and we will explore certain debates over how they are measured as well. Next, we analyze the *research*, especially on Finnish economic policies and inequality over time, as well as *discourses* on these topics in the media (Discourses on income inequality, mainly newspapers) in Finland and Sweden, to be followed by a discussion of the *policies* adopted (Nordic redistribution trends and welfare impacts). Finally, we will conclude with a broader discussion of the development trends and future prospects.

Data and methods: research, discourses, and policies

Our first goal here is to review some of the quantitative evidence, especially the various socio-economic indicators, to evaluate trends in polarization from the Nordic perspective. As shown recently via global comparisons by Leandro Prados de la Escosura,[2] the global polarization in terms of social well-being has declined steadily since World War I. Similarly, as discussed by Jan Luiten Van Zanden et al. (2014), global well-being on the whole has increased dramatically since the 19th century. Most of the indicators used in any analysis on well-being are correlated with GDP per capita, which is typically viewed as a key measure worth looking at when discussing inequality, similar to wealth. Such indicators, however, only tell part of the story of societal development and polarization, and here we will look at a limited number of indicators of Nordic development during the last century or so. Our working hypothesis is that the story is similar with all of the Nordic countries; although, here the main focus in the comparisons is on Finland and Sweden. However, even a cursory look at the data tells us that while the trends have been visible, there are differences between what we are measuring and between the countries as well. The Nordic countries did not necessarily form a coherent block in economic and social terms. Finally, the Nordic countries today have lower levels of inequality in its various forms than most Western nations.

The aim of this study is to analyze how research was setting an agenda to public debates, and how research and discussions affected the public policies. First, we characterize the main trends and findings in the international and national inequality research. Second, here we focus on some of the key Finnish research papers and reports on inequality as well as the major Finnish (*Helsingin Sanomat* (*HS*)) and Swedish (*Dagens Nyheter* (*DN*)) newspapers to gauge the dimensions of debates. Furthermore, we analyze some of the economic prognostications produced in the debates by analysts and pundits in the public sphere, namely through the lens of a key newspaper. In essence, we intend to analyze their views on future economic outlook as well as economic and societal polarization. We are using here mostly published sources and reports, and major newspapers via their digital collections, using keyword searches. Our initial hypothesis was that economic (or social) data and published research would not necessarily be reflected in these debates, and that national debates can be distorted by groupthink and lack of perspective. However, we had to refine our thinking based on the results, as the public discourse did in fact reflect some of the broader themes arising from scholarship, and on occasion some of the key studies made enough waves to penetrate the public discourse.

Third, we analyze the "changes" in policies vis-à-vis "facts" (research) as well as the debates (discourses). The main policy aspects of this study relate to redistribution policies through taxation and social transfers as well as education and other welfare state policies. We argue that the focus on facts/debates/change is a valuable tool to understand these processes. The so-called RDP model (research-discourses-policies model) is the theoretical model of our study (see Figure 4.1).

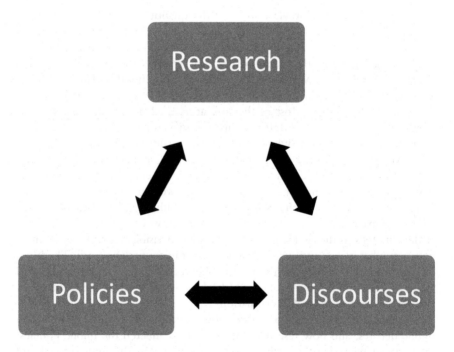

Figure 4.1 The theoretical model of the RDP framework.

Economic inequality: what do we know?

Top income shares

A certain amount of inequality is unavoidable in modern capitalist societies and economies – yet an increase in inequality may in time lead to severe challenges, even societal crises. European history alone has proved this time and again, with bloody revolutions and uprisings. Yet income inequality has also been a component of the most dramatic economic transitions in history, such as the industrial revolutions and globalization waves. In the recent political and scholarly debates, income inequality has become one of the key concepts to explore and to evaluate current-day problems from the perspective of historical development paths, and whether, for example, broad societal changes like welfare policies can temper tendencies toward inequality in its various forms.

In the very long run, there are relatively consistent series on economic inequality only for the top income shares (taxable incomes).[3] Economic inequality, measured on the basis of incomes or wealth, decreased in Western countries in the first part of the 20th century.[4] The inequality continued to decrease until circa the year 1980 (Figure 4.2). The phase of shrinking inequality was reversed after, first in the Anglo-Saxon countries and later in the Central Europe as well as in the Scandinavian countries. Thus, the trend has been toward lesser inequality in the 20th century; however, the experiences of sharp increases of inequality during the last decades have partly reversed that process. For example, in the United States the current-day inequality has reached the levels similar to the first decades of the 20th century. On the other hand, there are countries, for example, Denmark and the Netherlands, that have not experienced the sharp increasing tendency almost at all. Overall, the Anglo-Saxon countries have experienced much sharper increases in inequality when compared with the Central Europe and Nordic countries.

Gini coefficients

Next, we can further characterize the patterns of (income) inequality in the recent decades utilizing household survey data (Figure 4.3). The inequality measured by the disposable incomes at the household level (aka including received and paid transfers and payments) has relatively similar patterns compared with the top income shares calculated from tax statistics seen in Figure 4.2 (taxable incomes). The income inequality has increased significantly starting from the early 1990s to around year 2007, especially in Finland and Sweden. Furthermore, it is noticeable that Sweden was more unequal when compared with Finland in terms of income inequality after the year 1990. This might be explained with the higher capital gains in Sweden. After 2007, the perspective on the Finnish economic inequality depends on the indicators utilized: stagnated (absolute income inequality), decreased slightly (consumption inequality and income inequality), or increased (wealth inequality).[5]

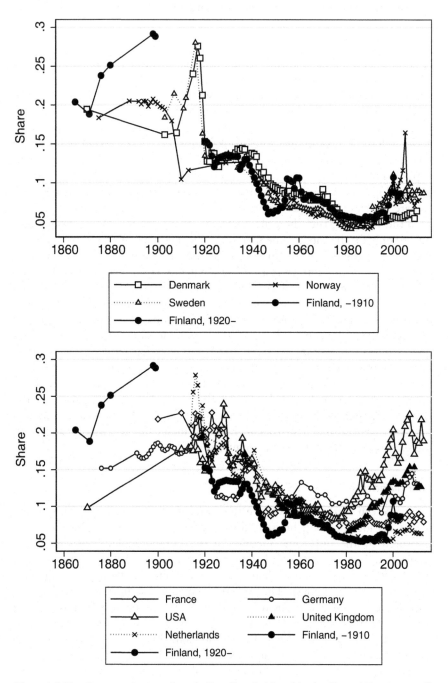

Figure 4.2 Top 1 percent income share in Scandinavia (a) and in the Central Europe as well as Anglo-Saxon countries (b).

Sources: Finland, 1865–1910 (Roikonen & Heikkinen 2018), Finland, 1920–2004 (Jäntti et al. 2010), Germany 1876–1880, USA 1870–1910 (Lindert & Williamson 2016, 173), other (WID database).

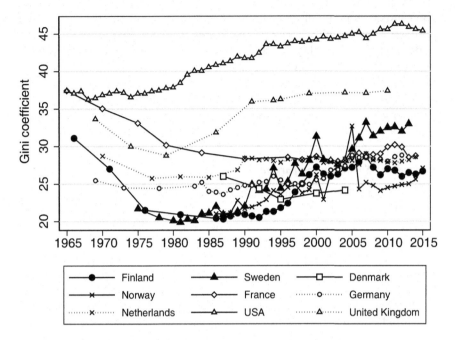

Figure 4.3 Gini coefficients for disposable incomes from 1965 to 2010.

Sources: Finland (Official Statistics of Finland 2019), Sweden (Statistics Sweden 2019), Denmark and the United Kingdom (LIS) (Milanovic 2016). Other (The Chartbook of Economic Inequality 2019).

Note: Swedish and Finnish data include capital gains.

The income inequality estimates from tax and survey data are slightly different, due to three obvious reasons: first, the concept of income is different, since the taxable incomes do not include taxes and transfers as well as other non-taxable income sources; second, the inequality measurements are different – that is, the top-income share versus Gini coefficient; and, third, the tax statistics are based on individual records, whereas the surveys were collected at the household level.[6]

The disparities with data raise questions about how we should handle these types of issues – especially since these types of subtle methodological and analytical differences are not obvious to politicians and the lay public – and which sources we should prefer to use. According to Burkhauser et al. (2012), the household surveys have severe problems in capturing the top incomes due to under coverage, underreporting, and top coding. In addition, there are many other sources of incomes that are not captured (such as capital gains in the USA). However, the tax statistics have limitations as well. The tax records are hampered by a changing concept of taxable income (e.g., deductions, preferences between income sources). Furthermore, tax evasion is a problem, especially among the top-income groups. In addition, the poorest people are missing in the tax filers' data. Regardless of these differences, according to empirical studies,[7] the top-income shares arising from tax data are relatively good proxies for overall inequality and can be a useful substitute for other measures of inequality.

Both types of inequality data and measures have possible pitfalls, and according to Alvaredo (2011), the survey-based Gini coefficients should be corrected by using the more complete top-income data from tax records. Therefore, some National Statistical Offices have decided to utilize registers to impute incomes in the income distribution surveys, including Statistics Finland; however, many statistical offices still rely on the answers presented in the interviews.

Finland and Sweden in comparison

As noted before, Finland and Sweden, as well as many other countries, have experienced a reversal of the equalization process from the 1990s onward. As seen in Figure 4.4, the growing difference between the average and median incomes (1) from the 1990s onward supports our earlier findings.[8] Poverty rates (2) followed similar patterns: the "harsh" Finnish recession during the 1990s resulted in a decline in the poverty rate, which is due to the automatic redistribution mechanisms of the welfare state and the decrease in the average incomes.[9] Furthermore, the poverty rates (2) increased in both countries, which indicates that part of the population "missed" the years of growth. The "harsh" recession after 2008 caused decreasing median incomes in Finland that partly lowered relative poverty rates; on the other hand, Sweden did not suffer such a drop in incomes or poverty rates. The increase in the gross earnings of the top decile as percentage median (3) as well as the top 1 percent wealth share (4) followed similar growth trends as noted before, despite the periods of recession in the early 2000s and 2008–2009.[10] Despite the rising contrast with the "haves and the have-nots" in Finland and Sweden, it is noticeable that the developments are significantly different from many other countries. For example, in the United States the average pretax real national income per adult increased roughly 60 percent from 1980 to 2014; on the other hand, the real incomes of the bottom half of the population stagnated during this period.[11] Thus, it is striking that half of the population did not reap the fruits of the economic growth at all during the last 30 years.

Discourses on income inequality

Societal planning and the question of inequality

One of the roles of human and social sciences today is to provide tools for societies and governments engaged in societal planning. A plethora of academic research, surveys, and statistics are produced daily to serve this goal. Since World War II, and especially during the past decades, the university sector alone has grown enormously globally. In addition, human and social sciences have grown as fields, which can be seen in the pure number of research

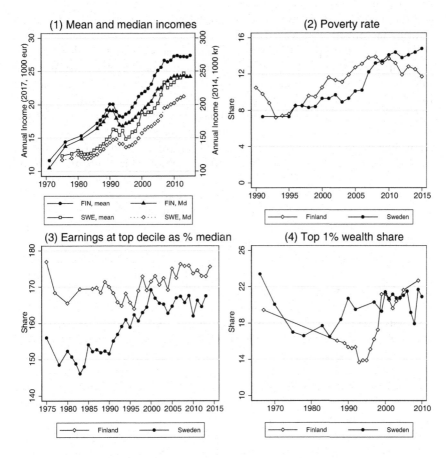

Figure 4.4 Finland and Sweden in comparison. Note: (1) Equivalent annual income (household income divided by modified OECD consumption units). (2) Percent living in households with equivalent disposable income below 60 percent median. (3) Personal gross earnings. (4) Share of top 1 percent in total individual net wealth.

Sources: The Chartbook of Economic Inequality (2019). Mean and median incomes from Finland (Official Statistics of Finland 2019). Mean and median incomes from Sweden (Statistics Sweden 2019).

outputs in terms of publications. Moreover, a whole industry of consultants has emerged to serve both private and public actors,[12] as well as research institutes and think-tanks of various kinds and with different political agendas to satisfy the need for information.[13] Thus, there is a massive, and growing, amount of information available for decisions-makers to use – even to the extent that the reliability of "politicized" information has been questioned time and again by both politicians and researchers. In essence, the problems and mediums faced by the scholars and policy-makers in the 1970s were completely different from today, as we now are living in an age of information overload and "fake news",[14] whereas 50 years ago there were fewer voices and the media landscape was simpler – and the impact of the Cold War was a limiting factor too.

This information provided by human and social sciences to understand our contemporary world and to make wise decisions for the future includes also information that is specifically aimed at predicting the future. Today, perhaps the most influential predictions are related to demography and climate change[15] – the latter, often thought to be the domain of mathematics and natural sciences, is also a topic that humanities and social sciences address using a variety of qualitative and quantitative methods. Using human and social sciences to predict the future emerged as an important part of societal planning during and after World War II. The Cold War era, particularly, produced projections, forecasts, scenarios, and other forms of predictions of world development that were essential when governments and corporations made decisions on current affairs – these predictions, in turn, have had and will have an impact on global politics today as well as in the future. Indeed, the Cold War era created ideologies suggesting, as Jenny Andersson (2012) has noted, that socio-economic and political problems might be "scientified" and predictable as "hard sciences". This development gave rise to new disciplines such as futures studies and futurology that changed the future as an object of science, whereas it previously had been more of a concept of utopian imagination. Only recently historians have also turned to the study of past visions of future.[16] Furthermore, in Sweden and Finland, future studies gained a role in societal debates early on.[17] Nevertheless, the bulk of this social forecasting has been conducted by "old" human and social science disciplines. While during the 1970s sociology paved the way for societal planning, it is economics that has been a vital force in forecasting during the past three decades or so.

These academic debates and "hot topics" on societal issues and forecasting were also highly cited in the public discussions featured in the newspapers. Thus, they made their way to influence the public opinion and consequently the political decision-making. This can be seen, for example, in the fact that the results of *some* academic research became widely referred to in major newspapers in the Finnish and Swedish cases, as we can see here. However, an open question is, though, why some research passes through the public and political spheres with barely a mention, whereas others do not.

From today's perspective, it is relatively easy to anachronistically show how "good" or "bad" the predictions made in the past were.[18] However, it is equally interesting to see in which conditions the analyses and predictions were made and which attributes they were based on. Moreover, even though information on societal developments and (good or bad) predictions for future did exist, all the information was not necessarily adopted into use due to political reasons or it was dismissed in the public discussions for one reason or another. Similarly, we have a number of cases of academic discussions that were dominating both the political and the public debates. As we can see in the following, income inequality is not an exception in this perspective: on the contrary, different aspects of income distribution were emphasized in different time periods, following (mainly) the results achieved in academic discussions. Moreover, some key politicians themselves actively wrote about income inequality – including such a prominent figure as Urho Kekkonen (1952).

Emergence of inequality as a topic in social sciences

In economics, the GDP (per capita) is the basic measure for research, and it is also used in societal planning and modelling[19]. Though the GDP has severe challenges as a metric, it still is "widely understood and respected" as the best measure of economic development so far developed.[20] The GDP is a measure of the aggregate economy constructed to help in the study and understanding of macroeconomic growth and its components, and the theory behind the measure was mainly developed in the 20th century, mostly during and after World War II. Since the 1950s, the distribution of this growth nationally and internationally has received a growing attention among economists, social scientists, and economic historians.[21] The 1950s also saw the rise of a research focusing on income and wealth distribution, including new journals such as *The Review of Income and Wealth* and *Economic Development and Cultural Change*.

The roots for studying the unequal distribution of wealth and income can be traced back to the mid-19th century, especially as a response to the Industrial Revolution, and to the writings of Karl Marx and his contemporaries.[22] The early studies of income inequality were also noted in Finland, and some influential studies were already made during the first years of the 20th century.[23] The most common metric to study inequality, the Gini coefficient, was developed by Corrado Gini (Ceriani & Verme 1912) – though it was more widely adapted as a tool in research to study income and wealth inequality only during the 1970s.[24] There were some early attempts to model income distribution in Finland, Sweden, Denmark, and Norway already in the 1940s, 1950s and 1960s[25] – as well as in studies published for international audiences.[26]

The quality of such research in general, and the ones dealing with income and wealth equality in particular, is dependent on the quality of data. The national statistical agencies were thus approached to compile suitable data, although in the Finnish case only from the late 1960s onward.[27] Also, the first historical studies since the early 20th century on income inequality were published in the early 1970s,[28] although it was not until the late 1970s when more adequate data were made available.[29] In the 1970s and the 1980s, Hannu Uusitalo (e.g., 1975, 1977, 1989) was especially actively publishing research on income inequality.

Internationally, comparable data to analyze income distributions have been produced in many countries since the early 1970s.[30] Studies by the OECD on income distribution were based on these data and also included Finland and Sweden.[31] The first international comparisons were made in Finland in the early 1970s.[32] International studies by, for example, Anthony B. Atkinson (1970) and Amartya Sen[33] influenced also the Nordic scholars during the 1970s. Subsequently, Erik Allardt (1976a, 1976b) compiled a comparative study on welfare dealing with Nordic countries in the 1970s. His study, as well as certain similar ones,[34] was only possible as the first statistics were compiled.

However, topics related to the income inequality did not rise to the center of the social science debates until the 21st century, not least because of the Pikettys famous *book Le Capital au XXIe siècle* (Piketty 2013) and its translated English version (2014). Especially in economics, the debates focusing on income distributions and inequality were almost instantly promoted from a category of "semi–interesting topics" to be alongside with the big questions such as the causes of the growth of GDP or other big debates about macroeconomic development.[35]

Public press reflecting the research

The first Finnish statistics and research on income inequality published during the 1970s also gained attention from the public press. The major Finnish newspaper, *HS*, published widely on topics related to income inequality during the first years of the 1970s (Figure 4.5), although during the latter part of the decade the topic ceased to interest it. On the other hand, before the late 1960s, there were hardly any newspaper articles on the topic. Thus, the new research managed to set the agenda and, moreover, introduced the concept also to the public debate. In fact, some of the first articles in *HS* directly referred to the

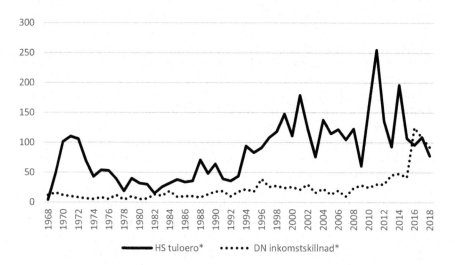

Figure 4.5 Articles on income inequality published in *HS* (Finland) and *DN* (Sweden), 1968–2018. Note: *HS* counted by pages (one occurrence per page) until the turn of the 1990s and thereafter by articles (one occurrence per article).

Sources: *HS*, The Päivälehti Archives, Helsinki (retrieved 14 January 2019); The Royal Swedish Library, The Dagens Nyheter Digital Archive (retrieved 10 January 2019).

new research and statistics.[36] Moreover, the statistics and research also interested the politicians, which, in turn, was discussed in the pages of newspapers as well. In particular, several left-wing politicians made statements about wishing to equalize the income distribution.[37] During the late 1980s, however, there were more right-wing politicians claiming that an increase in income inequality might be an option as well.[38] In Sweden, however, the topic did not hold similar appeal among the journalists, as shown by the number of articles published in *DN*, the major Swedish newspaper. Nevertheless, there were debates in the late 1960s and the early 1970s, especially on wealth distribution, in both Sweden and Finland.

Nevertheless, the academic research on income inequality was not widespread in the Finnish case during the 1970s, yet it contributed to an increasing trend during the 1980s, and especially during the 1990s, which is when income inequality increased as well (Figures 4.1–4.4). The discussions in the 1980s concentrated on topics such as spatial differences[39] in incomes, or differences between different groups in society, or, in the Finnish case, between farmers and factory employees.[40] Thus, scholarship was following, and amplifying, the interests of the two major political movements: the Centre Party (former Agrarian party) and the Social Democrats. Spatial differences in incomes, though, were discussed already in some studies published in the 1950s and the 1970s.[41] During the 1980s, research was reflected also in the pages of major newspapers.[42] Furthermore, the research on income inequality was slowly turning from sociology toward economics,[43] and even historical analyses appeared.[44]

During the turn of the 1990s, more specified analysis on income inequality were published on topics such as education,[45] taxation,[46] and generational differences.[47] However, perhaps the most influential stream of study emerged on the gender imbalance of incomes. The influential studies by Joan Acker were noted also in Finland and even translated into Finnish,[48] and several studies were published on the topic by scholars that have since been major contributors in the Finnish economic research circles.[49] Markus Jäntti's studies (e.g., 1993), for example, were especially influential at the time. These studies also gained public attention, which can be seen in the rising trend of related newspaper articles at the time. Nevertheless, it was not until the mid-1990s when the topic of income inequality really boomed in the Finnish public discussion, which can also be discerned from the output of articles in *HS* (Figure 4.5). This was mainly caused by concerns about the new statistics suggesting an increasing trend in income inequality; interestingly, a similar increase in public discussion in Sweden did not emerge until the 2010s. Furthermore, the Finnish case shows that the level of articles remained higher in the 2000s when compared with the 1980s. The 1990s was a decade of extremes in Finnish economic history too – the first half featured an intense recession, and the second half fast economic growth and the rise of the IT sector. These extremes likely also contributed to the public interest on inequality.

Was there, then, a link between the facts, research, and public discussion on income inequality? Based on the brief description of major trends in Finnish income inequality, research literature, and timing of published statistics, as well as the articles published in major newspapers, one might assume that the link does exist (Figures 4.1–4.5). On the other hand, the public interest toward inequality (articles published in *DN*) remained low in Sweden despite the increasing income inequality and the rising international debates on inequality in the social sciences. Our study here suggests that the main reasons for change in income inequality are relatively similar in Finland and in Sweden: capital incomes, taxation, and redistribution.[50] Why, then, did the discussion on income inequality get more space in Finnish newspapers than in the Swedish ones? One plausible reason might be the more rugged economic cycle in Finland: first the 1990s recession; then the rapid growth, with the rise of Nokia and the IT bubble; and lastly the recession in 2008 following the ten-year period of slow growth. Finland witnessed massive unemployment in the last 30 years; this was justly discussed in newspapers. Moreover, the welfare state creation had longer roots in the Swedish case, and the critiques of this political reality had large hurdles to overcome.

The topic of income inequality was introduced in Finnish academia especially during the turn of the 1960s and the 1970s when the first statistics appeared. This was also clearly shown in the pages of *HS* at the time. However, even though the number of academic studies increased in terms of both scale and scope throughout the 1970s and the 1980s, the issue was less debated in the public press – though there was a slight increase during the 1980s. In Sweden, the number of newspaper articles was even less significant. Here though, the keywords used might at least partly explain the difference. Nevertheless, it was not until the 1990s and the rising concerns over increasing income inequality in Finland that the number of articles published on the issue got a boost.[51]

There seemed to be a tendency of overestimating income inequality in both political and public discussion. For example, a newspaper article in 1973 claimed that income inequality was higher in Finland than in the other Nordic countries. Though this claim was based on research, it does not entirely hold if we look at the statistics compiled afterward (Figure 4.3). Moreover, inequality was on a declining trend at the time.[52] Six year later another article claimed that income inequality had declined slowly in Finland – although according to our Figures 4.3 and 4.4, the development was relatively fast.[53] Especially at the turn of the 1970s and the 1980s, newspaper articles referred to research showing that, indeed, the decline of income inequality was slowing down in Finland.[54] Moreover, more general discussion on "inequality" was more pronounced in both Finnish and especially Swedish press during this period, as can be detected from Figure 4.6. This, in turn, might have led to a confluence of both the public discussion and the political debates: whereas there is no statistical evidence of an increase in *income* inequality in Finland and Sweden during the 2010s (Figures 4.1–4.4), there certainly are many other types of inequalities present in the society that to a certain degree threaten the Nordic model, as discussed in a number of chapters in this volume.

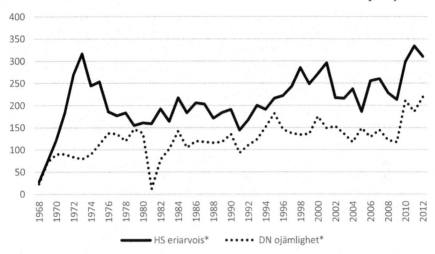

Figure 4.6 Articles on "inequality" published in *HS* (Finland) and *DN* (Sweden), 1968–2018.

Source: See Figure 4.5. Concepts such as *eriarvoisuus* (in Finnish) and *ojämlighet* (in Swedish) refer to inequality more broadly (like social, cultural, or educational) compared to *tuloero* (in Finnish) or *inkomst-skillnad* (in Swedish) in Figure 4.5. Both can be translated to mean "income inequality" in English. Thus, discussions on "income inequality" in particular and "inequality" in general have somewhat been mixed with each other in both public and political discussions, especially in Finland.

Nordic redistribution trends and welfare impacts

In this section we will discuss the broader trends in welfare state creation and tax policies and contemplate whether these deep structural societal changes were linked to the discourses and scholarly debates explored in the previous sections. Regardless, our aim is not to attempt an in-depth analysis of the political contexts linked to the discourse patterns, which would be too ambitious of an endeavor. As we can already see in some of the other chapters in this volume, the Nordic societies underwent dramatic transformations toward more egalitarian societies, mostly in the post–World War II period, based on broad societal and political compromises between major political parties. The early ideals of more egalitarian societies developed before World War II were slowly realized during the postwar decades, and these ideas evolved into fairly encompassing welfare states. Moreover, the critique of welfare states that emerged in the 1980s has also had a profound impact on Nordic welfare states and societies as a whole, since most of the left-wing or left-leaning parties[55] have come to accept some market-based solutions to welfare (and health care) provision and, respectively, the more right-wing or right-leaning parties have become defenders of the core principles of welfare states, albeit with more cautious fiscal policies that would sometimes even lead to government spending cuts and lower tax rates.

In general, the Nordic and other Western welfare states developed as a response to the rise of labor and socialist movements in the 20th century, as well as the slow democratization processes following the industrial revolutions and societal divisions they brought forth in the 19th century. Social spending increased rapidly between 1880 and World War II, and then boomed from the 1950s onward. The latter half of the 20th century witnessed the creation of various types of welfare state, ranging from the Anglo-American model of welfare restraint and individualism to the more universal Nordic welfare provision.[56] The creation of the Finnish welfare state did not begin in earnest until the 1950s, and it was built on the stable institutions and governmental organizations that had evolved over centuries, strong economic growth, and structural changes arising from the post–World War II period. In addition, the ideas and solutions offered by Finland's Nordic and other Western neighbors provided the building blocks of this emerging welfare state. The relatively rapid building of Finland's welfare state proves that it is possible to create such institutions quickly if there are the resources and opportunities to do so, especially as a response to developing societal harmony and equality. Furthermore, it is possible to sustain such institutions if the welfare policies contribute to the economic growth (e.g., by creating human capital). Building and extending the welfare state in Finland during the 1970s and the 1980s occurred despite political parties were relatively far from each other in many facets of policy issues; thus, the thread against this development during the recession in the early 1990s might be one of the explanations why income inequality gained so much attention in the public press at the time (Figures 4.5 and 4.6).

The Finnish, or Swedish for that matter, development was faster than elsewhere in Europe, although hardly unique. And the end result was an encompassing welfare state with highly progressive taxation. This can be seen in the central government spending levels among most Western countries; in fact, they showed little growth until World War I, although there were noticeable differences between them. Subsequently, in the interwar period, especially in the 1930s, the average central government spending increased. After World War II, the effect of the emerging welfare state can be observed until the 1980s. The last phase seems to represent a leveling-off stage (or at least a period of slower growth) for modern welfare states. Thus, the two World Wars appear to have imposed tremendous growth pressures on central government roles in most Western countries. Finland, however, seems to have experienced a strong period of growth in the 1950s, which differs from most of the others, thus catching up to Nordic levels of welfare provision and tax policies, while also entering a period of extremely rapid structural change for its economy. The United States, the embodiment of the Anglo-American welfare model, consistently spent less than the Europeans in the 20th century, whereas Sweden spent much more than Finland in the 1960s and the 1970s.[57]

Therefore, the emergence of welfare states in the postwar period took place in increments. For example, between 1937 and 1960, the percentage of GDP of public expenditures increased at a relatively slow pace, often more related to the increases in defense spending caused by the Cold War. This share was circa 23 percent in 1937 compared to roughly 28 percent in 1960. However, the period 1960–1980 could be described as the real golden age of public sector intervention, with a considerable macroeconomic consensus on the government's role. Criticism of this era of Keynesian dominance emerged in the aftermath of the economic crises of the 1970s, increasing in the 1980s and the 1990s with the arrival of fiscally more conservative governments, especially in the UK and the United States. Public choice and other institutional theorists have since been among the many critics of the welfare states. How extensive was this government growth? If we look at the development of general government expenditures (as a percentage of GDP) in the latter half of the 20th century, we see that the average share increased steadily from approximately 43 percent in 1980 to circa 46 percent in 1996. As Peter Lindert has pointed out, most Western nations did not cut their spending uniformly nor permanently, and globalization has since increased the demand for a government response. Finland certainly belongs in this group as well, having made only small welfare spending cuts in the 1990s and since the economic crisis of 2008.[58]

Furthermore, Finland closely followed the examples of Nordic (mainly Swedish) policy models in the post–World War II period, especially since the left-wing parties had gained significant momentum after the war and other parties would seek to bolster their electoral chances by collaborating with them on certain issues. Other factors that made this possible included the rapid economic growth and the structural changes in the Finnish economy in the 1950s and the 1960s. During the years 1948–1960, public expenditures, which now subsidized government-run health care, social security, and administration, grew at an annual average of 4.4 percent. The Finnish welfare state, however, really took off in the 1960s, when the growth of public expenditures accelerated. The Disability Pension Act and the Old Age Pension Act were passed in 1962, and the Health Insurance Act in 1964. These measures were followed by others, especially in education and health care in the 1970s, which increased the social spending role of the municipalities and local government. Education and health-care expenditures have generally grown fast, although the proportion of current transfers and subsidies increased even faster in the postwar period.[59] The growth in most areas of spending has continued since the 1980s, although the growth has slowed down. The periods of recession, such as the early 1990s and the period since 2008, have put more fiscal pressure, both domestically and from abroad, on the Nordic welfare states. In addition, the recent refugee crisis has added to the burden of the welfare bureaucracies in these countries, and it has led to a political backlash among the Nordic populations, as seen in the rise of nationalist/populist parties, such as in Finland and Sweden, and more stringent immigration policies, like in Denmark.[60]

However, on the aggregate, while the postwar Nordic societies have built up extensive social safety nets and invested in human capital, they have also enjoyed a high level of economic growth and living standards, something that Lindert has termed the free lunch puzzle. Why? According to Lindert, the Nordic societies have smartly focused on taxing mostly harmful behavior (i.e. enacting so-called sin taxes, on the use of tobacco, alcohol, gasoline, etc.) to provide societal gains, which has helped them redistribute money for more productive endeavors. In fact, one of the fundamental aspects of the durability and effectiveness of Nordic welfare states pertains to their redistribution policies. Thus, the factor income inequalities (capital, salary, and entrepreneurial incomes) are considerably higher when compared with the disposable income inequalities, such as when adding the social incomes to the factor incomes as well as subtracting taxes that were paid and other payments (Figure 4.7). The crucial fact is that factor income inequalities (1) increased significantly in both Finland and Sweden from the late 1970s to around year 1995; however, the disposable income inequalities remained at similar levels in Sweden until 1990 and in Finland until 1992. In other words, the redistribution activities of the welfare state held the inequalities at similar levels even as the factor or market inequalities increased.

However, the impact of the redistribution policies clearly diminished during the latter part of the observed period: the disposable income inequalities increased even though the factor income inequalities remained stagnant or slightly increased. Evidently, this process can be characterized by the following ratio: the disposable income inequality divided by the factor income inequality (2). Thus, this ratio (2) tells us how much the market income inequalities were decreased by redistribution policies. In both countries, the redistribution

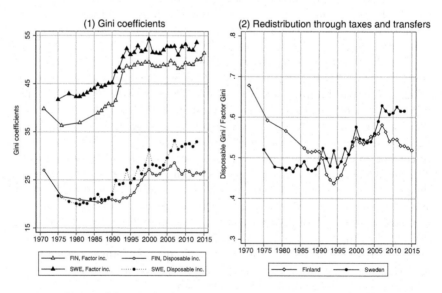

Figure 4.7 Gini coefficients and redistribution in Finland and Sweden (household, OECD-equivalence scale). Note: (1) Gini coefficients are calculated from factor (entrepreneurial + salary + capital incomes, including capital gains) and disposable incomes (factor incomes + social transfers − paid taxes and transfers). (2) Disposable Ginis are divided by Factor Ginis.

Source: Finland (OSF 2019: Income distribution statistics); Sweden (Statistics Sweden 2019: Household finances).

policies reversed around mid–1990s toward less equalizing policies. The next turning point occurred after 2008, when Finland and the rest of the world suffered a recession, unemployment increased, and the automatic welfare state social transfers increased in volume. In addition, the recession was not as severe in Sweden, and the development toward less equalizing policies was at least halted. Nevertheless, it is good to bear in mind that in terms of both of these figures, the level of unemployment and the "automatic" social transfer system were quite crucial, not necessary the policy changes.

One of the key changes in the redistribution policies in Finland was the separation between labor and capital income taxation in 1993, which meant that labor income tax rates were progressive and the capital income tax rates were flat (25 percent in 1993). In addition, the dividends from the rich closed companies were partly tax-exempt (Jäntti et al. 2010, Tuomala 2019). This strengthened the incentives to transform labor incomes to capital incomes since the top marginal tax rate on labor income was considerably higher. Thus, partly due to the changes made to the taxation, the share of the capital incomes in the top 1 percentage increased from 11 percent to about 63 percent between the years 1990 and 2004. Furthermore, whereas the average tax rates of the median incomes decreased only slightly from 22 percent to 21 percent between the years 1987 and 2004, on the other hand, the top 1 percent tax rates dropped considerably from 44 percent to 34 percent (Jäntti et al. 2010).

These redistribution policies were obviously not only aimed at keeping inequality in its various forms, especially income (or in some cases wealth) inequality but also aimed at societally acceptable levels – and what was considered acceptable or desirable obviously changed over time. In fact, the money arising from the redistribution policies also went toward investments in policies that would reduce inequality and provide economic mobility. These types of impacts can be seen in various indicators and outcomes in the Nordic cases. As seen in Table 4.1, in the beginning of the 20th century Finland was clearly

Table 4.1 Average years of schooling in Norway, Denmark, Finland, and Sweden, 1900–2010.

Year	Norway	Denmark	Finland	Sweden
1900	5.8	5.6	1.7	5.5
1910	6.0	6.0	2.0	5.9
1920	6.3	6.3	2.7	6.2
1930	6.5	6.6	3.6	6.6
1940	7.0	6.9	5.0	6.9
1950	7.6	7.6	6.0	7.4
1960	8.8	8.9	7.0	8.5
1970	10.0	9.8	7.6	9.7
1980	11.3	10.8	9.5	11.0
1990	12.1	11.4	10.6	11.8
2000	12.4	12.0	11.5	11.5
2010	12.6	12.1	12.0	11.9

Source: Clioinfra database. Available from: https://clio-infra.eu/. (Cited 1 March 2019).

a laggard in terms of schooling outcomes. However, by mid-century, this had changed already, and Finland had started to catch up. By the end of the century, Finland was on part with the other Nordic countries. In general, improvements in social well-being have come from many sources in the last 100 years among the leading Western economies, but one of the most important aspects has been the growth in human capital. Regardless, Finland was far behind until the 1960s and the comprehensive school reform, which put Finland eventually on par with the others, and even ahead in terms of achievements (PISA tests) in the 21st century.

In general, in most European countries education inequality decreased until the 1960s, and even beyond in some cases. However, in Finland the largest drops came before the new education laws in the 1960s, and the level of inequality even increased initially. In most countries this measure of inequality has decreased in the recent decades.[61] The Nordic countries were no exceptions to this general pattern. Another measure of human capital, numeracy, gives us a longer-term view of these trends in the Nordic countries. Norway caught up last among this group to the rest, but overall all these countries had high levels of numeracy by the early 20th century and that did not change by the later policies. The educational policies and expansion of the latter part of the 20th century simply reinforced the strength of the Nordic societies as highly educated polities,[62] which could be seen especially in Finland's superb performance in the PISA tests in the early 2000s.[63]

Finally, one important measure of societal inequality pertains to gender discrimination and status. It is much harder to obtain long-run data on such indicators. One way to look at this is through the representation of women in the Nordic parliaments (Figure 4.8). The most robust growth occurred from

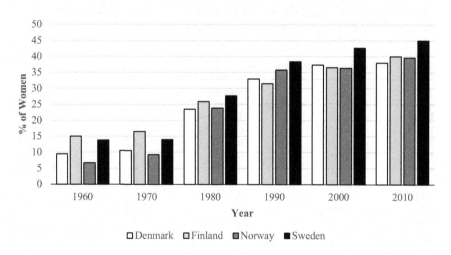

Figure 4.8 Number of female members in the parliament.

Source: Clioinfra database. Available from: https://clio-infra.eu/. (Cited 1 March 2019).

the 1970s onward. Overall, women MPs have quadrupled their share of parliamentary seats in the postwar era. As we noted earlier, gender imbalance on earnings became one of the focal points in the public discourse in the 1990s, and the voting patterns seem to be linked to this change as well. Overall, social, economic, and political mobility have become hallmarks of the Nordic societies, and the welfare and redistribution policies have certainly helped them along in this direction.

Discussion and conclusions

Inequality in its various forms has become a hot topic of broad societal discussion, in both the academic and policy circles, around the globe, most recently due to Thomas Piketty's work (e.g. 2001, 2014). However, we often perceive both public and policy discussions to be somewhat divorced from scholarly discourses, especially in determining what actual policy approaches would be desirable to achieve certain societal outcomes. Here we have displayed the broad trends in income inequality, and the Nordic countries are clearly still in the lower inequality group in the 21st century. Moreover, the Nordic trends have followed international patterns fairly well, namely high inequality in the late 19th century, lesser inequality after World War II, and rising trend since the late 1980s. Clearly the Nordic societies have converged over time economically, socially, politically, and culturally. We also discussed the redistribution and welfare state policies that have kept inequality lower in the Nordic societies, particularly in Finland and Sweden.

Our broad analysis of the topic of income inequality in the public sphere showed that the patterns were not entirely similar in Finland and Sweden, however. In Finland, it seems, certain academic debates also became public debates, and thus most likely had a greater impact on policy debates as well. In Sweden, in contrast, income inequality was discussed less until the recent years. Broader debates about welfare states and the role of the government in the aggregate economy were also parts of these discussions. In general, regardless of the occasional critiques of the welfare and redistribution policies, the broader Nordic societal agreement about the need for welfare state has been quite solid in poll after poll, even among the more conservative political parties. Our framework outlined a connection between research, policies, and discourses. We would argue here that in the last 50 years or so those connections have existed in Finland, although not always. In Sweden, the connections, at least in the context of income inequality, were less pronounced, perhaps also due to the earlier adoption of welfare and tax policies. Thus, the Nordic countries were not quite as homogenous as they sometimes appear.

Our goal here was to examine certain historical trends in income inequality and debates surrounding this topic, especially from the lens of redistribution and welfare state policies. It seems quite clear that politicians and the general public are aware of certain debates in for example in economics and economic history concerning income inequality; nonetheless, their understanding of the facts or data is often limited. Typically, many politicians would assume that income inequality is rising fast in countries like Finland, whereas it is actually remained relatively similar levels or only slightly increased in the 2000s after rapid increase in the 1990s.[64] Furthermore, Finland and other Nordic societies are much more equal when considering incomes, or other types of inequalities, than most places on this globe. The redistribution policies have been fairly effective in the post–World War II era, and the welfare state policies have created more equal opportunities for also minorities, yet the impact of those policies have waned somewhat in the 21st century.

Should scholars be more active in the public sphere, to provide deeper historical context for debates and point toward policy solutions? It is quite difficult to do that, especially in a way that various forms of media would find interesting enough. Moreover, it is also difficult in current climate of viral stories, fake news, and extensive social media networks. Regardless, while all those elements of modern media can distort "truths" and mislead debates, they can also amplify messages from scholars like Piketty, who can have a real impact on how societies evolve. And most universities and research centers today in fact value the idea of their employees having a public impact, even to the point of providing rewards for that, although they would equally be risk averse toward potentially negative publicity and embarrassment. This is the difficult balance that 21st-century scholars will face in their careers, and the topic of income inequality (or any other type of inequality) is a key topic of societal debate now and in the future.

Sources

The Chartbook of Economic Inequality: www.chartbookofeconomicine quality.com/about. (Retrieved 31 March 2019).

The Clioinfra database. Available from: https://clio-infra.eu/. (Retrieved 1 March 2019).

Dagens Nyheter (*DH*), The Royal Swedish Library, The Dagens Nyheter Digital Archive (Retrieved 10 January 2019).

Helsingin Sanomat (*HS*), The Päivälehti Archives, Helsinki (Retrieved 14 January 2019).

The Intergovernmental Panel on Climate Change (IPCC), pecial report. www.ipcc.ch/report/sr15/ (Retrieved 16 November 2018).

The Luxembourg Income Study (LIS), www.lisdatacenter.org/data-access/ [Accessed 2 August 2019].

Milanovic, Branko L. (2016). All the Ginis Dataset, World Bank Group. https://datacatalog.worldbank.org/dataset/all-ginis-dataset. (Retrieved 15 November 2018).

Official Statistics of Finland (OSF) (2019): Income distribution statistics [e-publication].

ISSN=1799–1331. Helsinki: Statistics Finland [Referred 1/4/2019].

Access method: www.stat.fi/til/tjt/index_en.html.

Official Statistics of Finland (OSF): Population projection [e-publication]. ISSN=1798–5153.2018. Helsinki: Statistics Finland [Referred 16/11/2018]. Access method: www.stat.fi/til/vaenn/2018/vaenn_2018_2018-11-16_tie_001_en.html.

Official Statistics of Finland (OSF): Gini coefficients and other income inequality measures in 1966–2017. Income distribution statistics, 015 (http://pxnet2.stat.fi/PXWeb/pxweb/en/StatFin/StatFin__tul__tjt/statfin_tjt_pxt_015.px// (Retrieved 2 August 2019).

Statistics Sweden (2019). Statistical database: Household finances. www.statistikdatabasen.scb.se/pxweb/en/ssd/START__HE__HE0103__HE0103A/DispInk8/?rxid=0309dbd3-a62c-45e7-a0c3-50650e04aca3#. (Retrieved: 31 March 2019).

The World Inequality Database (WID) (2018). Downloaded from wid.world on 29 May 2018 at 07:19:30. DOI: http://wid.world/data/.

Notes

1 See e.g. Lindert & Williamson 2016, Milanovic 2016, Piketty 2015a, 2015b, Piketty, Saez & Zucman 2018.
2 Prados 2018.
3 For summaries of the top income literature, see Atkinson & Piketty (eds.) 2007, Atkinson & Piketty (eds.) 2010. And earlier studies by Lindert 2000, Morrison 2000.
4 Roine & Waldenström 2015.
5 Törmälehto 2019, Riihelä & Tuomala 2019.
6 See e.g. Burkhauser et al. 2012.
7 Leigh 2007, Alvaredo 2011, Burkhauser et al. 2012.
8 See the growth rates between deciles in e.g. Jäntti et al. 2010.
9 For example, Riihelä & Suoniemi 2017.
10 Nevertheless, some studies show that wealth inequality and capital income inequality have grown more rapidly in Finland, e.g. Riihelä, Sullström & Tuomala 2017.
11 Piketty, Saez & Zucman 2018, 553.
12 Kipping 1999.
13 E.g. Kotilainen 2018.
14 Mihailidis & Viotty 2017.
15 Especially the 2018 Intergovernmental Panel on Climate Change (IPCC) was widely discussed. Similarly, the population projection by Statics Finland in November 2018 raised concerns. See: www.stat.fi/til/vaenn/2018/vaenn_2018_2018-11-16_tie_001_en.html (cited 16 November 2018) and www.ipcc.ch/report/sr15/ (cited 16 November 2018).
16 Andersson 2012, Ihalainen & Kinnunen 2018.
17 Andersson 2006, Roslin 2010, Kotilainen 2018.
18 Roslin 2010.
19 This article is not intended to give a definitive literature review on the research dealing with income inequality in Finland or Sweden during the 1970s–1990s; rather, we will provide some examples of the key literature published especially in Finland. – See also Baten & van Zanden 2008.
20 Broadberry et al. 2015.
21 E.g. Kuznets 1959, 1963.
22 See especially Milanovic 2016, 5, 55.
23 E.g. Renvall 1900.

24 Gini 1921, Ceriani & Verme 2012.

25 E.g. Bentzel 1952, Brummert 1963, 1965, Fougstedt 1948, Hagström 1944, Hemmilä 1960, Jylhä 1945, Wahlbeck 1955.

26 E.g. Bjerke 1957, Bentzel 1957, Aukrust 1957, 1970.

27 Kulutustutkimus   (http://pxnet2.stat.fi/PXWeb/pxweb/fi/StatFin/StatFin__tul__tjt/ statfin_tjt_pxt_015.px/?rxid=b5e03ef3-7a8c-440a-8eb5-ef756bd4cd76).   See also see also Linnaila 1969, Hjerppe 1972, Janhunen 1969, Salavuo 1970.

28 E.g. Hjerppe & Lefgren 1974.

29 See also Suominen 1979.

30 See especially: www.lisdatacenter.org/data-access/.

31 E.g. Sawyer & Wasserman 1976.

32 Partanen 1970.

33 E.g. Dasgupta, Sen & Starret 1973.

34 Noponen 1973, Suominen 1974, 1979, Pöntinen & Uusitalo 1975.

35 See section 3 for further details about literature.

36 *HS* 7 July 1969.

37 E.g. *HS* 29 December 1971.

38 E.g. *HS* 5 January 1986.

39 E.g. Lahdenperä 1987.

40 Tolvanen 1985a, 1985b, Puurunen 1987, Leppänen & Tolvanen 1987, Ylisippola 1989, Ringen & Uusitalo 1990.

41 E.g. Wahlbeck 1955, Kiiskinen 1958, Somervuori 1972.

42 E.g. Sailas 1987, Uusitalo 1988, Takala et al. 1988, Paananen 1988.

43 E.g. Sullström 1987, Pekkarinen 1988.

44 Especially Nummela 1987, 1988a, 1988b.

45 Laukkanen 1989, Tossavainen 1991, Asplund 1992.

46 Hagfors & Vartia 1989.

47 Sukupolvityöryhmä 1994.

48 Acker 1990.

49 E.g. Isotalus et al. 1989, Brunila 1990, Asplund 1995a, 1995b.

50 See e.g. Roine & Waldenström 2010, Jäntti et al. 2010.

51 A source critical note: The digital collections of Helsingin Sanomat count the frequency of the keyword per page until the turn of the 1990s, and per article from thereafter. Thus, the figures are not entirely comparable. Moreover, the articles dealing with income inequality both in Finland and in Sweden did not solely discuss the topic as a domestic issue. Nevertheless, articles discussing inequality as an international challenge were, on the whole, a minority.

52 *HS* 5 March 1973.

53 *HS* 29 March 1979.

54 E.g. *HS* 15 February 1985.

55 See Östberg in this volume.

56 Lindert 2004. On different types of welfare states and especially the Scandinavian "model", see e.g. Esping-Andersen & Korpi 1984.

57 Eloranta & Kauppila 2006, Hannikainen & Eloranta 2019.

58 Tanzi & Schuknecht 2000, 15, 197. On recent trends, see esp. Greve 2018, Kangas & Kvist 2018.

59 Alestalo & Uusitalo 1986, Hjerppe 1989, 130–131.

60 Heikkinen 2019. On rise of right-wing populism and immigration policies, especially in Denmark, see Heinze 2018. See several other contributions in this volume for further discussion of these discourses.

61 Van Zanden et al. 2014.

62 See e.g. Modalsli 2017 for discussion of Norway in the long run.

63 Cf. Sahlberg 2016.

64 See also Gustafsson & Uusitalo 1990, Haavisto 2018.

References

Acker, Joan, 1990: *Samanarvoinen työ. Tutkimus työelämän sukupuolistuneista rakenteista.* Tampere: Vastapaino.

Alestalo, Matti & Uusitalo, Hannu, 1986: "Finland" in Peter Flora (ed.) *Growth to Limits: The Western European Welfare States Since World War II.* Berlin: W. de Gruyter,

Allardt, Erik, 1976a: *Hyvinvoinnin ulottuvuuksia.* Porvoo: WSOY.

Allardt, Erik, 1976b: "Dimensions of Welfare in a Comparative Scandinavian Study" in *Acta Sociologica,* 19:3, 227–239.

Alvaredo, Facundo, 2011: "A Note on the Relationship between Top Income Shares and the Gini Coefficient" in *Economics Letters,* 110:3, 274–277. https://doi.org/10.1016/j.econlet.2010.10.008.

Andersson, Jenny, 2006: "Choosing Futures: Alva Myrdal and the Construction of Swedish Futures Studies, 1967–1972" in *International Review of Social History,* 51:2, 277–295.

Andersson, Jenny, 2012: "The Great Future Debate and the Struggle for the World" in *The American Historical Review,* 117:5, 1411–1430.

Asplund, Rita, 1992: *Education, Experience and Earnings in Finland. Data Analysis and Complementary Estimation Results.* Helsinki: Research Institute of the Finnish Economy.

Asplund, Rita, 1995a: *The Gender Wage Gap in Finnish Industry in 1980–1994. An Empirical Analysis of Non-Manual Workers.* Helsinki: Research Institute of the Finnish Economy.

Asplund, Rita, 1995b: "Palkkaerot Suomessa ja muissa maissa" in *Kansantaloudellinen aikakauskirja,* 91:4, 525–536.

Atkinson, Anthony Barnes, 1970: "On the Measurement of Inequality" in *Journal of Economic Theory,* 2:3, 244–263.

Atkinson, Anthony Barnes & Piketty, Thomas (eds.) 2007: *Top Incomes Over the Twentieth Century: A Contrast between Continental European and English-Speaking Countries.* Oxford: Oxford University Press.

Atkinson, Anthony Barnes & Piketty, Thomas (eds.) 2010: *Top Incomes: A Global Perspective.* Oxford: Oxford University Press.

Aukrust, Odd, 1957: "Trends and Cycles in Norwegian Income Shares" in *Review of Income and Wealth,* 6:1, 283–305.

Aukrust, Odd, 1970: "PRIM I: A Model of the Price and Income Distribution Mechanism of an Open Economy" in *Review of Income and Wealth,* 16:1, 51–78.

Baten, Joerg & van Zanden, Jan Luiten, 2008: "Book Production and the Onset of Modern Economic Growth" in *Journal of Economic Growth,* 13:3, 217–235.

Bentzel, Ragnar, 1952: *Inkomstfördelningen i Sverige.* Stockholm: IUI/Victor Petterssons Bokindustri Aktiebolag.

Bentzel, Ragnar, 1957: "Some Aspects of the Economic Interpretation of Changes in the Inequality of Income Distribution" in *Review of Income and Wealth,* 6:1, 269–282.

Bjerke, Kjeld, 1957: "Changes in Danish Income Distribution 1939–52" in *Review of Income and Wealth,* 6:1, 98–154.

Broadberry, Stephen et al., 2015: *British Economic Growth, 1270–1870.* Cambridge: Cambridge University Press.

Brummert, Raoul, 1963: "Henkilökohtaisten tulojen jakautumisesta Suomessa" in *Kansantaloudellinen Aikakauskirja,* 59:4, 235–265.

Brummert, Raoul, 1965: "Yksityisestä varallisuudesta ja sen jakautumisen tasoittamisesta" in *Kansantaloudellinen Aikakauskirja,* 61:4, 294–332.

Brunila, Anne, 1990: *Naisten ja miesten palkkaerot vuosina 1975 ja 1985.* Helsinki: Työväen taloudellinen tutkimuslaitos.

Burkhauser, Richard V. et al., 2012: "Recent Trends in Top Income Shares in the United States: Reconciling Estimates from March CPS and IRS Tax Return Data" in *The Review of Economics and Statistics*, 94, 371–388.

Ceriani, Lidi & Verme, Paolo, 2012: "The Origins of the Gini Index: Extracts from Variabilità e Mutabilità (1912) by Corrado Gini" in *The Journal of Economic Inequality*, 10:3, 421–443.

Dasgupta, Partha, Sen, Amartya & Starrett, David, 1973: "Notes on the Measurement of Inequality" in *Journal of Economic Theory*, 6:2, 180–187.

Eloranta, Jari & Kauppila, Jari, 2006: "Guns and Butter. Central Government Spending in the 20th Century" in Jari Ojala et al. (eds.) *The Road to Prosperity: An Economic History of Finland*. Helsinki: SKS, 216–243.

Esping-Andersen, Gösta & Korpi, Walter, 1984: *From Poor Relief Towards Institutional Welfare States: The Development of Scandinavian Social Policy*. Stockholm: Institute för Social Forskning.

Fougstedt, Gunnar, 1948: "Inkomstens fördelning i Finland" in *Ekonomiska Samfundets Tidskrift*, 1:4, 248–273.

Gini, Corrado, 1921: "Measurement of Inequality of Incomes" in *The Economic Journal*, 31:121, 124–126.

Greve, Bent, 2018: "Future of the Welfare State?" in *Routledge Handbook of the Welfare State*. London: Routledge, 525–533.

Gustafsson, Björn & Uusitalo, Hannu, 1990: "Income Distribution and Redistribution During Two Decades: Experiences from Finland and Sweden" in Inga Persson (ed.) *Generating Equality in the Welfare State. The Swedish Experience*. Oslo: Norwegian University Press, 73–95.

Haavisto, Ilkka, 2018: *Luultua parempi. Suomalaiset hahmottavat tuloerot todellista jyrkemmiksi ja vähättelevät omia tulojaan*. EVA analyysi 61. Helsinki: EVA, 27 February 2018.

Hagfors, Robert & Vartia, Pentti, 1989: *Essays on Income Distribution, Economic Welfare and Personal Taxation*. Helsinki: Research Institute of the Finnish Economy.

Hagström, K. G., 1944: "Inkomstutjämningen i Sverige" in *Skandinaviska Bankens kvartalsskrift*, 2.

Hannikainen, Matti & Eloranta, Jari, 2019: "Palveluiden ja tulonsiirtojen yhteiskunta" in Jaana Laine et al. (eds.) *Vaurastumisen vuodet. Suomen taloushistoria teollistumisen jälkeen*. Helsinki: Gaudeamus, 16–35.

Heikkinen, Sakari, 2019: "Julkinen talous, valtiontalous ja finanssipolitiikka" in Jaana Laine et al. (eds.) *Vaurastumisen vuodet. Suomen taloushistoria teollistumisen jälkeen*. Helsinki: Gaudeamus, 39–59.

Heinze, Anna-Sophie, 2018: "Strategies of Mainstream Parties Towards Their Right-Wing Populist Challengers: Denmark, Norway, Sweden and Finland in Comparison" in *West European Politics*, 41:2, 287–309.

Hemmilä, Pentti, 1960: *Fyysisten tulonsaajien tulotaso talousalueittain vuosina 1950 ja 1956*. Valtakunnan suunnittelutoimiston julkaisusarja, A:6. Helsinki: Valtakunnan suunnittelutoimisto.

Hjerppe, Reino, 1972: *Tulojen jakautumisen mittaluvuista, Yhteiskuntapolitiikan tavoitteita ja niiden mittaamista tutkiva jaosto*. Liite 2, Taloudellista eriarvoisuutta tutkivan työryhmän raportti. Helsinki: Talousneuvosto.

Hjerppe, Riitta, 1989: *The Finnish Economy 1860–1985. Growth and Structural Change*. Helsinki: Bank of Finland.

Hjerppe, Riitta & Lefgren, John, 1974: "Suomen tulonjakauman kehityksestä 1881–1967" in *Kansantaloudellinen Aikakauskirja*, 70:2, 97–119.

Ihalainen, Pasi & Kinnunen, Tiina, 2018: "Reform and Revolution in Scandinavia, 1917–1919: Entangled Histories and Visions of the Future" in *Scandinavian Journal of History*, 44:2, 143–149.

Isotalus, Päivi et al., 1989: *Sama palkka samanarvoisesta työstä. Kansainvälinen katsaus*. Helsinki: Sosiaali- ja terveysministeriö.

Janhunen, Olli, 1973: *Veronalaisten tulojen jakautuminen Suomen kunnissa v. 1969*. I. DETA 3, Helsingin yliopiston yleisen valtio-opin laitoksen tutkimuksia, Sarja C. Helsinki: Helsingin yliopisto.

Jäntti, Markus, 1993: *Essays on Income Distribution and Poverty*. Åbo: Åbo Akademi University Press.

Jäntti, Markus et al., 2010: "Trends in Top Incomes Shares in Finland" in Anthony B. Atkinson & Thomas Piketty (eds.) *Top Incomes: A Global Perspective*. Oxford: Oxford University Press.

Jylhä, Tauno, 1945: "Suomen kansan tulojakautumisesta" in *Matemaattisten aineiden aikakauskirja*, 9:4. Helsinki.

Kangas, Olli & Kvist, Jon, 2018: "Nordic Welfare States" in *Routledge Handbook of the Welfare State*. London: Routledge, 124–136.

Kekkonen, Urho Kaleva, 1952: "Toimeentulevaiset ja toimeentulemattomat" in *Kyntäjä*, 12.

Kiiskinen, Auvo, 1958: *Taloudellinen kasvu alueittain Suomessa vuosina 1926–1952. Tutkimus tuotosvolyymin, tuottavuuden ja reaalitulon alueellisista kasvusuunnista sekä kehityserojen syistä, lähinnä aineellisen tuotannon piirissä*. Helsinki: University of Helsinki.

Kipping, Matthias, 1999: "American Management Consulting Companies in Western Europe, 1920 to 1990: Products, Reputation, and Relationships" in *Business History Review*, 73:2, 190–220.

Kotilainen, Markku, 2018: *Ennustetoiminta Etlassa vuosina 1971–2018*. ETLA Muistio, No. 69. https://pub.etla.fi/ETLA-Muistio-Brief-69.pdf.

Kuznets, Simon, 1959: "Quantitative Aspects of the Economic Growth of Nations: IV. Distribution of National Income by Factor Shares" in *Economic Development and Cultural Change*, 7:3(2), 1–100.

Kuznets, Simon, 1963: "Quantitative Aspects of the Economic Growth of Nations: VIII. Distribution of Income by Size" in *Economic Development and Cultural Change*, 11:2(2), 1–80.

Lahdenperä, Harri, 1987: *Alueelliset tulo- ja hyvinvointierot Suomessa*. Espoo: Pellervo Economic Research PTT.

Laukkanen, Erkki, 1989: *Koulutuksen laajentamisen tulonjakovaikutukset Suomessa*. Helsinki: Ministry of Education.

Leigh, Andrew, 2007: "How Closely Do Top Income Shares Track Other Measures of Inequality?" in *The Economic Journal*, 117:524, 619–633.

Leppänen, Seppo & Tolvanen, Kari, 1987: *Toimialoittaiset palkkaerot vuosina 1960–1985*. Helsinki: Government Institute for Economic Research.

Lindert, Peter H., 2000: "Three Centuries of Inequality in Britain and America" in Anthony B. Atkinson & François Bourguignon (eds.) *Handbook of Income Distribution* (vol. 1). Amsterdam: North-Holland, 167–216.

Lindert, Peter H., 2004: *Growing Public. Social Spending and Economic Growth Since the Eighteenth Century*. Cambridge: Cambridge University Press.

Lindert, Peter H. & Williamson, Jeffrey G., 2016: *Unequal Gains. American Growth and Inequality Since 1700*. Princeton, NJ: Princeton University Press.

Linnaila, Jorma, 1969: *Vuoden 1966 kotitaloustiedustelun ennakkotietoja. Kotitalouksien tulot ja tulojen käyttö kulutukseen ja säästämiseen suuralueittain ja väestöryhmittäin*. Helsinki: Tilastollinen päätoimisto.

Mihailidis, Paul & Viotty, Samantha, 2017: "Spreadable Spectacle in Digital Culture: Civic Expression, Fake News, and the Role of Media Literacies in 'Post-Fact' Society" in *American Behavioral Scientist*, 61:4, 441–454.

Milanovic, Branko, 2016: *Global Inequality: A New Approach for the Age of Globalization*. Cambridge: Harvard University Press.

Modalsli, Jørgen, 2017: "Intergenerational Mobility in Norway, 1865–2011" in *The Scandinavian Journal of Economics*, 119:1, 34–71.

Morrison, Christian, 2000: "Historical Perspectives on Income Distribution: The Case of Europe" in Anthony B. Atkinson & François Bourguignon (eds.) *Handbook of Income Distribution* (vol. 1). Amsterdam: North-Holland, 217–260.

Noponen, Jyrki, 1973: *Tulojen epätasainen jakautuminen. Polkuanalyysin käyttö tulojen vertikaalisen jakautumisen syiden tutkimisessa*. Helsinki: University of Helsinki.

Nummela, Ilkka, 1988a: "Förmögenhetsskillnaderna i Finland under slutet av 1700-talet" in *Historisk tidskrift för Finland*, 73:1, 27–39.

Nummela, Ilkka, 1988b: "Varallisuuseroista Suomen kaupungeissa vuosina 1571 ja 1614" in *Historiallinen aikakauskirja*, 86:4, 301–303.

Nummela, Ilkka & Laitinen, Erkki K., 1987: "Distribution of Income in Kuopio 1880–1910" in *Scandinavian Economic History Review*, 35:3, 237–253.

Paananen, Seppo, 1988: *Pienituloiset kotitaloudet 1985*. Helsinki: National Board of Social Welfare.

Partanen, Juha, 1970: "Tuloerot Länsi-Euroopan maissa" in *Sosiologia*, 7:6, 307–312.

Pekkarinen, Jukka, 1988: "Kotitalouksien varallisuuseroista" in *Työväen taloudellinen tutkimuslaitos*, 16:1, 20–30.

Piketty, Thomas, 2001: *Les hauts revenus en France au 20ème siècle*. Paris: Grasset.

Piketty, Thomas, 2013: *Le Capital au XXIe siècle*. Paris: SEUIL.

Piketty, Thomas, 2014: *Capital in the Twenty-First Century*. London: The Belknap Press of Harvard University Press.

Piketty, Thomas, 2015a: "About Capital in the Twenty-First Century" in *American Economic Review*, 105:5, 48–53.

Piketty, Thomas, 2015b: "Putting Distribution Back at the Center of Economics: Reflections on Capital in the Twenty-First Century" in *Journal of Economic Perspectives*, 1:29, 67–68.

Piketty, Thomas, Saez, Emmanuel & Zucman, Gabriel, 2018: "Distributional National Accounts: Methods and Estimates for the United States" in *The Quarterly Journal of Economics*, 133:2, 553–609.

Pöntinen, Seppo & Uusitalo, Hannu, 1975: "Socioeconomic Background and Income" in *Acta Sociologica*, 18:4, 322–329.

Prados de la Escosura, Leandro, 2018: *Well-Being Inequality in the Long Run*. Centre for Economic Policy Research, Discussion Paper Series 12920. www.researchgate.net/profile/Leandro_Prados_de_la_Escosura/publication/324993375_WELL-BEING_INEQUALITY_IN_THE_LONG_RUN/links/5af086f5a6fdcc2436473b2d/WELL-BEING-INEQUALITY-IN-THE-LONG-RUN.pdf.

Puurunen, Maija, 1987: *Viljelijäväestön tulojen vertaaminen muiden väestöryhmien tuloihin*. Helsinki: Maatalouden taloudellinen tutkimuslaitos.

Renvall, Heikki, 1900: "Tulojen jaosta Suomen suurimmissa kaupungeissa 1875–1899" in *Kansantaloudellisen yhdistyksen esitelmiä*. Helsinki: Otava, 3.

Riihelä, Marja, Sullström, Risto & Tuomala, Matti, 2017: "Varallisuus ja Varallisuuserot Suomessa" in *Talous & Yhteiskunta*, 2, 38–46.

Riihelä, Marja & Suoniemi, Ilpo, 2017: "Miksi Suomen tuloerot ja köyhyys ovat kääntyneet kasvuun?" in Heikki Taimio (ed.) *Tuotannon Tekijät – Palkansaajien Suomi 100 vuotta*. Helsinki: Labour Institute for Economic Research, 190–233.

Riihelä, Marja & Tuomala, Matti, 2019: "Ovatko tuloerot Suomessa kasvaneet luultua enemmän?" in *Talous & Yhteiskunta*, 1, 30–37.

Ringen, Stein & Uusitalo, Hannu, 1990: "Income Distribution and Redistribution in the Nordic Welfare States" in *International Journal of Sociology*, 20:3, 69–91.

Roikonen, Petri & Heikkinen, Sakari, 2018: "A Kuznets Rise and a Piketty Fall: Income Inequality in Finland, 1865–1934" in *European Review of Economic History*. https://doi.org/10.1093/ereh/hey032.

Roine, Jesper & Waldenström, Daniel, 2010: "Top Incomes in Sweden Over the Twentieth Century" in Anthony B. Atkinson & Thomas Piketty (eds.) *Top Incomes: A Global Perspective*. Oxford: Oxford University Press, 299–370.

Roine, Jesper & Waldenström, Daniel, 2015: "Long-Run Trends in the Distribution of Income and Wealth" in Anthony B. Atkinson & François Bourguignon (eds.) *Handbook of Income Distribution* (vol. 2). London: Elsevier, 469–592.

Roslin, Bertil (ed.) 2010: *Ennustuksesta jälkiviisauteen*. Helsinki: Sitra.

Sahlberg, Pasi, 2016: "The Finnish Paradox: Equitable Public Education within a Competitive Market Economy" in Frank Adamson et al. (eds.) *Global Education Reform*. New York: Routledge, 110–130.

Sailas, Raija, 1987: *Köyhät keskuudessamme. Pienituloisimmat kotitaloudet vuoden 1981 kotital-oustiedustelussa*. Helsinki: National Board of Social Welfare.

Salavuo, Kari, 1970: "Tulonjaosta ja sen mittaamisen ongelmasta" in *Turun yliopiston sosiaal-ipolitiikan laitoksen tutkielmia*. B:10. Turku: Turun yliopisto.

Sawyer, Malcolm C. & Wasserman, Mark, 1976: *Income Distribution in OECD Countries*. Paris: Publications de l'OCDE.

Somervuori, Antti, 1972: *Elinkustannusten ja reaalitulojen alueelliset erot Suomessa*. Helsinki: Statistics Finland.

Sukupolvityöryhmä, 1994: *Sukupolvien välinen tulonjako: Sukupolvityöryhmän loppuraportti* [*Intergenerational Income Distribution: Report of the Working Group on Intergenerational Income Distribution*]. Helsinki: Prime Minister's Office.

Sullström, Risto, 1987: "Alimman tuloviidenneksen toimeentulo Suomessa vuonna 1981" in *Kansantaloudellinen aikakauskirja*, 83:1, 29–48.

Suominen, Risto, 1974: *Tulonsiirtoprosessin vaikutuksia eräissä maissa*. Helsinki: Ministry of Social Affairs and Health.

Suominen, Risto, 1979: *Tulonjako Suomessa vuonna 1976*. Helsinki: Statistics Finland.

Takala, Kari et al., 1988: *Kotitalouksien varallisuuserot Suomessa*. Helsinki: Labour Institute for Economic Research.

Tanzi, Vito & Schuknecht, Ludger, 2000: *Public Spending in the 20th Century: A Global Perspective*. New York: Cambridge University Press.

Tolvanen, Maija, 1985a: *Viljelijäväestön ja palkansaajien tuloeroja selvittävä tutkimus. Osa 1: Tulokäsitteet, tilastot ja tuloja koskevat laskelmat*. Helsinki: Maatalouden taloudellinen tutkimuslaitos.

Tolvanen, Maija, 1985b: *Viljelijäväestön ja palkansaajien tuloeroja selvittävä tutkimus. Osa 2: tulovertailut*. Helsinki: Maatalouden taloudellinen tutkimuslaitos.

Törmälehto, Veli-Matti, 2019: "Tulo-, kulutus- ja varallisuuseroista Suomessa" in *Kansanta-loudellinen aikakauskirja*, 115:1, 41–65.

Tossavainen, Pekka, 1991: *Koulutus ja ansiot*. Helsinki: VATT Institute for Economic Research.

Tuomala, Matti, 2019: *Markkinat, valtio & eriarvoisuus*. Tampere: Vastapaino.

Uusitalo, Hannu, 1975: "Tulonjako Suomessa ja muissa Pohjoismaissa" in *Sosiaalinen aikakauskirja*, 69:6, 575–580.

Uusitalo, Hannu, 1977: "Tulonjaon kehitys vuosina 1966–1975. Tosiasioita ja tulkinta-ongelmia" in *Sosiologia*, 14:2, 51–63.

Uusitalo, Hannu, 1988: *Muuttuva tulonjako. Hyvinvointivaltion ja yhteiskunnan rakennemuutosten vaikutukset tulonjakoon 1966–1985.* Helsinki: Statistics Finland.

Uusitalo, Hannu, 1989: *Income Distribution in Finland: The Effects of the Welfare State and the Structural Changes in Society on Income Distribution in Finland in 1966–1985.* Helsinki: Statistics Finland.

Van Zanden, Jan Luiten, Baten, Joerg, Mira d'Ercole, Marco, Rijpma, Auke, Smith, Conal & Timmer, Marcel (eds.) 2014: *How was Life? Global Well-Being Since 1820.* Paris: OECD Publishing.

Wahlbeck, Lars, 1955: *Om inkomstnivåns geografi i Finland år 1950. En undersökning av inkomstnivåns regionala variationer med hänsyn även tagen till möjligheterna att på grundval av dessa fälla omdömen.* Helsingfors: Söderström.

Ylisippola, Tiina, 1989: *Viljelijöiden ja pienyrittäjien tulovertailu.* Helsinki: Maatalouden taloudellinen tutkimuslaitos.

5 Liquid neutrality

Paradoxes of democracy in Finnish and Swedish NATO discussions?

Matti Roitto and Antero Holmila

> Fluids travel easily. They 'flow', 'spill', 'run out', 'splash', 'pour over', 'leak', 'flood', 'spray', 'drip', 'seep', 'ooze'; unlike solids they are not easily stopped – they pass around some obstacles, dissolve some others and bore or soak their way through others still.[1]

Zygmunt Bauman's famous conception of the modern condition as liquid modernity is in fact an apt description of Finland's and Sweden's security strategies during and after the Cold War. In order to understand the ways the Finnish and Swedish relationship to NATO has evolved since the end of the Cold War, we conceptualise Finland's and Sweden's security orientation as *liquid neutrality*.

Rather than the typical and publicly dominant 'solid' conceptualisations such as 'small-state realism'[2] and 'Finlandization', which put Finnish and Swedish foreign policy in a passive and reactive mode, 'liquid neutrality' implies an active, participatory, daring and deliberate policy orientation that – following Bauman – is able to pass around obstacles. Further, *liquid neutrality* nuances Finnish and Swedish foreign policy to show how small powers took advantage of cracks along the fault lines of superpower competition.

One area in which liquid neutrality becomes visible is the Finnish and Swedish post–Cold War policy formation regarding their relationship with NATO – the subject of this chapter. Typically, the Swedish and Finnish parliamentary democracies, often seen as a part of a wide and uniform Nordic model of democracy,[3] have enjoyed a solid reputation regarding the ideals of democracy.[4] However, during the recent crisis of democracy,[5] the Nordic democracies also, including Sweden and Finland, have been facing a crisis of legitimacy, efficiency and transparency, as discussed elsewhere in this volume.

An often overlooked aspect of the crisis of democracy is foreign and security policy. However, the matter was brought up already in 1975 by Samuel Huntington, Michel Crozier and Joji Watanuki as one of the contributing factors in the US crisis of democracy. The high costs of the war and unearthing of the US schemes that escalated the Vietnam conflict into a full-scale war meant a crucial loss of legitimacy for the US regime.[6] Foreign and especially security policy also pose a particular kind of challenge for the Nordic democracies. In this

DOI: 10.4324/9780429026690-5

chapter, we address this challenge with a historical analysis of the paradoxes in Finnish and Swedish policies vis-à-vis NATO.

Due to its double-faced nature, this side of politics is often overlooked. While issues such as budgets are debated in public, others – for example, the technological alignment of weapon systems or channels of information sharing – are kept hidden in the name of 'national interest'. Some fundamentals of the foreign and security policy are presented in the open in order to create identification and anchor points for politics, interests, values and ideas. Yet other issues are prepared in secrecy – more so in the phases of preparation as leaks can threaten the various national interests. However, a comprehensive analysis remains elusive, since many policy documents are still classified. Thus, we rely on public documents and other available sources and existing literature.

As ascribed to the archetypical realist Otto von Bismarck: 'laws, like sausages, cease to inspire respect in proportion as we know how they are made'. Although the quote was uttered by John Godfrey Saxe in 1869 and was only attributed to Bismarck in the 1930s,[7] it highlights a paradox of democracy, particularly in the realm of security policies. Paradoxically, the more transparent policy formulation and execution seem, the less creation of these policies seems to comply with democratic ideals. That holds true also in the case of Swedish and Finnish foreign and security policy, and even more so vis-à-vis their respective NATO relations and membership debates. Critics suggest that the two states have gradually aligned with NATO, to the brink of full membership, by various undemocratic double-dealings and technical arrangements.

On the one hand, those who study foreign and security policy are well aware of this great game of double-dealing. On the other, scholarship based on publicly available parliamentary sources tends to view foreign policy formation through the lenses of increased parliamentarisation and finds that to some degree, a certain constitutional role is often reserved for parliaments also in foreign policy.[8] These works have illustrated that certain parliamentary momentums have existed from time to time, even if the professionalisation of mass politics and the exponential increase in matters to be covered have shifted much of the parliamentary dealings behind closed doors.[9]

In 21st-century Sweden and Finland, the question of their cooperation with NATO has been one such challenge to democracy. Andrew Cottey has stated, referring to other scholars, that non-alignment has become a part of the identity of the European neutrals, and therefore it is rather unlikely that they would abandon this policy. Moreover, the neutrality policy has greatly affected European neutrals, including Sweden and Finland, to 'maintain their national integrity and political independence, while avoiding war, during and after the Cold War and can therefore be viewed as successful national security policy'. According to Cottey (and many others for that matter), the end of the Cold War triggered NATO expansion and cooperation outside the actual alliance, which is something Cottey describes as a quiet revolution.[10]

Indeed, the age-old discourse on neutrality and non-alignment has given way to a new discourse that goes against the grain of public opinion – or so the grand narrative of the two states inclining more and more towards NATO cooperation would suggest. This illustrates how liquid neutrality permeates Finland's and Sweden's foreign and security policy formulation. Particularly since the end of the Cold War, the long-lasting, outspoken political imperatives of neutrality and non-alignment, which have been true only in part, have been altered in response to the greater paradigm shifts in international relations. First, Finland and Sweden established much-coveted formal positions within the West by joining the European Union (EU) integration process.[11] Since then, they have also approached NATO, to the point that the two might become members rather rapidly.

However, even if this seems a novel situation in the two nations' foreign policy, that is not the case in historical perspective. The two formally non-aligned, neutral Nordic states had conducted a realist and 'liquid' security policy for nearly a century and quite successfully, if judged by the ultimate realist criterion: survival of the state.[12] The alleged neutrality (oriented to the West in Sweden and considerate towards the East in Finland) was a shield under which a pragmatic, active stance for the best possible security outcomes could be devised. Due to the geopolitical set-piece situation, the antagonistic Cold War blocs accepted their neutrality for the sake of stability. In other words, neither Sweden nor Finland was as neutral or non-aligned as they branded themselves as. Thus, the recent inclination towards NATO is building on a long-established tradition.

However, the state of interregnum in post–Cold War international relations has made these processes visible, which has shocked some observers. By 'interregnum' we mean a transformative phase in the international system during which the old conventions have lost their utility and new ones have not emerged.[13] The end of the Cold War – even if it was not the 'end of history' nor triumph of multipolarity[14] – and 'the return of geopolitics'[15] in the aftermath of the Russian annexation of Crimea were key events that heralded interregnums. The highlighting of the paradox between practice and policy declarations has contributed to the current challenges of Nordic democracy. The pursuit of vested national interests has become manifest, and the preparation for the worst is for the first time revealed and evident. Previously hidden information is now transmitted through constant media reporting. Security and foreign policy is subject to lobbying, despite the fact that most decisions are still made behind closed doors. From the point of view of democratic ideals, this might resemble a clandestine push towards NATO, despite the NATO-sceptic popular sentiment in both states. In Finland, the support for NATO membership would rise slightly if Sweden were to join.[16] As no major political decisions about membership application have been made, but a certain trajectory of alignment has been pursued, a sort of 'paradox of democracy' appears to exist. This provides a strong resonance board for various kinds of politicking and information operations, and might also foster a sentiment of alarm. Moreover, it might dissolve trust in political processes and culture.

Historical context: the Cold War era

Typically, the Nordic countries have been lumped together regarding welfare, economy, culture or foreign and security policy therefore obscuring diversity and dissimilarities that also exist within the Nordic nations. True, they share similar policies of progressive taxation and welfare, and an emphasis on what has been described as the 'Nordic model(s)' of democracy. Politics and policy are defined in a similar vein in all of the respective states, and the strategies of small-state realism they use to achieve this are very much alike.[17] Historically, this stems from a long trajectory of shared pasts that has affected the democratisation of both countries in political, economic and geopolitical terms.[18] Yet there are manifold differences, reported extensively in scholarly works published in the Nordic languages. These differences are particularly sharp regarding their foreign policy choices.[19]

With the outbreak of the First World War, the kings of Sweden, Norway and Denmark committed publicly to a joint policy of neutrality.[20] Likewise, due to geopolitical factors, a degree of small-state realism was practised in the Baltic region. Russia had for a long time been seen as a potential adversary. However, some differences were present then also.[21] During the 1920s and the 1930s, as a self-proclaimed regional leader Sweden promoted various forms of Nordic cooperation that never materialised. Other states opted for other solutions, which are rather well known, including the so-called border-states policy.[22] Since the Second World War, the Nordic line of neutrality or non-alignment has drastically changed and the 'Nordic model' has diversified even more. In the post-war situation, some of the Nordic states were more inclined to search security options from the West. Having been occupied in the war, Denmark and Norway opted for a NATO-backed security solution along with Iceland, instead of the 'Nordic cooperation' instigated by Sweden.[23] However, in much of the contemporary analysis, this difference between the countries has been overlooked and the Nordic countries have been lumped together to represent a 'third way' in post-war foreign policy between the major blocs. This has also been considered a typically pragmatic small-state realist approach.[24]

During the Cold War, both Sweden and Finland relied by necessity on publicly proclaimed neutrality and non-alignment.[25] In order to attain this status in the international system, while simultaneously keeping pace with Western trajectories, both countries, albeit sceptically at first, focused on international cooperation, mostly under the auspices of the United Nations (UN).[26] However, even in this multilateral form of internationalism, their experiences differed: Sweden joined the UN in 1945, while Finland, after a number of Soviet vetoes, was able to join only in 1956. Despite the multilateral orientation and small-state politics, both countries also had contingency plans, backed up by independent and strong armed forces.[27]

Although practically all states have several security policy options, generally only a few of them are publicly discussed or accessible.[28] Typically, one option is pursued as the preferred policy. In Sweden, this has, since the late 1950s, taken the form of a semi-clandestine partnership with the United States and NATO, while simultaneously branding neutrality as the core value of Swedish foreign and security policy.[29] Finland balanced between meeting the expectations of the USSR and identifying with the West through other means – especially through trade and culture. A number of scholars have pointed out that these Nordic double-dealings (*dubbelspel*) are already rather familiar.[30] Still, most scholars have studied them as part of individual national histories rather than using a comparative approach, with the notable exception of Johanna Rainio-Niemi.[31]

Finland, in particular, performed a high-wire balancing act between the East and the West, agreeing to a certain amount of Soviet influence in Finnish affairs in return for some freedoms. Sweden, in turn, continued to polish her defensive shield with declarations of non-alignment and neutrality – backed up by the most formidable armed forces among the Nordic states.[32] Behind the scenes, plans related to NATO and Western defence had been made since the 1950s. The Social Democrats dominated Swedish politics at this time, and because it was in the national interest, their *dubbelspel* was rarely challenged, only being used as minor leverage in domestic affairs by the political opposition.[33] This all changed drastically, however, with the fall of communist regimes. The Baltic States independence relieved some of the pressure on the Swedish shores of the Baltic Sea. While Finland in particular and Sweden to some extent were cautious to offer unequivocal support to the newly emerging Baltic States, they keenly supported the establishment of the armed forces of these states.[34]

Liquid neutrality and the alignment with the European community and NATO

The collapse of the USSR briefly brought about the advent of 'the unipolar world order' or 'unipolar moment'. In the Nordic countries, this shift in the early 1990s was not only perceived but also seized. In terms of security landscape, the question was not only primarily about NATO but also about the European Community (EC, later European Union, EU), which also included the element of common security. Finland was more careful but followed Sweden partially out of fear of being left behind or isolated. In 1991, after having followed Norwegian EC debate closely, Sweden opted to apply for membership of the EC. Sweden did this without notifying Finland first, much to the latter's surprise. In 1992, the Finnish-Soviet Treaty of Mutual Cooperation and Assistance from 1948 – which had been the defining feature of Finnish foreign policy throughout the Cold War – ceased to be in effect, and there was more room for general foreign policy deliberation. Not to be isolated and left out when the pieces of the geopolitical puzzle were shifting, Finland was forced to apply for EC membership as well in 1992.[35]

The Swedish non-notification traumatised Finland. Recognising this, the US Department of State and Defense noted that the intertwined defence and foreign policies of the two states meant that affecting one state would also affect the other and thus shaped US policies in the region.[36] If Sweden would align itself directly with NATO, it would demolish the core of the 'neutral buffer zone' in the region. For Finland, this would have been catastrophic, as the neutral zone was a prerequisite for Finland's attempts to pursue liquid neutrality and practise small-state realism.

In both countries, joining the EC/EU in 1995 was not directly related to security policy – or at least that dimension was toned down in the rhetoric. In foreign policy terms, the integration was part of a wider attempt to position formally within the West. To some extent the EU, to use the current acronym, was also seen as a possible 'third force' between the Soviet Union/Russia and the United States.[37] Already in 1992, Jaakko Iloniemi commented that in 'Finland it is still widely believed that joining the EC will not affect our security or defence policy. Such a thought is misleading.'[38] While the public remained ambivalent, Finland's positioning nevertheless acted as a signal for a willingness to align more deeply with NATO structures, which were seen as the backbone of the European defence landscape. By applying to the EU, both states also accepted shared responsibility for defending Europe. In 1994 – before the EU membership was agreed upon – both Sweden and Finland joined the NATO's Partnership for Peace (PfP) program, and they immediately began to enhance their NATO compatibility.[39] This can be seen as opening more options while staying aloof from binding commitments.

With increasing integration with the West, Cold War era contingency plans became less hidden – particularly in Sweden, but also in Finland. Changes in the geopolitical situation of the Baltic, underwritten by Russian weakness, meant that the limitations that had formerly prevented Nordic countries from having a more public alignment with NATO were now removed. As the leading Finnish weekly put it in 2001, 'Finland is already close to NATO's core' and was 'engaged with the Western security community that formed around NATO'.[40] This alignment was not a complete novelty, but already existing and well-developed ties could be strengthened.[41] The language of 'engagement' is in itself axiomatic about the ways Finland identified with the West.

Thus, for Finland, EU membership essentially meant claiming a much-coveted and clear identity within the West while simultaneously seeking to keep a strong national defence. For Sweden, the emergence of new independent Baltic buffer states meant that it opted for cost-effectiveness, meaning heavy disarmament, the closing of various military bases, and later abolishing national service. The decisions made in 1996 emphasised that Sweden remained non-aligned, while the defence decision in 2000 led to one of the greatest changes in the Swedish armed forces organisation, including disbanding numerous bases and forces.[42] This pattern was further developed in the defence decision of 2004, which was the last of the decisions oriented from territorial defence towards reactionary defence and crisis management.[43] In general, the new security paradigm entailed establishing professional military forces and reorienting its activities towards international crisis- and conflict-resolution projects under the auspices of NATO.[44] Liquid neutrality was massaged into the formulation of the policy, allowing Sweden to retain its neutral image while being fully integrated to NATO's structures.

While military-oriented NATO alignment was mainly conducted in the background, the public relations exercise opted to rebrand the Swedish military as a force for international crisis management and for preserving or projecting Western identity.[45] This shift was also a response to the detailed accounts of the Swedish clandestine cooperation plans with NATO during the Cold War – a topic of debate that emerged in public during the 1990s. Thus, amid public questioning of Sweden's Cold War militarisation, the next logical step to take was securing and strengthening the 'special relationship' while universally branding it as international crisis management.[46] To a lesser degree, Finland dovetailed Sweden but did not give up military conscription. In addition, Finland adopted the former Swedish policy of balancing between semi-formal non-alignment and enhancing NATO compatibility. Yet the sheer number of gradual changes and technical arrangements in this respect speaks for the policy of liquid neutrality once again. Through these measures, Finland and Sweden have become more NATO-compatible than most of those European states that have joined NATO since 1999.[47]

The Baltic area's security environment changed once again when Finland's and Sweden's smaller neighbours – the Baltic States – opted for full NATO membership in 2004. They followed the logic of alliances presented by Stephen M. Walt in 1987. Instead of bandwagoning with the great adversary, they allied against it.[48] Historically, Finland, Sweden, Estonia, Latvia and Lithuania have been cooperating and coordinating on security and defence issues (or matters related to security and defence). This cooperation is an example of pragmatic small-state realism (implicitly all of these states have practised pragmatic small-state realism). For the Soviet Union, and in recent times for Russia, this has caused annoyance at least. Until 2004, Swedish and Finnish support for developing the Baltic States' defences had been crucially important. This Baltic aspect is rarely addressed in analyses of Nordic defence cooperation.[49] The motives were essentially based on national interests: militarised Baltic States offered breathing space for Sweden and Finland, although it is a matter of debate whether the Baltic States' NATO memberships have a stabilising effect on regional security. Be that as it may, after 2004, Finland and Sweden continued their own NATO alignment – to the point that the option for joining NATO was solely dependent on political will, not military harmonisation. Yet thus far most of the Finnish political parties have not explicitly stated their opinion on Finland's NATO membership, save the conservative National Coalition Party that advocates membership. Subsequently, public considerations of potential NATO membership became a staple feature, especially in the multi-faceted media debates, but are noticeable also in official policy documentation.

NATO's development took a crucial turn after the 9/11 attacks, which transformed its role from that of international police and peace enforcer to a military and security organisation. Before the terrorist attacks, NATO had accepted most former Warsaw Pact States as its members, replaying the 1940s–1950s strategy of containment. The last members, including the Baltic States, were accepted in 2004. Some criticism, for instance about overreach, was voiced throughout the 'open door policy', but this did not change the decision.[50] At that point, Russia–NATO relations were still more amenable. Soon, however, Russia and NATO began to drift apart. Georgia's pro-Western developments since 2003 and an open willingness to join NATO finally forced Russia to act according to its historical fear of encirclement by hostile powers.[51] Even international cooperation against terrorism, also important for Russia, could not prevent a further divergence between the two. If the former Soviet satellites were clearly in the Russian sphere of interests, Georgia was part of the Russian backyard.

The Baltic Sea region sphere of interest contributes to the Finnish and Swedish defence dilemmas. To avoid having this natural maritime choke-point used against it, Russia might attempt to take over, occupy or at least incapacitate the Baltic States. The Åland Islands, Gotland and the Danish straits are also important in such a scenario.[52] By linking up with the enclave around Kaliningrad, Russia could also better secure sea access for St. Petersburg and would also have a further vantage point for the whole region. In many ways, the Baltic States offer an extension to the exclusion area protecting the important city and strategic base of St. Petersburg. This would also take some of the pressure off the Arctic region where Russia has its other important sea route to the west. As part of a larger Arctic strategy, which stated in 2008 that the Arctic would be its primary resource base, Russia has already improved its network of military bases in that region and has increased settlement in the region as well.[53] In the Kola Peninsula, for instance, there has been considerable military build-up and Russia has been seen to exert indirect pressure towards Norway, for instance.[54]

Russia's drive to reassert its position as a great power evidently conflicted with NATO's rapid enlargement to its borders in Northern Europe. The matter of security policy became more acute than it had been since the end of the Cold War. The first sign was the Georgian war in 2008, which was part of a stern Russian response to considerations of additional NATO members along its borders.[55] Later on, and due to numerous political, economic and strategic reasons, the same applied to Ukraine. These familiar events need not be repeated here. However, the NATO debate in Finland and Sweden now had a new urgency. From a Russian perspective, Nordic neutrality, in its liquid form, threatened to 'splash' from its fairly contained space into the quickly cracking security landscape.

In Finland, public opinion was against joining NATO, as were President Tarja Halonen and Foreign Minister Erkki Tuomioja. The official position was articulated in the government's security and defence policy statement to parliament in September 2004. Finland would continue its policy of military non-alignment until 2012; the main task would be the defence of the national territory and over 95 per cent of the defence budget would be devoted to it. The 2008 defence white paper, however, was due to include consideration of the pros and cons of NATO membership.[56]

As a response to the cracking security landscape, Nordic countries acted according to their own regional interests by tightening Nordic military cooperation. According to Malena Britz, after the rift caused by the Iraq conflict, political focus regarding Nordic cooperation in security politics has increased since 2007. The Nordic Battlegroup (NBG) was established in 2008. At the same time, Swedish and Norwegian military leaders co-authored an article discussing whether the Swedish and Norwegian armed forces should be organised regionally so that they could support each other. Another key theme in the article was the co-organising of defence material acquisitions. In June 2009, Sweden issued a declaration of solidarity for its Nordic neighbours: it would not stand aside if any of the neighbouring states faced an attack or catastrophe.[57] The Nordic Council covered defence cooperation in 2009 in line with a report from former Norwegian foreign secretary Jens Stoltenberg (current NATO Secretary General) and followed up with the Reykjavik Declaration in the summer of 2009. This was a new historical development, as during the 1970s and the 1980s security and foreign policy was not allowed on the joint Nordic agenda and only started to emerge during the first decade of the 2000s. Further discussions on security cooperation were pursued by the Nordic foreign secretaries in 2010. Subsequently, a statement on the idea of cooperation, 'the declaration of solidarity', was issued by the Nordic Council in Helsinki in 2011.[58]

Finland, Sweden, and the problem of EU-based security

In 2007, Finland's former Minister of Defence Jyri Häkämies said at the Center for Strategic and International Studies (CSIS) in Washington:

> In general, Finland is privileged to be located in one of the safest corners of the world. However, given our geographical location, the three main security challenges for Finland today are Russia, Russia and Russia. And not only for Finland, but for all of us.[59]

Such a statement was striking because it was so untypical. It not only raised eyebrows but also stirred up a storm in the 'teacup' of Finnish security policy. Criticisms came from various Finnish politicians, including the president and Ilkka Kanerva, the National Coalition Party's foreign minister; and it continued for some time in spite of Häkämies's assurances that the statement was based on formal policy documents and security estimates. Yet equally striking was the fact that it was only those three words that the media noted. After that line, Häkämies claimed that Russia nevertheless is not a direct threat to Finnish security; it posed not only a challenge but also an opportunity. However, this more nuanced contextualisation fell on deaf ears. According to the most nervous responses, Finland had three real security challenges: 'Häkämies, Häkämies, Häkämies'.[60]

Since the end of the Second World War in 1945, the security challenge that the Soviet Union/Russia posed for Finland has been treated with kid gloves – clearly evident in the response to the Häkämies incident. The other side of the coin is the question of security; if there is a potential threat, there must be also a potential security arrangement. In general, security discourse in Finland as well as in Sweden is dominated by attempts to obfuscate the extent to which Nordic countries are already thoroughly connected with NATO. This is related to the idea that publicly committing to one camp and giving up on the formally acknowledged, even if questionable, neutral or non-aligned status could push Russia into action that would require a direct answer or counter-move. Disregarding this paradox of saying one thing and doing the opposite in public debate can be seen, if not as a democratic deficit, at least as contributing to the scepticism towards defence debates in the parliaments – especially when what is actually happening has become more obvious. Thus, the security debate in the 2010s is 'smoke and mirrors' in which the truth of the situation – de facto (technical) NATO alignment – is obscured with reference to old and no-longer stable rhetoric, the key component being the question of a collective European security system through EU institutions.[61]

Since the initial attempts in the 1940s and the 1950s and up to today, the West European Union (WEU) that forms the security and military component of the Common Security and Foreign Policy (CSFP) has not come to fruition.[62] Cost efficiency has been among the main factors along with political will. The Maastricht Treaty and the 'pillar policy' that followed were existing factors, but in terms of collective security, they offered very little in terms of concrete means despite various attempts and promises.[63] Furthermore, as in the 1950s, NATO quickly emerged as the leading institution to guarantee European security. Establishing overlapping European schemes, organisations and plans would have increased overall defence costs, hampered organisation and perhaps even reduced the effectiveness of NATO.

The collapse of the USSR changed the European-level calculus. Not only did the main threat disappear – Russia was noticeably weak at the time – but the world-wide economic recession meant that there were fewer resources to allocate to European defence planning and capabilities, which remained modest. Further, after a brief period of intensified planning in the 2000s, the issue of broadening the Union took over at the expense of deepening and strengthening European security arrangements. For Finland, this development meant that although it had integrated itself deeply into the EU since the mid-1990s to the point that re-estimating the benefits of possible alliances within the European framework was brought up,[64] the European dimension of security was (and is) not a viable defence solution. Simply, it lacks the necessary military muscle. For Sweden, the situation was similar but even more troublesome, because it had abandoned its long-lasting security doctrine of total defence, driving down the level of society's militarisation.[65]

Since most EU countries are also members of NATO, their need for EU-based security is not acute, which is reflected in a lack of interest in developing a joint European defence and foreign policy. Further, doctrinal changes in the 1990s and the 2000s clouded the core function of NATO. Since the Balkan crises in the late 1990s, both NATO and the EU oriented themselves towards conflict resolution, peace-keeping and interventions in limited conflicts. Forces and capabilities utilised in these operations are very much the same, though the matter of which hats (or helmets in this case) – the EU or NATO – to wear is still present to some degree. As focus shifted to conflict resolution and peace-keeping, territorial defence and training in Europe were neglected. Neither experience from asymmetrical warfare nor evidence that victory through air power alone is not plausible has led to significant changes in NATO's European approach. Plans for changes exist on paper, but both within NATO and the EU, the will and funds have been lacking, and therefore more 'cost-effective' planning has been encouraged. In this respect, the organisations have lacked teeth. The EU's initial responses to the Georgian war and the events in Ukraine and Crimea were neither rapid nor stern.[66] Also, the EU member states' different economic and energy relationships with Russia hamper a unified security policy.

This lacklustre European defence system has led Finland and Sweden to evaluate the costs and benefits of their security policy. For instance, although the EU, especially the Common Foreign and Security Policy (CFSP) and its imaginary framework of structures, was repeatedly mentioned in Finnish security and foreign policy reviews, especially in 1995, as essential elements of Finnish policy, these mentions totally disappeared by 2016.[67] NATO's European members (and EU-members in general) have long been criticised for their low defence spending and 'freeloading' on the heels of the United States in 2020 by former US Vice President Mike Pence in Munich.[68] At the moment, the European states' capabilities for territorial defence are rather limited, even within NATOs own territory. Although Pence's utterances were no doubt related to arms trade efforts and the domestic pressure of Donald Trump's administration, statistics show that the decrease in defence costs in Europe has been remarkable until recently. From a Finnish and Swedish perspective, this does not portray a pretty picture of organised collective defence – a matter at the heart of the Nordic vision of collective security. Therefore, the possible gains from NATO membership would depend on US forces, while the European defence and security orientation of the late 1990s and the early 2000s has practically disappeared from public discourse, illustrating the total dismissal of a European security system independent of US influence. For example, the more recent Finnish defence and security policy documentation hardly mentions EU-based security, at least in comparison to the late 1990s and the early 2000s. The same applies to Sweden.[69] Moreover, although the Lisbon Treaty of 2007 provides certain theoretical guarantees of assistance from other members in the case of crisis, besides limited political will, capability is de facto lacking.

In addition, the NATO Charter gives some leeway of interpretation regarding the military commitments under Article 5. Even if (European) NATO members would spend more than the nominal 2 per cent of their GDP on defence, it is debatable what would actually be supplied by each member state in the event of a conflict.[70] Furthermore, even this deployment would require unanimous agreement, which might take some time.[71] Existing research actually reports that Denmark's and Norway's disarmament and development of a professional army is geared for rapid deployment in crisis and conflict management against lower-tier and asymmetrical adversaries and in counter-terrorism operations. Magnus Petersson, for instance, has estimated that Denmark and Norway have decreased their level of defence.[72] Instead, in the immediate pre-Crimean era, they heavily oriented their forces towards NATOs global role to such a degree that they might have difficulty defending their own territory, let alone intervene on behalf of the Baltic States. For instance, Denmark has given up her submarine fleet, affecting the ability to defend the Danish straits and therefore the Baltic Sea. Similarly, both countries have faced difficulties in providing aerial units for international operations.[73] For Sweden, this might decrease the interest in full NATO membership as it could cause more volatility and offer very little payback.

All this raises the question of how committed NATO is to the Nordic/Baltic region. European defence planning is in a state of flux for a number of reasons, such as Brexit, the rise of nationalism, internal power struggles and resource allocation towards climate change. Finding a joint political will is hard enough, let alone the relevant resources. NATO's 'Very High Readiness Joint Task Force' (VJTF) might, in spite of its name, not actually be as readily available or deployable as politicians would like. The NATO Response Force (NRF) is also still very much a work in progress and exists mainly on paper, as many member states have no troops or weaponry available for it. Additionally, maintaining the readiness of VJTF and NRF troops is also costly.[74] From the Swedish and Finnish point of view, this might mean that they would be gaining less in joining NATO to solve their security situation. By being a member, they would be considered a potential foe by Russia (and to a large extent by China), without necessarily securing the backup that was sought after. Thus, in the current state of affairs, it hardly serves Finland or Sweden's interests to join NATO. However, before any such conflict arose, the membership of the two countries would serve NATO's interests by adding to the security of the Baltic States. These conflicting considerations have not surfaced much in recent public membership debates, though they most certainly have been considered.

Liquid neutrality and developments since 2014

As stated earlier, since the end of the Cold War, both Sweden and Finland have altered their respective foreign and security policies. While becoming more interconnected with international security and foreign policy systems, they have also become more entangled with the global challenges. This, in turn, has affected their possibilities for pursuing new security policy options and coping with their shared security dilemmas.

The Russian occupation of Crimea in 2014 made the return of geopolitics imminent also in the Baltic Sea region, as previously distant problems were now at Finland's and Sweden's doorstep.[75] Unipolar use of strength to attain national interests was back on the agenda, backed up by the rising tide of information operations. Western hegemony was challenged globally by China and regionally in the Baltic Sea region, although not only there, by Russia. A state of flux, or interregnum, was evident in the international relations and a re-evaluation of existing policies was required. Finland's and Sweden's main response was a revision of the policies that they had been building since the 1990s. Liquid neutrality was very much back on the agenda.

Re-establishing national military capability returned to the political agenda. Sweden opted for returning to national conscription and scrapped its heavy disarmament program coined at FMI2020 (which could be translated loosely as "Ideas for Future Defence") in 1996.[76] Sweden also reversed the various downshifting processes that narrowed the whole command structure into a single command force. The doctrine of total defence was re-established. Heavy emphasis was given to the capabilities of the air force and the navy. The vulnerability of Gotland Island, a strategic base of operations aimed against the heartland of Sweden or for controlling the Baltic Sea, was duly noted. Russia's Baltic vantage point could also increase pressure directly on Finland and Sweden.[77] Moreover, the Baltic area would also be useful for Russia as a way to increase the anti-access, area denial (A2/AD) range to prevent an attack on St. Petersburg. Another point of consideration would be the recently resurfaced question of Russian intermediate range missiles situated in Kaliningrad and Russia abandoning the IMF treaty. Subsequently, in 2017, Sweden also announced its intentions to purchase Patriot missile systems, usually only sold to close US allies or NATO members.[78] The purchase of the antiballistic missile system is somewhat perplexing at first: Patriot missile systems have been reported to have serious flaws since the 1991 Gulf War, where the efficiency of the system appeared to be very limited. Although some of the data available have been classified, some of these evaluations are publicly available.[79] The system since has been improved, but this also raises considerations about what the actual purpose of the system is. It does provide the idea or feeling of security, something to be done to counter the reported Russian missile allocation. In the case of Sweden, this was no doubt a show of (political) will (and readiness) on several levels. As a response to Russia moving new, nuclear-capable medium-range Iskander ballistic missiles to Kaliningrad and supplementing them with heavy SAM protection since 2013 (and re-reported in 2018), it also signalled Sweden aligning with the United States and, to some extent, NATO. In turn, Finland was allowed to purchase air-to-ground cruise missiles in order to cope with various threats such as A2/AD or ballistic missiles. These have been hard to come by even for NATO members.

Sweden continued gearing up. Stationing a permanent garrison of troops in Gotland was put back on the agenda for 2016–2018.[80] The experiences from various international operations such as IFOR/SFOR, KFOR, ISAF, OUP, RSM and Iraq were also put to use. Although technical, organisational and other interoperability and compatibility with NATO had already been achieved, the capability to use military forces together with NATO was practised in the Swedish air operations over Libya in 2011 and in Afghanistan since 2014.[81]

While structural and operational alignment with the United States intensified, more emphasis was placed on Nordic cooperation. Above all, cooperation with Finland was considered a crucial way to strengthen the first line of Swedish defence, while the Swedes were rebuilding their own capability.[82]

However, these operational solutions were not considered sufficient. Despite potential Russian opposition, Sweden (like Finland) sped up its NATO alignment process. In the public sphere, NATO membership became a hotly debated option, even if public opinion was still against it. Like Finland, Sweden ordered a review of the questions related to a potential alliance. In 2014, Sweden, like Finland, participated in the NATO Summit in Wales for the Enhanced Opportunities Program, which allowed friendly states to deepen their cooperation with NATO, for instance through participation in operation planning, military exercises and consultations. The drafting of the NATO-host agreement was initiated in 2014. Thus, by this time, neutrality had become very fluid. This is exemplified more by the Finnish white paper on defence (2017), which stated that the Finnish defence system is developed in such ways that there would not be any practical obstacles for a potential military alliance (in the future).[83]

Yet, despite increasing alignment with NATO, the state of total, societal preparedness in Sweden was found wanting and could not be solved by either the means of potential defence and security cooperation or by alliances, as Björn von Sydow, the Chairman of the Swedish Defence Commission, pointed out. Although Article 3 of the NATO Charter recognises the importance of general societal resilience, this remains mainly a national responsibility. That Sweden is heavily reliant on imports of energy, food and other supplies and the whole economic structure is based on a 'just-in-time' model with limited storage constitute a considerable challenge for the doctrine of total defence and preparedness. This tendency is particularly illustrative in the case of Gotland – an exposed yet key strategic island in need of extensive logistical lines of supply. Gaining help or support might take weeks or months, were it be provided at all.[84]

It is against this backdrop that NATO's host-nation agreement sets in, as it focuses on enhancing capability to receive military supply, aid and assistance. Despite some public reservations, Sweden ratified the Host Agreement Treaty in 2016. Yet even if Sweden and Finland (which also signed) are not full NATO members through the agreement, in practice they are sucked into the vortex of NATO operations – a state of affairs that puts them in a pickle. Although the treaty has a reserve clause of NATO troops requiring governmental request from the host to utilise the reserved host areas, Sweden and Finland are indirectly almost totally committed to the defence of the Baltic States through NATO. The reason for this is that in a crisis NATO would use the host option and saying no might be difficult. The cold logic of *realpolitik* is that a superpower would take the necessary steps to fulfil its own security needs, irrespective of the views of Finnish or Swedish parliaments, as without Finland and Sweden, NATO would have a hard time defending the Baltic States.[85]

Even with higher military preparedness than Sweden, Finland also sped up its NATO alignment. Finland took part in various Western war games and trainings. In 1992, Finland selected US-made F-18s as the core of its air force, thus phasing out the old practise of making equal purchases from the East and the West alike (or from non-aligned states as an alternative to Western purchases).[86] These planes are estimated to end their service life in 2030, thus requiring somewhat rapid replacement plans (HX-project).[87] As of this writing, the consideration, bidding and evaluation are going on and lobbying on behalf of various respective candidates is somewhat heavy. Besides the actual cost of price per unit, the operating costs need to be assessed carefully or the chosen solution might become too costly. Moreover, also technical tactical, strategic, and above all, political consideration costs need to be assessed. Former Finnish Minister of Defence Elisabeth Rehn has, for instance, revealed that the decisions for the acquisition of F-18s were conducted behind closed doors by three key ministers, not the full government, and furthermore, without informing the parliament or engaging in parliamentary debate.[88]

In 2014, Jarmo Lindberg, the commander of the Finnish Armed Forces signed a host nation memorandum of understanding (MOU) on Finland's behalf. Mandate for this was given by the President of Finland Sauli Niinistö and the Ministerial Committee on Foreign and Security Policy, which operates under the Finnish Government.[89] In public, and as a response to the criticism of the agreement, the MOU was stated to be about receiving military assistance. Adhering to the idea of liquid neutrality, the Finnish Ministry of Defence's announcement of the agreement was as blunt as possible and revealed no details about the contents. A non-classified agreement was, however, attached to the issued statement – in English.[90] Sweden signed a similar host-nation agreement at the same time, thus underlining the intertwined policies of the two Nordic states. The most important features of the MOU were:

2.1 The purpose of this MOU is to establish policy and procedures for the establishment of operational sites and the provision of H[ost] N[ation] S[tatement] to NATO forces in, or supported from the HN, during NATO military activities.

2.2 This MOU and its follow-on documents are intended to serve as the basis for planning by the appropriate HN authority and by NATO Commanders anticipating HNS arrangements for a variety of NATO military activities. *These missions include those for which deploying forces have been identified and those for which forces are yet to be identified.*[91]

In other words, it appears that the agreement allows for any type of missions to be deployed on the host nation's soil. Moreover, the sites established for these missions are de facto under NATO command, and this is agreed to by the host nation, which will provide its fullest possible support for these missions.

Importantly, this agreement is in effect during peacetime and during conflicts, and it allows NATO forces to use the host's national airspace and territorial waters. A recent development is the setting up of a permanent communications cable network on Finnish soil, which was installed as a part of the secret 'Bold Quest' manoeuvres.[92] The aforementioned HX-fighter might also add to this series of technical arrangements, which can also serve as political security signalling. Furthermore, besides actual NATO alignment, other, bi- and trilateral arrangements and statements of intent have been prepared, the latest being the statement of intent of trilateral cooperation between Sweden, Finland and the United States.[93] This attests to the idea of liquid neutrality enhancing various capabilities and options without full commitment.

Public opinion in both states had been adamantly opposed to applying for NATO membership. This notion was further enhanced by fears that a membership in one of the newly emerging blocs might jeopardise the two states' national interests as well as their ability to conduct an independent and liquid foreign policy, acting as brokers between the two conflicting blocs. However, the change also brought forward heavy criticism of semi-clandestinely and deliberately moving to full NATO membership – a path taken gradually in previous years and decades.[94] Re-estimations of the possible effects of NATO membership was ordered by both states. The Swedish report by Krister Bringéus was much more detailed, feels more like a formal policy paper, and contains detailed estimates with sources mentioned, whereas the Finnish version, although commissioned by parliament and government and crafted by experts, was more like an executive summary and resembles an informal briefing paper.[95]

If Finland and Sweden were to exchange their current liquid resilience for joining NATO formally, it might provide a formal deterrent and add to the region's defence. It would not, however, remove the fact that even the tiniest change in the regional security puzzle would require some sort of response. This is clearly one of the reasons why the publicly promoted organisation of the Nordic Defence Cooperation (NORDEFCO) has once more become a viable (or at least stop-gap) solution, while also being a way to circumvent the question of full NATO membership. It has become much more than a practical and flexible attempt to cut back on costs and to complement wider arrangements on the EU and NATO level, as Håkon Lunde Saxi has proposed. Saxi has also mentioned that cooperation within the Nordic area itself has become a tool for bringing the Nordic states closer to NATO.[96] Wider Nordic cooperation includes two NATO members, thus enhancing the NATO compatibility of Sweden and Finland further. Subsequently, while the NATO alignment is under constant review, enhancing bilateral cooperation between Finland and Sweden appears to be at least the intermediate solution.[97]

Yet, there is one more point to bear in mind: potential membership is not guaranteed. President Donald Trump's view and policies vis-à-vis the future of NATO and even more traditional bilateral approaches are ambivalent to say the least. NATO is undergoing challenges related to: (i) the grand US strategy now emphasising the foreign policy importance of Asia; (ii) quarrels about members' defence budgets; and (iii) the conflicting political interests of its members noted by Finns and Swedes.[98] Interest in defending the Baltic States is ambivalent, and the capability to do so quickly enough is uncertain, even for those members who have committed to Article 5. This is even more the case, as while Finland and Sweden are not NATO members, they are obliged to take part in defending the Baltic States through the Lisbon Treaty.[99] Some analysts add that they are not obliged to provide this kind of assistance, but overlook the clauses of the NATO-host agreement that the two have signed.

That being said, an efficient defence of the Baltic States is important to the grand strategies of Finland and Sweden. As NATO members, the commitment to their defence would be even greater. In either case, the 'neutrality' of both states would be negotiable, risking involvement in a conflict between the great powers. In that respect, it might be more attractive to become full members to attain the umbrella of collective defence as deterrent. However, Russia would be expected to react negatively. Finland joining NATO could be interpreted by Russia as a containment or encirclement that would require reaction. Russia today is in a much stronger military position than in the late 1990s or early 2000s when it had to accept the rapid advancement of NATO and was more inclined to cooperate with it.

Conclusion

Sweden's partnership with NATO is now rather generally accepted to be a continuation of a secret arrangement established in the early 1950s. This has been dubbed a 'flexible foreign and security policy'[100] and is not so far removed from the small-state realism that had previously dominated Nordic foreign policies. However, as we have demonstrated throughout this chapter, 'flexible' can be taken even further, as flexible foreign policy denotes a degree of reactivity in the face of security challenges. Our neologism of liquid neutrality seeks to push the argument from reactivity to proactivity. Like liquid, Nordic security thinking flowed into the cracks in a deliberatively active manner. For Finland, the partnership took shape when the country joined the EU. In practice, it meant that Finland copied the Swedish security solution that has two obvious advantages: the informal security guarantees received from NATO, and the possibility to stay aloof in case a potential conflict with Russia would turn into open war in the Baltic region. This double standard has been noticed by the official member states of NATO and the Russians are also well aware of it.[101] According to some Swedish commentators, Sweden's informal NATO guarantees, presented in detail, for instance by investigate journalist Mikael Holmström in 2015, are not in effect anymore.[102]

If we read the Swedish and Finnish NATO alignment policy in light of liquid neutrality and the proper historical context of the two states' respective foreign and security policies, the decisions regarding NATO alignment appear to be contingent on the older policies, albeit with more nuances. Against the backdrop of navigating between the interests of great powers in the realm of geopolitics, the alignment with NATO can be seen as a pragmatic approach of enhancing security capability and negotiating more room to manoeuvre. Moreover, it is security and foreign policy in its own right: signalling that the two states are not passive pawns of great power politics. Instead, they are active, proactive, and subjects on their own merit, acting according to their own national interests. The most important of these interests is securing sovereignty and national survival by the means available and necessary. Therefore, the NATO policy of the two states continues the past politics in new surroundings with other means and therefore ought not raise the level of apprehension currently appearing in the public discussion.

If we, however, understand the shocks caused by the changes in the international system, namely Russian assertiveness, and consider this from the point of view of vested national interests and increased 'path dependency' on NATO, the formulation of Nordic security policies appear to be different. The current state of interregnum has revealed the gradual alterations to the age-old doctrine of non-alignment and neutrality. The revelation of changes that have taken place since the 1990s have occasionally caused shock effects in the population, leading to fading trust in political institutions. As the Cold War paradigm kept the more pragmatic foreign and security policy firmly outside public purview, relying on high-level official liturgy, it is all the more understandable that public reactions have varied widely.

The publicly presented estimates of the potential outcomes, plans and risk analysis of these plans appear as a clandestine inching towards NATO. As the majority of the population in both states are still against full membership, this causes alarm. This is not helped at all by the vast and multifaceted media coverage[103] on the matter, which includes all forms of information activity ranging from amateur pundits to scholarly analyses, outright lobbying, politicking and informal policy reviews often void of any deep insight. Finnish media has covered the NATO debate rather intensively. In his doctoral dissertation concerning the Finnish-NATO media coverage, Juho Rahkonen collected, in addition to radio and TV material, over 1,300 pieces of NATO-related print media pieces from 2003 to 2004 alone. Rahkonen stated that the membership debate started immediately after the dissolution of the Soviet Union in 1991 and media has been mostly marching to the beat of pro-NATO drum, stating membership is inevitable. One of the overlooked aspects Rahkonen mentions has been the logic within the media, which has enhanced the reporting due to requirements of gaining 'news wins' and dramatic headlines. These have been put together in various news pieces stating that Finland has been pushed towards full NATO membership against the will of the people and by clandestine and backroom deals. Another important feature Rahkonen mentions has been the lack of actual communication and exchange of views. Instead, the media coverage and political discussions have been talking past each other. In Finland, the recent mainstream NATO debate on the media has revolved mainly around the opinion polls and surveys about the pro and contra views of potential membership. The percentage of Finnish population supporting Finnish NATO membership has steadily declined. The highest percentage in favour of membership has never exceeded 30 per cent. Forty-nine per cent thought Finland was not non-aligned anymore, 52 per cent were opposed to joining NATO, and 59 per cent were against joining if Sweden joined.[104] However, some reporting has emphasised that the percentage of Finns opposing NATO membership has decreased, which testifies to the different framing of the topic per media alignment and pollsters.[105]

In Finland, the tendency to closely follow Swedish intentions (and vice versa, to lesser extent) and activities adds to the problematic situation. It partly diffuses agency from Finland's own hands into the hands of Swedish policymakers. Also, this deflects from the ideal of transparent Nordic parliamentary democracy in which the citizens have wide access to political participation and setting the agenda. However, the high-ranking experts who published a government-commissioned report on the possible effects of Finnish NATO membership considered in 2016 that the Finnish and Swedish NATO debates and policies were closely intertwined.[106]

In order to address this notion of a democratic paradox, a more concise and detailed analysis of the past activities, media coverage, interests, gains and risks needs to be made available for the greater public. Also the differences of the two states' situations and interests need to be acknowledged openly instead of almost alarmistically following the 'other'. Although this sense of alarmism, especially in Finland, originates from the historical experiences of 'being left alone', for example in the case of the EU membership applications, also the differences between Finnish and Swedish national interests needs to be addressed properly and information should be made available for the public.

Thus, besides the de facto security challenges and perpetual geopolitical dilemmas the two states are facing in this era of international interregnum, there is another paradox to consider. In order to foster the legitimacy of the political systems and culture, the existing paradoxes and issues mentioned in this chapter need to be addressed in detail. Otherwise, the multifaceted NATO debate might contribute to the deterioration of legitimacy for established representative political democracy. In addition, it needs to be made clear that the various, mainly technical arrangements that have been made in order to increase the two states' NATO compatibility have had political backing. No such technical arrangements could be made without policy guidance – and if they have been, alarmism is truly called for. A clarification of, for instance, the stances of the different political parties, at least, would enable the people to find out what their representatives are advocating, thereby enabling a democratic choice. The problems originating from the lack of trust in the international system during this era of interregnum and the subsequent liquid security policy responding to this situation might contribute in enhancing mistrust in domestic politics, political culture and politicians. One can sit on the fence only for so long. However, it will remain a balancing act how to combine such democratic procedures with the need to keep certain national interests classified.

Notes

1 Bauman 2000, 2.
2 BakerFox 1959 suggests that despite various challenges small states have a variety of approaches at their disposal in order to cope with and to resist the pressure of the great powers. The Swedish option was armed neutrality and Finland's 'fighting neutral'; see also Huldt 1977 who theorised that small states if threatened mostly align with a potential partner for cooperation and support. Walt 1987, agrees. See also Lindell & Persson 1986.
3 For instance, in Arter 2006, 2008. For variety and differences, see for instance Meinander, Karonen & Östberg 2018.
4 Dahl 1998, 2001.
5 For instance, Pharr & Putnam 2000, Runciman 2015, Streeck 2015. However, crises of democracy are not a novelty per se, neither as phenomena nor as a topic of research.
6 Huntington, Crozier & Watanuki 1975, 70–78, 97, 203–205; the roots of the decline of trust are deeper cf. 105–108.
7 Shapiro 2008.
8 See for instance the French Constitution of 1958. The Constitution of Finland 11 June 1999 (731/1999, amendments up to 817/2018 included): 'the Parliament accepts Finland's international obligations and their denouncement and decides on the bringing into force of Finland's international obligations insofar as provided in this Constitution. The President decides on matters of war and peace, with the consent of the Parliament.' Regarding Sweden: 'The Riksdag is guaranteed influence in important international agreements, however. All agreements that require a Riksdag decision in order to be implemented must be approved by the Riksdag. The Government must also obtain the approval of the Riksdag in regard to other important agreements. In such cases, however – if it is in the interest of the Realm – Riksdag approval may be replaced by consultation with the all-party Advisory Council on Foreign Affairs'. The Constitution of Sweden 2016, 42–44.
9 Brand 1992, Ihalainen & Matikainen 2016, Roitto 2015, 2016, in wider context cf. Wagner 2017, Häkkinen 2014.
10 Cottey 2018a, 1–4, 2018b, 211–212.
11 Forsberg & Vogt 2008, Saukkonen 2008.
12 Cf. Keohane 1969, Morgenthau 1978, Bull 2012.
13 For instance, see Pegram & Acuto 2015.
14 Murray 2013.
15 Diez 2004, Mead 2014.
16 For instance, Heinonen 2011, 150–151. For statistics concerning Finland, see Elinkeinoelämän Valtuuskunnan arvopankki.
17 Marcussen 2017, 240–244.
18 cf. Karonen, Roitto & Ojala 2018, Roitto, Karonen & Ojala 2018, Ojala, Roitto & Karonen 2018, Arter 2006, 2008, Nedergaard & Wivel 2017a, 1–2, 2017b, 306–312.
19 For instance, Kettunen, Lundberg, Österberg & Petersen 2015, also Meinander, Karonen & Östberg 2018, Gebhard 2017, 254–260.
20 Salmon 1997.
21 Ibid., Kalela 1971, Ahlund 2012, Holmén 1985, Jonasson 1973. For Swedish aspirations on greater role, see Gerner 2002.
22 Heikka 2005, Roiko-Jokela 1995.
23 For instance, Wivel 2013a, 2013b, 2014, Arter 2008, 263–266.

24 Tornudd 2005, 43–52, Archer, Alyson & Wivel 2014, Browning 2002, 2007, Pesu 2016, Westberg 2012, 93–94.
25 cf. Hanhimäki 1996, 1997, Kronvall & Petersson 2005, Bjereld 1992.
26 Jakobsen 2017, 281–293, Arter 2008.
27 Agrell 2000, Åselius 2005. Main part of the military manpower was based on conscription built reservist army. Same applies to Finland, too.
28 Brand 1992, Browning 2007.
29 Agrell 1991, Holmström 2015, 123–127, Tunander 1999, 2001, 2005, 2008, Silva 1999, Nilsson & Wyss 2016. Dalsjö 2014, mentions that recent scholarly works have started to challenge the dominating view of neutrality and have instead paid attention to the rationalist aspects of security and foreign policy arrangements made by Sweden in the 1950s. However, Wilhelm Agrell and Gunnar Åselius published relevant works on the theme in the 1990s.
30 In the case of Finland one of the key scholars in this 'revisionist' approach to the grand narratives has been Juhana Aunesluoma, who has also studied the alleged Swedish neutrality through the case of Swedish-British relations. Cf. Aunesluoma 2003, Aunesluoma & Rainio-Niemi 2016. Concerning the domestic sphere of this double play in both states, cf. Meinander 2018.
31 Rainio-Niemi 2014. Although the focus of this particular research includes Austria, the small neutral states are considered in detail in the comparisons.
32 The Swedish Air Force was one of the largest in Europe. In the 1950s, the Air Force consisted of some one thousand planes, whereas the mobilised reserves could field up to 850,000 people, at least on paper. Cf. Åselius 2005, 26–27.
33 Meinander 2018, 340–346.
34 Romanovs & Andžāns 2017, 14–15. Sweden supported the Baltic Defence Collegium and donated full equipment for one infantry brigade. Lithuania gained equipment for two infantry battalions from Sweden in 2001–2004. Swedish Project to Support Lithuanian Land Forces Completed' 3 December 2004. The Estonia project of the Finnish Armed Forces 1996–2003 donated to Estonia two fully equipped artillery batteries, 100 AAA-pieces and 54 mortars, communications and fire control equipment, and two coastal patrol vessels. In addition, 1,200 Estonians participated in military training organised by Finland, and 450 Estonians studied in Finnish military schools during the time. 'Viro–projekti päättyi' 2004. Statement by the Finnish General Staff, Blank 1996, (loc) 194–204, states that in Sweden Carl Bildt's conservative government renounced neutrality in 1992–1993 and went as far as to openly declare Sweden's interest in defending Baltic States against potential Russian invasion. Subsequent government committed again to neutrality.
35 Doeser 2012, 171–185, 186–199, Blank 1996, (loc) 90–204.
36 Blank 1996, (loc) 90–215.
37 Smith & Steffenson 2011, 405–408.
38 Iloniemi 1992, 43. About the rhetorics of these discussions cf. Särkkä 2019, 52–53.
39 For instance, in 1998, the tactical symbols, markings (and communications) were changed to be NATO compatible. cf. Sotilaslyhenteet ja merkit (SLM) 1998. In 'Sotilasmerkistö ja -lyhenteet' (SML) 2005, the NATO-based APP66 was recognised publicly as the basis of the symbols, p. 10. Sweden opted for NATO ammunition compatible rifle (AK-4) in the 1960s and in the 1970s – 1980s with the AK-5 opted for STANAG 4172 compatible NATO standard 5.56mm x 45 ammunition.
40 'Kohti Naton ydintä' 2001, citations from 30 and 32. Särkkä 2019, 126–127, 243–245, Rahkonen 2006, 23, 110–112 considers some of the pro-NATO media discourse as backlash from the Cold War era foreign political correctness. In Sweden, media debate increased vis-à-vis opinion polling and views are somewhat divided, Blix et al. 2016, 185–189. Giles & Eskola 2014, 13 consider that most of the Finnish press, including the leading daily newspaper *Helsingin Sanomat* have taken a pro-NATO stance.

41 Arter 2008, 289–294.

42 'Regeringens proposition 1995/96:12 – Totalförsvar i förnyelse, etapp 1'; 'Regeringens proposition 1996/97:4 – Totalförsvar i förnyelse, etapp 2'; 'Regeringens proposition 1999/2000:30 – Det nya försvaret'; 'Regeringens proposition 1999/2000:97 – Vissa organisatoriska frågor inom Försvarsmakten'; 'Regeringens proposition 2004/05:5 – Vårt framtida försvar'; 'Regeringens proposition 2004/05:43 – Försvarsmaktens grundorganisation'. Implementation was considered, for instance, in 'SOU 2005:092 Styrningen av insatsförsvaret'. These were followed up by Försvarsbeslutet 2009, Defence-decision 2009. The main decision was to give up national service (conscrip tion-based military) and followed through the cutbacks of the military budget from that of 2 per cent of GDP in 1997 (3.1 per cent in the 1970s) to 1.1 per cent (from 2011 onwards).

43 'Regeringens proposition 2004/05:5 – Vårt framtida försvar'; 'Regeringens proposition 2004/05:43 – Försvarsmaktens grundorganisation'.

44 Blix et al. 2016, 146–175.

45 Sjursen 2004. See also Kaplan 2004, 109–133. However, in 2018, Forsberg stated that neutral identity is still rather crucial stance, as it has served well and enabled certain room to maneuver.

46 Tunander 1999, Holmström 2015, Blix et al. 2016, 135–138, 159–170, Doeser 2012, 186–199, Gebhard 2017.

47 For Sweden cf. Blix et al. 2016, 156–171. For Finland cf. UTP 20/2007, 19–21, 37–38.

48 Walt 1987, 19–24.

49 Saxi & Friis 2018.

50 Petersson 2017, 99–101. Cf. Art 1998.

51 Bergquist, Heisbourg, Nyberg & Tiilikainen 2016, 47–53.

52 Coffey & Kochis 2016.

53 Dwyer 2013, 30–32, 35–41, Åtland 2011 mentions that Russian activities are also dependent on NATO and Arctic states although the scenario was rather different back in 2011. Konyshev & Sergunin 2014 however state that Russia is not seeking military superiority, but aims at protecting trade interests and economic spheres of interest and in showing great power capability in general.

54 Hayden 2017, loc 87–97, Bergquist, Heisbourg, Nyberg & Tiilikainen 2016, 51–52.

55 Clapper 2014, *Worldwide Threat Assessment of the U.S. Intelligence Community 2014*. See also Polikanov 2013, 82–87.

56 Arter 2008, 292.

57 Blix et al. 2016, 153–154. See also Proposition 2008/09:140.

58 Britz 2012, 223–225, 230–232.

59 Speeches 6 September 2007 09:47; Minister of Defence Jyri Häkämies at CSIS in Washington.

60 *Maaseudun tulevaisuus*, 12 September 2007, 4. Also Särkkä 2019.

61 cf. Forsberg & Vaahtoranta 2001.

62 Archer 1999a, 1999b, 55–59, Sydow 2012, 13. Split interests were evident in the 1990s: Britz 2012, 231, 241, 257.

63 McCormick 2013, 107–108, 111–113; then again according to McCormick and the works he cites, the EU has other forms of power that should not be overlooked, 115–117, 121, and the joint defence budget of the member states amounts to US$202 billion, second only to the United States, 122–123, table 5.2,

64 Valtioneuvoston selonteko eduskunnalle 1997.

65 Sydow 2012, 13, Britz 2012, 231, 241, 257.

66 Averre 2016, 699–704; also Howorth 2011.

67 The change from neutrality to non-alignment and non-allied is evident when comparing the various Government Reports on Finnish Foreign and Security Policy. Especially: VNS 1/1995, VNK Selonteko 2016. Also VNS 1/1997, VNS 2/2001vp. VNS

6/2004 mentions the EU framework as the basis of Finnish policy, VNS 11/2009, VNS 2012. In response, NATO and Nordic cooperation have become more prominent. The 'EU line of policy' has not been fully reinstated to its earlier level. See also Britz 2012, 257.

68 Karnitschnig & Herszenhorn 2019.
69 For Finland, Valtioneuvoston selonteko eduskunnalle 1997. For Sweden, Bergquist, Heisbourg, Nyberg & Tiilikainen 2016, SOU 2016:57, chapter 13 considers the EU level much more in detail than the Finnish NATO report, even if it is considered a work in progess in which Sweden might seek an ambitious role. See also Blix et al. 2016, Britz 2012, 257.
70 Petersson 2017, 99–102; also Saxi 2011, esp. n10.
71 Coffey & Kochis 2016.
72 Petersson 2017. SIPRI Military Expenditure Database for the period 1949–2018, however, reveals that since 2005 Norway has constantly increased its defence expenditures. On the change of Danish policy approach, cf. Wivel 2013b.
73 Petersson 2017, 104–106.
74 Coffey & Kochis 2016.
75 Åtland 2016, Winnerstig 2017.
76 Försvarsmakten, Försvarsmaktsidé 2020. Interestingly Finland also opted for downsizing its land forces considerably in the late 1990s, Valtioneuvoston selonteko eduskunnalle 1997.
77 SOU 2016:57. Försvarspolitisk inriktning – Sveriges försvar 2016–2020 Prop. 2014/15:109. *Resilience: The Total Defence Concept and the Development of Civil Defence 2021–2025* 2017.
78 'Sweden – Patriot Configuration-3+ Modernized Fire Units' 2018.
79 'Patriot Missiles are Made in America and Fail Everywhere' 2018. See also Hildreth 1992.
80 Försvarspolitisk inriktning – Sveriges försvar 2016–2020 Prop. 2014/15:109, see also Sydow 2018.
81 Blix et al. 2016, 156–159, Petersson 2018, Egnell 2015, 2016, 309–338.
82 Försvarspolitisk inriktning – Sveriges försvar 2016–2020 Prop. 2014/15:109.
83 VNK Puolustusselonteko 2017a, 16. 'Puolustusjärjestelmää kehitetään siten, että mahdolliselle sotilaalliselle liittoutumiselle ei muodostu käytännön esteitä'.
84 Sydow 2018. Also *Resilience* 2017.
85 Coffey & Kochis 2016. Bergquist, Heisbourg, Nyberg & Tiilikainen 2016, 52.
86 Forsberg 2018.
87 VNK puolustusselonteko 2017a, 2017b. Esiselvitys Hornet-kaluston suorituskyvyn korvaamisesta, Loppuraportti.
88 'Hornet-kauppojen taustalta paljastui "erittäin ruma temppu" – kolmen kopla junaili salaa koneet Suomeen' 2014.
89 Blix et al. 2016, 171–175. Also DS 2015:39 Samförståndavtal med Nato om värdlandsstöd.
90 *Finlex* 82/2014 www.finlex.fi/fi/sopimukset/sopsteksti/2014/20140082/20140082_1.
91 Memorandum of Understanding (MOU).
92 'Suomen johtamisjärjestelmäorganisaatio mahdollisti Bold Quest -tapahtuman toteuttamisen', *Pääesikunta* 16.5.2019 15.49.
93 Trilateral Statement of Intent 2018.
94 Cf. Särkkä 2019, Rahkonen 2006, Ydén, Joakim & Magnus 2019.
95 SOU 2016:57. Bergquist, Heisbourg, Nyberg & Tiilikainen 2016.
96 Saxi 2011, Saxi & Friis 2018. See also Forsberg 2013.
97 SOU 2016:57, 14–15 mentions this to be the most important Swedish security policy direction, though this idea overlooks the precarious geopolitical situation of Finland vis-à-vis Russia's border and different security interests, as the SOU report also emphasises

a direct threat to Sweden from Russia. Were a conflict to occur, Finland would serve as a buffer or eastern flank for Sweden.

98 Petersson 2017, 104–106. This is noted also in SOU 2016:57, 137–138, 141–142, 146–147.
99 Bergquist, Heisbourg, Nyberg & Tiilikainen 2016, 24–25, 30–31, 45–46.
100 Blombergs 2016, Haukkala 2013, Bjereld 1992.
101 Cf. 'Suomen huippusalaisen' 2020.
102 Cf. Holmström 2015, Bruzelius 2007.
103 Regarding Finland, cf. Rahkonen 2006, Särkkä 2019, Blix et al. 2016, 185–189, SOU 2016:57, 150, however notes that Finland wants to remain outside the Swedish domestic NATO-discussion.
104 'Survey: Finns Wary' 2013.
105 *Uusi Suomi* 3 February 2015. 'Kysely: Nato jakaa suomalaiset – joka kolmas empii'. The article mentions that more Finns are changing their views regarding NATO membership to more positive. The pro-NATO support has increased from 18 per cent to 26 per cent by 2015, based on the EVA polls regarding NATO membership opinion surveys. *Uusi Suomi* is an online news media, which claims to be politically non-aligned. Särkkä 2019 mainly agrees.
106 Bergquist, Heisbourg, Nyberg & Tiilikainen 2016, 55. The report was commissioned by Mats Bergquist (former high-ranking Swedish diplomat), François Heisbourg (diplomat and director of the IISS), René Nyberg (former high ranking Finnish diplomat) and Teija Tiilikainen (at the time the leader of the Finnish Institute of International Affairs, FIIA). Blix et al. 2016, 199, have considered the same, but mention that Finland applying NATO membership is very unlikely and were it to apply, Sweden might not follow suit, but were Finland to opt out, it would strengthen the reasons why Sweden should apply. Similar, but much more detailed report was crafted by Krister Bringéus in Sweden: SOU 2016:57, 148–150, which mentions that Finnish discussion is different due to Finns not perceiving a direct threat from Russia and Finland having less importance for Baltic seaways and thus not in the epicentre of potential conflict. Sweden, in turn, must observe the potential Russian threat for Baltic States in a different way.

References

Agrell, Wilhelm, 1991: *Stora lögnen*. Stockholm: Ordfronts förlag.
Agrell, Wilhelm, 2000: *Fred och fruktan: Sveriges säkerhetspolitiska historia 1918–2000*. Lund: Historiska Media.
Ahlund, Claes (ed.) 2012: *Scandinavia in the First World War. Studies in the War Experience of the Northern Neutrals*. Lund: Nordic Academic Press.
Archer, Clive, 1999a: "Nordic Swans and Baltic Cygnets" in *Cooperation and Conflict*, 34:1, 47–71. https://doi.org/10.1177/00108369921961771 [Accessed 30 November 2019].
Archer, Clive, 1999b: "The EU, Security and the Baltic Region" in *WeltTrends*, 23, 45–62.
Archer, Clive, Bailes, Alyson J. K. & Wivel, Andreas (eds.) 2014: *Small States and International Security: Europe and Beyond*. Abingdon: Routledge.
Art, Robert, 1998: "Creating a Disaster: NATO's Open Door Policy" in *Political Science Quarterly*, 113:3, 383–403.
Arter, David, 2006: *Democracy in Scandinavia: Consensual, Majoritarian or Mixed?* Manchester: Manchester University Press.
Arter, David, 2008: *Scandinavian Politics Today*. Manchester: Manchester University Press.
Åselius, Gunnar, 2005: "Swedish Strategic Culture After 1945" in *Cooperation and Conflict*, 40:1, 25–44. https://doi.org/10.1177/0010836705049732.

Åtland, Kristian, 2011: "Russia's Armed Forces and the Arctic: All Quiet on the Northern Front?" in *Contemporary Security Policy*, 32:2, 267–285. https://doi.org/10.1080/135232 60.2011.590354.

Åtland, Kristian, 2016: "North European Security after the Ukraine Conflict" in *Defense & Security Analysis*, 32:2, 163–176. https://doi.org/10.1080/14751798.2016.1160484.

Aunesluoma, Juhana, 2003: *Britain, Sweden and the Cold War, 1945–54. Understanding Neutrality*. Basingstoke: Palgrave Macmillan.

Aunesluoma, Juhana & Rainio-Niemi, Johanna, 2016: "Neutrality as Identity: Finland's Quest for Security in the Cold War" in *Journal of Cold War Studies*, 18:4, 51–78. https://doi.org/10.1162/JCWS_a_00680.

Averre, Derek, 2016: "The Ukraine Conflict: Russia's Challenge to European Security Governance" in *Europe-Asia Studies*, 68:4, 699–725. https://doi.org/10.1080/09668136.2016.1176993.

BakerFox, Anette, 1959: *The Power of Small States*. Chicago: Chicago University Press.

Bauman, Zygmunt, 2000: *Liquid Modernity*. Cambridge: Polity Press.

Bergquist, Mats, Heisbourg, François, Nyberg, René & Tiilikainen, Teija, 2016: *4/2016 The Effects of Finland's Possible NATO Membership. An Assessment*. Ministry for Foreign Affairs. https://um.fi/publications/-/asset_publisher/TVOLgBmLyZvu/content/arvio-suomen-mahdollisen-nato-jasenyyden-vaikutuksista.

Bjereld, Ulf, 1992: *Kritiker eller medlare? En studie av Sveriges utrikespolitiska roller 1945–90*. Stockholm: Nerenius & Santérus.

Blank, Stephen, J., 1996: *Finnish Security and European Security Policy* (Kindle edition). U.S. Department of Defense, Strategic Studies Institute, US Army War College.

Blix, Hans, et al., 2016: *Sverige, Nato och säkerheten: betänkande av Natoutredningen*. Lund: Celander.

Blombergs, Fred, 2016: "Johdatus Suomen turvallisuuspolitiikkaan kylmän sodan jälkeisessä Euroopassa" in Fred Blombergs (ed.) *Suomen turvallisuuspoliittisen ratkaisun lähtökohtia*. Maanpuolustuskorkeakoulu Julkaisusarja 1: Tutkimuksia nro 4. Helsinki: Maanpuolustuskorkeakoulu, 3–54.

Brand, Jack, 1992: *British Parliamentary Parties. Policy and Power*. Oxford: Clarendon Press.

Britz, Malena, 2012: "Ett oväntad uppvisning för nordiskt säkerhetspolitiskt samarbete" in Fredrik Doeser, Magnus Peterson & Jacob Westberg (eds.) *Norden mellan stormakter och fredsförbund. Nordiskt säkerhetspolitiskt samarbete i det gamla och nya Europa*. Stockholm: Santérus Academic Press, 223–260.

Browning, Christopher S., 2002: "Coming Home or Moving Home? 'Westernizing' Narratives in Finnish Foreign Policy and the Reinterpretation of Past Identities" in *Cooperation and Conflict*, 37:1, 47–72.

Browning, Christopher S., 2007: "Branding Nordicity: Models, Identity and the Decline of Exceptionalism" in *Cooperation and Conflict*, 42:1, 27-51.

Bruzelius, Nils, 2007: *"Near Friendly or Neutral Shores": The Deployment of the Fleet Ballistic Missile Submarines and US Policy Towards Scandinavia, 1957–1963*. Stockholm: KTH School of Architecture and the Built Environment.

Bull, Hedley, 2012: *The Anarchial Society* (4th edition). New York: Columbia University Press.

Clapper, James R., (Director of National Intelligence), 2014: *2014 Worldwide Threat Assessment of the U.S. Intelligence Community*. Senate Select Committee on Intelligence, Statement for the record, 29 January 2014.

Coffey, Luke & Kochis, Daniel, 2016: "The Role of Sweden and Finland in NATO's Defence of the Baltic States" in *Issue Brief*. The Heritage Foundation. http://report.heritage.org/ib4554 [Accessed 12 November 2019].

The Constitution of Finland, 1999: (731/1999, amendments up to 817/2018 included), 11 June 1999. www.finlex.fi/en/laki/kaannokset/1999/en19990731.pdf [Accessed 1 January 2020].

The Constitution of Sweden, 2016: *The Fundamental Laws and the Riksdag Act*. With an Introduction by Magnus Isberg. Sveriges Riksdag. www.riksdagen.se/globalassets/ 07.- dokument – lagar/the-constitution-of-sweden-160628.pdf [Accessed 12 November 2019].

Cottey, Andrew, 2018a: "European Neutrality in Historical Perspective" in Andrew Cottey (ed.) *The European Neutrals and NATO. Non-Alignment, Partnership, Membership?* Basingstoke: Palgrave Macmillan, 1–20.

Cottey, Andrew, 2018b: "The Europe Neutrals, NATO and Future Prospects" in Andrew Cottey (ed.) *The European Neutrals and NATO. Non-Alignment, Partnership, Membership?* Basingstoke: Palgrave Macmillan, 211–229.

Dahl, Robert A., 1998: *On Democracy*. New Haven, CT: Yale University Press.

Dahl, Robert A., 2001: "Democracy" in *International Encyclopedia of the Social & Behavioral Sciences*. Amsterdam: Elsevier Sciences.

Dalsjö, Robert, 2014: "The Hidden Rationality of Sweden's Policy of Neutrality during the Cold War" in *Cold War History*, 14:2, 175–194. https://doi.org/10.1080/14682745. 2013.765865.

Diez, Thomas, 2004: "Europe's Others and the Return of Geopolitics" in *Cambridge Review of International Affairs*, 17:2, 319–335.

Doeser, Fredrik, 2012: "Kalla krigets slut och utrikespolitisk förändring I Finland och Sverige" in Fredrik Doeser, Magnus Peterson & Jacob Westberg (eds.) *Norden mellan stormakter och fredsförbund. Nordiskt säkerhetspolitiskt samarbete i det gamla och nya Europa*. Stockholm: Santérus Academic Press, 169–202.

DS, 2015:39: *Samförståndavtal med Nato om värdlandsstöd*. Regeringskansliet, Försvarsdepartementet. www.regeringen.se/contentassets/c4f93c1e3479439c86f732a4b75b7a2b/ samforstandsavtal-med-nato-om-vardlandsstod-ds-2015_39.pdf [Accessed 12 November 2019].

Dwyer, William G., 2013: *The Evolving Arctic. Current State of U.S. Arctic Policy – Strategies of Other Arctic Nations, Russia, Canada, Denmark, Norway, Sweden, Finland, Iceland, Icebreakers, UNCLOS, SAR Assets*. Monterey, CA: Naval Postgraduate School, U.S. Government, Department of Defense.

Egnell, Robert, 2015: "The Swedish Experience: Overcoming the Non – NATO-Member Conundrum" in Karl P. Mueller et al. (eds.) *Precision and Purpose: Airpower in the Libyan Civil War*. Santa Monica, CA: RAND Corporation, 309–338.

Egnell, Robert, 2016: "The Swedish Decision to Participate in Operation Unified Protector" in Dag Henriksen & Ann Karin Larssen (eds.) *Political Rationale and International Consequences of the War in Libya*. Oxford: Oxford University Press, 174–191.

Elinkeinoelämän Valtuuskunnan arvopankki: www.eva.fi/arvopankki/kategoria.php?q=13 [Accessed 12 November 2019].

Forsberg, Tuomas, 2013: "The Rise of Nordic Defence Cooperation. A Return to Regionalism?" in *International Affairs*, 89:5, 1161–1181.

Forsberg, Tuomas, 2018: "Finland and NATO: Strategic Choices and Identity" in Andrew Cottey (ed.) *The European Neutrals and NATO. Non-Alignment, Partnership, Membership?* (Kindle edition). New Security Challenges. London: Palgrave Macmillan, 97–127.

Forsberg, Tuomas & Vaahtoranta, Tapani, 2001: "Inside the EU, Outside NATO: Paradoxes of Finland's and Sweden's Post-Neutrality" in *European Security*, 10:1, 68–93. https://doi. org/10.1080/09662830108407483.

Forsberg, Tuomas & Vogt, Henri, 2008: "Suomen ulkopolitiikan eurooppalaistuminen" in Pasi Saukkonen (ed.) *Suomen poliittinen järjestelmä – Verkkokirja*. University of Helsinki. https://blogs.helsinki.fi/vol-spj/ [Accessed 10 October 2019].

Försvarsbeslutet, 2009: *Defence-decision, 2009.* https://web.archive.org/web/201608020855 29/www.forsvarsmakten.se/sv/om-myndigheten/ekonomisk-planering-och-redovisning/forsvarets-andel-av-bnp/ [Archived; Accessed 10 October 2018].

Försvarsmakten, Försvarsmaktsidé 2020 (*FMI2020*), Högkvarteret, 3 June 1997. (Hkv 23210:68553).

Försvarspolitisk inriktning – Sveriges försvar 2016–2020 Prop. 2014/15:109.

The French Constitution, 1958: www.conseil-constitutionnel.fr/sites/default/files/as/root/bank_mm/anglais/constiution_anglais_oct2009.pdf.

Gebhard, Carmen, 2017: "Scandinavian Defence and Alliance Policies: Different Together" in Anders Wivel & Peter Nedergaard (eds.) *The Routledge Handbook on Scandinavian Politics*. London: Routledge, 254–268.

Gerner, Kristian, 2002: "North Eastern Europe and Swedish Great Power Policy. Reflections on Historical Consciousness" in *Journal of Baltic Seas Studies*, 33:4, 398–411.

Giles, Keir & Eskola, Susanna, 2014: *Waking the Neighbour. Finland, NATO and Russia.* Research & Assessment Branch, Defence Academy of the United Kingdom, September 2014. http://www.conflictstudies.org.uk/files/017.pdf.

Häkkinen, Teemu, 2014: *The Royal Prerogative Redefined. Parliamentary Debate on the Role of the British Parliament in Large-Scale Military Deployments, 1982–2003.* Jyväskylä Studies in Humanities 224. Jyväskylä: University of Jyväskylä.

Hanhimäki, Jussi, 1996: *Rinnakkaiseloa patoamassa: Yhdysvallat ja Paasikiven linja, 1948–1956.* Helsinki: SHS.

Hanhimäki, Jussi, 1997: *An Insecure Friendship. The United States and Scandinavia Since 1945.* Twayne's International History Series. New York: Twayne Publishers/Macmillan.

Haukkala, Hiski, 2013: "Finske diplomatimodeller: Er der en ny model på vej?" in *Økonomi & Politik*, 86:2, 34–44.

Hayden, Rory J., 2017: *Russia's Security Relations with Finland, Norway and Sweden.* Monterrey, CA: U.S. Government, U.S. Military, Department of Defense (DoD).

Heikka, Henrikki, 2005: "Republican Realism. Finnish Strategic Culture in Historical Perspective" in *Cooperation and Conflict*, 40:1, 91–119. https://doi.org/10.1177/001 0836705049736.

Heinonen, Veikko U. J., 2011: *The State of Finnish Security Policy. A Conceptual Analysis of the Finnish Debate on Security Policy in the Early 2000s.* Jyväskylä: University of Jyväskylä, Jyväskylä Studies in Education, Psychology and Social Research.

Hildreth, Steven A., 1992: *Evaluation of U.S. Army Assessment of Patriot Antitactical Missile Effectiveness in the War Against Iraq.* Report by Steven A. Hildreth Specialist in National Defense Foreign Affairs and National Defense Division Congressional Research Service, Prepared for the House Government Operations Subcommittee on Legislation and National Security, 7 April 1992. www.dtic.mil/dtic/tr/fulltext/u2/a344634.pdf [Accessed 2 February 2020].

Holmén, Hans, 1985: *Försvar och samhällsförändring. Avvägningsfrågor i svensk försvarsdebatt 1880–1925.* Meddelande från Historiska institutionen i Göteborg 29. Göteborg: Göteborgs universitet.

Holmström, Mikael, 2015: *Den dolda alliansen. Sveriges hemliga NATO-förbindelser.* Stockholm: Atlantis.

Howorth, Jolyon, 2011: "EU's Security and Defense Policy: Towards a Strategic Approach" in Christopher Hill & Michael Smith (eds.) *International Relations and the European Union* (2nd edition). Hampshire: Oxford University Press, 197–226.

Huldt, Bo, 1977: "Små stater i internationell politik" in Thomas Hörberg (ed.) *Aktörer I internationell politik*. Stockholm: Sekretariatet för framtidsstudier, 38–56.

Huntington, Samuel P., Crozier, Michel & Watanuki, Joji (eds.) 1975: *The Crisis of Democracy. Report on the Governability of Democracies to the Trilateral Commission*. New York: New York University Press.

Ihalainen, Pasi & Matikainen, Satu, 2016: "The British Parliament and Foreign Policy in the 20th Century: Towards Increasing Parliamentarisation?" in Pasi Ihalainen & Sati Matikainen (eds.) *Parliamentary History*, 35:1, Special Issue: *The British Parliament and Foreign Policy in the 20th Century*, 1–14.

Iloniemi, Jaakko, 1992: "Pohjola varustautuu. Miksi?" in *Suomen kuvalehti*, 25–26, 42–43.

Ilta-sanomat, 2014: "Hornet-kauppojen taustalta paljastui 'erittäin ruma temppu' – kolmen kopla junaili salaa koneet Suomeen." 15 October 2014.

Jakobsen, Peter Viggo, 2017: "The United Nations and the Nordic Four: Cautious Sceptics, Committed Believers, Cost-Benefit Calculators" in Peter Nedergaard & Anders Wivel (eds.) *The Routledge Handbook of Scandinavian Politics*. Abingdon: Routledge, 281–293.

Jonasson, Axel E., 1973: "The Crimean War, the Beginning of Strict Swedish Neutrality, and the Myth of Swedish Intervention in the Baltic" in *Journal of Baltic Studies*, 4:3, 244–253.

Kalela, Jorma, 1971: *Grannar på skilda vägar. Det finländsk-svenska samarbetet i den finländska och svenska utrikespolitiken 1921–1923*. Borgå: Söderström.

Kaplan, Lawrence S., 2004: *Nato Divided, Nato United: The Evolution of Alliance*. Westport, CT: Praeger.

Karnitschnig, Matthew & Herszenhorn, David, M., 2019: "Munich Insecurity Conference Transatlantic Differences Laid Bare at Annual Defense Powwow" in *Politico*, 16 February 2019, 7:43 PM CET, Updated 18 February 2019, 4:31 PM CET. www.politico. eu/article/munich-security-conference-angela-merkel-mike-pence/ [Accessed 2 January 2020].

Karonen, Petri, Roitto, Matti & Ojala, Jari, 2018: "Politiska kulturer 1430–1930" in Henrik Meinander, Petri Karonen & Kjell Östberg (eds.) *Demokratins drivkrafter Kontext och särdrag i Finlands och Sveriges demokratier 1890–2020*. Helsingfors: Svenska litteratursällskapet i Finland; Stockholm: Appell Förlag, 65–98.

Keohane, Robert, 1969: "Lilliputians' Dilemmas: Small States in International Politics" in *International Organization*, 23:2, 291–310.

Kettunen, Pauli, Lundberg, Urban, Österberg, Mirja & Petersen, Klaus, 2015: "The Nordic Model and the Rise and Fall of Nordic Cooperation" in Johan Strang (ed.) *Nordic Cooperation: A European Region in Transition* (vol. 8). Routledge Series on Global Order Studies. New York: Routledge, 69–91.

"Kohti Naton ydintä" in *Suomen Kuvalehti*, 10, 9 March 2001.

Konyshev, Valery & Sergunin, Alexander, 2014: "Is Russia a Revisionist Military Power in the Arctic?" in *Defense & Security Analysis*, 30:4, 323–335. https://doi.org/10.1080/147 51798.2014.948276.

Kronvall, Olof & Petersson, Magnus, 2005: *Svensk säkerhetspolitik i supermakternas skugga 1945–1991*. Stockholm: Santerus.

Lindell, Ulf & Persson, Stefan, 1986: "The Paradox of Weak State Power: A Research and Literature Overview" in *Cooperation and Conflict*, 21, 79–97.

Maaseudun tulevaisuus, 12 September 2007, "Häkämies on turvallisuuspoliittinen riski", in *Letters to the Editor*.

Marcussen, Martin, 2017: "Scandinavian Models of Diplomacy" in Peter Nedergaard & Anders Wivel (eds.) *The Routledge Handbook of Scandinavian Politics*. Abingdon: Routledge, 240–253.

McCormick, John, 2013: "The European Union: A Different Kind of Beast" in Donette Murray & David Brown (eds.) *Multipolarity in the 21st Century: A New World Order*. New York: Routledge, 80–106.

Mead, Walter Russel, 2014: "The Return of Geopolitics. Revenge of the Revisionist Powers" in *Foreign Affairs*, May–June.

Meinander, Henrik, 2018: "Inrikes utrikespolitik? Dubbelspel, finlandisering och demokratins gränser" in Henrik Meinander, Petri Karonen & Kjell Östberg (eds.) *Demokratins drivkrafter Kontext och särdrag i Finlands och Sveriges demokratier 1890–2020*. Helsingfors: Svenska litteratursällskapet i Finland; Stockholm: Appell Förlag, 295–324.

Meinander, Henrik, Karonen, Petri & Östberg, Kjell (eds.) 2018: *Demokratins drivkrafter Kontext och särdrag i Finlands och Sveriges demokratier 1890–2020*. Helsingfors: Svenska litteratursällskapet i Finland; Stockholm: Appell Förlag.

Memorandum of Understanding (MOU) between the Government of the Republic of Finland and Headquarters, Supreme Allied Command Transformation, as well as Supreme Headquarters Allied Powers Europe Regarding the Provision of Host Nation Support for the Execution of NATO Operations/Exercises/Similar Military Activity. www.defmin.fi/files/2898/HNS_MOU_FINLAND.pdf [Accessed 2 February 2020].

Morgenthau, Hans, 1978: *Politics Among Nations: The Struggle for Power and Peace* (5th edition). New York: Alfred A. Knopf.

Murray, Donette, 2013: "Introduction" in Donette Murray& David Brown (eds.) *Multipolarity in the 21st Century: A New World Order*. New York: Routledge, 1–16.

Nedergaard, Peter & Wivel, Anders, 2017a: "Introduction: Scandinavian Politics between Myth and Reality" in Peter Nedergaard & Anders Wivel (eds.) *The Routledge Handbook of Scandinavian Politics*. Abingdon: Routledge, 1–10.

Nedergaard, Peter & Wivel, Anders, 2017b: "Conclusions: Scandinavian Polities, Politics and Policies" in Peter Nedergaard & Anders Wivel (eds.) *The Routledge Handbook of Scandinavian Politics*. Abingdon: Routledge, 306–312.

Nilsson, Mikael & Wyss, Marco, 2016: "The Armed Neutrality Paradox: Sweden and Switzerland in US Cold War Armaments Policy" in *Journal of Contemporary History*, 51:2, 335–363. https://doi.org/10.1177/0022009414564804.

Ojala, Jari, Roitto, Matti & Karonen, Petri, 2018: "Tillväxt och demokrati Om ekonomins politiska långtidseffekter" in Henrik Meinander Petri Karonen & Kjell Östberg (eds.) *Demokratins drivkrafter Kontext och särdrag i Finlands och Sveriges demokratier 1890–2020*. Helsingfors: Svenska litteratursällskapet i Finland; Stockholm: Appell Förlag, 151–188.

"Patriot Missiles are Made in America and Fail Everywhere" in *Foreign Policy*, 28 March 2018. http://foreignpolicy.com/2018/03/28/patriot-missiles-are-made-in-america-and-fail-everywhere/ [Accessed 2 February 2020].

Pegram, T. & Acuto, M., 2015: "Introduction: Global Governance in the Interregnum" in *Millennium*, 43:2, 584–597. https://doi.org/10.1177/0305829814562017.

Pesu, Matti, 2016: "Kun pienvaltiorealismin hegemonia murtui: suomalaiset ulkopoliittisen koulukunnat kylmän sodan jälkeisen ajan alussa" in *Politiikka*, 59:4, 280–297.

Petersson, Magnus, 2017: "NATOs Territorial Defence: The Global Approach and the Regional Approach" in Rebecca R. Moore & Damon Coletta (eds.) *NATO's Return to Europe Engaging Ukraine, Russia, and Beyond*. Washington, DC: Georgetown University Press, 97–112.

Petersson, Magnus, 2018: "'The Allied Partner': Sweden and NATO through the Realist – Idealist Lens" in Andrew Cottey (ed.) *The European Neutrals and NATO. Non Alignment, Partnership, Membership?* (Kindle edition). New Security Challenges. London: Palgrave Macmillan, 73–96.

Pharr, Susan J. & Putnam, Robert (eds.) 2000: *Disaffected Democracies – What's Troubling the Trilateral Countries?* Princeton, NJ: Princeton University Press.

Polikanov, Dmitry, 2013: "The Russian bear" in Donette Murray & David Brown (eds.) *Multipolarity in the 21st Century: A New World Order.* New York: Routledge, 80–106.

Proposition, 2008/9:140: Ett användbart försvar.

Rahkonen, Juho, 2006: *Journalismi taistelukenttänä. Suomen Nato-jäsenyydestä käyty julkinen keskustelu 2003–2004.* Tampere: Tampere University Press.

Rainio-Niemi, Johanna, 2014: *The Ideological Cold War. The Politics of Neutrality in Austria and Finland.* Routledge Studies in Modern History. New York: Routledge.

Regeringens proposition, 1995/96:12: Totalförsvar i förnyelse, etapp 1.

Regeringens proposition, 1996/97:4: Totalförsvar i förnyelse, etapp 2.

Regeringens proposition, 1999/2000:30: Det nya försvaret.

Regeringens proposition, 1999/2000:97: Vissa organisatoriska frågor inom Försvarsmakten.

Regeringens proposition, 2004/05:5: Vårt framtida försvar.

Regeringens proposition, 2004/05:43: Försvarsmaktens grundorganisation.

Resilience: The Total Defence Concept and the Development of Civil Defence 2021–2025. The Swedish Defence Commission Secretariat – Unofficial Summary, 2017. www.govern ment.se/4afeb9/globalassets/government/dokument/ forsvarsdepartementet/resilience – report-summary – 20171220ny.pdf [Accessed 10 October 2018].

Roiko-Jokela, Heikki, 1995: *Ihanteita ja reaalipolitiikkaa. Rudolf Holstin toiminta Baltian maiden kansainvälisen de jure -tunnustamisen ja reunavaltioyhteistyön puolesta 1918–1922.* Studia Historica Jyväskyläensia 52. Jyväskylä: University of Jyväskylä.

Roitto, Matti, 2015: *Dissenting Visions: The Executive, Parliament and the Problematic Anglo – American Atomic Collaboration in the Changes of British Atomic Foreign Policy 1945–6.* Jyväskylä Studies in Humanities 268. Jyväskylä: University of Jyväskylä.

Roitto, Matti, 2016: "The Atomic Question of 1945–6 as an Attempt to Parliamentarise British Foreign Policy" in *Parliamentary History,* 35, 28–41. https://doi. org/10.1111/1750-0206.12182.

Roitto, Matti, Karonen, Petri & Ojala, Jari, 2018: "Geopolitik och identitet" in Henrik Meinander, Petri Karonen & Kjell Östberg (eds.) *Demokratins drivkrafter Kontext och särdrag i Finlands och Sveriges demokratier 1890–2020.* Helsingfors: Svenska litteratursällskapet i Finland; Stockholm: Appell Förlag, 99–150.

Romanovs, Ugis & Andžāns, Māris, 2017: *The Trilateral Military Cooperation of the Baltic States in the 'New Normal' Security Landscape.* Security in the Baltic Sea Region: Realities and Prospects. The Rīga Conference Papers.

Runciman, David, 2015: *The Confidence Trap: A History of Democracy in Crisis from World War I to the Present.* Princeton, NJ: Princeton University Press.

Salmon, Patrick, 1997: *Scandinavia and the Great Powers 1890–1940.* Cambridge: Cambridge University Press, EBSCOhost eBook Collection.

Särkkä, Iro, 2019: *Nato-retoriikka Suomen turvallisuuspoliittisessa keskustelussa.* Helsinki: University of Helsinki.

Saukkonen, Pasi, 2008: "Suomen kansainväliset suhteet ja ulkopolitiikka" in Pasi Saukkonen (ed.) *Suomen poliittinen järjestelmä – Verkkokirja* (e-book). University of Helsinki. https:// blogs.helsinki.fi/vol-spj/ [Accessed 10 October 2018].

Saxi, Håkon Lunde, 2011: "Nordic Defence Cooperation after the Cold War" in *Oslo Files on Defence and Security, No. 1*. Oslo: Norwegian Institute for Defence Studies.

Saxi, Håkon Lunde & Friis, Karsten, 2018: *After Crimea: The Future of Nordic Defence Cooperation*. NUPI Policy Brief, No. 6. Oslo: NUPI/IFS.

Shapiro, Fred R., 2008: "Quote. Misquote" in *New York Times Magazine*, 21 July 2008. www.nytimes.com/2008/07/21/magazine/27wwwl-guestsafire-t.html.

Silva, Charles, 1999: *Keep Them Strong, Keep Them Friendly: Swedish-American Relations and the Pax Americana, 1948–1952*. Stockholm: Stockholm University Press.

SIPRI Military Expenditure Database 1949–2018: www.sipri.org/databases/milex [Accessed 2 February 2020].

Sjursen, Helene, 2004: "On the Identity of NATO" in *International Affairs*, 80:4(1), 687–703. https://doi.org/10.1111/j.1468-2346.2004.00411.x.

Smith, Michael & Steffenson, Rebecca, 2011: "The EU and the United States" in Christopher Hill & Michael Smith (eds.) *International Relations and the European Union* (2nd edition). Hampshire: Oxford University Press, 404–431.

Puolustusvoimien koulutuksen kehittämiskeskus, 1998: *Sotilaslyhenteet ja merkit (SLM): luonnos*. Helsinki: Puolustusvoimien koulutuksen kehittämiskeskus.

Sotilasmerkistö ja -lyhenteet (SML), 2005: Pääesikunta/Operaatioesikunta, Ohjesääntönumero 829. Helsinki: Edita Prima Oy. https://puolustusvoimat.fi/documents/1948673/2258496/PEVIESTOS- Sotilasmerkist%C3%B6-ja-lyhenteet.pdf/cf80563e-9d4f-4702–8446-e2a7a0d85116/PEVIESTOS-Sotilasmerkist%C3%B6-ja-lyhenteet.pdf [Accessed 10 October 2019].

SOU, 2005:092: *Styrningen av insatsförsvaret*. Stockholm: Statens offentliga utredningar.

SOU, 2016:57: *Säkerhet i ny tid. Betänkande av Utredningen om Sveriges försvars- och säkerhetspolitiska samarbeten*. Stockholm: Statens offentliga utredningar.

Speeches, 6 September 2007, 09:47: *Minister of Defence Jyri Häkämies at CSIS in Washington*. www.defmin.fi/en/topical/speeches/minister_of_defence_jyri_hakamies_at_csi s_in_washington.3335.news?663_o=10 [Accessed 9 August 2019].

Streeck, Wolfgang, 2015: *Ostettua aikaa: Demokraattisen kapitalismin lykätty kriisi*. Tampere: Vastapaino.

"Suomen huippusalaisen tiedustelukeskuksen ex-pomo kertoo, mitä Venäjä oikeasti ajattelee meistä" in *Iltalehti*, 26 January 2020. An interview of the former deputy chief commander of the Finnish Military Intelligence Service, Martti J. Kari.

"Survey: Finns Wary of Following Sweden into NATO" in *YLE News*, 14 June 2013, 18:13. https://yle.fi/uutiset/osasto/news/survey_finns_wary_of_following_sweden_into_nato/6690400 [Accessed 12 November 2019].

"Sweden – Patriot Configuration-3+ Modernized Fire Units" in *Defense Security Cooperation Agency*, News Release, Washington, 20 February 2018. www.dsca.mil/major-arms- sales/sweden-patriot-configuration-3-modernized-fire-units [Accessed 2 February 2020].

"Swedish Project to Support Lithuanian Land Forces Completed" in *Defense Aerospace.com*, Briganti et Associés, 3 December 2004. www.defense-aerospace.com/articles- view/release/3/50069/baltics-received-donated-weapons-(dec.-8).html [Accessed 2 January 2020].

Sydow, Björn von, 2012: "Förord" in Magnus Peterson & Fredrik Doeser (eds.) *Norden mellan stormakter of fredsförbund. Nordiskt säkerhetspolitiskt samarbete I det gamla och nya Europa*. Stockholm: Santérus Academic Press, 11–16.

Sydow, Björn von, 2018: "Resilience: Planning for Sweden's 'Total Defence'" in *NATO Review*, 4 April 2018. www.nato.int/docu/review/articles/2018/04/04/resilience- planning-for-swedens-total-defence/index.html [Accessed 2 January 2020].

Tornudd, Klaus, 2005: "Finnish Neutrality Policy During the Cold War" in *SAIS Review of International Affairs*, 25:2, 43–52. Project MUSE. https://doi.org/10.1353/sais.2005.0044.

Trilateral Statement of Intent among the Department of Defense of the United States of America and the Ministry of Defence of the Republic of Finland and the Ministry of Defence of the Kingdom of Sweden, 2018. www.defmin.fi/files/4231/Trilateral_State ment_of_Intent.pdf [Accessed 2 February 2020].

Tunander, Ola, 1999: "The Uneasy Imbrication of Nation-State and NATO: The Case of Sweden" in *Cooperation and Conflict*, 34:2, 169–203. https://doi.org/10.1177/0010 8369921961825.

Tunander, Ola, 2001: "Swedish-German Geopolitics for a New Century Rudolf Kjellén's 'The State as a Living Organism'" in *Review of International Studies*, 27:3, 451–463.

Tunander, Ola, 2005: "Swedish Geopolitics. From Rudolf Kjellén to a Swedish 'Dual State'" in *Geopolitics*, 10:3, 546–566.

Tunander, Ola, 2008: "Geopolitics of the North: Geopolitik of the Weak. A Post-Cold War Return to Rudolf Kjellén" in *Cooperation and Conflict*, 43:2, 164–184.

UTP, 20/2007: vp. Ulkoasiainministeriö, Suurlähettiläs Antti Sierla Suomen mahdollisen Nato- jäsenyyden vaikutukset, 21 December 2007.

Valtioneuvoston puolustusselonteko, 5/2017a: Valtioneuvoston kanslian julkaisusarja. Esi-selvitys Hornet-kaluston suorituskyvyn korvaamisesta, Loppuraportti.

Valtioneuvoston puolustusselonteko, 5/2017b: Valtioneuvoston kanslian julkaisusarja. Valtioneuvoston kanslia, Loppuraportti.

Valtioneuvoston selonteko eduskunnalle, 1995: Turvallisuus muuttuvassa maailmassa Suomen turvallisuuspolitiikan suuntalinjat. Valtioneuvoston selonteko eduskunnalle, 6 June 1995. VEPS-tunnus VNS 1/1995 Valtiopäivät 1995 VNS 1.

Valtioneuvoston selonteko eduskunnalle, 1997: Euroopan turvallisuuskehitys ja Suomen puolustus. VNS 1/1997 Valtioneuvoston selonteko eduskunnalle, 17 March 1997.

Valtioneuvoston selonteko eduskunnalle, 2001: Suomen turvallisuus- ja puolustuspolitiikka. Valtioneuvoston selonteko eduskunnalle, 13 June 2001 VNS 2/2001 vp.

Valtioneuvoston selonteko eduskunnalle, 2004: Turvallisuus- ja puolustuspoliittinen selon-teko eduskunnalle. Valtioneuvoston selonteko VNS 6/2004. Valtioneuvoston kanslian julkaisusarja 16/2004.

Valtioneuvoston selonteko, Suomen turvallisuus- ja puolustuspolitiikka, 2009: Valtioneuvoston Kanslian julkaisusarja 11/2009.

Valtioneuvoston selonteko, Suomen turvallisuus- ja puolustuspolitiikka, 2012: Valtioneuvoston kanslian julkaisusarja 5/2012.

Valtioneuvoston ulko- ja turvallisuuspoliittinen selonteko, 2016: Valtioneuvoston kanslia, Valtioneuvoston kanslian julkaisusarja 7/2016.

"Viro–projekti päättyi: 'Suomi auttoi Viroa luomaan toimivan maanpuolustusjärjestelmän'" in *Suomen puolustusvoimien pääesikunnan tiedote*, 20 April 2004. www.mil.fi/paaesikunta/ tiedotteet/464.dsp (accessed through Internet Archive), [Accessed 10 October 2018].

Wagner, Wolfgang, 2017: "Parliaments in Foreign Policy" in *Subject: Political Institutions, World Politics Online*. https://doi.org/10.1093/acrefore/9780190228637.013.461.

Walt, Stephen M., 1987: *The Origins of the Alliances*. Ithaca, NY: Cornell University Press.

Westberg, Jacob, 2012: "Den nordiska småstatsrealismens rötter" in Magnus Peterson & Fre-drik Doeser (eds.) *Norden mellan stormakter of fredsförbund. Nordiskt säkerhetspolitiskt samar-bete I det gamla och nya Europa*. Stockholm: Santérus Academic Press, 67–94.

Winnerstig, Mike, 2017: "The Baltic Sea Area: A New Geopolitical Focal Point" in FOI Memo 6210, report published as a part of Cecilia Wiklund et al. (eds.) *Strategic Outlook 7*.

Perspectives on National Security in a New Security Environment. www.foi.se/en/foi/research/strategic-outlook.html [Accessed 10 October 2018].

Wivel, Anders, 2013a: "A Pace-Setter Out of Sync? Danish Foreign, Security and Defence Policy and the European Union" in Lee Miles & Andreas Wivel (eds.) *Denmark and the European Union*. London: Routledge.

Wivel, Anders, 2013b: "From Peacemaker to Warmonger? Explaining Denmark's Great Power Politics" in *Swiss Political Science Review*, 19:3, 298–321.

Wivel, Anders, 2014: "Still living in the Shadow of 1864? Danish Foreign Policy Doctrines and the Origins of Denmark's Pragmatic Activism" in Nanna Hvidt & Hans Mouritzen (eds.) *Danish Foreign Policy Yearbook 2014*. Copenhagen: Danish Institute for International Studies, 109–139.

Ydén, Karl, Joakim, Berndtsson & Magnus, Petersson, 2019: "Sweden and the Issue of NATO Membership: Exploring a Public Opinion Paradox" in *Defence Studies*, 19:1, 1–18. https://doi.org/10.1080/14702436.2019.1568192.

6 The decline of Nordic social democracy

Kjell Östberg

Social democracy's present crisis

Social democracy has generally been considered one of the most successful political forces of the 1900s. In particular, the 30 post-war "golden years" – the century's most prosperous period – have been closely associated with social democracy and seen as the standard bearer of modernization and the solidaric welfare society. The Nordic countries have taken an obvious leading position in this development and are viewed in a special light.[1] The Nordic model, building on the institutionalized, corporatist collaboration between capital, labour and state and long extolled as a successful compromise between a communist planned economy and free market capitalism, has close links to Nordic social democracy.

Twenty years ago, social democracy was Europe's leading force. Its leaders were Gerhard Schröder, Tony Blair, Lionel Jospin – and Nordic leaders Göran Persson, Paavo Lipponen, Jens Stoltenberg and Poul Nyrup Rasmussen. Twelve of the prime ministers who made up the Council of the European Union were Social Democrats, and the so-called Third Way promised to give answers to the challenges of a globalized society.[2]

The organizational home of Nordic social democracy has been the Social Democratic parties; working-class dominated mass parties with deep roots in trade unions and popular movements. Today, international social democracy is in deep crisis, ideologically, politically and organizationally. In recent years, Social Democrats have suffered dramatic defeats in a series of parliamentary elections. The German Social Democratic Party, which for long periods of time has been the most powerful in Europe, has been overshadowed by Angela Merkel since 2005. In the fall election of 2017, it lost 5 per cent of its votes, ending up at a record low of 20 per cent. In the European election of 2019, it sank to 15 per cent. The French socialists had a catastrophic election in 2017, getting a mere 6 per cent of the votes in the presidential election; their mandates in the national assembly dropped from 280 to 30. In the Netherlands, the party went from 25 per cent of the vote to 5.7 per cent. In Austria in 2016, the social-democratic presidential candidate received 11 per cent of the votes and was defeated in the first round.

DOI: 10.4324/9780429026690-6

Nordic social democracy, long viewed as the jewel in the crown of international social democracy, is no longer an exception.[3] It is true that Sweden, Finland and Denmark in the summer of 2019 have Social Democratic prime ministers, but the election support for all three is at a historic low. In Sweden, the Social Democratic Party has lost 40 per cent of its voters and two-thirds of its members over the last decades. To be able to lead a fragile coalition government together with the Green Party, the Swedish Social Democrats were forced to accept harsh political concessions to bourgeois parties, in the same way the Danish party did when it accepted much of the immigration policy of populist and xenophobic Dansk Folkeparti.

This chapter will, by focusing on Sweden, discuss the situation of Nordic social democracy against the backdrop of the developments of recent decades. Despite some clear distinctions between them, the parties will all be seen to share a special Nordic tradition. By way of introduction I will formulate two possible explanations for the development of international social democracy. The analysis will follow two red threads, one political and one organizational.

In the mid-20th century, to follow the political thread, social democracy formulated an objective that found more mass support than any other leftist idea: to offer citizens protection against the inequalities created by an unregulated market.[4] According to one thesis, social democracy's decline is associated with the fact that it has abandoned this policy.

Social democracy's ability to translate its ambition into reality, to follow the organizational thread, is also dependent on the party's historical ability to build strong movements with deep social anchors that offered significant potential for implementing its policy.[5] My thesis is that these movements are, at present, eroding. Underlying these questions is the role of social democracy in the democratization of society.

What is social democracy? An organizational definition

When researchers try to describe what social democracy is, they have sometimes made use of a "broad" definition and a "narrow" one. One might say that these correspond to the aforementioned political and organizational levels.[6]

The narrow definition is based on the movement and its history. Its point of departure describes parties that have their roots in the (industrial) working class but at the same time are part of a larger movement. Trade unions have often been a central part of this movement, as have a number of other citizen organizations. The pattern varies from nation to nation. For a century, the working class in Nordic countries has been among the world's best organized. At its peak, the Swedish Social Democratic Party had 1.23 million members, in a country with a population of 8 million. Three-fourths of the party members were affiliated through the trade-union movement. For a long time, between 80 and 90 per cent of workers were members of the LO, the Swedish Trade Union Confederation.

The party's Youth League was long dominated by the working class. There was a Women's League, and children were organized into the Young Eagles (Unga örnar). At its height, the so-called A-Press published some 30 social democratic daily newspapers. However, the social democratic family extended still further. Most important was the LO with more than 2 million members in the 1980s. The Workers' Educational Association (ABF) organized up to a hundred thousand study circles and lectures in a single year, and there were 1,000 people's houses around the country. Organizations such as the Swedish National Pensioners' Organization (PRO) and the Swedish Union of Tenants (Hyresgästföreningen), with hundreds of thousands of members, could also unquestionably be seen as part of the movement. Furthermore, an extensive cooperative consumer movement (KF) collaborated closely with the party as did the insurance company Folksam; HSB, a cooperative housing society; a film production company; advertising firms; and even a national chain of undertakers. Hundreds of thousands of members held positions in local politics.[7] People could spend their whole lives, from cradle to grave, within the social democratic movement.

Even though Social Democratic Party influence in other Nordic countries has not been equally hegemonic, particularly in Finland and Denmark, social democracy has often been described as the "people's movement party". The parties can be characterized as socially imbedded institutions that are bearers of a specific political culture with clear democratic functions. The parties succeeded in organizing, mobilizing and socializing large groups that had previously been without political influence, first and foremost the working class. They contributed actively in creating a collective identity that became the basis for political activity. But they also contained a broader democratic potential, exceeding parliamentary institutions. In these milieus political demands and projects could be discussed, formulated and implemented between elections and the limits of politics could be challenged and widened.

A political definition

The broad definition of social democracy is, meanwhile, used in an attempt to single out some central features of a common reformist ideology that Social Democrats tried to translate into political action. Several terms inspired by the English Social Democrat Anthony Crossland sum it up: democracy, mixed economy, welfare state, equality. To this we usually add further specifications: on the one hand, *corporatism*, the institutionalized cooperation between capital, labour and state; on the other *decommodification*, a welfare state limiting the influence of markets.[8]

After the Second World War there was a sort of symbiosis between capital's wish for mass production and the people's wish for mass democracy. The strength of the economy, it was argued, depended on the welfare of the wage labourers.[9] Economic development was driven by the 30 golden years of the post-war era, the longest and strongest boom in international capitalism.

The Fordist welfare state developed into something that, from different political standpoints, was seen as a legitimate means by which the state could intervene in developments on behalf of democracy, social security and efficient markets. This intervention was seen as the solution to problems posed by capitalism and industrial society.[10]

But in that case, what distinguished the Social Democrats from other liberal and bourgeois forces? The latter were willing to put up with greater government intervention in exchange for stimulated productivity and an infrastructure appropriate to the new conditions of production. For the Social Democrats, Keynes made it possible to merge the interests of the working class with the goal of national growth. Economic planning, full employment, expansion of the welfare state with a clear general building programme, redistribution of resources to compensate for inequalities created by the market, greater equality – all this could be located, at least as stated goals, within the framework of the reformist project.[11]

In the Nordic countries, this was social democracy's greatest moment. In Sweden, Denmark and Norway, the party was in government for most of the 1950s and the 1960s. The working class was larger than ever, and three-fourths of the workers voted for the Social Democrats. In Finland, the situation was different, but in the 1970s the party gained influence both politically and organizationally.

A clever reform policy, which gained international notoriety, also caused significant portions of the middle class to share the reformist ambitions of the party. These fitted nicely into basic capitalist structures. Real departures from the market economy were yet to take place. Left-wing critics could, with strident bitterness, ask if a class compromise during an economic boom was all social democracy could accomplish.

Around 1970, things took a new, more radical course, especially where the Swedish welfare state was concerned. This can, to a large degree, be explained by a forceful shift in the spirit of the time. In Sweden, as elsewhere, the radicalization of the 1960s began with a youth movement characterized by international solidarity, new Marxist thinking and the appearance of a series of new social movements. These groups often criticized the Social Democrats for being bureaucratic and ideologically shallow. Instead of flagging after 1968, radicalization deepened and spread to additional sections of society, reaching a climax in the mid-1970s. The new women's movement also affected traditional women's associations, while the environmental movement succeeded in putting a stop to the expansion of Swedish nuclear power.

The workers' movement was also greatly affected. A notorious mining strike in 1969/70 triggered a wave of wildcat strikes, showing that central parts of the Swedish working class had joined the radical movement. At the same time, the social democratic workers' movement had never been larger, stronger, or better organized. Forty years in power had given the party experience, competence and self-confidence.

The reforms undertaken during these years were the most extensive ever implemented in Sweden. The manner in which the welfare state was organized was also of great importance. There was a striking degree of movement away from market dependence and toward an increasingly decommodified system. Everything from schools to day care to healthcare and care of the elderly was financed, owned and run by the public sector. The public sector became the spearhead of the social transformation.[12]

The best indication of how far the workers' movement was willing to go is the fact that the LO, which traditionally belonged to the less radical part of the workers movement, endorsed the proposal to create so-called employee funds. This proposal, had it had been implemented, would have meant that the major part of today's Swedish business sector would have been owned by trade unions.[13] A similar development, if less dramatic, took place in the other Nordic nations.

The welfare regimes dominated by social democrats were far from unproblematic from a democratic point of view. They gained their power from structures organized by and for the masses. But they were led by bureaucracies. These were necessary if the parties were to function as mass organizations, in order to maintain ties to the masses – but also fulfilling their functions as parliamentary and corporate structures. As the years passed, and the workers' movement expanded its influence in various public agencies, critical voices were raised against a growing tendency towards autocracy.[14]

The end of the golden years: politics and market

As suddenly and unexpectedly as post-war social democracy had entered its golden age, suddenly – and unexpectedly, at least to many Social Democrats – the decline set in. The long-lasting post-war boom petered out and a series of crises took its place. They were structural crises associated with great changes taking place in global capitalism. They had serious consequences for the employment rate and standards-of-living, and also led to extensive ideological shifts, not least in perceptions of the welfare state. Keynesian economic policy no longer worked. Stagflation, a combination of the two worst alternatives, inflation and economic stagnation, became a new phenomenon.[15]

A central tenet of the perception developed by bourgeois actors was the idea that politics had gained too much influence in the market. The solution was to let loose capitalism's self-healing powers, to emphasize the primacy of the market rather than politics. Once again, global economic developments greatly influenced democracy. In this context, the broad-based mass democracy associated with the welfare states was seen as a particularly great problem. Such a view stood in direct contraposition to the ideal that had come to be associated with post-war social democracy.

The issue of the relationship between market and democracy has, during recent years, received much attention and has been critically examined by leading social scientists.[16] One focus concerns the gradual move away from redistributive mass democracy.

The welfare state has shrunk and, to a large degree, been integrated into the market economy. The efforts toward decommodification, which had been notable in Sweden, have diminished or ceased altogether. A series of social regulations introduced during the post-war years has been repealed, as was the case where labour laws are concerned, which has resulted in precarity, wage dumping and the suppression of union rights. Another factor is the effect of growing state debt. This has contributed to a situation in which less and less of the state's resources could be used for financing new reforms.

Politicians also made important decisions divesting themselves of power over economic policy. In Sweden, this development began in the second half of the 1980s, with symbolically significant decisions to deregulate banking and to allow the exchange rate to float. In 1990, it was decided that the goal of a maximum of 2 per cent inflation was to take priority over low unemployment. When the national bank became independent of political regulation in 1999, the politicians left crucial parts of macro-economic policy up to economists, often recruited from the banking sector.

Another sign of circumscribed space for extensive political intervention in the market economy is the trend towards increasing regulation of political activity. This is meant to tie the hands of supposedly irresponsible and meddlesome politicians. The Swedish budgetary legislation is an example of this. When Sweden joined the EU in 1994, many decisions were moved beyond the purview of democratically elected politicians.[17]

Challenges to reformist politics

Clearly all this hit social democracy hard. It was a challenge to their strongest card – Keynes and the attempts to regulate the market, using an expanding public sector as a lever for reducing market power. The crisis has also directly hit the movement's base, the industrial working class. This was, in part, a result of a significant decline in the number of industrial jobs; it was also in part because the common experience of shared struggle that had played such a large part in the creation of the workers' movement had become somewhat motheaten during the golden years. It was further diluted as the trade unions were weakened and increasingly attacked.

It was a rude awakening. In one country after another, the Social Democrats have been forced – or have chosen – to adapt to these new conditions, usually as a result of acute political and/or economic crises. Instead of nostalgically looking backwards towards the policies of a different era, European Social Democrats, initially inspired by New Labour, entered into a dialogue concerning the important issues of this new era, such as globalization, information technology and individualization. In order to participate in this discourse, they accepted its fundamental conditions: monetarism; a freer, deregulated market; a balanced budget; low inflation rather than less unemployment; diminished income transfer (that is, greater gaps in income); and privatization. The welfare system and the public sector had to be streamlined, slimmed down, shrunk but not abolished. Capitalism was to be streamlined and the Social Democrats were once again to be the bearers of modernism.[18]

At the same time, the EU was seen as an opportunity to implement part of the programme that seemed impossible to accomplish at the national level. However, the hopes raised by the social dimensions of various EU treaties, from Amsterdam and Lisbon to Gothenburg 2017, have only to a very small extent translated into binding agreements. It is a common perception among researchers that the crucial obstacle hampering the realization of a social Europe is built into the structures of the EU. As a matter of fact, according to the Greek social scientist Gerassimo Moschonas, the EU undermines three of the classic, fundamental features of social democracy: faith in the state, faith in the primacy of politics and a welfare policy related to the working class.[19]

In the introduction, social democracy was sketched out in general terms. This broad definition was an attempt to capture some central features of a common reformist ideology. It was based on the assumption that Social Democrats and capitalists shared an interest in creating the best possible conditions for economic growth including both state regulation and the welfare state. This, in turn, could take forms that allowed politics to limit the power of capital. Clearly the preconditions for this platform have been undermined. Today, to put it mildly, capital's wish to join in common projects with the workers' movement is minimal, and social democracy's programme for curbing the market is not particularly concrete. After the financial crisis of 2008–2009, the European Social Democrats were to pay the price for this.

The crisis of the 1930s had been the beginning of the social democrat success story. An important reason was that Social Democrats succeeded in offering a successful alternative to the economic liberalism of the time. The Social Democrats had no such alternative to propose in 2008. Clearly the EU has played an important role in this context.

The EU has gradually developed from being an economic-political union to being primarily a tool for the implementation of neo-liberal policy. In the Maastricht and Lisbon treaties, monetarism was codified as a foundation for EU economic policy. When the euro was introduced, most countries were formally bound to implement a monetary economic policy and far-reaching market reforms. With the arrival of the troika – which includes not only the ECB and the EU Commission but also the IMF, an authority over which the EU has no control at all – the final say in European politics has been placed with a hydra without formal judicial or political standing and beyond democratic oversight.[20]

The post-financial crisis policy, imposed by Brussels and Frankfurt with an iron hand, has torn Europe apart. The severe cutbacks forced upon those in the periphery of the monetary union have led to income gaps and social misery of a kind that had not been seen in Europe for decades – without succeeding to put an end to the economic turbulence that began with the financial crisis nearly ten years ago.

In none of these cases have the Social Democrats raised objections. On the contrary, all the leaders of the European social democracy have assented to this development. In many cases, indeed, they have been the ones to crack the whip over countries that could not sufficiently meet the demands of the market. As is well known, Greece is an especially pitiful example. The European Social Democrats have acted in like manner when it comes to the EU's other great failure, the refugee question. The refugee crisis, to a substantial extent a result of EU intervention in the Middle East – from the invasion of Iraq and onwards – is a humanitarian and social catastrophe. It is also an expression of a moral collapse on the part of the EU, which has not only refused to take responsibility for preventing further human suffering, but whose cynical behaviour has further contributed to strengthening the rapidly growing xenophobic forces in Europe.[21]

Social Democrats have simply abandoned what was, during their years of success, their strongest talking point – the prioritizing of political concerns over market interests. They have consciously refrained from proposing any kind of alternative policy and have actively contributed to tying their own hands. And they have made a virtue out of this necessity. By concentrating entirely on trying to win over the middle class, Social Democrats have tried to erase differences between the political blocs. In countries like Germany and Finland, Social Democrats have formed coalitions with bourgeois parties. In other countries, such as Spain and the Nordic countries, right- and left-wing parties take turns being in power, without either making significant political changes.[22]

A decreasing movement

But the narrow definition of social democracy has also been affected by the neoliberal turn. The space in which traditional mass parties – not least the Social Democrats – operate has changed fundamentally.[23] This neoliberal turn created a larger gap between citizens and their representatives. What had previously made the party members essential – the election of party leaders, financing activities, input into policy formation and implementation – is no longer necessary. Sponsorships and state subsidies have made membership fees less important to party budgets. Public surveys have replaced input from membership organizations. Media and PR consultants spread the parties' messages more effectively and directly than the members can.

Party leaders are being recruited from an increasingly narrow social circle, different from those of party members and voters. Party leadership has become professionalized and career paths become more and more alike from party to party. The loyalties of the leaders also increasingly lie with the political class. The tendency to form a new political class is reinforced by a general consensus on policy, or from there being, at least, little scope for a change of political course.[24] A fight for the middle has, of course, characterized politics for the last decades. Engagement in political parties has dwindled. Voter loyalty to a party has also weakened significantly, as it has become increasingly common to change party preferences between elections. The post-war mass parties have developed into professional "catch-all-parties".[25]

This development has had obvious socio-economic consequences. Those who first and foremost have lost confidence in politics and have distanced themselves most from political participation are those who are hardest hit by the growing social gaps that have developed in the wake of policy changes. The emergence of populist right-wing parties can, to a certain degree, be seen as a reaction to this development. This, of course, has particular consequences for the social-democratic mass parties.[26] Large sectors of what used to be social democracy's base of popular movements have weakened, even eroded.

There are several reasons for this. One has to do with changes in class structure and social composition. The size of the industrial working class that had formed the social base for social democracy has diminished greatly. This is due to the almost complete disappearance of the many factory towns – often built around one factory – in which social democracy had been hegemonic. Voting according to class, with two-thirds of the LO's members voting social democrat and most of the remainder voting for other left-wing parties, has dwindled in the new millennium. In the election of 2018 only 40 per cent of the LO's members voted for Social Democrats.

The social composition of the party's membership has changed. Workers are very much underrepresented in political congregations of party members, and even more as a proportion of voters. Their relative scarcity becomes more palpable the further up the hierarchy one goes. The proportion of "political broilers" – party leaders who have never been part of the workforce – has grown dramatically.[27]

For a long time, values based on the workers movement's egalitarian ideals were dominant, even within the right-leaning strata of the Social Democratic Party. As the party's recruitment base changed, the hold these values have on the party has loosened. This may also be in response to the party's policies becoming increasingly adapted to the market. When they leave politics, social-democratic top politicians continue their careers within the private sector, something that was unimaginable a few generations ago.

Another central factor is the weakening of the social movements from which social democracy sprang. Sweden's LO has lost half a million members over the last ten years. For the first time since the 1930s, the proportion of organized workers in the party is below 70 per cent. Social-democratic cooperatives have been commercialized, People's Houses to a large extent have been sold or shut down, and the social-democratic press has gone bankrupt.

All the parties' memberships have collapsed. A crucial change took place when the LO, in the early 1990s, abolished collective membership in the Social Democratic Party. Until then, the party had had more than 1.2 million members. In 1992, the number was still a quarter of a million. Today, the number has sunk to 90,000, and the average age of its members is 60. With the partial collapse of the social-democratic youth association (SSU), the party lost what had traditionally been its most important source of leadership recruits for different leadership levels. In Finland, social-democratic membership has shrunk by more than a half over a couple of decades, and the workers movement's "red machines" have suffered a severe loss of power.[28]

The EU's two major failures – first, its inability to hold the Union together socially and economically after the financial crisis of 2008 and, second, the migration question – led to the consequences mentioned previously. In Sweden, the Social Democrats have found themselves trapped within frameworks created by these two issues.

While the Swedish economy has grown in recent years, Sweden's economic and social gaps have increased more than in most OECD countries. The series of tax reforms that were implemented by social-democratic governments before 2006 and by the conservative government between 2006 and 2014 benefited primarily society's upper echelons.[29]

At the same time, the foundation of the solidaric welfare state has eroded. Social security increases, as well as increases in subsidies such as child benefits, have lagged behind inflation.[30] The continued privatization of care and education has undermined the political control of a previously public-run welfare apparatus and has created new fissures, especially within the educational sector. The return of a social democratic government in 2014 merely led to minor adjustments of this policy.

The most spectacular outcome of the 2014 election was the rise of the right-wing, populist Sweden Democrats. They succeeded in doubling their votes to 13 per cent, which meant that none of the traditional political blocs was able to form a majority. Unlike their sister parties in Denmark and Norway, the Sweden Democrats have their roots in openly racist and pro-Nazi organizations.[31] Since the late 1990s, a new generation of young leaders has successfully managed to build an effective party organization, starting from local strongholds in southern Sweden. Xenophobia and anti-immigration have been the party's main ideological platforms and the main reasons they have been able to win votes. With increasing parliamentary influence, the party has made efforts to downplay its more openly racist rhetoric, expelling some of its most enthusiastic representatives. The party has also lately tried to stress the national-conservative features of its programme, in imitation of similar trends in Poland and Hungary. The Sweden Democrats' economic and welfare policies, in fact, resembled those of the Conservative Party. For a long time there was a de facto agreement between the traditional parliamentary parties that the Sweden Democrats should be isolated; all were to refrain from involving them in negotiations. This was one reason why Sweden's right-wing parties accepted the red-green coalition in 2014.

The huge numbers of refugees in 2014 and 2015 – Sweden received 80,000 in 2014, 160,000 in 2015 – changed the political situation almost overnight. Before October 2015, there was broad consensus that Swedes were prepared to "open their hearts" – to quote former Conservative Party leader Fredrik Reinfeldt. Initially, only Sweden Democrats criticized the massive immigration. When the party started to grow and shortcomings in the organization of the reception of refugees became obvious, most leading parties, including the Social Democrats, agreed to put an immediate stop to the influx and re-adjust Swedish immigration policy to conform to the EU's minimum criteria. This change was more than a formal adaptation to new conditions. It was accompanied by a rise in anti-immigrant sentiments, anti-Muslim agitation and demands from the traditional parties – including the governing Social Democrats – for tougher legislation against what were claimed to be crimes committed by immigrants.[32]

Just before the election of 2018, the Social Democrats' policies took a turn to the right, not only concerning immigrant-related legislation but also in terms of attitudes towards law and order. In 2017, Sweden was hit by a terrorist attack. At the same time, attention was drawn to a series of fatal shootings that became associated with criminal gangs of immigrant background. Now the Sweden Democrats were no longer alone in demanding more severe penalties for crimes that were alleged to be linked to immigration.

Clearly one reason for the change in policy was the threat posed to both Social Democrats and Conservatives by the Sweden Democrats. As could have been predicted by looking at experiences in other countries, the change of tac-tics did not work. The Sweden Democrats continued to grow at the expense of these two parties in particular. The result of the most recent election in 2018 confirms this conclusion. The Social Democrats' votes fell to 28 per cent, their lowest result since the introduction of universal suffrage in 1921. The Conservatives lost even more, falling by 3.5 per cent. Meanwhile, the Sweden Democrats reached 17.5 per cent, an increase of almost 5 per cent.

A majority of the working class is not voting left any more. Thirty years ago 70 per cent of the working class voted Social Democrat (and another 10 per cent Communist). In 2014, 53 per cent of the members of the LO voted Social Democrat; in 2018, only 40 per cent (and another 10 per cent for the Left party).[33] The outcome changed the political landscape in several regards. The result led to a stalemate between the two traditional political blocs. To be able to take over the government, the Conservatives together with the Christian Democrats were prepared to pass the demarcation line that until then existed between the traditional political parties and the xenophobic right-wing popu-lists and form a government with a de facto support of the Sweden Democrats.

This attempt was blocked by the two liberal parties who broke up a long-time alliance with the Conservatives and decided to support a social democratic government. The support was not without costs. The Social Democrats had to accept a political agreement forcing the government to carry out a robust neoliberal programme, including increased privatization of the welfare sector, lower taxes for the wealthy and higher rents for tenants. Perhaps most contro-versial was an agreement that threatened to weaken the influence of the trade unions.

The political development of the last few decades has been discussed mainly from a top-down perspective. Few of the reforms and political course changes implemented by the Social Democrat leaders were instituted due to pressure from below. On the contrary, each departure from traditional social-democratic policy has met with extensive protests. When the first step was taken toward a neoliberal policy focused on deregulation in the 1980s, the result was the so-called War of the Roses, with the LO leading the critical charge. A majority of the social-democratic electorate voted against joining the EU in the 1990s. The new, individual-based and market-oriented pension system that was implemented at the same time failed to get support from any of the social-democratic party congresses that discussed the issue. In spite of its great efforts, the social-democratic government did not manage to push through Sweden's inclusion in the European Monetary Union (EMU) after the turn of the 21st century. Over the last years, opposition to further erosion of the public sector has primarily focused on education, healthcare and other care activities and the emergence of large, for-profit organizations within the tax-funded welfare sector.[34]

The outcome of the 2018 elections has created further protests among trade unions and rank-and-file members of the party. However, this has not had any deeper impact on the party leadership. It is obvious that the Swedish Social Democrats have chosen to continue the road also taken by several other European Social Democrats. There are few reasons to believe that the results would be different in Sweden.

In Finland, the Social Democrats after the 2019 parliamentary elections were able to form a centre-left government. The party made some gains and became the largest, but only got 17.7 per cent of the vote and came in just slightly ahead of the right populist True Finns. The result is far below the vote levels of what the party used to attract a couple of decades ago.

The combination of the strengthening positions of the global market economy, the declining space for political decisions, the decreasing ambitions of the social democratic leadership and the gradual vanishing of the movement that once constituted the democratic core of the social democratic movement has led to a fundamentally altered condition for political mobilization and actions and, by extension, for the future of democracy.

Notes

1 Misgeld, Molin & Åmark 1992.
2 Waele, Escalona & Vieira 2013, 17–18.
3 Östberg 2012, 205.
4 Schmidt 2016, 251–252.
5 Östberg 2012, 207–208.
6 Moschonas 2002, 64.
7 Östberg 2018, 403–244.
8 Esping-Andersen 1990.
9 Crouch 2004.
10 Judt 2012, 324–359.
11 Sejersted 2011.
12 Östberg 2017, 36–37.
13 Östberg 2012.

14 Östberg 2008, 406–407.
15 Notermans 2000.
16 Mair 2013.
17 Östberg 2012, 222.
18 Andersson 2010.
19 Moschonas 2009.
20 Ibid.
21 Barlai 2017.
22 Schmidt 2016.
23 Mair 2013.
24 Hermansson 2010, Bergström & Järliden Bergström 2013, Östberg 2014.
25 This process was discussed in a theme issue of *Statsvetenskaplig tidskrift* in 2010. *Statsvetenskaplig tidskrift*, 112:2.
26 Östberg 2018, 418–419.
27 Garsten, Rothstein & Svallfors 2015.
28 Östberg 2018, 412–418.
29 OECD 2019.
30 Lindbom 2011.
31 Jungar 2017.
32 Dahlstedt & Neergaard 2016.
33 VALU 2018.
34 Östberg 2017, 62.

References

Andersson, Jenny, 2010: *The Library and the Workshop. Social Democracy and Capital in an Age of Knowledge*. Stanford: Stanford University Press.

Barlai, Melani, Fähnrich, Birte, Griessler, Christina & Rhomberg, Markus (eds.) 2017: *The Migrant Crisis. European Perspectives and National Discourses*. Zürich: Lit Verlag.

Bergström, Jeanette & Järliden Bergström, Åsa-Pia, 2013: *Makteliten. Klyftorna består*. Stockholm: LO.

Crouch, Colin, 2004: *Post-Democracy*. Cambridge: Polity Press.

Dahlstedt, Magnus & Neergaard, Anders, 2016: "Crisis of Solidarity? Changing Welfare and Migration Regimes in Sweden" in *Critical Sociology*, 45:1, 121–135.

Esping-Andersen, Gøsta, 1990: *The Three Worlds of Welfare Capitalism*. Cambridge: Polity Press.

Garsten, Christina, Rothstein, Bo & Svallfors, Stefan, 2015: *Makt utan mandat. De policyprofessionella i svensk politik*. Stockholm: Dialogos.

Hermansson, Jörgen & Beckman, Ludvig, 2010: *Regeringsmakten i Sverige. Ett experiment i parlamentarism 1917–2009*. Stockholm: SNS förlag.

Judt, Tony, 2012: *Postwar: A History of Europe Since 1945*. New York: Penguin Press.

Jungar, Ann-Cathrine, 2017: "Continuity and Convergence: Populism in Scandinavia" in Peter Nedergaard & Anders Wivel (eds.) *The Routledge Handbook of Scandinavian Politics*. London: Routledge.

Klaus Misgeld, Karl Molin & Klas Åmark (eds.) 1992: *Creating Social Democracy. A Century of the Social Democratic Labor Party in Sweden*. University Park: Pennsylvania State University Press.

Lindbom, Anders, 2011: *Systemskifte? den nya svenska välfärdspolitiken*. 1. uppl. Lund: Studentlitteratur.

Mair, Peter, 2013: *Ruling the Void: The Hollowing of Western Democracy*. London: Verso.

Moschonas, Gerassimos, 2002: *In the Name of Social Democracy. The Great Transformation, 1945 to the Present.* London: Verso.

Moschonas, Gerassimos, 2009: "Reformism in a 'Conservative' System. The European Union and Social Democratic Identity" in John Callaghan (ed.) *In Search of Social Democracy: Responses to Crisis and Modernisation.* Manchester: Manchester University Press.

Notermans, Ton, 2000: "Europeanization and the Crisis of Scandinavian Social Democracy" in Robert Geyer, Christine Ingebritsen & Jonathon Wayne Moses (eds.) *Globalization, Europeanization and the End of Scandinavian Social Democracy?* London: Palgrave Macmillan, 23–44.

OECD, 2019: *OECD Economic Surveys: Sweden 2019.* Paris: OECD Publishing. https://doi.org/10.1787/c510039b-en.

Östberg, Kjell, 2008: "Sweden and the Long'1968'. Break or Continuity?" in *Scandinavian Journal of History*, 33:4, 339–352.

Östberg, Kjell, 2012: "Swedish Social Democracy after the Cold War. Whatever Happened to the Movement?" in Ingo Schmidt & Bryan Evans (eds.) *Social Democracy after the Cold War.* Edmonton, AB: AU Press.

Östberg, Kjell, 2014: "Politikens ändrade villkor" [Changing Conditions of Politics] in Anders Ivarsson Westerberg et al. (eds.) *Det långa 1990-talet. När Sverige förändrades.* Umeå: Boréa.

Östberg, Kjell, 2017: "Den solidariska välfärdsstaten och förändringarna i den politiska dagordningen" in Torsten Kjellgren (ed.) *När skiftet äger rum. Vad händer när den politiska dagordningen ändras.* Stockholm: Tankesmedjan Tiden.

Östberg, Kjell, 2018: "När ingen längre kokar kaffet" in Henrik Meinander, Petri Karonen & Kjell Östberg (eds.) *Demokratins drivkrafter. Kontext och särdrag i Sveriges och Finlands demokratier 1890–2020.* Stockholm: Appell förlag.

Schmidt, Ingo (ed.) 2016: *The Three Worlds of Social Democracy: A Global View.* London: Pluto Press.

Sejersted, Francis, 2011: *The Age of Social Democracy: Norway and Sweden in the Twentieth Century.* Princeton, NJ: Princeton University Press.

Statsvetenskaplig tidskrift, 2010, 112:2.

VALU. SVT:s valundersökning 2018, 2018: www.svt.se/omoss/media/filer_public/5c/17/5c17fc91-31c4-4e0a-a17f-b42318edf4a4/valuresultat_riksdagsval_pk_2018_vagda_0912.pdf.

Waele, Jean-Michel de, Escalona, Fabien & Vieira, Mathieu (eds.) 2013. *The Palgrave Handbook of Social Democracy in the European Union.* Basingstoke: Palgrave Macmillan.

7 Conservatives at the crossroads

Cooperating or resisting extremism and populism?

Torbjörn Nilsson

Right-wing populist parties have gained support and been successful in national elections in the past few decades, including in the formerly stable Nordic party systems. This is challenging not only for the traditional democratic right, but for the Nordic Model as well. Established in the authoritarian 1930s and helped by the successful concept "the People's Home", the model now fights for its survival. In this chapter, I will compare how the conservative parties reacted to threats from right-wing extremism in the 1930s and in the first decades of the new millennium, analyzing how they balanced strategies of cooperation and resistance and how they tried to modify or isolate the new parties.

During the 1930s, the Nordic democracies were threatened by the rise of National Socialism and various other forms of right-wing extremism. Most vulnerable were the conservative parties and especially their youth leagues, where many members listened to the siren calls from Italy and Germany.

Without discussing the concept of populism in this chapter, "right-wing populist" will be used for today's parties that also can be described as "national conservative" or "extreme right" That does not prevent elements of social radicalism – at least favoring the ethnic majority.

The tensions between liberal-conservative parties and right-wing populists are rarely studied in a historical perspective. My intention is to compare the past few decades with the 1930s when parts of the conservative parties became pro-Nazi. Undoubtedly, the older opponents differed from today's parties that are trying to become legitimate parts of the system. However, the problem of the democratic right has been the same: distance themselves from the new parties or cooperate with them? By taking-off in the 1930s and ending in contemporary politics, this study at the same time illuminates conservative strategies and the difficulties for the Nordic Model.

Varying strategies have been used in the Nordic countries, and there are differences between the strategies of today and those of the 1930s. How crucial to the decision-making process were the overall differences between the 1930s and post-2000, for example the emergence and strengthening of the Nordic model in the intervening period, and what is the role of differences in national political cultures?

DOI: 10.4324/9780429026690-7

I will first discuss the conservative parties and the right-wing extremism in each country in the 1930s.[1] How strong were the new challengers? This is followed by a corresponding discussion about the past few decades. Then the two periods can be compared to explore similarities and differences. Are there elements of a Nordic conservative consensus in how to act against extreme parties to the right? If so, did or does any country tend to diverge from the pattern, either in the 1930s or today? The wider question of how vulnerable the Nordic model is to the progress of the extreme parties will also be discussed.

Conservatism and right-wing extremism in the 1930s

The established conservative parties

Denmark. The Conservative People's Party (Konservative Folkeparti, KF) was established in 1915, succeeding the more aristocratic and traditional Right Party (Høyre).[2] The new party mixed liberal and conservative positions, mostly supporting the liberal farmers' Left party (Venstre). With John Christmas Møller as chairman, a more independent course was introduced in 1929. Christmas Møller, supported by the Conservative Youth League (Konservative Ungdom, KU), gained new sympathizers by stressing social and national matters. The membership of the KU doubled from 1932 to 1936, from 15,000 to 30,000. The KF gathered 60,000 members, so the Youth League was an important part of the conservative family, especially in the election campaigns. In the elections in 1932–1938, the conservatives reached 17–19 percent of the vote.

Norway. The Right party (Høyre) was already established in 1884, much earlier than other Nordic conservative parties.[3] The main opponent, the Left Party (Venstre), became the leading party, but when the Workers party (Arbeiderpartiet, Ap) made progress in 1906 after the change in voting rights, the Right party for a time succeeded in becoming the strongest party in the parliament (Stortinget). In the 1930s, the conservatives upheld second place, securing 21–29 percent in the elections. The joint election campaign with a former splinter group from the Left Party, the Liberal Left (Frisinnade Venstre), ended in 1931. Instead, that small group with its slightly misleading name began to cooperate with various extreme right-wing groups. However, very few of the conservatives were attracted by the extreme right.

Sweden. The Conservative party (Allmänna Valmansförbundet, AVF) was hesitatingly formed in 1904, still opposing a modern party system, full democracy and parliamentary rule (and, until 1913, female members).[4] After the democratic breakthrough in 1917–1921, the party managed to keep an important position, gaining 18–24 percent in the elections to the parliament (Riksdag) during the years 1932–1940. The Swedish National Youth League (Sveriges nationella ungdomsförbund, SNU) significantly increased its membership, reaching approximately 40,000 in 1932. However, the political initiative had from that point on been taken over by the Social Democrats.

After the conservative Prime Minister Arvid Lindman's resignation in 1930, no conservative politician would participate in a government until 1976 (except in the 1939–1945 wartime coalition government).

Finland. The National Coalition Party (Kansallinen kokoomus/Nationella samlingspartiet) has its roots in two parties from Finland's period as part of the Russian empire: the moderate Old Finns and to a certain degree in the Young Finns, who had advocated more active resistance against russification.[5] After independence in 1917 and the subsequent civil war, the Coalition Party worked energetically for a monarchical constitution. However, due to Germany's collapse, a republic with a strong presidency was established. The Coalition Party had sympathizers in many of the extreme right organizations, especially the Lapua Movement (Lapporörelsen) and the Academic Karelian Society (Akademisk-Karelska Sällskapet, AKS). An agreement with the new right-wing, fascist-oriented party IKL (Fosterländska folkrörelsen), was reached in 1933. However, the result of the election was a disappointment and the contacts with IKL became increasingly frosty. In 1939, the Coalition Party politically dissociated itself from IKL. It is also important to mention the conservative minority in the Swedish People's Party (Svenska folkpartiet, Sfp) that tried to establish a coalition with sympathizers to the Lapua Movement.

The challengers

In general, the various extreme right-wings groups were not serious challengers to mainstream conservatism in the Nordic countries, except in Finland. The Danish National Socialist Workers Party reached 1.8 percent in the 1938 election; in Sweden the results were even worse, 1–1.5 percent (depending how different groups are classified); and in Norway Vidkun Quisling's National Coalition (Nasjonal samling, NS), founded in 1933, did not manage more than 1.8 and 2.0 percent in 1933 and 1936, respectively.

The real problem in Denmark, Norway and Sweden turned out to be their youth organizations. National Socialism, fascism and other extremism was to a high degree a youth protest against traditional society and the political system, attracting teenagers, male and female, with collective and often violent actions. Disregarding differences in other aspects, in this sense there are similarities with the radical protests in the 1960s.

Denmark. "Young Denmark" had been a widespread concept already in the middle of the 19th century.[6] It was neither a movement nor a program. Instead, it has been seen as an intellectual conception, interpreting how to be truly Danish. The core of "Young Denmark" was an anti-liberal, organic nationalism. To be Danish was incompatible with being liberal. Both young conservatives and the old school of classical conservatism were influenced by this way of thinking. However, the party chairman Christmas Møller was too nationalistic to accept the new German vision and too much of a democrat to brush aside the parliamentary system.

Anyway, the antagonism between anti-system and system-friendly conservatism increased. As a result of profound contacts with SNU, the program of Danish Youth League was a nearly complete translation of the Swedish program. In a couple of years, the tension among the three Nordic conservative organizations would lead to splits and a new conservative Nordic landscape.

Norway. Despite the fiasco for NS in the elections, right-wing extremists could cause problem – recruiting younger people and attacking the old conservative traditional politics. Besides NS there were other right-wing organizations that failed for different reasons. Fridtjof Nansen, the well-known explorer, scientist and Nobel Peace Prize laureate, died in 1930. No one could replace him, although not a fascist, as potential leader of a broad authoritarian movement.[7]

Sweden. SNU had been formed in 1915, and soon became very important during the conservative election campaigns, although not formally belonging to the party organization. Young persons in academia, especially in Uppsala and Lund, were attracted by conservative ideas. From the beginning of the 1930s, SNU became more critical of the democratic political system. Some members had never really accepted the democratic breakthrough in 1917–1921. Also other extreme positions were integrated, like economic collectivism and the wearing of party uniforms. The SNU increasingly distanced itself from the main party. The right-wing in the SNU was stronger than in Norway. A clear majority in SNU supported the turn to the right and the positive view of the regimes in Italy and Germany. In 1934, the chairman of the Conservative Party Arvid Lindman broke contact with SNU. Afterward, this can be interpreted as a crucial moment for the development of democratic conservatism in Sweden.[8]

Finland. In contrast with the other countries, the young conservatives in Finland were less attracted by National Socialism and other extreme views than the older generation that had been formed by the civil war in 1918. However, as a whole, right-wing extremism was stronger in Finland than in the Nordic region generally. The Academic Karelian Society had sympathizers among Finnish-speaking students and intellectuals, and the Lapua Movement was established by landowners in Ostrobothnia, although dissolved after the violent actions in 1932 (in Mäntsälä). Instead, the dominant party became IKL, uniting various extreme groups and participating in the election of 1933, allied with the conservatives in the National Coalition Party. Right-wing tendencies could also be found in Sfp, in the faction that worked for an alliance with groups to the right in order to neutralize the communists.[9]

The decisive moments: agreement or confrontation?

The developments in Denmark, Norway and Sweden were quite similar. Opposition groups among the young conservatives were defeated by the established party machines. In that struggle, the contributions of esteemed conservative leaders like John Christmas Møller (Denmark), Carl-Joachim Hambro (Norway) and Arvid Lindman (Sweden) were decisive. They despised pro-fascist and antidemocratic ideas and strongly defended a conservative tradition that integrated democracy and nationalism.[10]

In Denmark, the party opposition was defeated. The Conservative Youth League kept its loyalty to the main party, and in the end leading opponents had to leave the party. In Norway, some district organizations participated in electoral alliances with NS, for example in Bergen where the two parties worked together in 1933. However, the party executive strongly criticized all such collaboration and afterward succeeded in isolating the NS and other groups. In that way, the Conservative party also saved the contributions from the industry that for a couple of years had been divided between the party and right-wing groups.[11]

SNU was too strong to be defeated. When Lindman cut ties with SNU in 1934, only a minority among the members stayed loyal to him. The majority continued as an independent party, soon changing its name to Sweden's National League (Sveriges Nationella Förbund, SNF). However, the youthful character of the organization should not be overestimated. Many members had stayed in the SNU, notwithstanding of age, in the late 1920s when SNU increasingly became an oppositional right-wing organization. Lindman had to build a new Youth League (Ungsvenskarna). In some places, Conservatives and SNU/SNF formed electoral alliances (Norrköping, Helsingborg, 1934–1938). However, SNF never succeeded in building a strong party. The three members of the parliament that belonged to the organization were not re-elected in 1936. Therefore, SNF became merely one of several pro-Nazi parties, competing for the small group of Swedish Nazi sympathizers.

In Finland, the election in 1933 was a disappointment for the conservatives. The alliance with IKL gathered fewer votes than the Conservatives alone had reached in 1930. The adaption of some of the more extreme positions was strongly criticized and the electoral alliance was not repeated. However, IKL held its position and participated in the government 1941–1944. IKL was characterized by anticommunism, corporatism, ultra-national foreign policy, pure Finnishness, an ideal of the strong leader ("the Führer principle"), and a traditional Christian faith. The best election result was 8.3 percent in 1936. During the Continuation War (1941–1944), pro-German views were widespread and not limited to IKL.[12]

As already mentioned, Denmark, Norway and Sweden share a common history in the 1930s, at least regarding the relations between the Conservative parties and various extremist challengers. Opponents in the Youth Leagues were tolerated to a certain degree. But when they went too far and tried to establish themselves as more independent factions, repressive measures were taken. KU in Denmark was overtaken by more loyal elements, and soon the opposition was defeated. Norway shares the same history, and Swedish SNU was excluded from the conservative family. In all three countries, the party leaders were decisive in the struggle against fascist and other extreme elements. Such groups outside the parties were seldom considered coalition partners, and local agreements were strongly counteracted by the central executives. However, some exceptions could be found in Sweden, where some local arrangements were upheld for a couple of years, not causing much trouble.

In the middle of the 1930s, the conservative parties had triumphed. By linking democracy to old national traditions, fascism and National Socialism were characterized as un-national and incompatible with Nordic traditions.[13] The antifascist contributions by the conservatives have seldom been taken into account when analyzing the failure of right-wing extremism in the Nordic countries. However, the efforts by John Christmas Møller, Carl-Joachim Hambro and Arvid Lindman motivate their places in a hypothetic Nordic pantheon of antifascism. Of course, they should share their glory with liberals as well as the Social democrats, succeeding to stabilize society with broad coalition agreements that weakened extreme elements in the farmer's organizations and generally turned depression and unemployment to stability and belief in the future.

Finland has a very different story. The civil war, the communist activities in the 1920s in order to start a revolution and the frontier to the Soviet Union polarized society. Strong authoritarian groups combatted the communist threat with legal as well as illegal methods. Liberal politicians, especially in the Swedish People's Party, and Social Democrats engaged themselves against the fascist threat, but that never became a consensus view in Finland. The Conservative party accepted some of the new, extreme ideas, but the formal alliance with IKL turned out to be a failure. The reactions from conservative statesmen like Juho Kusti Paasikivi (president 1946–1956) against the right-wing violence were important, but did not more than temporarily deter extremist strength.

Conservatism and right-wing populism in the past few decades

Needless to say, the political landscape in the Nordic countries has changed in a profound way since the 1930s. In particular, the welfare state and other elements of the Nordic model have been decisive for these changes. The former conservative parties are more liberal than before, not least on economic issues. At the same time, differences between conservatives and liberals to some extent have been blurred. Also the relative strength inside the nonsocialist bloc (if there is such a thing) has been changed. In Denmark, the Conservative Party nowadays is a small party, receiving only 6.6 percent of the votes in the 2019 election. Instead the Left Party, liberal/right-wing, has succeeded the Conservatives as the leading party on the established right. However, both parties will be discussed, and similarities as well as differences observed.

Nowadays, the challengers of the right in the Nordic countries are of a different kind, in comparison with those 60 or 70 years ago. They have been developing outside the traditional conservative parties, outside the traditional party system as such. Generally, they have appeared as protest or populist parties, critical to elements of the Nordic model such as taxes, bureaucracy, centralization and progressive values. An anti-immigrant policy was integrated after some time and has grown to be the most important issue for these parties.[14] However, characterizing the new parties as fascist is misleading. Populism, authoritarian, national conservative, or sometimes ultraliberal are more useful concepts. An exception is the early phase of the Swedish Democrats (Sverigedemokraterna, SD) with its roots in the Nazi milieu in the 1980s, ideas that nowadays have disappeared.[15] On the other hand, the party has been relatively successful in connecting its policy to the concept of the People's Home.

In contrast to the crisis in the 1930s, losing party organizations to the challengers has not been the main problem for the conservatives. Instead, the debate has circled around the strategies of the parties. Which relationships were desired or feasible? Could the new parties be reliable as supporters of the government, or maybe even as a part of coalition governments?

The established conservative parties

Denmark. In the 1990s, various groups had been criticizing the liberal Danish immigrant policy. Some restrictions were instituted and when a center-right coalition of the Liberal and Conservative parties assumed power in the 2001 elections, a radical change of policy was introduced. The government was supported by the populist, anti-immigration, nationalist Danish People's Party (Dansk Folkeparti, DF) that had been successful in the election. The new government policy was popular domestically, but criticized by international observers. In the cultural-ideological field, the left paradigm was seriously challenged by right-wing conservatives, especially by the priest Sören Krarup. His Christian thinking is built on nationalism. By stressing the struggle between Christianity and Marxism, Christianity and science, and not least, Christianity and Islam, he rejects the modern homage to the individual. For some years Krarup was a member of parliament (Folketinget) for the Danish People's Party. His aggressive attitude to Islam became very influential for the changing of Danish immigration policy after the year 2000.[16]

The Liberal-Conservative coalition, under Prime Minister Anders Fogh Rasmussen (V), was re-elected in 2005 and 2007. When Rasmussen was appointed secretary-general of NATO in 2009, he was replaced by the foreign minister, Lars Løkke Rasmussen. The restrictive immigration policy was not changed, not during the Social Democratic government 2011–2015, and not during the following governments dominated by Venstre. In the 2015 election, it reached 19.5 percent and the coalition partners, the Conservatives and the Liberal Alliance, each received 3.4 and 7.5 percent of the vote respectively. DF received 21.1 percent, but stayed outside the government. Although Venstre kept its share in the 2019 election, the Social Democrats took over, supported by RV and two left parties in Folketinget.

Norway. During the past few decades, the Conservative Party has usually been second in parliamentary strength after the social democrats in the Workers Party (Ap). However, the left has been weakened, and in 2013, Conservative leader Erna Solberg became the first prime minister from her party since

1990. She headed a minority coalition government with the Progress Party (Fremskrittspartiet, FrP). The small parties in the middle (the liberal Left Party and the Christian People's Party) chose not to join the new government, but agreed to support it in return for some softening of the restrictive immigration policy that for a long time had been the core issue for the Progress Party. After the 2017 election, the coalition managed to stay in power, although with a narrower margin. In 2018, the Left Party accepted a place in the government and in 2019 the Christian People's Party after a trying party debate followed suite.

Sweden. The liberal-conservative Moderate Party (former Right party) turned to the middle after a disappointing election in 2002. The new party chairman Fredrik Reinfeldt abandoned many of the party's former core issues: a strong defense, reforms of the laws inspired by social democratic values in the labor market and cuts in the welfare system. He also proclaimed a more open and generous immigration policy and at the same time clearly dissociated the party from the anti-immigration Swedish Democrats.[17] No collaboration whatsoever with SD was possible during his reign. Reinfeldt was prime minister from 2006 to 2014, jointly with three smaller center-right parties. After the 2014 election, he resigned. The successor, Anna Kinberg Batra, did not succeed in formulating a trustworthy political line when the refugee crisis turned many traditional ideas upside down.[18] To avoid uncontrolled immigration to Sweden, the Social Democratic-led government instituted a much more restricted policy, transforming the unique Swedish immigrant policy to one resembling a mainstream European one. In October 2017, Kinberg Batra was replaced by Ulf Kristersson. In the election of 2018, the Moderate Party was one of the losers, although with 19.8 percent of the votes it was still the strongest party in the non-socialist Alliance and second after the Social Democrats with 28.3 percent of the vote.

Kristersson had accepted being prime minister with the help of SD, although at the same time refusing further cooperation with the party. However, his candidacy was voted down and instead the Social democratic chairman Stefan Löfvén reestablished the coalition with the Green party. This time with the support of the Liberal and the Center parties from the former non-socialist alliance. The new collaboration was possible due to the weakening of the Social democrats and the clear opposition of the two middle parties supporting a government in any way dependent on SD. The relations with SD are still controversial in the Moderate party, although the role as opposition party might bring the two parties closer to each other.

Finland. The conservatives in the National Coalition Party have kept its position as one of the leading Finnish parties. It has participated in most of the governments during the last 20 years, sometimes also filling the post of prime minister (Holkeri, Katainen, Stubb). One explanation is the Finnish tradition of majority governments, including parties of the right, center and left at the same time. In the 2015 election, the conservatives reached 18.2 percent, a decline from the 20.4 percent of votes they had in the previous election.

The decrease continued in 2019, 17.0 percent. For the first time since 2007, the Conservatives were left out from the coalition government.

The challengers

Denmark. In the sensational 1973 election, the Progress Party (Fremskridtspartiet) became one of five newcomers to the parliament. The controversial lawyer Mogens Glistrup had established it just one year before. Until his death in 2008, Glistrup would remain a spectacular figure in political debates, most of the time as leader of his anti-bureaucratic and soon also anti-immigration party. Muslims were a particular target for Glistrup's scoffing. However, in later years he could not lead his party due to his imprisonment for tax evasion. At that time, the party had lost its seats in the parliament.[19] In 1995, Pia Kjærsgaard and other leading members broke with the party and established the Danish People's Party (Dansk Folkeparti, DF). They wanted to form a party that would be more acceptable to other parties, and using that strategy, influence society, especially immigration policy. In the 2001 election, DF came in third with 12 percent of the votes. The governments led by the Left Party (V) were dependent on DF from 2001 to 2011. Agreements between the government and DF were made before the proposals were sent to parliament. Therefore, the nationalistic policy of DF regarding immigration as well as the EU became official Danish policy. The strong hostility toward a multicultural society has continued to be the core element in DF's ideology during the chairmanship of Kristian Thulesen Dahl, who succeeded Pia Kjærsgaard in 2012.[20] In the 2015 election, DF reached its all-time high with 21.1 percent of the vote, surpassed only by the Social Democrats (26.3 percent). In 15–20 years, DF had an important position in Danish politics, without participating in the government. This situation ended abruptly after the 2019 election when the Social Democrats took over. DF lost more than half of its voters, reaching only 8.7 percent.

Norway. In 1973, an equivalent to Glistrup's party was established, named a bit narcissistically the Anders Lange Party (Anders Langes parti). The platform was also reminiscent of Glistrup's creation: lower taxes, less bureaucracy and a populist critique of the authorities in general. It immediately won four mandates in parliament. However, Lange died in 1974 and after choosing a new party name, the Progress Party, and the appointment of Carl I. Hagen as chairman in 1978, the party became an important force in the Norwegian party system.[21] Sometimes the economic policy was characterized by neo-liberalism, sometimes by promises of welfare reform, especially for the elderly. More continuity can be found in the immigration issues, where the party established a strong resistance against refugees, especially those from outside Europe. Hagen led the party for 30 years and left behind an established party with extensive experience in national politics and local government. However, it was his successor Siv Jensen that led the Progress Party in a coalition with the Conservatives after the 2013 election (16.3 percent), a coalition that stayed in power after the 2017 election (FrP 15.1 percent), still dependent on the smaller parties in the middle. Jensen has been minister of finance in the coalition government since it was established in 2013.[22]

Sweden. The first successful populist party in Sweden, New Democracy (Ny demokrati, ND), was established in 1991. Thanks to widespread media coverage, well-known party leaders and a growing dissatisfaction with Swedish immigration policy, ND received 5.7 percent of the vote in the 1991 election, enough to get 25 seats in the parliament. Disagreements inside the party and controversial statements made by some of the leading politicians broke down the party and it eventually fell out of parliament already in the 1994 election. No agreements between the center-right government and ND had been made, but secret negotiations between the Moderate party secretary and ND helped the government when ND fell apart.[23]

The Swedish Democrats have formed a more stable party, although every now and then the party is hit by accusations of crime or political scandals concerning racist or other remarks by leading members. SD's roots are in neo-Nazi groups from 25 to 30 years ago. Although quite successful in forming a more modest and democratic image ("national conservative" or "social conservative"), its history still casts a shadow over the party. It managed to get 5.7 percent of the vote in the 2010 election, a share that was increased to 12.9 percent in 2014. In the 2018 election, the increase continued to 17.5 percent, which, however, was not as much as predicted.

In June 2002, all seven parties in the parliament (except SD) had published a joint proclamation against the SD. Neither the center-right government of Reinfeldt nor the Social Democratic/Green Party government of Löfvén made agreements or negotiated with SD when in power. Even informal political talks with SD representatives were out of the question.

However, due to the strengthening of the Swedish Democrats in 2014, claims for a different attitude to the challengers were raised in the Moderate Party. Particularly at the local level, various forms of cooperation have been established. In the build-up to the 2018 election, this current became more outspoken, at least outside the party-executive. The party chairman Ulf Kristersson explained that his first option was an Alliance government. However, he also declared that he would accept SD's passive support in order to form a government containing Moderates and Christian Democrats. After the election in 2018, a couple of local alliances were formed by the Moderate Party and SD, defying the official party line.

Finland. The first populist party in the Nordic countries, the Smallholder Party (Småbondepartiet), was established in 1959 as a splinter group of the Agrarian Party. (Cf. Emilia Palonen's article in the book). Its leader, Veikko Vennamo, had participated in the government of Urho Kekkonen, later the president of Finland, but became critical of the situation for the Karelian people who had come to Finland after the War of Continuation. In 1966, the name was changed to the Countryside Party (Landsbygdspartiet/Suomen Maaseudun Puolue, SMP).

The 1970 election was successful, 10.5 percent of the vote. Thereafter, strong internal divisions, defections and other trouble weakened the party. In the 1980s, it made a strong comeback with Pekka Vennamo, son of the founder, as party leader. The party participated in various governments but again faced trouble when it went bankrupt in 1995. The party was formally dissolved in 2003. The Finns, formerly the True Finns (Sannfinländarna/ Perussuomalaiset), was founded in 1995 as a successor party, but did not reach the parliament before 2003. With his anti–EU, anti–NATO and anti–immigration policy in 2011, Timo Soini led the party to a sensational result of 19 percent of the vote (in 2007, it was 4.05 percent). After the 2015 election, the party became a member of the government with Soini as foreign minister. When Soini resigned in 2017, the far-reaching opponent of immigration, Jussi Hallo-aho, was elected chairman. Some of his opponents broke with the party and founded a separate, more moderate, group in the Riksdag. However, the hard line faction clearly won the competition. In the 2019 election it gained 17.0 percent – but was not invited to the government – while the moderate group only got 1.0 percent.

The decisive moments: agreement or confrontation?

The four main challengers discussed here demonstrate differences as well as similarities. Three of them have a long history, founded in the 1950s (Finland) or the 1970s (Denmark and Norway), if original party creations are included. Sweden is an exception, also in view of the first challenger in the 1990s, New Democracy. The backgrounds differ. When the populist, anti-bureaucratic character was obvious in the Danish and Norwegian parties, for a long time carrying synonymous names, the anti-urban trait was more important in Finland. SD in Sweden has a completely different background due to its roots in the neo-Nazi tradition.

The strategies of the Nordic conservative parties display clear differences. One side is represented by Finland, Denmark and Norway. The challengers have been handled much in the same way as other parties in the political system. The Countryside Party participated in the Finnish government in 1966. However, the party was not so controversial, compared to the two forms of the Progress Party from the 1980s. Immigration was a non-issue in Finland during the Cold War. However, while never a governmental party, DF's supporting position strongly influenced (some might say decided) the government's policy on immigration, which is the best example of political success for the challengers. Participation in the Norwegian (2013–) and Finnish (2015–2019) governments marks still more progress for right-wing populist members of the Nordic party family.

The coalitions and other forms of collaboration do not seem to have caused any sharp tensions in the conservative parties. Also the Danish Social Democrats have accepted most of the new policy. In a nearly desperate bid to win back its former voters, they have declared a general agreement with DF on many political issues. It seems that the conservatives have easily accepted the restrictive immigration policies that have come from the right. If so, the price to pay for letting in the populists has been moderate.

The exception is, of course, Sweden. SD has been seen as not "house-trained", a spiteful remark about DF made by Poul Nyrup Rasmussen, Danish prime minister (1993–2001) and leader of the Social Democrats. Accepting the party in government is unthinkable in political debate in traditional parties, at least on the national level. Agreements with or formal dependency on SD for gaining a majority are also hard to accept. In the past few years, any hint of consideration for the party's existence has been criticized from either the right or the left. The difficulties concerning SD have made it difficult for the Moderate party to establish a clear policy on the relationship. The election in 2018 did not give enough mandates to build a non-socialist government based solely on the four parties in the Alliance. The Moderate party did not succeed in persuading the middle parties to support Kristersson as prime minister if this required the votes from SD. The party had to stay in opposition after four months of complicated party negotiations.

From internal threats to external help?

By comparing the 1930s with the beginning of the 2000s, some differences have been brought forth. The new parties are much stronger than the old fascists groups. It was, of course, easier to isolate small parties in the 1930s than treating today's parties representing 15 to 25 percent of the voters the same way.

The threat that stands before the conservative parties today is external, not like the internal threat in the 1930s when certain elements of the movements stepped out of the democratic field. The modern right-wing populist parties do not share a common conservative or liberal-conservative idea of society and politics, although tax reductions, anti-bureaucracy and anti-socialism often are common platform points. By adapting their policy, the conservatives could use the new situation as a strategic weapon, transforming the general threat to a threat against the left, thereby challenging aspects of the Nordic Model that they consider too socialist.

The party conflicts in the 1930s resulted in a polarization between conservatism and extremism. Today, some important ideas have been accepted by conservatives, and to some degree also by center and left parties. Most obvious is the new agenda regarding immigration policies. With the exception of Sweden, the new parties have been accepted in government (Norway, Finland), or as an auxiliary force for the government, with strong influence on governmental policy (Denmark). By getting votes from the working class, populist parties have diminished the left's chances to lead the government. On condition that the conservative parties continue to collaborate with them, strong center-right or right governments could be the Nordic model in the future. However, the development is not determined. For the moment, in September 2019, three of the Nordic Prime Ministers are social democrats. The result of the Swedish 2018 election was a Social Democratic-Green government, supported by the liberal parties. The four-party alliance that governed Sweden 2006–2014 has broken down. Instead, the government has promised to carry through important liberal demands. The Swedish Democrats won't hold the balance of power as long as the left – liberal collaboration remains.

Of course, there are other options: the populist parties may start falling apart when some of their ideas have been realized. Or, perhaps, they will sharpen their demands and try to change more fundamental elements of society. Based upon the situation in Denmark, one should not leave aside the possibility of a social democratic – populist alliance. Both parties are dependent on support from the lower classes and consequently share some social demands. Today the challenging parties work inside the system, determined to change as much as they can in the area of "multiculturalism", a concept that besides "liberalism" can be seen as their main enemy.

The extreme right parties in the 1930s, influenced by fascism and National Socialism, turned their backs on the relatively young democracy. Today, the new parties have accepted the democratic system, although leading politicians and ordinary members, not only in Sweden, have shown negligence concerning human rights.

Maybe the democratic system is not at stake today, but populist parties have learnt to use democratic means to change society. That could be fateful, not only for the Nordic model – what still remains of it – but for all forms of rational, human and tolerant systems. Democracy is after all mainly a system for majority decisions, not a guarantee for tolerance and human reforms.

Notes

1 Uglevik Larsen 1990, 240–263, Girvin 1994, ch. 3.
2 Egander Skov 2013, Jensen 1983, Winther 1966.
3 Seip 1987, 45–104, Kaartvedt 1984.
4 Nilsson 2004, 130–175.
5 Waltå 1993, Schauman & Lilius 1992, Djupsund & Karvonen 1984, Bonsdorff 1947, 1984, 1994, Andreen 1980.
6 Egander Skov 2013, 51–55.
7 Norland 1973, 152–155, Danielsen 1984, 448–451.
8 SNU and the conflict with the mother party, Nilsson 2002, 77–107, Wärenstam 1965.
9 Nilsson 2017, 157–182, Schauman & Lilius 1992, 49–71.
10 Nilsson 2002, 77–107.
11 Danielsen 1984, 196–202, Brevig & de Figueiredo 2002.
12 The extreme right, especially in the Church: Murtorinne 1982, 272–278. IKL in government: Karvonen 2006, 129–152, Meinander 2009, 2013, Djupsund & Karvonen 1984, 18.
13 Nilsson 2002.
14 Hellström & Lodenius 2016, 19–25.
15 Jungar 2017, Lindroth 2016, Jungar & Jupskås 2014.
16 Denmark: Schjørring & Jannerp 2018, Friisberg 2016.
17 Nilsson 2004, 295–298, Nilsson 2018, 72–80.
18 Sweden: Jylhä, Rydgren & Strimling 2018, Oja 2015, Kiiskinen & Saveljeff 2010. On Kinberg Batra, *Svenska Dagbladet* 30 October 2016, 22 September 2017, 6 February 2018.

19 Nielsen 2013.
20 Schjørring & Jannerp 2018, Friisberg 2016.
21 Larsen 2015, 23–90, 90–98 (Conclusions).
22 Norway: Todal Jenssen 2017, Bjerkem 2016, Simonnes 2013, Jupskås 2013, Notaker 2013.
23 Nilsson 2004, 284–289.

References

Andreen, Per G., 1980: *Finland i brännpunkten. Mars 1940–juni 1941*. Stockholm: Lindfors.

Bjerkem, Johan, 2016: "The Norwegian Progress Party" in *European View*, 15:2, 233–243.

Bonsdorff, Göran von, 1947: *Samlingspartiet. Skrifter utgivna av Nyliberala studentförbundet 10*. Helsingfors: Söderström.

Bonsdorff, Göran von, 1984: *Svenska folkpartiet II. Från självständighet till Lappo 1917–1929*. Helsingfors: Svenska folkpartiet/Schildt.

Bonsdorff, Göran von, 1994: *Svenska folkpartiet IV, Krigstid och återuppbyggnad 1939–1956*. Helsingfors: Svenska folkpartiet, 81–128.

Brevig, Hans Olaf & de Figueiredo, Ivo, 2002: *Den norske fascismen: Nasjonal samling 1933–1940*. Oslo: Pax.

Danielsen, Rolf, 1984: *Høyres historie 2. Borgerlig oppdemmingspolitikk 1918–1940*. Oslo: Cappelen.

Djupsund, Göran & Karvonen, Lauri, 1984: *Fascismen i Finland. Högerextremismens förankring hos väljarkåren 1929–1939*. Åbo: Akademi.

Egander Skov, Christian, 2013: *Konservatismens ideologiske udvikling i mellemkrigstiden*. Århus: Universitetsforlag.

Friisberg, Claus, 2016: *Dansk demokrati og politik 1973–2015 i en verden i hastig forandring*. Varde: Vestjysk Kulturforlag.

Girvin, Brian, 1994: *The Right in the Twentieth Century: Conservatism and Democracy*. London: Pinter.

Hellström, Anders & Lodenius, Anna-Lena, 2016: *Invandring, mediebilder och radikala högerpopulistiska partier i Norden*. Rapport 2016:6. Stockholm: Delegationen för Migrationsstudier.

Jensen, Erik, 1983: *Mellem demokrati og fascisme. Traek af Konservativ Ungdoms organisatoriske og ideologiske nyorientering 1932–34*. Odense: Universitetsforlag.

Jungar, Ann-Cathrine, 2017: *Populism i Norden. Från marginalen mot den politiska mittfåran*. Helsingfors: Tankesmedjan Agenda.

Jungar, Ann-Cathrine & Jupskås, Anders Ravik, 2014: "Populist Radical Right Parties in the Nordic Region: A New and Distinct Party Family?" in *Scandinavian Political Studies*, 37:3, 215–238.

Jupskås, Anders Ravik, 2013: "Mangfoldig mobilisering og velsmurt valgkampsmaskineri. Fremskrittspartiet under 40 år" in *Nytt Norsk Tidsskrift*, 30:1, 5–17. Oslo.

Jylhä, Kirsti, Rydgren, Jens & Strimling, Pontus, 2018: *Sverigedemokraternas väljare: vilka är de, var kommer de ifrån och vart är de på väg?* Stockholm: Institutet för framtidsstudier.

Kaartvedt, Alf, 1984: *Drømmen om borgerlig samling. Høyres historie I*. Oslo: Cappelen.

Karvonen, Lauri, 2006: "I stormens öga" in Siv Sandberg (ed.) *Svenska folkpartiet genom 100 år*. Helsingfors: Schildt.

Kiiskinen, Jenny & Saveljeff, Sigrid, 2010: *Att dansa i otakt med väljarna. Socialdemokraternas och Moderaternas strategiska bemötande av Sverigedemokraterna*. Malmö: Högskolan.

Larsen, Fredrik Bøyesen, 2015: *Til høyre for Høyre – Hvordan Høyre forholdt seg til Fremskrittspartiet 1973–1990*. Master's thesis. Oslo: Universitetet.

Lindroth, Bengt, 2016: *Väljarnas hämnd. Populism och nationalism i Norden.* Stockholm: Carlssons.

Meinander, Henrik, 2009: *Finland 1944: krig, samhälle, känslolandskap.* Helsingfors: Söderström.

Meinander, Henrik, 2013: *A History of Finland.* Oxford: Oxford University Press.

Murtorinne, Eino, 1982: "Den finska kyrkans inställning till högerradikala rörelser och till den tyska kyrkokampen under 1930 – talet" in Ingun Montgomery & Stein Uglevik Larsen (eds.) *Kirken, krigen og krisen.* Bergen: Universitetsforlaget, 259–265.

Nielsen, Flemming Christian, 2013: *Glistrup. En biografi om en anarkist.* København: Gyldendal.

Nilsson, Torbjörn, 2002: "Med historien som ledstjärna – Högern och demokratin 1904–1940" in *Scandia*, 68:1, 77–107. Lund.

Nilsson, Torbjörn, 2004: *Mellan arv och utopi. Moderata vägval under hundra år, 1904–2004.* Stockholm: Santérus.

Nilsson, Torbjörn, 2017: "Gustav II Adolf: Finlandssvenskarnas härförare under 1900 – talet" in *Personhistorisk Tidskrift*, 113:2. Stockholm.

Nilsson, Torbjörn, 2018: "Högerns vägskäl – med eller mot ytterhögern?" in *Fortid*, 15:1, 72–80. Oslo.

Norland, Andreas, 1973: *Hårde tider. Fedrelandslaget i norsk politikk.* Oslo: Dreyers Forlag.

Notaker, Hallvard, 2013: "Høyres ideologiske spenninger" in *Norsk Statsvitenskapelig Tidsskrift*, 29:2, 111–119.

Oja, Simon, 2015: *Sverigedemokraternas budskap 2005–2010: en retorisk studie av ett annorlunda parti.* Örebro: Universitet.

Schauman, Henrik & Lilius, Patrik, 1992: *Svenska folkpartiet III:1–2, 1930–1939.* Helsingfors: Svenska folkpartiet.

Schjørring, Esben & Jannerp, Michael, 2018: *Værdikæmperne, slaget om danskernes sjæl: VK – regeringerne 2001–2011.* København: Gyldendal.

Seip, Jens Arup, 1987: "Høyre gjennom hundre år 1880–1980" in *To linjer i norsk historie.* Oslo: Universitetsforlaget, 45–104.

Simonnes, Kamilla, 2013: "I stjålne klær? En analyse av endringer i Høyres, Arbeiderpartiets og Fremskrittspartiets innvandrings – og integreringspolitikk fra 1985 til 2009" in *Norsk statsvitenskapelig tidsskrift*, 29:2, 144–158.

Todal Jenssen, Anders, 2017: "Norsk høyrepopulisme ved veis ende? Fremskrittspartiets gjenfødelse som høyreparti" in *Nytt Norsk Tidsskrift*, 34:3, 230–242. Oslo.

Uglevik Larsen, Stein, 1990: "Conservatives and Fascists in the Nordic Countries. Norway, Sweden, Denmark and Finland, 1918–1945" in Martin Blinkhorn (ed.) *Fascists and Conservatives. The Radical Right and the Establishment in 20th-Century Europe.* London: Routledge, 240–263.

Waltå, Göran O:son, 1993: *Poet Under Black Banners. The Case of Örnulf Tigerstedt and Extreme Right-Wing Swedish Literature in Finland 1918–1944.* Uppsala: Universitet.

Wärenstam, Eric, 1965: *Sveriges nationella ungdomsförbund och högern 1928–1934.* Uppsala: Universitet.

Winther, Jens, 1966: "Det Konservative folkepartis historie i et halvt århundrede: 1915–1965" in *2. Fra krise til krig 1929–1940.* København: Nyt Nordisk Forlag.

8 Nordic populists as hegemony challengers

Emilia Palonen and Liv Sunnercrantz

This chapter explores populism in Nordic countries where there is a long tradition of heterogeneous, populist parties with incompatible political ideologies transforming over decades. Between the anti-communism, anti-elitism, anti-tax-paying, anti-immigration, and agrarian features, little unites these parties. We argue, however, that at least one feature fits: they were all hegemony challengers. This may indeed be a feature of populism as such following the theory of Ernesto Laclau.[1] Hence, a particular study of Nordic populists would reveal hegemony as the particular shared social imaginary horizon in each of the Nordic countries. The chapter develops a Laclaudian understanding of populism and provides a chronological narrative of the populist parties in Finland, Denmark, Norway, and Sweden, and a discussion of hegemony as it emerges and transforms over time. Populist parties have emerged as a reaction to dominant thinking in each of the political contexts. Our study explores alternatives or points of contestation regarding key issues emerging during the studied period, most notably relations to the Soviet Union and market deregulation as well as migration and welfare chauvinism.

There are several ways to approach populism, and Nordic populist parties have been studied from ideational perspectives as well as a party family.[2] Our post-Gramscian approach to populism includes an idea of hegemony and counter-hegemony: populist parties are challengers of the status quo who seek to offer a new alternative vision, question, or basis of argumentation for a political 'us'.[3] Two features mark Nordic politics: the strong position of Social Democratic parties and a culture of consensus in coalition governments, as stressed by David Arter.[4] Despite the potential for conflict, overriding social democratic ideals enabled a political culture where issues were settled through compromise. Low levels of conflict over the basic rules of the political process and the exercise of power combined with a high degree of concertation in public-policy creation characterise this culture of consensus.[5] While we do not study consensus politics per se, we do investigate how hegemony challengers have fertilised and used the powerful myth of a social democratic consensus (although in Finland this position has been occupied by the Centre Party).[6] The emergence of populist parties has to be analysed with view to this initial setup. The most prominent feature that we find when exploring Nordic populist

DOI: 10.4324/9780429026690-8

parties is that they challenge a status quo that transforms over time. Studying populist parties in the Nordic countries not only reveals – often unsuccessful – alternatives these parties pursued in politics, but what they sought to challenge. Until now, the research on populist parties has focused on their ideology or style, or on voters, in line with dominant trends such as the ideational approach in political science.[7] While we recognise similar topoi as ideological contents like some previous researchers,[8] our contribution lies in the logic of populism. The logic is not reducible to a tool kit, although it might benefit from it or the hybrid media system.[9] Furthermore, adding to research on the radical right, we insist that anti-immigration is not synonymous with populism, although it may entangle it.[10]

From our perspective, populism is not an ideology or substance. It is debatable whether it is ideological at all.[11] Political theorists Ernesto Laclau and Chantal Mouffe conceptualise populism as a logic of articulation. Accordingly, the substance of populism is a particular logic or form.[12] It is composed of three ingredients – an abstract content of identification: 'us'; a dichotomy with 'them'; and an element that grips the audience – through passion or an emotional attachment. We have simplified this into the following formula: *Populism* $= us^{affect1} + frontier^{affect2}$. Rather than looking for particular ideas tied to populism, the formula allows us to analyse populism as a performative process. In a given rhetorical situation, the 'us' category of identification can be substituted with various forms of universal and inclusive forms of 'us' that can take up the representation of the political subject that integrates disparate identities and demands into temporary unity. Who gets defined as 'them' or what lies beyond the 'frontier' also constitutes 'us'. As hegemony is constituted through otherness, in this study we demonstrate that it is not constant. Over time and through different political actors and movements, the contents of 'us' and the 'frontier', alongside the affects and emotions that heighten them, transform.[13]

Theoretically, generating a typology between populist parties, we divide populist parties into mainstream and fringe populist parties. Mainstream populists seek to take over political space as a whole from a central position in the core of politics, as one of the larger and often traditional parties. Fringe populist parties and movements would challenge all the other parties from a supposed outside. They seek a position outside the core: they operationalise the 'frontier' against the other established parties. It is typically fringe populist parties we discuss in this case of Nordic countries. If they attempt to advance their positions, fringe-leaning parties face challenges such as how to claim a mainstream position and successfully represent the whole political field. To further develop the understanding of populism, we argue that populism is not constant but emerges in moments. Here, we analyse particular 'populist' movements and political parties and recognise the form of populism in their rhetoric and articulations.[14] The study of Nordic populism stresses the particularity of Nordic countries as a particular region in Europe with its historical contingencies.

The Nordic countries differ from the Latin American countries Laclau studied. There, the populist party were the parties of the people rather than the elites, and workers rather than industries dominated the spectrum. Yet their power became institutionalised while the political spectrum polarised. They became mainstream populist parties. Laclau sought to theorise on a more universal level taking examples from the Russian Revolution and the workers' movements: populism has to do with mobilisation and becoming, temporarily, the people.[15]

Our analysis shows that the emergence of Nordic populist parties has, in particular, to do with a reaction against the hegemony, which could also manifest itself as overall shared imaginary rather than particular policy positions. Hegemonic discourses or imaginaries with overarching concepts in the Nordic countries could, of course, be seen from different angles, just as Götz and Markund with their colleagues have demonstrated studying Nordic 'openness'.[16] Consensus may also refer to the lack of diversity of opinions; contesting it would mean calling for plurality over polarisation or single-vision.[17] From the discourse-theoretical perspective hegemony is something that becomes consensual, unquestioned and sedimented through political practice. It is distinct from a set of practices of power sharing and policy-making – although these may play a part in the process of hegemonisation. Furthermore, we analyse how populist parties have contested sedimented and institutionalised practices (including consensual decision-making) in the Nordic countries.

In her work from the 1990s and the 2000s, Chantal Mouffe, Laclau's partner and co-theorist, drew on experiences from her native Belgium and another country she frequents, Austria. In Austria, the emergence of the Freedom Party (FPÖ) with their leader Jörg Haider was a reaction from the regions against the consensus of the Viennese elites; rather than a racist vote as it had been interpreted by those elites, she explained.[18] Similar regionalism can be found in our Nordic set. We see it in the Finnish Rural Party (Suomen maaseudun puolue, SMP) – as the name would indicate,[19] and in the Danish national election of 2015, when the Danish People's Party's (Danske Folkeparti) success in rural areas can be attributed partly to their representation of the rural region against the capital.[20] Likewise, the emergence of the Finns Party (Perussuomalaiset) and the Sweden Democrats (Sverigedemokraterna) has been reduced to racism and anti-immigration of the left-behinds of global capitalism, rather than an anti-elitist and anti-consensus response. Although, as Ainur Elmgren has highlighted in her chapter, the anti-consensus Finns Party has indeed called for openness challenging the Finnish elites on their own ground, just as they perform consensus as closure.[21] Digging deeper into the background of populists in Finland and Sweden, we see that racism and anti-elitism intertwine, but there are also other features to challenge and contest. In neighbouring Norway and Denmark, populist parties have focused first and foremost on issues of taxation. While nation-centrism and a focus on the people were present in those parties, it was only in the late 1980s that they adopted an anti-immigration discourse.[22]

Consensus culture in politics is present in all Nordic countries but political systems differ. In countries like Sweden, left-right coalition ('bloc') voting has divided the political spectrum and often results in minority governments.[23] Forming a government had been rather simple until 2014, as Kjell Östberg discusses in his chapter. By contrast, in Finland, elections give voice to individual candidates on party lists, and can cause bottom-up ordering of policy-makers. Yet, there had traditionally – until the elections in 2015 – been three major parties, two of whom had invariably been in a majority coalition government: the former agrarian Centre Party (Centre), the Social Democratic Party (SDP) and the right-wing bourgeois National Coalition Party (NC). Until 2015, this praxis had generated some continuity in politics. For example, none of the governments have sought to radically alter the Finnish welfare state, and this continuity has been praised as a key feature of Finnish democracy. In both Finland and Sweden, the strong status of trade unions and the praxis of negotiation between the employers' and workers' representatives has further sedimented consensus. It has been difficult for a single political party to challenge the power of three large parties and corporatism[24] and demonstrate whether these are society-wide phenomena, as the SMP and Green Party examples show.[25]

Nordic populist parties have experienced waves of popularity related to different grievances and protests: from elitism in the 1960s to taxes in the 1970s–1980s and to immigration from the 1980s and onward. A common thread through these cases is the welfare state as a point of contestation.[26] The exact rise, decline and forms of expression of populist challengers in the Nordic countries vary within the social context. While populist parties emerged in Denmark, Norway, and Finland in the late 1970s; Sweden only caught up with this trend many years later.[27] Researchers have questioned why it took such a long time for a markedly populist party to gain ground in Sweden, in comparison to neighbouring countries.[28] We explain how, in the early 1990s, Swedish New Democracy (Ny Demokrati) utilised the populist appeal of the broader neoliberal movement, which lacked direct parliamentary representation at the time.[29] In this study, we particularly look at the hegemony challengers' emergence in Sweden.

1950s–1960s and onwards: emergence of the Finnish rural party

The Finns Party's predecessor Finnish Rural Party (SMP) emerged as an anti-Soviet, anti-bourgeoisie, anti-elitist front as a response to both the Agrarian Party's affluent small-holder tradition, and the socialism of both anti-Soviet and pro-Soviet left. Founder Veikko Vennamo was elected to the Finnish Parliament Eduskunta in the 1940s and 1950s representing the predecessor of the Agrarian Party (Maalaisliitto) today's Centre Party. He deviated from the mainstream of the party backing Urho Kekkonen, and ultimately joined a new party of the small-holders that was formed into the SMP. The new party gained from Vennamo's networks as he was leader of the office administering the post-war settlement to the current borders of Finland, Eastern Karelia. They established themselves mostly in rural communities and suburbs, but were set apart from the locals due to their dialect, and rural communities were not always inclusive. Vennamo drew support from the party from his formal employment where he took care of settling the Finnish refugee population after the war. Attention to the marginalised and excluded, and the anti-elitist rhetoric defending the 'ordinary people' was characteristic to the Finnish Rural Party, with Vennamo as the key orator.

Among the Finnish parties, the SMP sought to provide an alternative to the Agrarian Party led by Urho Kekkonen, who eventually became the longest serving president of Finland and was a keen negotiator with the Soviets from the 1950s. The anti-Soviet stance was a useful tool for Vennamo.[30] It would resonate among the settlers, contest the hegemony of Kekkonen's Agrarian Party, and challenge so-called Finlandisation, which was becoming a norm. Much of the polarisation was personified between Vennamo and Kekkonen. In the historical landslide elections of 1970, SMP went from 1 to 10 per cent of the vote and demanded a non-communist government. The Agrarians went back and forth in negotiations with Vennamo: some in the Agrarian Party thought that if SMP stayed in opposition they would become too strong. The Communists (SKP) protested the possibility of SMP in the government, which fuelled Kekkonen's worries that SMP could play the card of old parties being against them.[31]

Leading contemporary analysts, such as Risto Sänkiaho, locate the SMP between the Left and Right and discuss urbanisation and the use of recognisable and strong rhetoric.[32] As Aarni Virtanen demonstrates in his thorough study, Vennamo and his movement were branded systematically as fascist in *Kansan Uutiset*, the newspaper of the party of the left SKDL and communist SKP. Kekkonen also supported this view, and this kind of branded *cordon sanitaire* made it difficult for the political right to collaborate and associate with them. Virtanen's analysis brings to the fore the combination of clear non-socialism, anti-communism, and the left-wing policies and right-wing conservative values in Vennamo's SMP. The party sought to represent the rural poor (the *lumpenproletariat*, one could say). Moving to the suburbs and the increasing fluidity of party identification enabled support for a relatively new party.[33] Around the 1970 elections, the SKP informed East German comrades about the fascist SMP and the reactionary National Coalition Party (Kokoomus). Non-socialist coalition building, however, always failed. The party put their faith in SDP's Mauno Koivisto and got a victory from their arch opponent Kekkonen when Koivisto (once the favourite of Kekkonen) was chosen as his successor.[34]

In terms of socio-economic groups, the SMP's main competition was from the further left-wing parties, and here anti-communism set them apart. It also challenged the Agrarian Party, which could be seen as too liberal or representing the more well-off people. In 1970 Kokoomus leaned to the left in their social policy. Both Kokoomus and SMP were eager to get into government. This meant collaborating with the Agrarian-Centre Party. For both of them, challenging the status quo *did not target* the welfare state, but objected to the power of the KGB and Soviet influence in Finnish internal affairs. While under

Holkeri's leadership, Kokoomus was moving towards collaborating with Kek-konen's Centre, and when he saw a change, Vennamo began to collaborate. On many occasions in the 1960s and the 1970s, parliamentarism was more visible in contrast to Kekkonen's presidentialism (in a semi-presidential system): SMP was an extremely active party in the parliament, and what Vennamo and his colleagues were getting in trouble for was speaking too much in parliament. So the label of populist anti-parliamentarism does not hold here. Koivisto finally launched the long legislative process of increasing the power of the parliament over the president.

Although this negative branding about the emergence of a fascist movement existed, it is difficult to argue that the roots of the Finns Party would have been outright nationalist-xenophobic,[35] in part because immigration was not a salient issue or policy field.[36] None of the other Nordic countries witnessed anti-immigration right-wing populism from the start.

1970s: emergence of right-wing tax populism in Denmark and Norway

Right-wing populist parties emerged in both Denmark and Norway in the 1970s. Their points of contestation were bureaucracy and tax burdens, which they framed as unjust and out of proportion. These parties' discourses were initially not concentrated around the national people, nor did they mobilise an active opposition against immigration until the 1980s.

Lawyer Mogens Glistrup became known to the Danish public when he, on live television in 1971, revealed that he, lawfully, circumvented all income tax – thus exposing the shortcomings of the existing system. A year later, he founded the Danish Progress Party (Fremskridtspartiet) in the fight against income taxes, bureaucracy, and the extent of the public sector. The Progress Party burst into parliament as the second-largest party in the 'landslide election' of 1973 and remained in parliament until 1999. Although Glistrup's rhetoric was somewhat xenophobic from the outset, the anti-immigrant message became more promi-nent in the 1980s.[37]

The precursor to the Norwegian Progress Party is usually traced to the estab-lishment of Anders Lange's Party for a Strong Reduction in Taxes, Duties and Public Intervention (Anders Langes Parti til sterk nedsettelse av skatter, avgifter og offentlige inngrep; ALP) in 1973. Lange, inspired by Glistrup, opposed bureaucracy, state capitalism, and socialism. He was a strong supporter of neo-liberalism. When Carl I. Hagen took leadership in 1978, the ALP became the Progress Party (Fremskrittspartiet) and quickly gained swing-vote leverage.[38]

Nordic countries experienced similar discussions even though populists were not everywhere in the forefront of liberalising economy. Meanwhile, in Finland, the Korpilahti meeting brought 'consensus': it mainstreamed the idea of shrinking the role of state companies, sustained criticism of the welfare state and highlighted the need to improve competitiveness. Meeting up in a hotel in a remote part of Espoo, a city neighbouring Helsinki, was enough to mainstream several ideas among the political elites. The move from the welfare state system towards the right happened within the existing political parties and their mutual balance[39] rather than through a new or anti-welfare statist populist actor.

1980s: towards xenophobia from mainstreaming neoliberalism

During the 1980s, the Danish Progress Party was torn by internal factions. Glistrup served time for tax evasion and upon his release in 1985 railed against Muslims as a threat to Danish identity. In the meantime, the party experienced their worst election results ever in 1984 under Pia Kjærsgaard, who officially became party leader in the mid-1980s. While the Danish Progress Party had started out as a populist-libertarian project, they took a more xenophobic turn around this point.[40] Simultaneously, radical right-wing protest groups and racist subcultures gained ground in Denmark during the 1980s (inspired by radical right-wing projects in Germany and France). The Left suffered from visionary disorientation and demobilisation as the Eastern Bloc started to collapse. Radical right-wing rhetoric gained disproportionate media attention. The Progress party used the momentary attention on the EU and immigration as well as the consensus among mainstream parties (who nevertheless failed to hegemonise the public discourse) to take up a contesting, alternative position.[41]

Swedish business interpreted the employee funds in 1983 as a breach from the old consensus between labour and capital.[42] Business, think tanks, and intellectuals joined forces as Swedish neoliberals mobilised against contemporary hegemony: the social-democratic welfare state.[43] They challenged the status quo and offered a new alternative vision and basis of argumentation centred on private and individual (rather than public and collective) ownership. Swedish neoliberalism took shape around the specific purpose to question the consensual norm in politics. As expressed in a neoliberal analysis of the failing bourgeoisie political project (in 1987):

> The more [the bourgeoisie] disliked the class struggle – the more they advocated consensus. There is of course a limit where consensus is no longer possible. But psychological mechanisms easily work in a way that one who is inclined to confrontation compromise less than one who wants consensus. . . . They want so much consensus and wish to see as little political struggle that they gradually accept adaptation to an all the more politicised climate. They defend the proposals that they opposed yesterday as a desperate chance not to have to give in to further demands.[44]

Neoliberal intellectuals sought to challenge the social democratic hegemony and renegotiate what was 'politically impossible'.[45] Through historical analyses of the 'privilege to define problems',[46] they concluded that the labour movement had successfully defined the political agenda for the 20th century.

Inspired by the Left, they developed strategies to redefine the social field as divided between two opposing camps: the individual (the underdog, the people, the 'common man', the oppressed masses, 'you', 'I', 'we', and so on) versus the welfare state (the establishment, power, social democracy, and so on). At the core of the neoliberal discourse that followed was not literally 'the people' but other inclusive forms of 'us' such as 'individuals' or 'human beings'. Paradoxically, the 'individual' which functioned as addressee, subject, *and* appeal was a collective, universal individual everyone could identify with.[47] Neoliberalism represented the interest of 'ordinary people' while parliamentary parties (i.e. 'the establishment') represented the special interests of one class or another, it was argued.[48] Much like the first wave of populism in Norway and Denmark, Swedish neoliberal populists protested against the strong taxation of the welfare state system. In Finland, there were only minor parties emerging with the (neo)liberal economic agenda with anti-Sovietism – for example, Liberal party, Georg C. Ehrnrooth's SPK/POP.[49] These have been largely marginalised and disappeared in contemporary Finnish politics.[50]

The Valco corruption scandal in 1979 gave a boost to the SMP who contested the rich elites and their abuse of power. A non-socialist government was not formed, but four years later, the party, hyperactive in their parliamentary activities, made it to the government in 1983. They were brought into a coalition with the SDP and Centre Party – but they saw themselves in the middle of the two.[51] It may have been better to keep them in parliament rather than active in opposition. Their support shrunk by 1987, but they joined the first post-war government led by the National Coalition and SDP. The 1980s were economically a boom in Finland with opening regulations and the 'casino economy' (*kasinotalous*) overheating the market. The anti-elitist party being a junior partner in government led to criticism in terms of the metaphors of the softness of the seats of ministerial Audi's and accusations of party ministers having spines made of banknotes – the latter trope, *seteliselkärankainen*, actually signified a split in the party. In the 1980s, the bases for corporatisation of state-owned companies were laid.[52]

The Norwegian Progress Party was redefined as a libertarian party in 1983 under the leadership of Carl I. Hagen. According to Swedish neoliberals, Hagen and his party did not measure up to mainstream media's descriptions of '"neoliberalism" or "populism"'.[53] The party took aim at immigration in time for the 1987 local elections, when Hagen used a (now infamous) forged letter to portray a Muslim threat against Norwegian culture and Christianity.[54] Still, Hagen argued as late as 1989 against 'insane' media accusations of xenophobia: 'Our profile has initially been, from the start in 1970, that we were against taxes, fees, and public intrusions. . . . but we have long been in favour of an immigration stop, as long as we have a socialist welfare state'.[55] It was not until the 1990s that the party discourse would be rephrased around cultural differences and integration as key concerns.[56] Meanwhile, neoliberal actors treated the Norwegian Progress Party as a fellow anti-welfare-state actor and downplayed their xenophobic tendencies.[57] Just as the Finnish Rural Party was losing their connection with the people in the minds of many when they were in the government in the 1980s, similar criticism was directed at the Finns Party when in power in 2015–2017. The Sipilä government, analytically termed as a three-legged Aalto chair – well-integrated but wobbly – carried out anti-welfare state policies and tightened immigration policies.[58]

By 1989, Sweden was on the road to a fiscal, social, and political crisis that knocked the social democratic welfare-state project off its foundations. The minister of finance, social democrat Kjell-Olof Feldt, played a central role in the years and decisions leading up to the crisis. Feldt was generally recognised as a right-leaning economist. Swedish neoliberals applauded his inspirations from Thatcher and Reagan, welcomed him as 'the high priest of Neoliberal-ism' and described the following tax reforms as 'a form of Glasnost'.[59] Neolib-eral challengers to the social-democratic hegemony attempted to construct a chain of equivalences between the Swedish Social Democrats, the Soviet state, and politics in dissolution. In parallel to the Soviet Union, the Social Demo-crats attempted to save the system through reforms aimed at higher efficiency. Feldt, like the Soviet leaders, embarked on an extensive reform programme. Hence, the failing system and its rulers were constructed as the main offenders in the counter-hegemonic critique at the time.[60]

1990s: neoliberalism – from fringe to mainstream

The Soviet Union's collapse and the end of the Cold War brought an end to the bipolar conflict. Neoliberal forces utilised this opportunity to administer economic shock therapy, and a wave of privatisation rolled across Northern and Eastern Europe. In several countries, neoliberal networks mobilised popu-lar support, built coalitions, and framed privatisation as the only alternative to discredited statist systems. Social-democratic regimes (e.g. Poland, Sweden) launched economic reforms to transform and privatise state enterprises. Neo-liberal emphases on private property and individualism shaped major aspects of these processes.[61]

Most analyses of Nordic populism focus exclusively on parliamentary party politics.[62] From such a perspective it is easy to conclude that New Democracy were the only populists in Sweden and that they were largely unsuccessful – especially when compared to the electoral success of Danish and Norwegian People's Parties. Yet, at the same time, neoliberal populists were able to move quickly from the margins to the mainstream, managing in the process to insti-tutionalise political demands for decreased taxation and increased privatisation. They did so, however, without founding a parliamentary party. Instead they relied on extra-parliamentary ways of doing politics (think tanks, business asso-ciations, etc.).[63] Their demands gained parliamentary support because they were taken up by conservative and social democratic MPs who felt compelled to partially align their views with the neoliberal movement. When analysts won-der at the seeming lack of populism in Sweden, they have simply been looking in the wrong place. Populism did indeed leave substantial marks on Swedish politics in the 1990s, but it did so largely through the extra-parliamentary politics of radical neoliberals who succeeded in their stated aim to make the 'politically impossible possible'.[64]

Sweden's first right-wing populist party, New Democracy, rolled in on a wave of populism created by the Swedish neoliberal movement. The party program was presented in 1990 in a context of severe fiscal and social crisis. While New Democracy mobilised against immigration policies from the out-set, the xenophobic tendencies grew and became more apparent through the years.[65] In 1991, the Swedish Social-Democratic party experienced their worst election since 1921; a right-wing government took office after nine years in opposition; and New Democracy, with their populist appeal, went from non-existent to parliamentary success in less than a year (although their decline was nearly as swift). A shift in politics marked the end of the social democratic ide-ology that had permeated Swedish politics since 1932. The social democratic hegemonisation of politics and society had assured a political consensus on the Swedish democracy and welfare model, but, as neoliberal ideas permeated the public debate, this model was described as a problem rather than a solution. Affective appeals and emotional engagement abounded in neoliberal rhetoric. Mainstream public political debate was, however, characterised by rational rea-soning and managerial concerns. Social Democrats defended the administrative systems.[66] They argued in terms of efficiency, instead of formulating a politics for the masses against 'a few capitalists', as chairman of the Social Democrats and two-time prime minister Per Albin Hansson put it in the famous 'People's Home-Speech' (*Folkhemstalet*) of 1928.[67]

The Scandinavian populist parties all experienced crises in the mid-1990s. In 1993, conflicting factions were tearing the Norwegian Progress Party apart. So far, conservatives and radical neoliberals had been united by common interests in market economy and liberal alcohol policies. Opposition grew between an older generation of 'reactionaries' proposing 'large restrictions on immigration' and a younger generation of 'true liberals' in favour of 'completely free immi-gration, dismantling the welfare state',[68] and so on, according to contemporary analysis by neoliberal intellectuals. Internal oppositions were even flaunted in televised debates in the aftermath of the poor election results of 1993. By 1997, immigration was framed as a threat to the existing socio-cultural harmony. With a rhetoric centred on ethnicity and difference, 'ethnic Norwegians' were coupled with norms and values like equality, peace and harmony, while immi-gration was linked to conflict and loss of equality. On top of re-gaining voter support from losses in 1993, the Progress Party became Norway's second-largest party in the 1997 national elections.[69]

In parallel, New Democracy's populist leader abruptly left the party after internal conflicts in 1994. With new leadership, the core signifiers of the party's discourse turned from taxes to immigration and electoral support plummeted. Like the Norwegian Progress Party and others that experience sudden success, New Democracy was unprepared for the number of seats they needed to fill. If the party had been better organised and less dependent on the two charismatic founders, it might have retained support. While the Progress Party in Norway was able to build alliances and reinvigorate their rhetoric, New Democracy failed at both.[70]

Likewise, internal conflicts and power struggles eventually spelled the end of the Danish Progress Party's success story. Kjærsgaard and her allies abandoned the party in the mid-1990s, and founded the Danish People's Party. In People's Party rhetoric, the ordinary people were positioned against the elite of well-to-do experts, intellectuals, and socialists. Much like the Swedish neoliberal discourse, the right-wing populist message of the Danish People's Party met little resistance from the Left. While the Danish People's Party shared many of the demands initially posed by the Danish Progress Party, the former promoted welfare chauvinism (for 'real' Danes) against public sector reductions and privatisations. The nationalist tendencies of the People's Party were clear, but they have nevertheless positioned themselves as equal to established right-wing parties. Simultaneously, right-wing nationalists attacked leftist values and ideals at all levels of society.[71]

If populist parties in the Scandinavian countries were able to challenge social democratic hegemonies through demands for increased privatisation and decreased taxes in the 1970s, 1980s and early 1990s, these notions became hegemonic themselves in the end. Therefore, we can speak of a hegemony that emerges and transforms over time. The central issues emerging from the 1970s to the 1990s are the relations to the Soviet Union and market deregulation. Populist parties have emerged as a response to dominant thinking in each of the political contexts. Yet these parties (and movements) take form around different points of contestation at different times, to contest cultures of consensus.

In Finland, the SMP spent the 1980s working inversely against unemployment and poverty, for example, through taxation. They were strongly anti-elitists, but having held power, their support was collapsing. In the early 1990s, the economic recession steepened due to collapsing Eastern trade with the collapse of the Soviet Union. SMP and its party newspaper consequently went bankrupt.[72] In 1995, some of its key actors reinvented the party as the Finns Party (Perussuomalaiset). Simultaneously, in the ethnically relatively homogeneous Finland, the arrival of Somalian refugees and even the Ingrian people from the former Soviet Union neighbouring areas – the latter especially welcomed by Mauno Koivisto, whom the SMP supported for Finnish president – provoked some Finns Party politicians, notably Sulo Aittoniemi.[73] For the Finns Party leader, Timo Soini (from 1997), the key point of contestation became the other parties and the European Union, which started to fill the hegemonic narratives in Finland in the 1990s. In complete contrast with the thinking of Veikko Vennamo, the original founder, the party adopted a stance against European integration and a critical perspective towards immigration and refugees.[74] Welfare chauvinism became an entangled feature of the new party.[75] This transformation could be attributed to the collapse of the Soviet other and Finlandisation of the Finnish self-image, and the need for new narratives.

Other potential populist parties in Finland at this point included the Greens and the liberals, although the roots of the Green movement in Finland are longer. The emblematic populist environmental moment was the Koijärvi movement in 1979 that inspired a generation and boosted the organisation of a political party in the shape of a fringe populist force contesting all the existing parties to offer an alternative.[76] The Greens have been strong in Helsinki for a long time as the third and then the second-largest party, but attained national relevance only in the late 2010s. This was partly due to the success of a veteran from the 1980s, Pekka Haavisto, and confrontational, even populist, rhetoric by their then leader Ville Niinistö. In 1973–1992, the small liberal party on the style of Scandinavian populists, Constitutional Right Party (Perustuslaillinen oikeistopuolue, POP), led by Georg C. Ehrnrooth originally of the Swedish People's Party,[77] was right-wing particularly in terms of being anti-communist and against Kekkonen line.[78] As SMP grew softer under Veikko Vennamo's son Pekka Vennamo's leadership, in particular, and joined governments, POP kept their 'fringe populism' going – until Ehrnrooth's point of contestation disappeared in the early 1990s.

2000–2010s: mainstreaming fringe populism

Euroscepticism has been relevant to some degree for all the Nordic populist parties.[79] In the case of the Danish People's Party and Sweden Democrats, immigrants had been the source of identity after the hegemonic shift to the right in economic policies. This thinking also started to spread in Finland. One could also say that the Vennamo heritage on left-wing policies was lost and only the anti-elitist rhetoric (in the style of *rötösherrat kuriin*) remains in the renewed Finns Party programme. In the Nordic countries, populist parties moved more steadily from the fringe to the mainstream and other parties appropriated their ideas.

The 2000s saw the establishment of the Finns Party. In his master's thesis in 1988, the Finns Party chairman Timo Soini discussed Scandinavian populism. He also named Pia Kjærsgaard as his reference point in his opinion pieces in the *Helsingin Sanomat* in the 2000s.[80] His rhetoric confirmed how the duality of anti-elitism and anti-EU overshadowed anti-immigration; yet the tension remained. In the early 2000s, the voice of the suburbs, Tony Halme, an iconic boxer, became an MP for the Finns Party in Helsinki. Meanwhile, Timo Soini was elected as one of the representatives of the Helsinki Region at the Finnish parliament. The real breakthrough came only after the 2007 general elections, and in particular in 2008, when the scandal of election funding and the Law of the Land (*maantapa*) was debated. Established political parties had developed practices through which they could avoid unveiling their sources of electoral funding. Set against the 'old parties', the Finns Party emerged as a novel alternative: it did well in the 2008 local elections, and it gained a landslide in the 2011 and 2015 elections. The voices of anti-immigration, with Jussi Halla-aho first elected to the Helsinki City Council in 2008, became intertwined with anti-elitism. However, as Arter argues, the party was for the so-called 'Finns' but not as aggressively as the Scandinavian counterparts.[81]

In Sweden, the Social Democratic Party turned right to navigate the crisis of the 1990s. The political playing field became increasingly crowded around the centre. All the more so when the conservative party incorporated former social democratic slogans into their rhetoric in the early 2000s. The four right-wing parties formed a common alliance in the mid-2000s, and the voters' political options were narrowed down to a choice between two 'blocs'. In addition, voters experienced that the difference between the established parties shrunk to such a degree that it hardly mattered which party you voted for.[82] In this sedimented political culture, the Sweden Democrats gained attention as an alternative to the established order. The Sweden Democrats successfully exploited the political vacuum and presented themselves as the only viable political alternative to the disrupted consensus-oriented political elite. They adapted to the mainstream technical-rational political discourse by speaking of the costs of immigration, while mobilising voters with more affective appeals in their political propaganda. The organising principle of the Sweden Democrats' politics has always been the opposition between a national 'us' and the immigrant/non-Christian 'them' – unlike other Nordic populist parties, who initially focused on tax issues. In comparison with populist parties in Denmark, Norway, and Finland, the Sweden Democrats have lagged behind and only emerged as a real political contender since 2010–2014.[83]

The three populist alternatives in Sweden (the New Democracy, the extra-parliamentary neoliberals and the Sweden Democrats) share similar political strategies. *Folklig* is a term in Swedish (*folkelig* in Danish and Norwegian) that signifies practices that are popular, plebbish, or 'like ordinary people'. Politicians may strive to appear *folkliga*. When political spokespersons appear as ordinary people do – in sweatshirts and bucket hats in the case of New Democracy; with flaws or petty criminal behaviour (be it moonshining, tax evasion, gambling or drunk and disorderly behaviour) in the case of neoliberals or Sweden Democrats – their popularity increases. Both New Democracy and extra-parliamentary neoliberals emphasised fun, alcohol consumption, and common sense. New Democracy's campaign film from 1991 was even titled 'Common Sense'.[84] They bragged about their vast number of volunteers but limited finances. They toured the country in boats and cars, and spoke on fun fairs, campsites, and squares.[85] Stressing the need to 'listen to the people' on national television in 1990, party founder Bert Karlsson appeared as 'a man of the people' who sympathised with the less fortunate. In congruence with our point about the post-foundational understanding of populism, a populist party is not by definition representing the 'underclass' or represented by it. The co-founder and party leader Ian Wachtmeister stood in stark contrast with his upper-class roots and ideological message of radical market liberalism coupled with anti-immigration. It has since been 'the count' Wachtmeister, rather than 'the valet' Karlsson, who the Sweden Democrats have consulted in their election campaigns.[86]

New Democracy used rhetorical tropes that had been prominent among neoliberal radical intellectuals for many years: to take from the state and give to the individual, and so on. Their rhetoric positioned common people against politicians and their 'contempt for people'. In short, they contested the political status quo through affective arguments that appeal to the audience's sense of neglect. New Democracy's populist logic built on an 'us' that integrated disparate identities under a common identity: 'the common people'. It identified established politicians as 'them'. In the preceding, broader neoliberal discourse, the populist logic is even clearer. There, the unifying 'us' mobilised against the system was the people as individuals, and the political 'frontier' was set against the social-democratic welfare state.[87]

As long as Sweden was characterised by a social-democratic hegemony, populism was voiced as an opposition to the social-democratic welfare state. Lately, the Sweden Democrats have begun to frame their politics as a more traditional version of social democracy – in contrast to the contemporary Social-Democratic Party. Since the social-democratic welfare state has lost its hegemonic standing in Swedish politics, it no longer functions as the main opponent of populist politics. Consequently, these actors are left grappling for a new frontier. In positioning themselves as the true Social Democrats, spokespersons for the Sweden Democrats have made use of the old concept *Folkhemmet* (the people's home).[88] *Folkhemmet* is a 'shining example'[89] of the culture of consensus mentioned at the beginning of this chapter and was produced by a historic compromise between capital and labour. However, it was also an important metaphor for the successful social democratic hegemonisation of Swedish political discourse, as argued by Erik Åsard and W. Lance Bennett.[90] It has long since been obsolete in social democratic rhetoric.

The *folkhem* metaphor has now been re-activated by the Sweden Democrats to appeal to traditional social democratic voters – all the while articulating a nostalgic vision for the Swedish nation. The Social Democratic Party represents the political elite, just as it did in the neoliberal populist discourse of the 1980s and 1990s.[91] The argument is that the Social Democratic Party has betrayed their ideological roots as well as the Swedish people.[92] The Sweden Democrats' financial politics have turned increasingly towards a market liberal agenda during the past decade. Paradoxically, the party's attitude to trade unions and workers' rights have simultaneously taken a turn to the left, as voter support among unionised blue-collar workers increasingly favour the Sweden Democrats.[93]

Remembering the emptiness at the core of populism, we should also consider left populism. Recently, leftist aspirations in Sweden challenge the neoliberal hegemony through conscious and explicit populist politics inspired by Chantal Mouffe's advocacy for a left populism.[94] That is, a logic of articulation that places the universal identification 'us' in a dichotomy with 'them'. Moving on from an attempt to re-assert class as the central signifier in political discourse,[95] social democratic think tank intellectuals recently initiated a new group within the Swedish Social Democratic Party: 'the Reformists' (*Reformisterna*). These Reformists challenge the neoliberal hegemony in and outside the Social Democratic Party. With demands to 'reinstate the monetary system', they attempt to construct a political frontier between 'ordinary people' and 'the economic elite'.[96] Through the articulation of a reform program that highlights a Green New Deal, they link together multiple environmental and economic struggles around a demand for equality and social justice against the status quo.[97] Using the 'ordinary people' as a point of identification enables them to reclaim voters from the Sweden Democrats – without constructing the latter or their voters as the enemy.

The Reformists actively challenge the status quo in both politics and media. Swedish news media have adopted a cultural valuation scale (GAL-TAN) from the political sciences in attempts to explain the successes of what they call populism: the Sweden Democrats, Brexit, Trump, the Finns Party, and so on. According to mainstream media, 'the old battle between right and left'[98] has been replaced by one between liberal globalists and conservative nationalists. In contention, the Reformists expose hegemonic practices that cover up redistributive concerns. That is to say, they have emerged as a response to dominant thinking in Swedish politics and contest the status quo where cultural concerns are said to have replaced economic concerns.

The Finns party had a landslide in 2011 but remained in opposition. In Finland, the Finns Party went to a neoliberal austerity government in 2015 with the Centre Party and the National Coalition. The millionaire faction in power in the Centre moved quite far from some of their traditional values, and after the failure in 2019 and steep decline in the party membership, the party changed leadership. The Finns Party term in office led to the decline of its support. Some also argued that the government did not succeed in containing immigration. The leadership was challenged and changed by a faction that mobilised on social media and *Hommafoorumi* online platform in the party congress in June 2017. The congress elected Jussi Halla-aho, an MEP known for his strong anti-immigration and civilisationist stance and founder of the platform, as party leader. None of the five ministers or those close to the founding member and chairman of the FP were chosen in the leadership. This faction, comprising half of the parliamentary caucus, stepped out and by autumn 2017 established a new party: Blue Reform (Sininen tulevaisuus).

With the transformed leadership, the Finns Party succeeded in the 2019 elections becoming one of the three largest parties. After the elections, fierce debates over whether or not they should be sitting at the right-wing end of the parliament where they were now assigned, as their economic policy resembled the early versions of Nordic right-populist parties. The earlier seat in the centre originated from the SMP, a splinter from the Agrarian Party, and an economic policy between the Left and the Right – until Juha Sipilä's austerity government (2015–2017) and leadership change. The Blue Reform were, however, not successful in the polls in the 2019 elections and did not run in the elections to the European Parliament, and Finns Party, while becoming the main opposition party and the most popular party in the polls in the summer 2019, did not do as well in the Euroelections as those for *Eduskunta*.

The week preceding the European parliament elections of 2019 were over-shadowed by the question of Russian influence in the newly forming nationalist bloc that included cooperation between Italian Lega, Freedom Party of Austria, and others with Nordic populist parties. The issue of hegemonic struggle with the eastern neighbour re-surfaced. It became apparent that several European populist parties, such as Matteo Salvini's Lega in Italy or the Austrian FPÖ, with video-exposed leader Heinz-Christian Strache, had close ties to Vladimir Putin's Russia. Considering the anti-Soviet heritage, this could have contrib-uted to their poor result in comparison to the polls in general. As the tradi-tional national identity in Finland is formed through what it is not (Russian or Swedish), questions remain to what extent the Finnishness in the renewed Finns Party is defined through opposition to Russia or the European Union or simply the migrants. The Sweden Democrats did not join this coalition.

In Norway and Denmark, the Progress Party and People's Party respectively managed to secure increased voter support through the 2000s despite a series of scandals.[99] Both have survived changes in leadership, replacing long-term leaders Hagen and Kjærsgaard, respectively. Widespread scepticism among the other Norwegian parliamentary parties initially made it difficult for the Pro-gress Party to practice its theoretical leverage. The Danish People's Party and the Sweden Democrats alike have transformed themselves by adapting social democratic ideals and rhetoric. Simultaneously, more radically right-wing and anti-immigrant or anti-Muslim parties emerge to challenge already-established populist parties from even stronger fringe positions. In the 2019 parliamentary elections, the Danish People's Party suffered a significant setback – halving their voter support – which can, if only in part, be attributed to the rise of new fringe parties. This is largely due to the Social Democrats adapting their lost rhetoric and combining it with a tough-on-immigration stance that had now become mainstream.

Addressing the overall transformations and political logics in different con-texts, it is easy to see that the contents of demands and policies vary much more than the forms of their presentation do. Like the neoliberal movement, early right-wing populist parties in Norway and Denmark were neither ethno-nationalist nor mobilised against immigration (until the 1980s). The Sweden Democrats have, on the contrary, always been ethno-nationalist and anti-immigration but never neoliberal: they vote with the Social Democrats and Left party in many instances concerning labour market policies and workers' rights. One thing is clear, however: the fringe populist parties mainstreamed themselves in the 2000s. However, many of them either fell back to a fringe position, such as in Finland, or were pushed there by more popular parties, as in the Danish case.

Transforming hegemony

There are several conjunctures that we can draw on that also have to do with international politics and are transnational. Going back to the 1960s, the

Finnish populist SMP was born out of the direct reaction against the Soviet-friendly politics epitomised in the figure of Urho Kekkonen as the head of the Agrarian party, and finally the longest-serving president. The coupling of the Soviet developments and the domestic politics in the Nordic countries continued in terms of populist parties. As the Washington Consensus was establishing and the Soviet model crumbling, the populist parties also sought to question either the foreign policy related to it (in Finland) or the economic models that gained their raison d'être from the response to those models (Sweden and Scandinavia). In both Sweden and Finland, market deregulation discussions started in the 1980s. In the geographically more western Scandinavian countries Norway and Denmark, populist parties had already contested the idea of high taxation as a basis of the welfare-state model. As market liberalism was declared the winner in the Cold War global ideological contest, Soviet-style economies crumbled, welfare states were transformed, and communism no longer provided a political Other, the populist parties and movements were losing their point of contestation. In the 1990s, while the Finnish economy was in recession, in Sweden some claimed that the Soviet economy was privatising 'too fast'; others believed that it was not fast enough; but all agreed that privatisations were necessary.[100]

The intertwining of neoliberalism and anti-immigration discourses often goes unexplained as a curiosity in Nordic populism research. The rationalising argument that supported neoliberal reforms, stressed as a given that the welfare state is not affordable. This led to nationalism coupling with the welfare chauvinism that tries to rescue what is left of the welfare state and safeguard it from the newcomers. The recent turn of the Danish People's Party to early social democratic ideals and the Sweden Democrats' emphasis on the nostalgia of *Folkhemmet* that includes the welfare state testify to this process. Going back to the theoretical framework and our formula $Populism = us^{affect1} + frontier^{affect2}$, we ask ourselves what picture of populism is emerging? Clearly each period has its own contents, but overall we argue that in the Scandinavian countries, the frontier feature to be opposed became welfare statism, to which individualism and market economy were contrasted; while in Finland, the confrontation thrived with anti-Sovietism:

Scandinavian Populism (1970–2000) = people-as-individuals$^{anti-system}$ + welfare statism$^{past-system}$

Finnish Populism (1970–2000) = ordinary people^{inclusion} + Soviet-lead$^{loss of independence}$

Affects are a dimension we have not closely studied here – we add here anti-system confrontation and the naming of something as past and allusion of independence as potentials. The rhetoric of neoliberalism was affective in that it provided a vision of a new era and recognised of the individuals rather than a system (with clear anti-Soviet tones). In the Finnish case, one could hypothesise that populism provided healing for the loss. Moving to the 2000s, it was replaced by nationalism that highlighted the Nordic people versus immigrants axis. However, even here, it is about livelihoods: transforming neighbourhoods or surroundings as well as the foreign element of religion heightened the frontier concept.[101] However, welfare returns to the side of the 'us', as an affective dimension where welfare could also feature alongside nationalism. One interpretation could look like this:

$$Nordic\ Populism\ (2000\text{–}2010s) = Nordic\ people^{welfare\text{-}nationalism} + immigrants^{transforming\text{-}communties}$$

We argue that welfare chauvinism restores the belief in the welfare state. In the Scandinavian countries, populists, and in Finland, some other parties spoke for years against the welfare state as a luxury to be afforded on a global scale, which has paved the way for welfare chauvinism. Fear of losing the welfare state in the face of the newcomers could explain a particular transformation that took place. In a sense, this fear was used by neoliberals in the 1980s – but their solution was to cut welfare expenditure and support for all, not just for a few. In short, the argument on the need to cut welfare provision in terms of economic efficiency and ageing populations provokes responses that are welfare chauvinism. This is how neoliberalism and anti-immigration can get entangled in populist meaning-making.[102]

We conclude that, using the framework of the formula of populism, it is easy to see that the political Other has transformed: the frontier used to mark a contrast to the welfare-statist regulated market, or the collaboration with the USSR in Finland, but as marked deregulation mainstreamed, the contestation focused on the suspicion of newcomers, sometimes with welfare-chauvinist undertones. The political 'us' emerged from this contestation as a relatively monoethnic constellation.

Notes

1 Laclau 2005.
2 Hawkins, Carlin, Littvay & Kaltwasser 2018, Jungar & Jupskås 2014.
3 Laclau 2005, Laclau & Mouffe 1985, Mouffe 2018, Palonen 2021.
4 Arter 2010.
5 Arter 2013, Elder, Thomas & Arter 1988.
6 Östberg 2018. See also Kjell Östberg's chapter in this volume.
7 E.g. Arter 2013, Hagelund 2005, Wingborg 2016.
8 E.g. Rydgren 2006.
9 Ylä-Anttila 2017, Hatakka 2019.
10 Palonen 2018, Palonen & Saresma 2017.
11 Cf. Freeden 2017.
12 Laclau 2005, 2014, Laclau & Mouffe 1985, Mouffe 2018.
13 See also Palonen 2020.
14 Palonen 2018, 2020.
15 Laclau develops on Claude Lefort's democratic theory in Laclau 2005. See also Lefort 1988 and Näsström 2007.
16 Götz & Marklund 2014.
17 Polarisation may mean a bipolar hegemony, where two camps would be apparently consensual and single-voiced, each camp co-constituting the other (Palonen 2009).

18 Mouffe 2000.
19 Jungar 2015.
20 Møller Hansen & Stubager 2017.
21 Elmgren 2014. See also Rainio-Niemi 2014 in the same volume.
22 Andersen & Bjørklund 1990, Jens Rydgren 2010.
23 Rydgren & van der Meiden 2018, Taggart 1996. Historically, Swedish right-wing parties had to form majority coalitions to take government office. The Social Democrats used to be able to form minority governments, but their voter support has dwindled in the past decades. The left-right divide between parties willing to cooperate has long been clear but was sharpened in the 2006 election. In the mid-2000s, the four right-wing parties agreed to run for office together in an 'alliance for Sweden'. Since, only two government alternatives have been represented in Swedish politics, despite the existence of various parties in a party-list proportional system.
24 Rainio-Niemi 2014.
25 Virtanen 2018, Aalto 2018.
26 See also Roikonen, Eloranta & Ojala in this volume.
27 Rydgren & van der Meiden 2018.
28 Fryklund 2018, Rydgren 2006.
29 Sunnercrantz 2017.
30 Virtanen 2018.
31 Ibid., 170–171
32 Sänkiaho 1971.
33 Virtanen 2018, 265.
34 Ibid.
35 Ibid., Arter 2010.
36 Ethnic homogeneity has been significant in Finland, where other ethnic groups have been small. Migration policy, apart from settling the Eastern Karelian population, and especially strategy hardly existed as Tilli (2019) explains. With the arrival of immigrants in Finland from Somalia, racism emerged in the 1990s as an explicit political issue. This is not to say there had not been racism before in Finland or the Nordic countries. Rather, particularly against the Sami minority in Sapmi (which stretches across Norway, Sweden, and Finland) and Inuits in Greenland, this had been carried out even at the level of policy. Other historical minorities such as the Roma and Tatars in Finland were not exempted from (institutionalised) racism.
37 Aarhus University 2019, Jens Rydgren 2010, Stubager et al. 2016, Taggart 1996, Ydling Brunbech 2011.
38 Kvanmo & Rygnestad 1993.
39 E.g. Nevalainen 2018.
40 Jens Rydgren 2010, Ydling Brunbech 2011.
41 Karpantschof 2006.
42 Hort 2014. See also Östberg's chapter in this volume for further discussion on the employee funds.
43 Sunnercrantz 2017.
44 Westholm 1988, 39.
45 Segerstedt 1988.
46 Westholm 1988, 26.
47 Sunnercrantz 2020.
48 See e.g. Borg 1992, Norberg 1993a, Westholm 1988.
49 Keski-Rauska 2015.
50 Yet this legacy somehow prevails with the celebrity politician and parliamentarian Harry Harkimo of Movement Now (*Liike Nyt*) – formerly of the National Coalition (*Kokoomus*), who has been establishing his movement in the model of the Five Star Movement in Italy.
51 Virtanen 2018.

52 Nevalainen 2018.
53 Du Reitz 1989, 14; cf. Schoolland 1993.
54 Hagelund 2005.
55 Du Reitz 1989, 14.
56 Hagelund 2005.
57 See Wingborg 2016, cf. Du Reitz 1989, Schoolland 1993.
58 Palonen 2017.
59 Varveus 1989.
60 See e.g. Ibid.: 'rid the system of the worst perversions'.
61 Bohle & Neunhöffer 2006, Sunnercrantz 2017.
62 Cf. Betz 1994, Fryklund 2018, Rydgren 2006, Taggart 1996.
63 Cf. Fryklund 2018, Jens Rydgren 2010, Taggart 1996.
64 Segerstedt 1988.
65 Taggart 1996, Widfeldt 2015.
66 Sunnercrantz 2017.
67 Hansson 1928.
68 Norberg 1993b, 7. Furthermore, the author argues:

> If the conservatives were to win the struggle, the party would become more tra-
> ditionally social-democratic combined with xenophobia and moralism. One can
> at least be glad that a conservative Progress Party would slowly but surely wither,
> without the youthful regeneration and intellectual capacity that only the young neo-
> liberals have.

69 Hagelund 2005.
70 Taggart 1996, Widfeldt 2015.
71 Karpantschof 2006, Stubager et al. 2016, Taggart 1996, Ydling Brunbech 2011.
72 Virtanen 2018.
73 Prindiville & Hjelm 2018.
74 Virtanen 2018.
75 Keskinen 2016, Kuisma 2013.
76 Aalto 2018.
77 Despite the name, the Swedish People's Party defended the Swedish minority in Fin-
    land, and while they may have populist undertones at times, they were an ethnic minor-
    ity party.
78 Keski-Rauska 2015.
79 Herkman 2017, Raunio 2007.
80 Palonen 2017.
81 Arter 2010.
82 Hellström & Nilsson 2010.
83 Widfeldt 2015. Inspired by the Danish populist right, the Sweden Democrats toned
    down their nationalistic elements. Despite established parties' and mass media's convic-
    tion that parties like the Danish Progress Party and the Sweden Democrats would never
    become 'potty trained' both parties have strived to disprove them. See Dahlerup 2008,
    Lindberg 2011, Wingborg 2016.
84 Cederquist 1991.
85 Ibid., Dahlbäck 2013.
86 Dahlbäck 2013, Widfeldt 2015, Wingborg 2016.
87 Sunnercrantz 2017.
88 With reference both to Per-Albin Hansson and the more nationalist politician and polit-
    ical scientist Rudolf Kjellén. See Hellström 2010.
89 Arter 2013, 152.
90 Åsard & Bennett 1997.
91 Sunnercrantz 2020.
92 Hellström 2010, Hellström & Nilsson 2010, see also '*Torehammars supervalår*', 140813.

93 Hellström & Lodenius 2016, Sundell 2015, Wingborg 2016.
94 See e.g. Greider & Linderborg 2018, Suhonen & Gerin 2018.
95 Katalys, Klass i Sverige.
96 Socialdemokratiska föreningen Reformisterna.
97 Ibid.
98 '[A] prerequisite for both the traditional block policy and the alliance building', according to Marmorstein 2019.
99 Herkman 2018.
100 See Sunnercrantz 2017.
101 In the case of Denmark, the frontier has partly ceased to be external to the country. Instead, it has been reconstructed and manifested internally through the state's designation of 'ghettos' and the more recent policy programme against 'parallel communities'.
102 Palonen 2018.

References

Aalto, Sari, 2018: *Vaihtoehtopuolue: Vihreän liikkeen tie puolueeksi.* Helsinki: Into Kustannus.
Aarhus University, 2019. *The Danish Election Database.* https://valgdatabase.dst.dk/ [Accessed 8 October 2019].
Andersen, Jørgen Goul & Bjørklund, Tor, 1990: "Structural Changes and New Cleavages: The Progress Parties in Denmark and Norway" in *Acta Sociologica*, 33:3, 195–217.
Arter, David, 2010: "The Breakthrough of Another West European Populist Radical Right Party? The Case of the True Finns" in *Government and Opposition*, 45:4, 484–504.
Arter, David, 2013: *Scandinavian Politics Today.* 2nd ed. Manchester: Manchester University Press.
Åsard, Erik & Bennett, W. Lance, 1997: *Democracy and the Marketplace of Ideas: Communication and Government in Sweden and the United States.* Cambridge: Cambridge University Press.
Betz, Hans-Georg, 1994: *Radical Right-Wing Populism in Western Europe.* London: Palgrave Macmillan.
Bohle, Dorothee & Neunhöffer, Gisela, 2006: "Why is there no Third Way? The Role of Neoliberal Ideology, Network and Think Tanks in Combating Market, Socialism and Shaping Transformation in Poland" in Dieter Plehwe, Bernhard Walpen & Gisela Neunhöffer (eds.) *Neoliberal Hegemony: A Global Critique.* London and New York: Routledge.
Borg, Anders E., 1992: *Generell välfärdspolitik – bara magiska ord?* Stockholm: City University Press.
Cederquist, Peter, 1991: *Ny Demokratis valfilm 'Sunt förnuft'.* www.youtube.com/watch?v=KAlghcy6_TU [Accessed 27 September 2019].
Dahlbäck, Vincent, 2013: "Händelser som skakat Sverige: Ny Demokrati" pt. 4:8, 'Svenska händelser – De ville förändra svensk politik radikalt' in *SVT 2*, 2 April 2013. www.svt.se/svenska-handelser/de-ville-forandra-svensk-politik-radikalt.
Dahlerup, Drude, 2008: "En politisk tragedi" in *Aftonbladet*, 29 June 2008. www.aftonbladet.se/a/ng9rEQ [Accessed 11 March 2019].
Du Reitz, Einar, 1989: "Carl I Hagen – Libertarian eller opportunist?" in *Nyliberalen*, 1989:3, 14–15, 17.
Elder, Neil Thomas Alastar H. & Arter, David, 1988: *The Consensual Democracies? The Government and Politics of the Scandinavian States.* Oxford: Basil Blackwell.
Elmgren, Ainur, 2014: "The Nordic Ideal: Openness and Populism According to the Finns Party" in Norbert Götz & Carl Marklund (eds.) *The Paradox of Openness: Transparency and Participation in Nordic Cultures of Consensus.* Leiden: Brill, 91–119.

Freeden, Michael, 2017: "After the Brexit Referendum: Revisiting Populism as an Ideology" in *Journal of Political Ideologies*, 22:1, 1–11.

Fryklund, Björn, 2018: "Populism in the Nordic Countries 1965–2015: The Swedish Case as an Ideal Type or Comparative Yardstick for the Development of Populism" in Urpo Kovala, Emilia Palonen, Maria Ruotsalainen & Tuija Saresma (eds.) *Populism on the Loose.* Jyväskylä: Jyväskylän yliopisto.

Götz, Norbert & Marklund, Carl (eds.) 2014: *The Paradox of Openness: Transparency and Participation in Nordic Cultures of Consensus.* Leiden: Brill.

Greider, Göran & Linderborg, Åsa, 2018: *Populistiska manifestet: för knegare, arbetslösa, tandlösa och 90 procent av alla andra.* Stockholm: Natur & Kultur.

Hagelund, Anniken, 2005: "The Progress Party and the Problem of Culture: Immigration Politics and Right Wing Populism in Norway" in Jens Rydgren (ed.) *Movements of Exclusion: Radical Right-Wing Populism in the Western World.* New York: Nova Science.

Hansson, Per Albin, 1928: *Folkhemmet, medborgarhemmet.* Speech in Second Chamber Parliament, 18 January 1928. www.peralbinhuset.se/folkhemstalet.html [Accessed 5 December 2018].

Hatakka, Niko, 2019: *Populism in the Hybrid Media System.* Turku: University of Turku.

Hawkins, Kirk A., Carlin, Ryan E., Littvay, Levente & Kaltwasser, Cristóbal Rovira, 2018: *The Ideational Approach to Populism: Concept, Theory, and Analysis.* London: Routledge.

Hellström, Anders, 2010: "Det nya folkhemspartiet" in *Fronesis*, 34, 110–124.

Hellström, Anders & Lodenius, Anna-Lena, 2016: *Invandring, mediebilder och radikala högerpopulistiska partier i Norden.* Stockholm: Delegationen för migrationsstudier.

Hellström, Anders & Nilsson, Tom, 2010: "'We are the Good Guys': Ideological Positioning of the Nationalist Party Sverigedemokraterna in Contemporary Swedish Politics" in *Ethnicities*, 10:1, 55–76.

Herkman, Juha, 2017: "Articulations of Populism: The Nordic Case" in *Cultural Studies*, 31:4, 470–488.

Herkman, Juha, 2018: "Old Patterns on New Clothes? Populism and Political Scandals in the Nordic Countries" in *Acta Sociologica*, 61:4, 341–355.

Hort, Sven E. O., 2014: *Social Policy, Welfare State, and Civil Society in Sweden. Vol. 1, History, Policies, and Institutions 1884–1988.* Lund: Arkiv.

Jungar, Ann-Cathrine, 2015: "Agrarian Populism in Finland: Continuity and Change" in Dirk Strijker, Gerrit Voerman & Ida Terluin (eds.) *Rural Protest Groups and Populist Political Parties.* Wageningen, NL: Wageningen Academic Publishers.

Jungar, Ann-Cathrine & Jupskås, Anders Ravik, 2014: "Populist Radical Right Parties in the Nordic Region: A New and Distinct Party Family?" in *Scandinavian Political Studies*, 37:3, 215–238.

Karpantschof, René, 2006: "Højreradikalismen i Danmark – en politik model på historisk-sociologisk grund" in *Dansk Sociologi*, 14:3, 25.

Katalys, Klass i Sverige: *Om Katalys stora klassutredning: Klass i Sverige – Katalys.* www.katalys.org/klass/ [Accessed 13 February 2019].

Keskinen, Suvi, 2016: "From Welfare Nationalism to Welfare Chauvinism: Economic Rhetoric, the Welfare State and Changing Asylum Policies in Finland" in *Critical Social Policy,* 36:3, 352–370.

Keski-Rauska, Riku, 2015: *Yksinäinen Ehrnrooth. Georg C. Ehrnrooth YYA-Suomen puristuksessa.* Helsinki: Otava.

Kuisma, Mikko, 2013: "'Good' and 'Bad' Immigrants: The Economic Nationalism of the True Finns' Immigration Discourse" in Umut Korkut et al. (eds.) *The Discourses and Politics of Migration in Europe.* New York: Palgrave Macmillan, 93–108.

Kvanmo, Hanna & Rygnestad, Arild, 1993: *Anders Langes saga*. Oslo: Norske samlaget.

Laclau, Ernesto, 2005: *On Populist Reason*. London: Verso.

Laclau, Ernesto, 2014: *The Rhetorical Foundations of Society*. London: Verso.

Laclau, Ernesto & Mouffe, Chantal, 1985: *Hegemony and Socialist Strategy: Towards a Radical Democratic Politics*. London: Verso.

Lefort, Claude, 1988: *Democracy and Political Theory*. Cambridge: Polity Press.

Lindberg, Anders, 2011: "SD är inte rumsrena" in *Aftonbladet*, 11 July 2011. www.afton bladet.se/a/0EL73G [Accessed 11 March 2019].

Marmorstein, Elisabeth, 2019: "Utdragen maktkamp med given utgång" in *SVT Nyheter*, 3 March. www.svt.se/nyheter/inrikes/utdragen-maktkamp-med-given-utgang [Accessed 13 February 2019].

Møller Hansen, Kasper & Stubager, Rune, 2017: *Oprør fra udkanten: folketingsvalget 2015*. København: Jurist- og Økonomforbundet.

Mouffe, Chantal, 2000: *The Democratic Paradox*. London: Verso.

Mouffe, Chantal, 2018: *For a Left Populism*. London: Verso.

Näsström, Sofia, 2007: "The Legitimacy of the People" in *Political Theory*, 35:5, 624–658.

Nevalainen, Pasi, 2018: "Deadlock in Corporate Governance: Finding a Common Strategy for Private Telephone Companies, 1978–1998" in *Business History*, 60:6, 908–929.

Norberg, Johan, 1993a: "Välfärdspolitikens teoretiska grunder vacklar" in *Nyliberalen*, 1993:4, 66–67.

Norberg, Johan, 1993b: "Sönderfallande Fremskrittsparti" in *Nyliberalen*, 1993:7, 7.

Östberg, Kjell, 2018: "När ingen längre kokar kaffe – eller vad har hänt folkrörelsepartierna?" in Henrik Meinander, Petri Karonen & Kjell Östberg (eds.) *Demokratins drivkrafter: kontext och särdrag i Sveriges och Finlands demokratier 1890–2020*. Stockholm: Appell förlag.

Palonen, Emilia, 2009: "Political Polarisation and Populism in Contemporary Hungary" in *Parliamentary Affairs*, 62:2, 318–334.

Palonen, Emilia, 2017: "Finland" in *European Journal of Political Research: Political Data Yearbook*, 92–98.

Palonen, Emilia, 2018: "Performing the Nation: The Janus-Faced Populist Foundations of Illiberalism in Hungary" in *Journal of Contemporary European Studies*, 26:3, 308–321.

Palonen, Emilia, 2020: "Ten Theses on Populism" in Emmy Eklundh & Andy Knott (eds.) *The Populist Manifesto*. London: Rowman & Littlefield, 55–69.

Palonen, Emilia, 2021: "Democracy vs. Demography: Rethinking Politics and the People as Debate" in *Thesis Eleven*. https://doi.org/10.1177/0725513620983686

Palonen, Emilia & Saresma, Tuija (eds.) 2017: *Jätkät & jytkyt: Perussuomalaiset ja populismin retoriikka*. Tampee: Vastapaino.

Prindiville, Nicholas & Hjelm, Titus, 2018: "The 'Secularization' and Ethnicization of Migration Discourse: The Ingrian Finnish Right to Return in Finnish Politics" in *Ethnic and Racial Studies*, 41:9, 1574–1593.

Rainio-Niemi, Johanna, 2014: "A Nordic Paradox of Openness and Consensus? The Case of Finland" in Norbert Götz & Carl Marklund (eds.) *The Paradox of Openness: Transparency and Participation in Nordic Cultures of Consensus*. Leiden: Brill, 27–49.

Raunio, Tapio, 2007: "Softening but Persistent: Euroscepticism in the Nordic EU Countries" in *Acta Politica*, 42:2–3, 191–210.

Rydgren, Jens, 2006: *From Tax Populism to Ethnic Nationalism: Radical Right-Wing Populism in Sweden*. New York: Berghahn Books.

Rydgren, Jens, 2010: "Radical Right-Wing Populism in Denmark and Sweden: Explaining Party System Change and Stability" in *SAIS Review*, 30:1, 57–71.

Rydgren, Jens & van der Meiden, Sara, 2018: "The Radical Right and the End of Swedish Exceptionalism" in *European Political Science*, 18:3, 439–455.

Sänkiaho, Risto, 1971: "A Model of the Rise of Populism and Support for the Finnish Rural Party" in *Scandinavian Political Studies*, 6:1, 27–47.

Schoolland, Ken, 1993: "A Libertarian Odyssey" in *Freedom Network News*. http://rkba.org/libertarian/isil/fnn/fnn02.txt [Accessed 11 March 2019].

Segerstedt, Torgny T., 1988: *Det politiskt omöjliga*. Stockholm: Ratio.

Socialdemokratiska föreningen Reformisterna, 2019. *Reformprogram Reformisterna*. www.reformisterna.se/reformprogram [Accessed 26 September 2019].

Stubager, Rune, Møller Hansen, Kasper, Callesen, Kristoffer, Leed, Andreas & Enevoldsen, Christine, 2016: *Danske vælgere 1971–2015: en oversigt over udviklingen i vælgernes holdninger mv.* Aarhus: Det danske valgprojekt, Aarhus University.

Suhonen, Daniel & Gerin, Enna, 2018: "Socialdemokraterna måste lära av vänsterpopulisterna" in *Dagens Nyheter*, 18 November 2018. www.dn.se/debatt/socialdemokraterna-maste-lara-av-vansterpopulisterna/ [Accessed 15 January 2019].

Sundell, Anders, 2015: "Sverigedemokraterna röstar oftare med Socialdemokraterna än med Moderaterna" in *Politologerna*, 22 May 2015. https://politologerna.wordpress.com/2015/05/22/sverigedemokraterna-rostar-oftare-med-socialdemokraterna-an-med-moderaterna/ [Accessed 10 March 2019].

Sunnercrantz, Liv, 2017: *Hegemony and the Intellectual Function: Medialised Public Discourse on Privatisation in Sweden 1988–1993*. PhD dissertation. Lund: Lund University.

Sunnercrantz, Liv, 2020: "Vom Gegner lernen. Der anti-etatistische und nicht-nationalistische Populismus der neoliberalen Rechten in Schweden" in Seongcheol Kim & Aristotelis Agridopoulos (eds.) *Populismus, Diskurs, Staat*. Baden-Baden: Nomos.

Taggart, Paul A., 1996: *New Populism and the New Politics: New Protest Parties in Sweden in a Comparative Perspective*. Basingstoke: Palgrave Macmillan.

Tilli, Jouni, 2019: "Finnish Discourses on Immigration, 2015–2016: Descendants of Ishmael, Welfare Surfers, and Economic Assets" in Jouni Tilli & Clarke Rountree (eds.) *National Rhetorics in the Syrian Immigration Crisis: Victims, Frauds, and Floods*. East Lansing: Michigan State University Press.

Torehammars supervalår, 'Utfrågning och livequiz med Jimmie Åkesson (SD)', 140813.

Varveus, Anders, 1989: "Glasnost på finansdepartementet?" in *Nyliberalen*, 1989:1, 3.

Virtanen, Aarni, 2018: *Vennamo: mies ja hänen puolueensa*. Helsinki: Art House.

Westholm, Carl-Johan, 1988: "Borgerligheten som kyrkoruin" in Torgny T. Segerstedt (ed.) *Det politiskt omöjliga*. Stockholm: Ratio.

Widfeldt, Anders, 2015: *Extreme Right Parties in Scandinavia*. London: Routledge.

Wingborg, Mats, 2016: *Den blåbruna röran: SD:s flirt med Alliansen och högerns vägval*. Stockholm: Leopard förlag.

Ydling Brunbech, Peter, 2011: "Fremskridtspartiet 1972–2001" in *danmarkshistorien.dk*. https://danmarkshistorien.dk/leksikon-og-kilder/vis/materiale/fremskridtspartiet/ [Accessed 10 February 2019].

Ylä-Anttila, Tuukka, 2017: *The Populist Toolkit: Finnish Populism in Action 2007–2016*. Helsinki: University of Helsinki.

9 Cultural policy and cultural diversity

Pasi Saukkonen

Policies reflect societal realities as well as political ideas and ideologies. There-fore, policies are in a state of constant change. Cultural policy makes no excep-tion. In modern times, both the more narrow arts policy and the broader cultural policy have developed in relation to what has been taking place in their local and national environments, with regard to international agreements and in the context of the proliferation of ideas and innovations. In addition to the promotion of arts and creativity, policies regarding arts and culture have always had other, more instrumental, societal functions.

The first half of the 20th century was characterized in Europe by the consol-idation of nation-building processes, and cultural policy instruments were used to strengthen national feelings and enhance national esteem. In the second half of the century, especially in the 1960s and thereafter, cultural policy increas-ingly became a tool to enhance welfare and well-being. At the same time, the cultural needs and rights of traditional minorities and the value of the diversity of cultural expressions received more attention.

Meanwhile, immigrants from other parts of Europe and from other parts of the globe began to arrive. In the final decades of the century, practically all European countries had become destinations of international mobility. As immigrants formed families, new ethnic groups and cultural minorities were established. Many countries acknowledged the diversification of societies; some of them even celebrated multiculturalism. Gradually, national cultural policies started accommodating their principles and operations in relation to changing demographic and ethno-cultural structures.

In the 1990s, however, different forms of neo-nationalism appeared on the political scene, challenging multiculturalist ideas of responding to the new diversity. Nationalist forces have been able to occupy influential positions in many countries and this development has had repercussions for national cul-tural policies. Moreover, the global financial crisis that started in 2008 has put additional pressure on the funding of public services. In many countries, cul-tural policies and arts policies have suffered from austerity measures.[1] In times of affluence, it is also easier to allocate resources for minorities and other devia-tions from mainstream culture than in periods of resource scarcity.

DOI: 10.4324/9780429026690-9

In this chapter, I will take a closer look at the development sketched previously by focusing on four Nordic countries: Denmark, Finland, Norway and Sweden. The main questions guiding the analysis are the following: what has been the national cultural policy reaction towards the increasing ethnic and cultural diversity in these countries? Have neo-nationalist political ideas, parties and movements during the last few decades already influenced national cultural policies? Is there a Nordic cultural policy model, and if yes, is this model under pressure?

Nordic nations and the diversification of societies

Nordic countries have traditionally had a reputation of being nation-states, that is, societies where the national community and the political unit, the state, are congruent. There are differences between them, though. Sweden and Denmark belong to older European states where the nation-building process has been state-led. Norway and Finland are, in turn, countries that gained full independence in the early 20th century. The 19th-century nation formation took place at the same time as a state-seeking process was going on. In comparison with many Eastern European nations that belonged to the Russian, Austro-Hungarian, or Ottoman empires, in both cases there was nevertheless an autonomous unit before independence within which the consolidation of the state-nation relation could develop: the personal union between Norway and Sweden since 1814 and the autonomous Grand Duchy of Finland since 1809.

These four Nordic countries never had completely homogeneous populations – that is, there have always been ethnic, linguistic, religious and cultural minorities.[2] The Sámi, speaking many different languages, are considered an indigenous people with age-old origins in the region. The Roma diaspora was also established in Scandinavia centuries ago. In larger cities, there was often a Jewish community and other minorities and ethnic or national groups. At the end of the 19th century, many Tatars moved to Finland thereby forming one of the oldest Muslim communities in Western Europe.

In literature concerning nationalism and the treatment of minorities, it has often been mentioned that the state-led (often Western European) version of nation-building has been more benign towards minorities, whereas in the state-seeking (often Eastern European) countries there has more often been hostility and even persecution. Assimilation has been a frequently applied model of integration in both cases, but in the more radical nationalism, it has often been carried out with clearly oppressive means.[3]

If we look at these Nordic countries from the perspective of minority rights, the picture is, however, more complicated. In the first half of the 20th century, minority rights were best guaranteed in Finland. Finland became an officially bilingual state right from the beginning of independence and the state church system was abandoned in the 1860s. Denmark recognized the cultural rights of Germans in South Jylland after the plebiscite in 1920, but otherwise minorities had few rights before the second half of the 20th century. Norway also became bilingual, with two variations of the Norwegian language, *nynorsk* and *bokmål*. Sweden was characterized by what has been called *folkhem*-nationalism in which the basic idea was that it would be better for the members of minority groups and communities to assimilate into the majority, ethnically and culturally.[4]

Generally speaking, there was positive development in the position of minorities and in the provision of individual and collective rights for members of minority communities after the Second World War. Especially since the mid-1960s, a kind of general mental or theoretical framework was developed within which the recognition of minority rights was combined with the concession made by many minorities not to challenge state integrity. Instead of full independence, the objective became different kinds of autonomy solutions, either territorial or non-territorial, or at least the provision of cultural rights for the representatives of minorities.[5] In Norway, Sweden and Finland, the position of the Sámi, in particular, started improving in this period.[6]

At the same time, ethnic and cultural structures have undergone significant changes. Europe had been a continent of emigration for centuries, and in the last decades of the 19th century vast numbers of people from the Nordic countries left their places of origin to search for a new life and opportunities elsewhere, mainly in the United States, Canada, Australia and New Zealand. After the Second World War, as a result of the collapse of colonial empires and of the post-war reconstruction and rapid economic development, many European countries started either receiving immigrants from former colonies or recruiting a foreign labour force and sometimes both.

With regard to post-war immigration, there are again some important differences between the Nordic countries. The most obvious exception is Finland that remained a country of emigration until the 1970s, much longer than the other three Scandinavian states. The main country of destination for Finnish emigrants was Sweden that, in turn, has received more newcomers than any other Nordic country. In 2000, the percentage of that population that were foreign-born was in Finland only 2.6 per cent, and Finns constituted the largest group of immigrants in Sweden. At that time, there were about one million foreign-born people in Sweden (11.3%). In Denmark and Norway, the foreign-born population stood at 5.6 and 6.8 per cent, and in absolute numbers, the size of the immigrant population was similar (about 300.000), too.

Since the turn of the millennium, the Nordic countries have also followed different paths in immigration and immigration policy. Denmark started restricting its immigration policy, especially concerning those seeking international protection. Sweden, in turn, remained an important destination of international mobility until the political turnover in 2015, and the share of those with a refugee background of all immigrants is high in international comparison. Finland became a country of immigration in the early 1990s, and immigration from Estonia, Russia and other countries continued to diversify the population rapidly in the 2000s. Norway also has recently received many asylum seekers. In addition, the country has become an important destination of labour migrants from countries that joined the European Union in 2004 such as Poland and Lithuania. In terms of the share of migrants in population, Norway has approached Sweden, whereas Finland has come closer to Denmark (Table 9.1). If we would include those born in the country of residence to parents born abroad (the so-called second generation), the figures would be much higher, and the gap between Finland and the other countries significantly wider.[7]

This development means that the Nordic countries of today are unquestionably ethnically and culturally diverse. There are hundreds of languages spoken, privately and publicly, especially in the metropolitan areas. All major world religions with their belief systems and ceremonies are present in Nordic spiritual life. A vast number of cultural traditions are reproduced in smaller and larger circles. Lots of people have some kind of combined, mixed or hyphenated identity, many individuals also feel like living in a third space outside of all ethno-cultural or national categories. Calling these countries nation-states in the meaning stated here is no longer correct.

Nordic multiculturalism

Before analysing the cultural policy development in Denmark, Finland, Norway and Sweden more closely, it is worthwhile to take a more detailed look at different approaches to ethnic and cultural diversity in these four countries. Nationalism was, after the Second World War, discredited as an ideology, especially in its most extreme, fascist forms. However, there are significant

Table 9.1 Top ten foreign-born populations by country of birth in 2017.

Denmark		Finland		Norway		Sweden	
Poland	39.400	Former USSR	56.476	Poland	97.553	Finland	153.620
Germany	35.660	Estonia	45.659	Sweden	48.316	Syria	149.418
Syria	33.530	Sweden	32.147	Lithuania	37.686	Iraq	135.129
Turkey	32.45	Iraq	13.825	Somalia	28.720	Poland	88.704
Romania	24.42	Russia	13.668	Germany	27.965	Iran	70.637
Sweden	22.85	Somalia	11.102	Denmark	24.762	Former Yugoslavia	66.539
Iraq	21.22	China	10.447	Iraq	22.524	Somalia	63.853
Norway	20.19	Thailand	10.184	Philippines	22.211	Bosnia and Herzegovina	58.181
United Kingdom	19.54	Viet Nam	7.468	Syria	20.833	Germany	50.189
Bosnia and Herzegovina	17.14	Former Yugoslavia	7.307	Pakistan	20.138	Turkey	47.060
Foreign-born population, N	**641.3**		**357.541**		**799.797**		**1784.497**
Foreign-born population, %	**11.2**		**6.5**		**15.1**		**18.0**

Source: OECD.

differences between states with regard to the cultural rights of minorities and newcomers even within the relatively homogeneous group of Nordic countries. Some Nordic countries have been more nationalist and less multiculturalist than others.[8]

In literature concerning minority rights and immigrant integration, there is usually a distinction made between assimilationist countries and multiculturalist countries.[9] In an assimilationist strategy, historical minorities are hardly recognized, and immigrants are supposed to leave behind their old identity and cultural traditions and markers. Multiculturalism, in turn, recognizes different forms of ethnic and cultural diversity. The state regards this diversity positively, or at least neutrally, and feels obligated to support at least some minorities in the realization of cultural rights.

The Multiculturalism Policy Index (MCP) developed at Queens University in Canada is helpful in comparing the Nordic countries with regard to the cultural rights of national minorities, indigenous people and immigrant groups. The MCP Index monitors the evolution of multiculturalism policies in 21 Western democracies. It has been designed to provide information about multiculturalism policies in a standardized format concerning the three types of minorities mentioned previously. Each policy indicator captures a policy dimension where liberal-democratic states face a choice about whether or not to take a multicultural turn and to become more accommodating and supportive of minorities.[10]

The Swedish post-war approach was assimilationist until the late 1960s after which the country took a conspicuous multiculturalist turn concerning both more traditional and more recent minorities (Table 9.2). Instead of assimilation, the key words of the new policy became equality, co-operation and freedom of choice. The last point referred to the right of newcomers and their descendants to choose whether they would like to become Swedish or to maintain their previous identity and culture. Nowadays, it is the most multiculturalist country regarding immigrant groups in Europe.

When it comes to the total score, Finland comes first. This is because the MCP Index does not recognize Nordic minorities other than the Swedish-speakers in

Table 9.2 Multiculturalism policies in Denmark, Finland, Norway and Sweden.

	Total score for immigrant minorities				Total score for indigenous people			Total score for national minorities		
	1980	*1990*	*2000*	*2010*	*1980*	*2000*	*2010*	*1980*	*2000*	*2010*
Denmark	0	0	0	0	6	7	7	N.B.	N.B.	N.B.
Finland	0	0	1.5	6	3.5	3.5	4	4	4.5	4.5
Norway	0	0	0	3.5	0.5	4	5	N.B.	N.B.	N.B.
Sweden	3	3.5	5	7	1	2	3	N.B.	N.B.	N.B.

Source: Multiculturalism Policy Index.

Finland as a national minority.[11] The Sámi policy is most advanced in Norway, but the Danish policy with regard to the rights of the population of Greenland is even better assessed. Denmark turns out to be the least multiculturalist. In relation to immigrant integration, there has been multiculturalist development between 2000 and 2010 in Finland, Norway and Sweden, whereas the Danish approach has remained strictly assimilationist.[12]

Cultural policy development

The development of modern Nordic cultural policy has taken place in the general context of the construction of the Nordic welfare state.[13] The autonomy of the field of the arts has occupied a central position, and the arm's length principle in making many policy decisions has been guaranteed. Cultural policy, arts policy in particular, has been regarded as a means to promote aesthetic values in a society according to a humanistic rationality that emphasizes artistic quality as the most important assessment criteria. Under the slogan or cultural democratization, arts of high quality were made accessible to all citizens regardless of their social status or geographical location.

Together with the expansion of financing of culture and the arts by public authorities, other aims, objectives, rationalities and discourses have emerged. Dorte Skot-Hansen[14] has in the Danish context and from the point of view of local cultural policy written about a social rationality emphasizing social and cultural emancipation, and the Swedish scholar Jenni Johannisson[15] has written about welfare discourse enhancing citizenship participation. Cultural democracy became, especially in the 1970s, one of the keywords of cultural policy, denoting an increasing recognition of group-based cultural activities and of different forms or artistic and cultural expressions. Local cultural initiatives were increasingly stimulated, and everyday culture was given more credit. In this heyday of Nordic welfare states, cultural policy was also legitimized as an important instrument in the fight against the negative impacts of commercialization and cultural industry.[16]

Nordic scholars also seem to be quite unanimous in their judgments that in the last few decades, since the 1980s, the instrumentalization of cultural policies has become all the more prominent.[17] Instead of having an intrinsic value, arts and culture are increasingly seen as assets that can be used for social, economic and even political purposes. The role of markets has become stronger and international visibility is appreciated more than before. Commercial culture is not shunned any more. Quite the contrary, economic success is increasingly taken as a sign of high quality. As a result, different rationalities and discourses are now overlapping in Nordic cultural policies making these policies quite multifaceted.

Despite of these similarities in overall cultural policy development, based on the differences between the four Nordic countries with regard to minority rights and the integration of immigrants, we can expect that there should also be clear differences between Denmark, Finland, Norway and Sweden when it comes to the adaptation of arts policy and cultural policy to the more diverse societal realities. In the following, I shall briefly look at the development in each of these four countries separately. I will mainly concentrate on the policy principles and policy implementation concerning immigrants and new ethnic groups.[18]

Sweden: from celebration of diversity to mainstreaming

In the Swedish Government Bill on Culture in 1974, immigrants and members of minority groups – together with children, handicapped people and other marginalized people – were regarded as disadvantaged groups whose position should be improved. Immigrants and minorities were also thought to give inspiration to Swedish society if they had a chance to maintain their own culture and identity. State institutions were expected to give groups and communities as much autonomy as possible in managing their own affairs.[19]

This reasoning was in line with the changes in the overall approach of Swedish society towards minorities and immigrants. In practice, however, concrete action remained quite modest, and for the most part, located outside official cultural policy. Swedish schools started giving native language instruction to immigrants and to members of minority groups. Newcomers and members of minority groups were also encouraged to form their own associations and media organizations and to apply for public funding. Immigrant and minority cultural activities were supposed to take place mainly within these organizational frameworks.

In the 1990s, Swedish integration policy and cultural policy were almost simultaneously reformed. Immigrants and minorities were now regarded as an intrinsic part of Sweden, and diversity (*mångfald*) became a key concept.[20] The emphasis of policy moved from a group-based to an individual-based approach. The national cultural policy reform also introduced a new concept, world culture (*världskultur*), which took a central place in diversity-related cultural policy and mainly referred to non-Western cultures.[21] Furthermore, there was a proposal to establish regional world culture consultants.[22]

The commission report that preceded the government's 1997 proposition on integration policy urged the Swedish cultural policy and cultural landscape to better reflect society's diversity. Swedish cultural arenas and institutions were challenged to broaden their operational framework and offerings. Specific state allowances to promote the cultural activities of ethnic or linguistic groups were also suggested. In the final proposition, concrete ideas were, nevertheless, either omitted or profoundly reformulated.[23]

The next major step was taken in 2004 when the Swedish Government decided to proclaim 2006 a specific Year of Cultural Diversity (*Mångkulturåret* 2006). The main idea was that publicly funded cultural institutions and organizations have a responsibility to address and include the whole Swedish population.[24] Studies conducted as preparatory work for the special year had shown that there was a wide gap between those people who were regularly involved in publicly financed cultural activities as practitioners or audiences and those who were rarely or never involved.[25]

In the final report regarding the accomplishments during *Mångkulturåret*, the national coordinator, Yvonne Rock, found it promising that there exists a strong and growing will to promote ethnic and cultural diversity in the publicly financed cultural sector.[26] However, the Year of Cultural Diversity was also treated with criticism in the Swedish media and among artists and cultural workers. For example, instead of the original aim of generating long-lasting, structural changes, the year was often considered something special and temporary, sometimes even as something that disturbed already existing activities and development.[27]

Swedish cultural policy was once again reformed in 2009. According to the Government Bill on cultural policy, culture in Sweden should now be a dynamic, challenging and independent force based on freedom of expression. Everyone should be able to participate in cultural life, and creativity, diversity and artistic quality should mark society's development. Under the heading, 'diversity and inter-cultural co-operation', the bill discusses discrimination, participation in culture and the arts, gender equality, national minorities and other forms of diversity. Cultural policy should contribute to increasing diversity and to a multifaceted cultural supply and thus to everyone's increased freedom of choice.[28]

So close to *Mångkulturåret*, references to ethnic and cultural diversity are strikingly short, superficial and ambiguous. Jenny Johannisson has also pointed out that there is a clear rank order in the Swedish cultural policy that also reflects the tensions between particularism and universalism and between democratic and aesthetic values, favouring the latter.[29] Nina Edström and Charlotte Hyltén-Cavallius, in turn, argue that integration policy and cultural policy have moved further away from each other.[30] At the same time, integration policy initiatives have since been, at least rhetorically, included in the cultural policy. An illustration of this might be that the Swedish Arts Council (Kulturrådet), which allocates state funding to many arts and cultural institutions, now points at promoting the cultural diversity perspective as one of their central tasks.

Finland: multiculturalism in principle with little concrete impact

Finnish cultural policy adapted to the societal change quite swiftly when immigration started to increase in the early 1990s. The first policy guidelines of the Ministry of Education and Culture concerning immigration were published in 2003. In this document, cultural services and the support mechanisms in the field of culture and the arts were considered important means to advance integration. The needs of minority cultures should be better taken into account in the general system for supporting arts and culture and in the functioning of cultural and art institutions. Furthermore, the cultural needs of immigrants should be taken care of by increasing the financial means for supporting minority cultures to correspond with the changes caused by immigration. Finally, systems for supporting professional artists that belong to ethnic minorities and their organizations should be developed.

These guidelines can be seen as a key document that has laid the general framework for Finnish cultural policy regarding cultural diversity. Other strategic documents have also displayed a positive view to ethnic and cultural diversity and to the cultural rights of immigrants. For example, the national strategy for cultural policy that was published in 2009 clearly affirms the positive attitude towards diversity and multiculturalism:

> Finland is a multicultural country with a strong cultural identity. The cultural diversity springs from a wealth of diverse regions, languages, indigenous cultures and cultural heritage – diverse cultural expressions and mores. . . . Immigrants are a new creativity and talent resource, and the positive effects of multiculturalism add to the vitality of Finnish culture.[31]

There have been concrete instruments to achieve the stated policy goals in the 2003 guidelines. At the national level, the main channel to financially support the maintenance of language, culture and identity has been the state grants for supporting multiculturalism and combating racism. Another important measure has been the establishment of the Helsinki City Library to function as the national Multilingual Library. The cultural needs of immigrants and cultural minorities have also been included into general efforts to secure everyone's equal opportunity to participate in culture and to express creativity. In order to achieve this task, the Ministry of Education started financing Culture for All Service in 2003. An independent association later took over this service. The state-funded Cultura Foundation supports the maintenance and development of the linguistic and cultural identity of the Russian-speaking population in Finland and also otherwise promotes bidirectional and multi-dimensional integration.

In 2009, The Arts Council of Finland (later the Arts Promotion Centre) started distributing grants for art projects promoting multiculturalism in Finland. The overall aims were, on the one hand, to strengthen the opportunities for immigrant artists and for artists belonging to national ethnic minorities to engage in artistic activities and to take part on an equal basis in Finnish artistic life. On the other hand, the objective was to support the multicultural work of other artists and working groups and art projects promoting intercultural interaction in Finland.[32] The Arts Promotion Centre also later distributed the grants for supporting multiculturalism and combating racism.

It would thus be unfair to say that multiculturalism in Finnish cultural policy would be mere rhetoric. However, similar to the Swedish situation, a closer look reveals some qualifications to the general picture. For example, we can observe a discrepancy between the general and specific level of cultural policy documents. Immigration, minorities and the overall ethnic and cultural diversity, and the new challenges that these changes pose for national cultural policy, were easily discernible in the general cultural policy documents, such as the cultural policy strategy. In policy documents closer to the implementation of cultural policy and arts policy, such as policy plans and programs for music, visual arts and performing arts, these questions were much weaker and far less systematically answered.[33]

This observation is also in line with the results of a survey carried out in 2007 in which arts and cultural institutions in the Helsinki region were asked how they take immigration and the ethnic and cultural diversification of Finland into account.[34] The survey revealed that there undoubtedly was much goodwill in the Finnish arts and cultural institutions to do something. However, there were very few examples of concrete action. In many cases, these activities were considered something additional that one can start implementing if there is extra funding available.[35]

It is also relevant to ask how much money there has been in the Finnish cultural policy to achieve the stated policy objectives regarding cultural diversity. Based on the available sources, one can conclude that the amount of money for the maintenance of language and culture and for multicultural arts projects has been relatively small. Public funding has mainly been sufficient to relatively small-scale and project-like activities only.[36]

Norway: slow acceptance of the change

According to Trevor Davies[37] (2007), Norwegian cultural policy started paying more attention to the ethnic and cultural diversification of the society at the end of the 1990s. Before that, activities had usually been limited to separate, often short-term, projects and initiatives without sufficient funding. In 1996, it was officially acknowledged that Norwegian society has always been culturally diverse and will also increasingly be so in the future. As in Sweden and Finland, diversity was then in Norway generally seen as an enriching element and an asset in society.

An important specific investment was the *Mosaikk* programme from 1998 to 2000. The main purpose of this programme was to promote multicultural and intercultural expressions in the established arts and cultural policy arrangements and in the daily operations in culture and the arts. Furthermore, the programme strived for improving minority groups' opportunities for self-defined creativity and for enhancing the participation of members of minority groups in the arts as artists and as audience.

As a whole, *Mosaikk* was considered a success. However, the incorporation of diversity issues into the ordinary operations of arts institutions proved to be difficult also in Norway. In addition, the aims and objectives of the programme were criticized for being not clear enough and the scope of the programme for being too large. The demarcation of multicultural projects into a category of its own, in which rules different from the rest of the arts world and arts policy would apply, was also criticized.[38]

Furthermore, inspired by the Swedish Year of Cultural Diversity and the European Union Year of Intercultural Dialogue, Norway decided to celebrate 2008 as a specific Year of Cultural Diversity (*Mangfaldsår*). The aim of this thematic year was to stimulate both traditional and new cultural actors to work for the sake of cultural diversity and to strengthen the cooperation of established institutions with artists and audiences with a minority background. In addition, there was an effort to incorporate a multicultural perspective into different operations and to institutionalize arenas in which people representing different views could challenge each other. Similar to the Swedish *Mångkulturåret*, cultural diversity was supposed to have sustainable impact on Norwegian cultural policy.

However, also in this case, the development has been slow and cumbersome. In 2013, an extensive cultural policy report examined the role of cultural policy in the Norwegian nation-building process, analysed contemporary challenges and proposed recommendations. According to this *Kulturutredningen*, cultural diversity has become an important characteristic in Norwegian society. However, this demographic fact is not properly reflected in culture and the arts, in the professional and institutionalized part of cultural life, in particular. People belonging to minority groups are clearly underrepresented in culture and the arts. The authors of the report point out that in the future it would be essential to enhance the accessibility of cultural services and to give support to such forms of arts and culture that different groups find interesting and meaningful.[39]

Denmark: ignorance of diversity issues

Knowing the general anti-multiculturalist approach of Denmark to the cultural rights of immigrants, it is not surprising to notice that issues related to the diversification of Danish society have largely been ignored in Danish cultural policy.[40] Not completely, though. In the 1970s, at the same time cultural democracy (the equality of different forms of cultural creativity and expressions) and cultural democratization (increased equality in the participation in 'high culture') were important catchwords in cultural policy, cultural activities of ethnic and cultural minorities, and the intrinsic value of these activities, were also increasingly recognized.

However, Dorte Skot-Hansen[41] has remarked that this recognition-in-principle had little practical impact. The promotion of cultural democracy was mostly delegated to Danish municipalities. In some cases, local communities incorporated activities by immigrant or minority groups or by immigrant artists to the operations of local cultural centres or community houses. At the national level, 'multiculturalist' cultural policy activities were located into the social sector or into humanitarian organizations that, in the final instance, aimed at a one-way integration of newcomers into society. Of these activities, many remained separate from other operations and of short duration.

At the end of the 1990s, there was a short period when the general attitude seemed to be changing. Minister of Culture Jytte Hilden felt the need to better recognize the existence of different subcultures, including those of immigrant groups. A series of publications on cultural policy (*Kulturens politik*) included a subchapter on culturally diverse Denmark. The authors of this chapter suggested that the national government should initiate concrete action to benefit immigrants. The Hilden's successor, Ebbe Lundgaard, also pointed out that Danish cultural policy should 'provide possibilities for the new Danes to cultivate their cultures, preferably in a form which invites other Danes to gain more familiarity with them'.[42]

These suggestions did not receive much positive response nor did they lead to concrete implementation. In addition to small-scale activities, one can notice the mentioning of ethnic and cross-cultural art among the two focus areas of a specific development fund (*Kulturministeriets Udviklingsfond*) established in 1998. Its role, however, remained modest. According to Skot-Hansen, this was partly a result of the lack of goals clear enough to promote concrete action.[43] Furthermore, there were difficulties in combining the traditional notion of quality emphasizing universalist and aesthetic values and a more group-based notion of quality that recognizes different cultural contexts in making value judgments.

Neo-nationalism and cultural policy

The brief analysis of cultural policy development in the four Nordic countries here reveals, on the one hand, that there are differences between Denmark, Finland, Norway and Sweden. Accommodation to new and more diverse demographic realities is traceable especially in Finland and Sweden and to a growing extent also in Norway whereas in Denmark societal change caused by immigration has been approached with hesitation if not reluctance. On the other hand, however, even in the more multiculturalist countries, the inclusion of diversity issues into mainstream cultural policy has been cumbersome.

During the last 25 years or so, the Nordic political landscape has been complemented with new parties and movements that have sometimes been labelled right-wing populist parties, radical right parties, or xenophobic politics.[44] In this context, I will call these actors neo-nationalist because of the importance of restrictions to immigration, critique of multiculturalism and the emphasis on traditional 'national' culture on their political agenda.[45] Can we trace any impact of neo-nationalism in Nordic cultural policy during the last few decades?

In Sweden, the electoral support of neo-nationalism, in the shape of Sweden Democrats, long remained at a low level, but it has recently started rising. In the 2014 parliamentary election, the party received almost 13 per cent of the vote, and in 2018, the electoral support rose to 17.5 per cent. Until now, the established parties have refused to co-operate with them, thus isolating the party from decision-making. Therefore, we can, at least for the time being, notice that Swedish cultural policy has had a rather anti-populist and anti-nationalist character even though there have not been any notable new openings towards the incorporation of diversity into cultural policy or arts policy either.

The Finnish nationalist-populist party, the True Finns (later the Finns Party) received a big victory in the 2011 national elections and was able to maintain its level of support in the 2015 and 2019 elections. In 2015, the party also joined the government coalition together with the moderate conservatives (National Coalition) and the Center Party. A representative of the party, Sampo Terho, was nominated as the minister of culture in May 2017.[46] In public, Terho was frequently interpreted as a conservative willing to support culture with a national or traditional character. This possibility to exercise power has not, however, caused major repercussions to national cultural policy. When the law for the Finnish Public Broadcasting Company was reformed, the tasks of the company were slightly modified to a more nationalist and less multicultural direction.[47]

The Norwegian Progress Party, which represents Nordic nationalist populism in Norway, has been a partner in two consecutive governments since 2013. This has not, however, led into dramatic changes in the Norwegian cultural policy from the point of view of ethnic and cultural diversity. According to Per Mangset and Bård Kleppe, the main reason behind the fact that there are now fewer programmes emphasizing multiculturalism in the arts is the growing emphasis on the autonomy or the arts. Guidelines promoting multiculturalism, for example, have been abolished from the funding agreements of national cultural organizations.[48]

The most obvious impact can be discovered in Denmark where, after the 2001 election, a ten-year period of Centre-Right minority governments leaning on the support of the nationalist and populist Danish People's Party started. This led to cuts in the state cultural budget, including the closing down of the development fund mentioned earlier. Danish language and traditional Danish culture were emphasized in culture policy, the launch of the Danish cultural canon as the most concrete indication of this approach. None of the works of art included in the canon was made by an immigrant artist or reflected immigrant experiences in Danish society.[49]

In 2011–2015, two left-wing cabinets led by the Social Democratic prime minister governed Denmark. According to Dorte Skot-Hansen,[50] a more liberal attitude towards diversity prevailed and there was an explicit wish to depart from a strict division between the Danish 'us' and the foreign 'them'. However, these ideas never resulted as major concrete action. In 2015–2019, two right-wing governments again strongly emphasized national values and traditions in cultural policy. According to the Government Declaration of the third government of Lars Løkke Rasmussen: 'Culture is a decisive element of our identity as a nation and as a people.'

Conclusion

Nordic countries have often been classified as states where the political unit and the national community are congruent, but this nation-state characterization is no longer correct. All four countries are ethnically and culturally diverse and continue to be ever more so. The largest cities, in particular, are home to lots of ethnic, national, linguistic and religious groups and communities from all over the world. Majority-minority situations where the native population no longer exceeds the 50 per cent threshold are increasingly common.

No unified Nordic model exists to respond to this ethno-cultural diversification. Sweden embraced multiculturalism in the late 1960s whereas Denmark has until today been reluctant to accept this societal change and to provide immigrants with group-related cultural rights. When immigration to Finland started increasing, this country also took a positive view towards multicultural solutions. Norway has also gradually started delivering more rights and freedoms to newcomers and their communities, getting closer to Sweden and Finland and further away from Denmark.

Focussing on cultural policy development, we can also trace differences between the Nordic countries. There has been more cultural policy multiculturalism in Sweden and in Finland whereas Danish cultural policy has not accommodated cultural policy in an increasingly diverse society. In contrast, the governments have often explicitly expected newcomers to assimilate to Danish values. The Norwegian development has again taken a position in between, gradually approaching the Swedish and Finnish recognition of the need for policy adjustment.

However, it is also important to notice that the implementation of multiculturalist cultural policy has often turned out to be slow and problematic. In particular, it has been difficult to incorporate diversity issues into regular arts policy and cultural policy. Even though mainstreaming has been the explicit target, special arrangements have been the most frequently applied solution. Resources allocated to diversity programmes and practices have been modest, fragmented and usually short-lived. Therefore, the difference between Denmark and the rest of the Nordic countries appears wider at the level of policy principles than policy practices. Sweden and Finland have never been as multiculturalist as it might seem if we made judgments based solely on policy discourse.

It also seems that the climax (at least so far) of cultural policy multiculturalism was at the end of the 1990s and during the first years of the new millennium. During the last 10–15 years, we have witnessed far less noteworthy initiatives or openings than in the years preceding this period. Neo-nationalism has also been growing in popularity, but its influence to cultural policy development has, again with Denmark as an exception, been quite modest. Therefore, it seems that there has been a general change of atmosphere towards diversity in general and multiculturalism in particular. Instead of celebration, ethno-cultural differences are nowadays treated with hesitation if not suspicion.

Both ethno-cultural diversification in society and the strengthening of neo-nationalism are challenging traditional self-understanding and national identity in the Nordic countries. Multicultural diversity renders the assumption of demographic homogeneity problematic, and many Nordics look to the future with anxiety when they see their society drifting further away from the old nationalist ideal. In contrast, there also are a lot of inhabitants in the Nordic countries that experience nationalist and radical right parties and politicians threatening the pluralistic values of openness, tolerance and mutual trust. In these circumstances where gloomy future visions prevail, it is not easy to make progressive cultural policy that also would be properly implemented.

A previous version of this chapter has appeared in Swedish in *Kulturanalys Norden 2017*. I am thankful to Linnéa Lindsköld, Per Mangset and Dorte Skot-Hansen for their valuable comments regarding the recent development in Sweden, Norway and Denmark.

Notes

1 Inkei 2019.
2 See e.g. Cordell & Wolff 2004.
3 See e.g. Alcock 2002.
4 See e.g. Kivisto & Wahlbeck 2013.
5 Alcock 2002, 139–147.
6 See e.g. Sillanpää 1994.
7 For more information, see e.g. Karlsdottìr et al. 2018.
8 See e.g. Borevi 2013, Lœgaard 2013, Brochmann & Britt Djuve 2013.
9 See e.g. Favell 2001, Geddes & Scholten 2016.
10 There is more information about how the MCP Index works in practice at the index web site, www.queensu.ca/mcp/home.
11 Sweden has since 2010 had legislation concerning national minorities and minority languages. The position of these groups and languages is not, however, comparable with the position of Swedish-speakers and the Swedish language in Finland.
12 See also Kivisto & Wahlbeck 2013, Saukkonen 2013a.
13 Duelund 2003.
14 Skot-Hansen 1999.
15 Johannisson 2006.
16 Cf., Kangas 1999.
17 Skot-Hansen 1999, Johannisson 2006, Kangas 1999.
18 On a wider European development, see e.g. Bennett 2001, Meinhof & Triandafyllidou 2006. A more detailed analysis of the countries in question can be found from Saukkonen 2010, 2013b, 2013c. On Nordic cultural policy regarding the Sámi, see e.g. Gaup 2007. On policies regarding national minorities, see e.g. country-specific monitoring on the implementation of the Council of Europe Framework Convention for the Protection of National Minorities and the Council of Europe European Charter for Regional or Minority Languages.
19 Egeland 2007, 63, Tawat 2014, 10; see also Edström & Hyltén-Cavallius in Kulturanalys 2017.
20 On the concept of *mångfald*, see Lindsköld in Kulturanalys 2017.
21 Egeland 2007.
22 This plan was finally realized in 2002 when the Government allocated SEK 3.0 M. for regional multicultural consultants, Edström 2006, 9.

23 Edström 2006, 11.
24 SOU 2005, 9–10.
25 Pripp, Plisch & Printz Werner 2004.
26 SOU 2007, 28–29.
27 Edström & Hyltén-Cavallius 2011, 5–12.
28 Regeringens Proposition 2009, 22–24.
29 Johannisson 2012, 48–49.
30 Edström & Hyltén-Cavallius 2011, 11.
31 Ministry of Education 2009, 16.
32 See also Paula Karhunen's contribution in Kulturanalys 2017.
33 Saukkonen 2010, 97–102.
34 Saukkonen, Ruusuvirta & Joronen 2007.
35 Cf., Myndigheten för kulturanalys 2017.
36 Saukkonen 2010, 222.
37 Davies 2007.
38 Marsio 2005, 40.
39 NOU 2013, 15.
40 Cf., Lœgaard 2013.
41 Skot-Hansen 2002, 199–200.
42 Quoted from Skot-Hansen 2002, 201.
43 Skot-Hansen 2002, 204, 206–207.
44 See e.g. Widfeldt 2018.
45 On Scandinavian radical right parties and cultural policy, see also Linsköld 2015.
46 In June 2017, the Finns Party split into two fractions after a change of the party's chairperson. The dissident group, called the New Alternative (later forming a new Party, Blue Reform), remained in the Government. Terho continued at his post as the Minister of Culture.
47 Previously, one of the public tasks of the Finnish YLE was to support tolerance and multiculturalism. The new regulation first emphasizes the need to foster Finnish cultural heritage, and after that mentions tolerance, equity, equality, and cultural diversity that also deserve support.
48 Mangset & Bård Kleppe 2016, 19.
49 Tawat 2014, 9.
50 A speech given by Skot-Hansen at the Nordic cultural policy research conference in Helsinki, 23 August 2017.

References

Alcock, Anthony, 2002: *A History of the Protection of Regional Cultural Minorities in Europe*. Houndmills: Palgrave Macmillan.

Bennett, Tony, 2001: *Differing Diversities. Transversal Study on the Theme of Cultural Policy and Cultural Diversity*. London: Council of Europe Publishing.

Borevi, Karin, 2013: "Understanding Swedish Multiculturalism" in Peter Kivisto & Östen Wahlbeck (eds.) *Debating Nordic Multiculturalism in Nordic Welfare States*. Houndmills: Palgrave Macmillan, 140–169.

Brochmann, Grete & Britt Djuve, Anne, 2013: "Multiculturalism or Assimilation? The Norwegian Welfare State Approach" in Peter Kivisto & Östen Wahlbeck (eds.) *Debating Nordic Multiculturalism in Nordic Welfare States*. Houndmills: Palgrave Macmillan, 219–245.

Cordell, Karl & Wolff, Stefan (eds.) 2004: *The Ethnopolitical Encyclopedia of Europe*. Houndmills: Palgrave Macmillan.

Davies, Trevor, 2007: *Kulturel mangfoldighed set i forhold til Kunstrådet. Inspirationsrapport*. København: Kunstrådet.

Duelund, Peter, 2003: *The Nordic Cultural Model.* Copenhagen: Nordic Cultural Institute.

Edström, Nina, 2006: *Har du sett på mångkulturkonsulenten! Utvärdering av verksamheten med regionala konsulenter för mångkultur.* Botkyrka: Kulturrådet/Mångkulturellt centrum.

Edström, Nina & Charlotte, Hyltén-Cavallius, 2011: *Osmos – inkluderingprocesser i kulturlivet.* Botkyrka: Mångkulturellt centrum.

Egeland, Helene, 2007: *Det ekte, det gode og det coole. Södra teatern og den dialogiske formasjonen av mangfolddiskursen.* Linköping: Linköpings universitet.

Favell, Adrian, 2001: *Philosophies of Integration. Immigration and the Idea of Citizenship in France and Britain.* London: Palgrave Macmillan.

Gaup, Karin Mannela, 2007: *Samisk kulturpolitik i ett nordiskt perspektiv.* Umeå: Vaartoe – Centrum för Samisk forskning.

Geddes, Andrew & Scholten, Peter, 2016: *The Politics of Migration and Immigration in Europe* (2nd edition). London: Sage Publications.

Inkei, Péter, 2019: *Public Funding of Culture in Europe, 2004–2017.* Budapest: The Budapest Observatory.

Johannisson, Jenny, 2006: *Det lokala möter världen: kulturpolitiskt förändringsarbete i 1990-talets Göteborg.* Göteborg: Skrifter från Valfrid.

Johannisson, Jenny, 2012: "Kulturpolitik som redskap för mångfald" in *Den utmanande diskussionen. Debattskrift om kulturpolitik och identiteter i Norden.* Köpenhamn: Nordiska Ministerrådet.

Kangas, Anita, 1999: "Kulttuuripolitiikan uudet vaatteet" in Anita Kangas & Juha Virkki (eds.) *Kulttuuripolitiikan uudet vaatteet.* Jyväskylä: Jyväskylän yliopisto.

Karlsdottìr, Anna et al., 2018: *State of the Nordic Region 2018: Immigration and Integration Edition.* Copenhagen: Nordic Council of Ministers.

Kivisto, Peter & Östen Wahlbeck (eds.) 2013: *Debating Nordic Multiculturalism in Nordic Welfare States.* Houndmills: Palgrave Macmillan.

Kulturanalys Norden, 2017: *Vem får vara med? Perspektiv på inkludering och integration i kulturlivet i de Nordiska länderna.* Stockholm: Kulturanalys Norden.

Linsköld, Linnéa, 2015: "Contradicting Cultural Policy: – A Comparative Study of the Cultural Policy of the Scandinavian Radical Right" in *Nordisk Kulturpolitisk Tidskrift,* 18:1, 8–26.

Lœgaard, Sune, 2013: "Danish Anti-Multiculturalism? The Significance of the Political Framing of Diversity" in Peter Kivisto & Östen Wahlbeck (eds.) *Debating Nordic Multiculturalism in Nordic Welfare States.* Houndmills: Palgrave MacMillan, 170–196.

Mangset, Per & Bård, Kleppe, 2016: "Country Profile: Norway" in *Compendium of Cultural Policies and Trends in Europe* (13th edition). Strassbourg: Council of Europe/ERICarts.

Marsio, Leena, 2005: *Cultural Diversity Programme: Challenges and Solutions in Scandinavia.* MA thesis. Arts Management. Helsinki: Sibelius Academy.

Meinhof, Ulrike Hanna & Triandafyllidou, Anna (eds.) 2006: *Transcultural Europe: Cultural Policy in a Changing Europe.* Basingstoke: Palgrave Macmillan.

Ministry of Education, 2009: *Strategy for Cultural Policy.* Publications of the Ministry of Education 45/2009. Helsinki: Ministry of Education.

Myndigheten för kulturanalys, 2017: *Vilken mångfald? Kulturinstitutioners tolkningar av mångfaldsuppdraget.* Stockholm: Myndigheten för kulturanalys.

NOU, 2013: *Kulturutredningen 2014.* Norges offentlige utredninger 2013:4. Oslo: Kulturdepartementet.

Pripp, Oscar, Emil Plisch & Printz-Werner, Saara, 2004: *Tid för Mångfald. En studie av de statligt finansierade kulturinstitutionernas arbete med etnisk och kulturell mångfald.* Botkyrka: Mångkulturellt centrum.

Regeringens Proposition, 2011: *Tid för Kultur.* Regeringens Proposition 2009/10:3. Stockholm: Sveriges regering.

Saukkonen, Pasi, 2010: *Kotouttaminen ja kulttuuripolitiikka. Tutkimus maahanmuutosta ja monikulttuurisuudesta suomalaisella taiteen ja kulttuurin kentällä.* Helsinki: Kulttuuripoliittisen tutkimuksen edistämissäätiö.

Saukkonen, Pasi, 2013a: *Erilaisuuksien Suomi. Vähemmistö- ja kotouttamispolitiikan vaihtoehdot.* Helsinki: Gaudeamus.

Saukkonen, Pasi, 2013b: "Multiculturalism and Cultural Policy in Northern Europe" in *Nordisk Kulturpolitisk Tidskrift,* 16:2, 178–200.

Saukkonen, Pasi, 2013c: *Monikulttuurisuus ja kulttuuripolitiikka Pohjois-Euroopassa.* Helsinki: Kulttuuripoliittisen tutkimuksen edistämissäätiö.

Saukkonen, Pasi, Ruusuvirta, Minna & Joronen, Tuula, 2007: *"Tulossa on jotain juttuja". Kyselytutkimus pääkaupunkiseudun taide- ja kulttuuritoimijoiden suhteesta maahanmuuttoon ja monikulttuurisuuteen.* Helsinki: Kulttuuripoliittisen tutkimuksen edistämissäätiö & Helsingin kaupunki.

Sillanpää, Lennard, 1994: *Political and Administrative Responses to Sami Self-Determination. A Comparative Study of Public Administrations in Fennoscandia on the Issue of Sami Land Title as an Aboriginal Right.* Commentationes Scientiarum Socialium 48. Helsinki: Finnish Society of Sciences and Letters.

Skot-Hansen, Dorte, 1999: "Kultur til tiden – strategier i den lokale kulturpolitik" in *Nordisk kulturpolitisk tidskrift,* 2:1, 7–27.

Skot-Hansen, Dorte, 2002: "Danish Cultural Policy – from Monoculture Towards Cultural Diversity" in *International Journal of Cultural Policy,* 8:2, 197–210.

SOU, 2005: *Agenda för mångkultur. Programförklaring och kalendarium för Mångkulturåret 2006.* Delbetänkande från kommittén för samordning av mångkulturåret. Statens Offentliga Utredningar 91. Stockholm: Sveriges regering.

SOU, 2007: *Mångfald är framtiden.* Statens Offentliga Utredningar 50. Stockholm: Sveriges regering.

Tawat, Mahama, 2014: "Danish and Swedish Immigrants' Cultural Policies between 1960 and 2006. Toleration and the Celebration of Difference" in *International Journal of Cultural Policy,* 20:2, 202–220.

Widfeldt, Anders, 2018: *The Growth of the Radical Right in Nordic Countries: Observations from the Past 20 Years.* Washington, DC: Migration Policy Institute.

10 Managing moods

Media, politicians, and anxiety over public debate

Anu Koivunen

The notion of interregnum captures a mood: a sense of change and an anxiety regarding what will come and when. Interregnum is a state of waiting and anticipating, as it, in the Gramscian sense, denotes a period that lies between an old, declining system and an emerging new one. In the words of Wolfgang Streeck, interregnum is 'a period of tremendous insecurity in which the accustomed chains of cause and effect are no longer in force, and unexpected, dangerous and grotesquely abnormal events may occur at any moment'.[1] In Streeck's analysis, this illustrates the contemporary crisis of neoliberalism and global capitalism, as evidenced by the world-wide rise of populisms. However, it also serves to depict what Andrew Chadwick calls 'a time of fundamental change' and 'a chaotic transition period' caused by the increased influence of digital media in how political life is lived and mediated.[2] Digital technologies have profoundly altered how political actors, publics, and media interact. In the context of hybrid media and networked publics, politicians and journalists have been repositioned and now face new challenges.[3] Competing with the amplified influence of social media and PR, journalists have lost much of their power as agenda-setters and gatekeepers. Politicians are both benefiting from and agonising over the multitude of public arenas. While 'the disrupted public sphere'[4] allows them to bypass journalistic gatekeeping and to address different audiences in distinct and direct ways, the disintegration of a national public sphere challenges any attempt to mobilise a national sense of a 'we'. With the weakening of mass communication, the media as an institution and a key facility of national imagination is changing, which in turn affects the use and the force of nationalism as a principle of legitimation.[5] Characteristic of an interregnum is the absence of given interpretive frames: the waning of the old order entails not only an epistemological crisis but also an ontological one. If not imagination, what holds a nation together?

In this chapter, the notion of interregnum is invoked to identify a language of concern among Swedish and Finnish politicians and journalists and to interpret it as a response to the disintegration of national public spheres in the wake of globalised, digital media. It is the context of digital disruption, the chapter at hand suggests, that frames the recurrent debates in Sweden and Finland

DOI: 10.4324/9780429026690-10

regarding the problems of public debate and concerns over the tone. Whereas fear as an emotion has an object, anxiety as an affective state does not; rather, it connotes 'an approach to objects'.[6] In the context of the disrupted public sphere and networked publics, this chapter suggests that politicians and journalists have sought new identities and increasingly positioned themselves as analysts and managers of the nation's mood.

The 2010s entailed recurrent debates regarding debates, with a special focus on the tone and the attitudes of the participants. In 2016, *Dagens Nyheter* contended that the tone in Swedish politics was harsher than during what is known as 'hatred for Palme', referring to the strong feelings aroused by the late Social Democratic Prime Minister Olof Palme.[7] According to political scientist Stig-Björn Ljunggren, there was now a double political polarisation: on the one hand, between extreme positions in the public debate and, on the other hand, between those who enjoyed the harsh tone and those who disliked it and left the debate. He described the following historic change: whereas the conflicts in the Palme era, namely the 1970s and the 1980s, existed between political parties, they now were 'among people out in reality', with the parties trying to 'dampen the atmosphere'.[8] A similar diagnosis of the present public discussion as exceptionally polarised was proposed in Finland, where a think tank reported that over 90 per cent of Finns witnessed an increase of 'deliberate provocations' in public debate and 50 per cent disliked the polarisation to the extent of withdrawing from the public debate.[9] In addition, while both Sweden and Finland are countries where trust in democratic institutions is traditionally high, both countries have seen a debate concerning growing media distrust, with the legacy media increasingly being accused of violating social trust through partisanship, political bias, or a polarising media logic. At the same time, after having been a horizon of enhancing democracy, social media has increasingly been discussed in negative terms in relation to polarisation, filter bubbles, echo chambers, hate speech, and disinformation.[10]

Analysing a set of Swedish and Finnish media texts (journalism, opinion pieces, and a documentary), parliamentary debates, and speeches by government members, party leaders, and heads of state from 2014 through 2017, this chapter focuses on three key figurations capturing an anxiety over the public sphere.[11] After discussing the Swedish debate on 'corridor of opinion' (*åsiktskorridor*) as a case of media distrust and democratic challenge, the chapter then analyses the Finnish debate on 'the extremes' (*ääripäät*) and 'the sensible folk' (*tolkun ihmiset*) as threats to the national security. While different as metaphors, the Swedish one pointing to a lack of diversity and the Finnish one calling for a middle ground, all the metaphors capture an anxiety over the national public sphere. They highlight the interdependencies of media and politics, placing media at the centre and calling it out as an agent of power and politics. Responding to a diminishing trust in the media in both countries, the journalistic media has refashioned itself as an arena for curing the ills of polarisation and as an agent of affective pedagogy in the service of national cohesion.

This attitude is summarised by the Swedish notion of improving the quality of public debate by having 'more adults in the room' (*fler vuxna i rummet*).

The anxiety over the national public sphere, the chapter finally suggests, is linked to the key importance of trust at the heart of both Swedish and Finnish national imaginaries and of the Nordic model as a transnational identity narrative. The erosion of social and political trust is a threat to both, and the metaphors discussed not only articulate new roles and sources of legitimacy for politicians and journalists in the age of interregnum but also point to attempts to maintain and reinstate trust and to reproduce the national imagination.[12]

The corridor of opinion: media power called out

In December of 2013, Professor of Political Science Henrik Ekengren Oscarsson coined a term that would become a key metaphor in Swedish politics and media: he described the Swedish public debate as a 'corridor of opinion' (*åsiktskorridor*) that is narrowing to the extent of marginalising classic social democratic, liberal, and conservative positions as a 'danger to the public' (*samhällsfarlig*) or as twisted ideologies. In a blog post describing how election studies scholars treat all voting behaviour as intelligible, he lamented that Swedish public debate instead lacked the intellectual curiosity and desire to understand political opponents; conversely, 'categorical rejection, often in seconds, of divergent descriptions of reality and deviant opinions is becoming a norm'. He described the contemporary public debate as 'a corridor of opinion' in which 'the sore toes' are many, and leeway for expressing deviant opinions has diminished.[13] Ekengren Oscarsson noted that annual surveys of Swedish public opinion have clearly shown that voters hold an array of opinions concerning, for example, abortion, asylum seekers, animal rights, gay adoption, death penalty, wolves, or school ceremonies in churches, which are rarely voiced in the public sphere. Arguing for a classic liberal notion of a rational public sphere, he called for 'a more moderate and respectful' public debate.

In a context where the support for the Sweden Democrats (*Sverigedemokraterna*) was steadily growing, while excluded from political collaboration with other parties, the corridor metaphor caught immediate attention. It was adopted by both critics of the Swedish political status quo (those criticising Swedish refugee policies or those advancing religious arguments in public debates) and those questioning the actual existence of a 'corridor of opinion'.[14] Indeed, the Language Council of Sweden included it in its list of neologisms of the year. It was widely circulated and commented on by journalists. The public service Swedish Radio responded quickly by asking, in a prestigious actualities programme, whether a corridor of opinions actually exists and what it entails. The editor-in-chief of *Expressen* announced that his tabloid would start publishing more 'counter-voices', introducing the tagline 'Expressen is wrong!' to encourage improving the quality of public debate and to celebrate the diversity of opinions.[15] The editor-in-chief of *Dagens Nyheter* also acknowledged that in the age of hybrid media, established news outlets shoulder an important role in defining the debate climate and ensuring access to information in a country.[16] In his assessment,

> trust in the established media requires that we resist the trend to mainly publish that which gets our readers to click the like-button. The market-place of ideas must be as broad as possible, and also contain what hurts in the society.[17]

Whereas some journalists adopted a notion of 'opinion elite' to describe the existence of 'a corridor', others refuted the idea, highlighting the power of Twitter to turn 'ordinary people to rulers'.[18] Debates regarding the 'corridor of opinion' have also encouraged several prominent Swedish journalists in press and television to make penitence and engage in public self-criticism.[19]

The metaphor captured and gave expression to media distrust, which in the 2010s became a topic of public discussion both in Sweden and in Finland; in both countries, this was propelled by the rise of populist parties. Whereas overall trust in the media concerning many topics – issues of health care, for instance – remained high in Sweden, mainstream media coverage of immigration and crime was increasingly questioned by populist parties and anti-immigration groups establishing 'alternative' or 'counter-media' outlets. Media trust in both countries correlated strongly with political ideology: in Sweden, the distrust in the media did not characterise all citizens, but instead, surveys showed that a high percentage of Swedes continued to have trust in radio, television, and daily press. Those with low trust were generally more right-wing, and in Sweden, the Sweden Democrats were overrepresented among those with mistrust.[20] In 2018, according to the Pew Research Center, populist divides in media attitudes were strong in Sweden: 49 per cent of people with populist views stated that they trust the news media, compared with 74 per cent of those without populist views.[21]

The 'corridor of opinion' metaphor demonstrated the power of social media to challenge the agenda and news values of professional journalism. How-ever, while offering a tool for calling out ideological bias and politicising news media, thereby shattering the role of professional journalism, the metaphor simultaneously offered support to the old structures of political information. It materialised the inseparability of media and politics, reproducing a sense of the public sphere as one place, as opposed to a complex, unruly, and unstructured network. Calling out the power of journalists and addressing them as gatekeep-ers, the metaphor reproduced the agenda-setting power, suggesting its contin-ued relevance, placing the old architecture of public discussion in the centre, and reproducing a position not self-evidently owned anymore.

The extremes: invoking 'the sensible folk' as a civic ideal

'Eat shit, racists and fascists!' 'Traitors, why don't you eat shit! You defend rapists, killers, and bestiality!' Elina Hirvonen's documentary feature film *Kiehumispiste/*

Boiling Point (Elina Hirvonen 2017) depicted Finland in the mid-2010s as a pressure cooker. The film opens with scenes from a demonstration in central Helsinki, where the heavily armed riot police control anti-immigration groups and counterdemonstrators slandering one another. Offered as a diagnosis of the present, the film provided a snapshot of a nation's mood, transitioning between northern and southern Finland, between the city and suburbs of Helsinki and the small towns of Kemi, Tornio, Kajaani, Rovaniemi, Forssa, and Petäjävesi. It depicted activists from various anti-immigration groups (*Suomi ensin!/Finland First!, Rajat kiinni!/Close the Borders!*) protesting outside reception centres and in suburbs with notable immigrant communities. In the film's narration, these groups' battle cries against 'diseases of tolerance' as an 'epidemic' that 'is about to destroy whole nations' clashed with counterdemonstrators' interference and cries of 'Shame on you! Shame on you!'. As a counterpoint to these scenes, with relatively few participants but fierce rhetoric, the film featured footage from *Peli poikki!* (Game Over!) and other mass demonstrations against racism and fascism filling the streets of central Helsinki. Interjected in between the crowd scenes, the film's protagonists – a young male anti-immigration activist, a retired female teacher assisting asylum seekers, and two men debating immigration in a public sauna in Helsinki – provide their perspectives, as talking heads, on what is happening in Finland.

In its narration, *Boiling Point* employed the cinematic technique of montage to create a sense of a nation's mood, mapping different parts of the country and representing recurring confrontations between opposing views and clashing perspectives. Documenting the different reactions to the 2015 migration crisis, the film depicted a drama of accelerating affective intensity, disagreements and passions, fear, disappointment, resentment, and outright rage. Interpreting the conflict as a symptom of social polarisation wherein one disenfranchised group (marginalised Finns) attacked another one (refugees) and wherein the conflict becomes one between different Finnish citizens, it dramatised a national narrative in dissolution. At the same time, it used drone images scanning empty landscapes to suggest a third position: one beyond or outside the intense polarisation.

In identifying the public debate as a social and political problem, the film echoed a broader concern over polarised opinions weakening national coherence. In the Finnish public debate, concern regarding political and social polarisation has been captured by the figure of the extremes (*ääripäät*) – in plural, implying two opposing ends – and the related figure of 'the sensible folk' (*tolkun ihmiset*).[22] As a metaphor for political life, the image of the two extremes implies a fugitive point or an outsider's view. When using it, the speaker or writer posits him- or herself as being beyond the political debate, without an opinion, and as someone who has a full grasp of 'the big picture'. This position as an outsider, a moral judge of the tone of the debate, has been highly idealised and positively valued. In the Finnish context, it reads as a figure of the anxiety over polarisation and the dissolution of national consensus that is rooted in both contemporary security politics and history.

The figure of the sensible folk was coined as a political metaphor in early 2016, when President of the Republic Sauli Niinistö shared on Twitter a column published in a small local newspaper which celebrated the idea of the silent majority of Finns as 'the sensible folk' who are alienated by 'the extremes' in discussions of the refugee crisis.[23] The presidential embrace meant that the notion of 'the sensible folk' stuck and became a counter-image to 'the extremes'. Public service broadcasting news media asked its audience to help the 'silent sensible majority' to get more airtime, but the figure also became an object of political struggle and contestation.[24] 'We Finns are the people of sense and restraint', said the then Prime Minister Juha Sipilä (Centre Party) in 2015, endorsing the notion as a civic ideal and claiming it as a national virtue. It was employed by the then Minister of Justice Jari Lindström to frame voters of the populist Finns Party not as racist but as 'ordinary sensible folk'. It was also invoked by MP Pekka Haavisto (Green Party), who made an effort to resignify the term as connoting not passivity but activism and a will to interfere in social wrongs.[25] In the lively public debate, the figure of the 'sensible folk' was criticised as a slogan of political cynicism and an attempt to co-opt right-wing populism and anti-immigration sentiment. It was, furthermore, critiqued for evading political responsibility and envisioning ideal citizens as onlookers, rather than participants, in a political struggle.[26] In the discussion, some debaters attempted to go beyond the polarising metaphors: 'There are not two extremes. There are sensible persons and only one extreme: the criminals.'[27]

Throughout the 2010s, mounting polarisation was discussed as an increasing internal security risk in government reports.[28] In parliamentary debates, the figure of 'the extremes' was repeatedly invoked as a threat. 'It is better that we are all ordinary average Finns rather than polarise and divide ourselves to the extremes', stated a Social Democratic MP in a discussion of internal security.[29] Political affect was explicitly securitised by President Niinistö, as he, after the Russian overtaking of Crimea and Donbass, regularly described conflicts of opinion as threats to trust and as sites of hybrid warfare. Today, he warned, the war does not start with guns and troops marching but with information, infiltration, and hate-mongering. 'If we would ward off all this, we would all be members of national defence', he stated.[30]

In his televised New Year speech of 2016, President Niinistö contended the following: 'It is my idea that Finland should not meet the spring in the spirit of internal quarrelling and disagreement. I want to remind again that social cohesion is our best resource.'[31] Addressing the parliament a month later, he returned to the topic of public discussion, stating that Finns had over the past months learnt to tell each other off: 'The men have been told off, the women likewise. The tolerant and the intolerant have been told off, and then as, a conclusion, the police. We have thoroughly told off ourselves.'[32] He again characterised affective discipline as an act of national defence: 'The challenge of migration cannot be met so that we are internally out of order.'[33] In his New Year speech of 2018, President Niinistö repeated the message, quoting *Seitsemän veljestä/Seven Brothers* (1870) by Aleksis Kivi (2005), the first Finnish novel and a foundational narrative for national imagination: 'all will go well, if everyone strives for peace and harmony. But if we look for a fight, there will always be a reason for neckhairs to bristle.'[34]

The danger of polarisation was a recurrent theme in 2018, when Finland commemorated the civil war of 1918. The centenary served as a frame for discussions of where extreme polarisation and hate in the public sphere may lead, thus drawing from and adding to a rich narrative legacy, given the centrality of 1918 for the Finnish national imagination.[35] This was the recurrent topic in the many speeches of both President Niinistö and the then Prime Minister Juha Sipilä. In the words of President Niinistö, 'The lesson of 1918 is that the most important task for a nation is to take care of its cohesion and stability.' Beyond serving as a warning, the memory of the civil war served to underline the importance of democracy in managing different and conflicting ideological positions and political goals: 'Even if there are differences, and while people have divergent backgrounds, convictions and goals, they nevertheless have the right to disagree. And this must be respected, no matter how differently oneself thinks.'[36]

Similar rhetoric was practised by the editor-in-chief of *Ilta-Sanomat*, a major Finnish tabloid, in equating the critics of the notion of 'the sensible person' with 'extremists', describing 'hatemongers' as a security threat and critiquing anti-fascist demonstrations as 'narcissistic projects' for the organisers.[37] Addressing her readers in an obliging tone, she adopted the position of 'the sensible person' beyond the political disagreements. Invoking the civil war as a disciplinary fiction two years before the centenary, she described an anti-fascist demonstration as an 'agitation of ordinary people into a polarisation':

> One would hope that each of us would pause for thinking what we do and what we participate in. Do you by any chance, without intending it, throw gas into flames, or do you attempt to scold your rage? Do you press like on writings agitating to polarisation or do you support objectivity? Do you generalise? Do you blame those who are not to be blamed? Do you distort? Do you scream with others or do you scream stop?'[38]

While the President's concern was related to national security, the editor-in-chief fought a moral war: beyond defending 'the sensible person' as a civic ideal, she was engaged in framing the critics of the ideal as immoral.

Whereas the Swedish debate on 'the corridor of opinion' problematised the power over agenda-setting and questioned the gate-keeping power of the journalists, in Finland, concern over 'the extremes' read as concern over too much debate, idealising the position of a distant, if morally invested, onlooker.[39] While 'the extremes' as a figure articulated a concern over polarisation, it simultaneously suggested a disbelief in the value of public debate. In the narrative of the extremes, the 'silent majority' was imagined as a non-political middle ground, whose thoughts and values the speaker nevertheless alledgedly knew. As a model citizen, paradoxically, 'the sensible person' invoked an idealistic figure whose major characteristic was its lack of any characteristics. It read as a figure of consensus, but not political consensus in the sense of supporting negotiations between different interests.[40] In the 2010s, it rather issued a moral obligation and, drawing from history lessons (the legacy of 1918), made a call not to disagree.

The adults in the room: affective pedagogy in the media

Both 'the corridor of opinion' and 'the extremes' were outspokenly critical figures of speech, and both placed the media and the mediatised debate at the centre of political life. Both metaphors plotted politicians and journalists as protagonists of the national imagination, casting them as gatekeepers or guardians of the tone of the debate. The tone became a political slogan in 2017, when Ulf Kristersson, appointed as the chair of the Swedish Moderate Party, made a call for 'more adults in the room' to improve the quality of the public discussions.[41] Cautious not to express a desire to police the subjects of the public debate, Kristersson – and other politicians in both Sweden and Finland – emphasised instead a desire to police and discipline the tone.

In the media, the concern over tone transformed into active measures of affective pedagogy. The Finnish documentary feature *Boiling Point* serves as an example, as its release was accompanied with a civic education project, flag-shipped as offering a means to engage in a constructive dialogue, to enhance respect and prevent the incitement of hatred. For this project, the production company Mouka Filmi had prestigious collaborators: the Ministry of Justice, the Ministry of Economic Affairs and Employment, the Finnish Innovation Fund Sitra, the Finnish Red Cross, and Aalto University.[42] On the one hand, the different protagonists in the documentary offered a range of perspectives, complicating any one narrative viewpoint. On the other hand, the film offered, through high-angle drone images, a momentary respite from the cacophony of opinions on the soundtrack. As a pedagogical project, first and foremost, the documentary underlined the importance of respectful dialogue, inviting its viewers to engage in one and even issuing an obligation to do so. The sauna discussions between Tapio Salminen and Oula Silvennoinen were offered (and also hailed in the film's appreciative reception) as exemplary: two men who have strongly opposing views on immigration but are committed to continuing their dialogue, respecting one another.[43]

In the 2010s, dialogue as an ethical and political form was offered as a recipe for enhanced democracy, but it was also reinvented as a legitimising discourse in the press and in television.[44] As a concrete sign of a 'disrupted public sphere' in both Sweden and Finland, public service television struggled to find a format for its debate programmes to meet the demands of their remit to serve democracy. In Finland, the long-term YLE concept of A2-theme nights was terminated in 2017, after fierce public debates regarding its dramaturgical choices and casting: while founded on the idea of multiple voices and a democratic marketplace, the programme had for long been criticised for increasing rather than alleviating conflicts and polarised opinions. In the fall of 2015, A2 Pakolaisilta (*A2 Refugee Night*) was structured around a strong opposition between 'us' (Finns) and 'them' (the refugees); in 2016, for A2 Turvattomuusilta (*A2 Insecurity Night*) the chair of the Finnish Defence League was invited as a discussant in a debate where 'the extremes' were supposed to meet each other.[45] In Sweden, the debate programmes *SVT Debatt* and *Opinion Live* were similarly criticised for confrontational setups – for fostering polarisation rather than encouraging dialogue.[46]

Responding to the criticisms, the Swedish Public Broadcasting Company SVT closed its weekly debate programme in 2019, and as a new gesture, it adopted a concept developed by *Die ZeitOnline* for assembling persons with different views on topical, divisive issues. In the process, the media outlet first invites its readers and viewers to sign up for live meetings, answering a series of test questions, and then being coupled through an algorithm with someone holding different opinions and finally meeting in person.[47] 'When was the last time you met someone who does not think like you', SVT asked its viewers and was met with enthusiasm.[48] The series *Sverige möts (Sweden meets)* was broadcast in the spring of 2020. In Finland, *Die ZeitOnline*'s concept – ironically called Political Tinder – was adopted in the spring of 2019 by *Helsingin Sanomat*, the largest national newspaper. With *Suomi puhuu (Finland talks)*, *Helsingin Sanomat* wanted to 'bring disagreeing Finns together so that we would better understand each other'.[49] In the managing editor's words, 'The opponent is not evil, even if he or she disagrees – welcome to the outside of your bubble!'[50]

Reacting to the weakening of gatekeeping and agenda-setting power, hence, traditional news media has reinvented itself as a manager of the disrupted public sphere. While accused of increasing polarisation due to media logic focusing on confrontations, legacy media has cast itself as offering a remedy to the problem it is deeply implicated in. At the core of this affective national pedagogy is the moral obligation to engage in dialogue and to break one's 'bubble' – the filter bubble being a pejorative metaphor for the company of the like-minded. In 2018, the Finnish Public Broadcasting Company YLE launched its project on *Kuplat (Bubbles)*, staging encounters between 'two persons living in different worlds': a right-wing MP meets an unemployed person, two persons with opposing views on immigration; a person living in Helsinki meets someone living in a remote countryside; a priest meets an atheist; a vegan meets a pig farmer; and a downshifter meets a career-oriented leader.[51]

A similar notion of speaking across a divide informed a series of articles published by *Svenska Dagbladet* in Sweden: playwright and pundit Stina Oscarson was to meet 'persons who in different ways divide Sweden with their statements and actions'.[52] The ensuing series of dialogues aroused a range of media commentary. Some celebrated it – 'more people should step outside their filter bubbles' – whereas others wondered whether 'the dream of the open dialogue can be fulfilled', whether there is 'an exaggerated reliance on dialogue with right-wing extremists', or whether 'dialogue activism' is merely another meta-debate about debate.[53]

The public sphere, trust, and the (trans)national imagination

The 2010s debates about debates were more than metacommentary. At stake in them was a concern over not only the national public sphere or the roles of politicians and journalists in the new hybrid media context of political life but, importantly, trust as a key element in both the Swedish and the Finnish national imaginary and in the transnational narrative of the Nordic model.

While the Nordic model is claimed to have lost its distinctiveness as a consequence of various social policy and labour market reforms, it nevertheless continues to be exceptional in one sense. In the European Social Survey and other studies of public opinion, the Nordic countries are associated with a high level of trust, making them distinctive and comparable to no other region in the world.[54] Despite the narrative battle in Sweden about the country 'becoming broken' or 'systems collapse', annual surveys showed 'no signs of weakened social cohesion'.[55] Trust is often described in rational terms, and a 2017 report by the Nordic Council of Ministers called trust the 'Nordic gold', summarising its perceived worth.[56] In the narrative of the Nordic model, trust is valued for both its economic and social effects and is described as what connects them: 'Underpinning this virtuous interaction of security and flexibility is the widespread feeling of trust – among citizens and in public institutions – and a sense of fairness related to the egalitarian ambitions of the welfare state (education, social policy).'[57] On the one hand, trust is described as 'a lubricant for the economy', increasing efficiency and economic growth. On the other hand, trust is valued as an ingredient of social capital, increasing individual happiness, simplifying collaboration, promoting political engagement, stimulating democratic development, counteracting corruption, and reducing criminality.[58] While striving for political consensus has often been criticised as an obstacle to social and economic reforms or even a sign of undemocratic corporatism, in the Nordic countries, the ability to survive and stabilise changes and to maintain continuity remains key to national imaginaries and to the narrative about the Nordic model.[59]

All of the metaphors of the 'corridor of opinion', 'the extremes', and 'the sensible folk' operated within the historical legacy of engendering cohesion and inviting consensus. It is the work of the national and, in the context of Nordic countries, transnational imagination to reproduce a sense of being, in some sense, 'in the same boat' that is crucial to cohesion and trust.[60] In the context of global, networked media, the discourse of concern among politicians and journalists over the public discussion articulated a concern over the future of imagination and hence what international relations scholars term 'ontological security'. As narrative analyses of state policies posit, states are as much concerned about their ontological security, 'the security of a consistent self', as they are about material, physical security, and the necessity of a narrative is particularly acute in contexts of crisis.[61]

In debating the tone of debates, Swedish and Finnish politicians and journalists responded to the disrupted public sphere by offering constructive solutions, while simultaneously establishing new roles and new grounds of legitimation for themselves. Casting themselves as managers of a nation's mood, they placed themselves in the centre as guardians of social cohesion and as pedagogues of proper affect, thus reimagining the future beyond interregnum not as a new world but rather as an upgrade of the old order. In so doing, they also reproduced the key 'ontological' or 'foundational' narrative of the Nordic model which over the decades has offered stability beyond policy changes, providing a sense of past and a direction for the future.

Notes

1 Streeck 2017, 14.
2 Chadwick 2017, 4. See also Hallding et al. 2013; Ohlsson, Oscarsson & Solevid 2016.
3 Papacharissi & de Oliveira 2012.
4 Bennett & Pfetsch 2018, see also Koivunen 2018.
5 Mihelj 2011, 20–21.
6 Ahmed 2004, 64–65.
7 Eriksson 2016. See also, e.g., Holmqvist 2015.
8 Eriksson 2016.
9 Pitkänen & Westinen 2016a, 2016b.
10 E.g. Jones 2016a, 2016b.
11 The analysis is based on keyword searches in the Svenska Dagstidningar database (Swedish daily newspapers) at the Swedish Royal Library as well as online archives of Swedish Television (SVT), Swedish Radio (SR), *Dagens Nyheter*, Svenska Dagbladet, *Helsingin Sanomat* (HS), Finnish Broadcasting Company (YLE), Ilta-Sanomat (IS), Iltalehti (IL) as well as searches in Sveriges Riksdag (Swedish Parliament) and Suomen Eduskunta (Parliament of Finland). Furthermore, speeches by Prime Ministers Juha Sipilä and Stefan Löfven as well as President of the Republic Sauli Niinistö have been studied.
12 For discussions of trust in Sweden and Finland in the 2010s, see Esaiasson, Martinsson & Sohlberg 2016, Bäck & Kestilä-Kekkonen 2019.
13 Ekengren Oscarsson 2013.
14 Sandlund 2014.
15 Godmorgon, världen! 2014, Mattson 2014.
16 Wolodarski 2013.
17 Ibid.
18 Madon 2014, Fadakar 2014.
19 Neuding 2014, Marteus 2015.
20 Truedson 2017, Andersson & Weibull 2018. On Finland, see Reunanen 2019.
21 Pew Research Center 2018.
22 Hämäläinen 2016, Huhta 2015, Ranta 2016a.
23 Paretskoi 2016, Niinistö 2016b.
24 Pöntinen 2016.
25 Sipilä 2015, Suomen Eduskunta 2016b.
26 Raatikainen 2017, Kovalainen 2017, Ranta 2016b.
27 Appelsin 2017, Martela 2016.
28 Sisäministeriö (Ministry of Interior Affairs) 2017.
29 Suomen Eduskunta (Parliament of Finland) 2016a, Sisäministeriö (Ministry of Interior Affairs) 2016, Suomen Eduskunta (Parliament of Finland) 2015, Sipilä 2016.

30 Niinistö 2015.
31 Niinistö 2016a.
32 Niinistö 2016b.
33 Ibid.
34 Niinistö 2018a.
35 For an overview of the meanings of 1918 in Finnish history and memory culture, see Tepora & Roselius 2018.
36 Niinistö 2018b, Sipilä 2018. For invoking 1918 as a reference for public debate before the centenary, see e.g. Appelsin 2015.
37 Appelsin 2016a, 2016b.
38 Appelsin 2015.
39 For a historic legacy of the Finnish nation as 'one mind', see Pulkkinen 1999. See also Pitkänen & Westinen 2018.
40 On consensus, see Rainio-Niemi 2015.
41 Laaninen, 2016, Linnaeus 2017, Teodorescu 2017.
42 Mouka 2018.
43 Lindberg, 2016, Virkkula 2017.
44 For a Finnish discussion of the promise of dialogue for democracy, see Männistö & Wilhelmsson (eds.) 2017.
45 YLE 2015, 2016, Mattinen 2016, Hellman & Lerkkanen 2017.
46 Åhbeck 2017.
47 Kiel 2018, Reinhard 2018.
48 Atallah 2019, SVT Nyheter 2020, SVT 2020, Burström 2019.
49 Hartikainen & Saarikoski 2019, Hartikainen 2019.
50 Saarikoski 2019.
51 YLE 2018, Upola, Ali-Hokka & Orispää 2018.
52 Irenius 2018.
53 Madon 2019, Werner 2019, Stakston 2019, Klenell 2019.
54 Andreasson 2017, 13–14; see Delhey & Newton 2013.
55 Strömbäck 2016, 2017; Solevid 2017. For political debates, see e.g. Ljungholm 2014, Åkesson 2015.
56 Andreasson 2017.
57 Andersen et al. 2007, 14.
58 Andreasson 2017, 11–12. For the notion of social capital, see Putnam 2000.
59 For criticisms, see Rainio-Niemi 2015, Palonen & Sunnercrantz in this volume.
60 Andersen et al. 2007, 65.
61 Subotić 2016, 613–614; see also Koivunen & Vuorelma, forthcoming.

References

Åhbeck, Öhrman, Myra, 2017: "Programmet som skrämmer bort alla seriösa debattörer" in *Dagens ETC*, 2 March 2017.
Ahmed, Sara, 2004: *The Cultural Politics of Emotion*. Edinburgh: Edinburgh University Press.
Åkesson, Jimmie, 2015: *Handlingsplan till följd av migrationskrisen*. Motion till riksdagen 2015/16:3279. http://data.riksdagen.se/dokument/H3023279 [Accessed 10 May 2020].
Andersen, Torben M., Holmström, Bengt, Honkapohja, Seppo, Korkman, Sixten, Honka-pohja, Söderströmm Hans Tson & Vartiainen, Juhana, 2007: *The Nordic Model: Embracing Globalization and Sharing Risks*. Helsinki: ETLA.
Andersson, Ulrika & Weibull, Lennart, 2018: "Polariserat medieförtroende" in Ulrika Andersson, Anders Carlander, Elina Lindgren and Maria Oskarsson (eds.) *Sprickor i fasaden: SOM-undersökningen 2017*, 71–92. Göteborg: SOM-institutet.

Andreasson, Uld, 2017: *Trust – The Nordic Gold.* Copenhagen: Nordic Council of Ministers. https://www.norden.org/en/publication/trust-nordic-gold.

Appelsin, Ulla, 2015: "Meidän suomalaisten tulisi muistaa Halme" in *IS.fi*, 14 August 2015. www.is.fi/kotimaa/art-2000000976171.html [Accessed 10 May 2020].

Appelsin, Ulla, 2016a: "Suomi ja riidankylväjät" in *IS.fi*, 12 March 2016. www.is.fi/koti maa/art-2000001137010.html [Accessed 10 May 2020].

Appelsin, Ulla, 2016b: "Suomessa olisi hyvä muistaa satu sudesta ja paimenpojasta" in *IS.fi*, 3 October 2016. www.is.fi/kotimaa/art-2000001274402.html [Accessed 10 May 2020].

Appelsin, Ulla, 2017: "Millaista on se vihapuhe jota ei huomata" in *Ilta-Sanomat* 1 January 2017. https://www.is.fi/kotimaa/art-2000005028792.html.

Atallah, Carol, 2019: "SVT lanserar nytt projekt där människor med olika åsikter kan mötas" in *SVT Nyheter*, 17 May 2019. www.svt.se/nyheter/inrikes/svt-lanserar-nytt-projekt-for-att-forena-manniskor-med-olika-asikter [Accessed 10 May 2020].

Bäck, Maria & Kestilä-Kekkonen, Elina (eds.) 2019: *Poliittinen ja sosiaalinen luottamus Polut, trendit ja kuilut.* Helsinki: Publications of the Ministry of Finance, 31.

Bennett, W. Lance & Pfetsch, Barbara, 2018: "Rethinking Political Communication in a Time of Disrupted Public Spheres" in *Journal of Communication*, 68:2, 243–253.

Burström, Hasse, 2019: "Stort intresse för Sverige möts – över 1500 anmälda på bara en dag" in SVT, 20 September 2019. https://www.svt.se/nyheter/inrikes/stort-intresse-for-sverige-mots-over-1500-anmalda-pa-bara-en-dag.

Chadwick, Andrew, 2017: *The Hybrid Media System: Politics and Power.* 2nd edition. Oxford: Oxford University Press.

Delhey, Jan & Newton, Kenneth, 2013: "Predicting Cross-National Levels of Social Trust in Seven Societies: Global Pattern or Nordic Exceptionalism?" in *European Sociological Review* 21:4, 311–327.

Ekengren Oscarsson, Henrik, 2013: "Väljare är inga dumbommar" Blog post at Politologerna, in *Wordpress.com*, 10 December 2013. https://politologerna.wordpress.com/2013/12/10/valjare-ar-inga-dumbommar/ [Accessed 10 May 2020].

Eriksson, Karin, 2016: "Tonen i svensk politik hätskare än på Palmehatets tid" in *Dagens Nyheter*, 21 February 2016.

Esaiasson, Peter, Martinsson, Johan & Sohlberg, Jacob, 2016: *Flyktingkrisen och medborgarnas förtroende för samhällets institutioner.* Stockholm: Myndigheten för samhällsskydd och beredskap.

Fadakar, Ehsan, 2014: "Twitter gör vanligt folk till makthavare" in *Aftonbladet*, 8 January 2014.

Hallding, Karl; Hallding, Karl; Eriksson, E. Anders; Mobjörk; Malin; Nilsson Måns; Alfredsson, Eva; Skånberg, Kristian; Sonnsjö, Hannes; Benzle, Magnus; Carlsen, Henrik & Kemp-Benedict, Eric, 2013: *Sweden in a World of Growing Uncertainties: Background Report 10 to the Commission on the Future of Sweden.* Stockholm, Sweden: Fritzes.

Hämäläinen, Unto, 2016: "Hallitsevatko ääriryhmät liikaa keskustelua?" in *Helsingin Sanomat. fi*, 11 April 2016. www.hs.fi/blogi/perassahiihtaja/art-2000004877191.html [Accessed 10 May 2020].

Hartikainen, Jarno, 2019: "Yli 2 000 ihmistä mukana HS:n Suomi puhuu -tapahtumassa" in *Helsingin Sanomat*, 10 March 2019. www.hs.fi/kotimaa/art-2000006030653.html [Accessed 10 May 2020].

Hartikainen, Jarno & Saarikoski, Laura, 2019: "HS tuo erimieliset suomalaiset yhteen, jotta ymmärtäisimme toisiamme paremmin: Tule mukaan Suomi puhuu -tapahtumaan ja tapaa vastakohtasi" in *Helsingin Sanomat*, 19 February 2019. www.hs.fi/politiikka/art-2000006005520.html [Accessed 10 May 2020].

Hellman, Matilda & Lerkkanen, Tuula, 2017: "Construing Oppositions, Demarcating Awe-Ness: The Dramaturgy of a Live TV Debate on the Refugee Crisis" in *European Journal of Cultural Studies*, 22:1.

Hirvonen, Elina, 2017: *Kiehumispiste/Boiling Point*. Mouka Filmi Oy, 2016.

Holmqvist, Annette, 2015: "Löfven markerade mot näthat och polarisering" in *Aftonbladet*, 16 August 2015.

Huhta, Kari, 2015: "Pakolaiskriisissä ääripäät eivät ole suomalainen enemmistö" in *Helsingin Sanomat*, 14 October 2015.

Irenius, Lisa, 2018: "Historien bakom SvD Kulturs samtalsserie" in *Svenska Dagbladet*, 7 April 2019.

Jones, Evelyn, 2016a: "Internets filterbubblor kan öka polarisering" in *Dagens Nyheter*, 14 December 2016.

Jones, Evelyn, 2016b: "SVT vill sticka hål på bubblorna" in *Dagens Nyheter*, 14 December 2016.

Kiel, Viola, 2018: "Festival der Meinungsverschiedenheit" in *Die ZeitOnline*, 23 September 2018. www.zeit.de/gesellschaft/zeitgeschehen/2018-09/deutschland-spricht-frank-walter-steinmeier-sascha-lobo-harald-martenstein-mely-kiyak [Accessed 10 May 2020].

Kivi, Aleksis, 2005: *Seven Brothers*. Translated by Richard A. Impola. Beaverton, Ontario: Aspasia Books, Inc.

Klenell, Johan, 2019: "Är samtalsaktivismen den nya skrikdebatten?" in *Arbetet*, 11 March 2019. https://arbetet.se/2019/03/11/ar-samtalsaktivism-den-nya-skrikdebatten/.

Koivunen, Anu, 2018: "Bortom nationella medieoffentligheter? Mediepolitik och demokratins framtid" (Beyond National Public Spheres? Media Politics and the Future of Democracy) in Henrik Meinander, Petri Karonen & Kjell Östberg (eds.) *Demokratins drivkrafter: Kontext och särdrag i Finlands och Sveriges demokratier, 1890–2020*. Helsingfors: Svenska Litteratursällskapet, 359–390.

Koivunen, Anu & Vuorelma, Johanna, forthcoming: *Trust and Authority in the Age of Mediatised Politics*.

Kovalainen, Heikki A., 2017: "Ääripäiden kumoaminen ja tolkun harha" in *Etiikka.fi*, 7 April 2017. https://etiikka.fi/aaripaiden-kumoaminen-ja-tolkun-harha/.

Laaninen, Timo, 2016: "Toivoa pelon tilalle" in *Suomenmaa*, 8 April 2016. www.suomenmaa.fi/puheenvuoro/toivoa-pelon-tilalle-6.19.100021.6da544c982.

Lindberg, Anders, 2016: "Vi måste skapa ett nytt samtal" in *Aftonbladet*, 21 November 2016.

Linnaeus, Olle, 2017: "Sverige är inget Dawnton Abbey" in *Helsingborgs Dagblad*, 2 July 2017.

Ljungholm, Markus, 2014: "Löfven: Sverige håller på att gå sönder" in *SVT Nyheter*, 2 September 2014. www.svt.se/nyheter/val2014/socialdemokraterna-presenterar-sitt-val manifest [Accessed 10 May 2020].

Madon, Sakine, 2014: "Tyckareliten lider bristen av självinsikt" in *Expressen*, 25 April 2014.

Madon, Sakine, 2019: "Fler borde kliva ur sina filterbubblor" in *Upsala Nya Tidning*, 11 April 2019.

Männistö, Liisa & Wilhelmsson, Niklas (eds.) 2017: *Demokratiassa kuplii. Dialogin mahdollisuus suomalaisessa digiyhteiskunnassa*. Helsinki: Oikeusministeriö.

Martela, Frank, 2016: "Tolkun ihminen hyväksyy vihapuheen ja väkivallan" in *Keskisuomalainen*, 25 September 2016. www.ksml.fi/teemat/sunnuntaisuomalainen/Tolkun-ihminen-hyv%C3%A4ksyy-vihapuheen-ja-v%C3%A4kivallan/842748.

Marteus, Ann-Charlotte, 2015: "Det är jag som är åsiktskorridors" in *Expressen*, 13 February 2015.

Mattinen, Johanna, 2016: "Ylen A2-illan tuottaja pahoittelee ääripää-termiä: 'Erittäin huono sanavalinta'" in *Iltalehti.fi*, 3 March 2016 [Accessed 10 May 2020].

Mattson, Thomas, 2014: "Vi ska publicera fler motröster" in *Expressen*, 5 January 2014.

Mihelj, Sabina, 2011: *Media Nations: Communicating Belonging and Exclusion in the Modern World*. Houndmills: Palgrave Macmillan.

Mouka, Filmi, 2018: *Kiehumispiste-vaikuttavuuskampanjan loppuraportti: Elokuva käynnisti rakentavan keskustelun kymmenilletuhansille ihmisille*. http://mouka.fi/wp-content/uploads/2018/04/Kiehumispisteen-kampanjaraportti.pdf [Accessed 10 May 2020].

Neuding, Paulina, 2014: "Åsiktskorridoren är för smal" in *Magasinet Neo*, 2. https://maga sinetneo.se/artiklar/asiktskorridoren-ar-for-smal/.

Niinistö, Sauli, 2015: *Tasavallan presidentti Sauli Niinistön tervehdys Talvisodan kansallisen muistomerkin peruskiven muuraustilaisuudessa 13.3.2015*. www.presidentti.fi/puheet/tasavallan-presidentti-sauli-niiniston-tervehdys-talvisodan-kansallisen-muistomerkin-peruskiven-muuraustilaisuudessa-13-3-2015/.

Niinistö, Sauli, 2016a: *Tasavallan presidentti Sauli Niinistön uudenvuodenpuhe 1.1.2016*. www.pre sidentti.fi/puheet/tasavallan-presidentti-sauli-niiniston-uudenvuodenpuhe-1-1-2016/.

Niinistö, Sauli, 2016b: *Tasavallan presidentti Sauli Niinistön puhe valtiopäivien avajaisissa 3.2.2016*. www.presidentti.fi/puheet/tasavallan-presidentti-sauli-niiniston-puhe-valtiopaivien-avajaisissa-3-2-2016/.

Niinistö, Sauli, 2018a: *Tasavallan presidentti Sauli Niinistön uudenvuodenpuhe 1.1.2018*. www.pre sidentti.fi/puheet/tasavallan-presidentti-sauli-niiniston-uudenvuodenpuhe-1-1-2018/.

Niinistö, Sauli, 2018b: *Tasavallan presidentti Sauli Niinistön puhe Sovinnonpuheen juhlassa Nivalassa 5.5.2018*. www.presidentti.fi/puheet/tasavallan-presidentti-sauli-niiniston-puhe-sovinnonpuheen-juhlassa-nivalassa-5-5-2018/.

Ohlsson, Jonas, Oscarsson, Henrik & Solevid, Maria, 2016: "Ekvilibrium" in Jonas Ohlsson, Henrik Ekengren Oscarsson & Maria Solevid (eds.) *Ekvilibrium*. Göteborg: Göteborgs universitet, SOM-institutet.

Papacharissi, Zizi & de Oliveira, M., 2012: "Affective News and Networked Publics: The Rhythms of News Storytelling on #Egypt" in *Journal of Communication*, 62:2, 266–282.

Paretskoi, Jyri, 2016: "Tolkun ihmiset" in *Iisalmen Sanomat*, 28 January 2016. www.savon sanomat.fi/iisalmensanomat/mielipide/kolumnit/Tolkun-ihmiset/1142186.

Pew Research Center, 2018: "In Western Europe, Public Attitudes Toward News Media More Divided by Populist Views Than Left-Right Ideology" in *Pew Research Center*, May 2018. www.journalism.org/2018/05/14/in-western-europe-public-attitudes-toward-news-media-more-divided-by-populist-views-than-left-right-ideology/.

Pitkänen, Ville & Westinen, Jussi, 2016a: *Provokaatioita ja vastakkainasetteluja – kuka innostuu, kuka vetäytyy?* https://e2.fi/publication/12 [Accessed 10 May 2020].

Pitkänen, Ville & Westinen, Jussi, 2016b: *Kenen mitta on täysi? Tutkimus yhteiskunnallisesta ilmapiiristä Suomessa*. Helsinki: e2. https://e2.fi/publication/13 [Accessed 10 May 2020].

Pitkänen, Ville & Westinen, Jussi, 2018: *Samat huolet, eri näkökulmat. Tutkimus suomalaisten asenteista ja identiteeteistä*. Helsinki e2 & Suomen Kulttuurirahasto. https://e2.fi/publica-tion/50 [Accessed 10 May 2020].

Pöntinen, Anu, 2016: "Kuinka hiljainen tolkun enemmistö saataisiin ääneen? – Anna ehdotuksesi!" in *Yle.fi*, 1 February 2016.

Pulkkinen, Tuija, 1999: "One Language, One Mind" in T. M. S. Lehtonen (ed.) *Europe's Northern Frontier. Perspectives on Finland's Western Identity*. Jyväskylä: PS-Kustannus, 118–137.

Putnam, Robert, 2000: *Bowling Alone. The Collapse and Revival of American Community*. New York: Simon & Schuster.

Raatikainen, Panu, 2017: "Miksi puhe 'kahdesta ääripäästä' herättää ärtymystä?" in *Kansan Uutiset*, 22 July 2017. www.kansanuutiset.fi/artikkeli/3752350-panu-raatikainen-miksi-puhe-kahdesta-aaripaasta-herattaa-artymysta.

Rainio-Niemi, Johanna, 2015: "A Nordic Paradox of Openness and Consensus? The Case of Finland" in Norbert Götz & Carl Marklund (eds.) *The Paradox of Openness: Transparency and Participation in Nordic Cultures of Consensus.* Leiden: Brill, 29–47.

Ranta, Ville, 2016a: *Demokraatti.fi,* 26 January 2016. www.demari.fi/?p=59506 [Accessed 10 May 2020].

Ranta, Ville, 2016b: "Tolkun ihmiset. Cartoon" in *Kirkkojakaupunki.fi,* 8 February 2016. www.kirkkojakaupunki.fi/-/ville-ranta-tolkun-ihmiset#d173011b   [Accessed   10 May 2020].

Reinhard, Doreen, 2018: "Wir holen uns einen Haufen Sorgen ins Land" in *Die ZeitOnline,* 24 September 2018. www.zeit.de/gesellschaft/2018-09/deutschland-spricht-diskussion-dresden-taxifahrt-meinungsverschiedenheit/komplettansicht.

Reunanen, Esa, 2019: *Uutismedia verkossa. Reuters-instituutin Digital News Report Suomen maaraportti.* Tampere: Media-alan tutkimussäätiö & Journalismin, viestinnän ja median tutkimuskeskus COMET.

Saarikoski, Laura, 2019a: "Vastapuoli ei ole paha, vaikka olisi eri mieltä – tervetuloa kuplasi ulkopuolelle!" in *Helsingin Sanomat,* 19 February 2019. www.hs.fi/politiikka/art-2000006006043.html [Accessed 10 May 2020].

Sandlund, Elisabet, 2014: "Offer för trång åsiktskorridor" in *Dagen,* 17 June 2014.

Sipilä. Juha, 2015: "Puoluejohtajien yhteinen kannanotto oikeusvaltion kunnioittamisesta ja pakolaiskriisin asianmukaisesta hoitamisesta", Blog post, 29 November 2015. https://www.juhasi.fi/blogi/puoluejohtajien-yhteinen-kannanotto-oikeusvaltion-kunnioittamisesta-ja-pakolaiskriisin-asianmukaisesta-hoitamisesta-29-11-2015/.

Sipilä, Juha, 2016: "Ei väkivallalle, ei vihapuheelle, ei rasismille" Blog post, 19 September 2016. www.juhasi.fi/blogi/ei-vakivallalle-ei-vihapuheelle-ei-rasismille/.

Sipilä, Juha, 2018: "Sisällissodan perintö velvoittaa vaalimaan eheyttä" Blog post, 26 January 2018. www.juhasi.fi/blogi/sisallissodan-perinto-velvoittaa-vaalimaan-eheytta/.

Sisäministeriö, 2016: *Valtioneuvoston selonteko sisäisestä turvallisuudesta.* Sisäministeriön julkaisu 8/2016. Helsinki: Sisäministeriö. https://julkaisut.valtioneuvosto.fi/bitstream/handle/10024/74957/Sisaisen_turvallisuuden_selonteko_SUOMI_18052016.pdf.

Sisäministeriö, 2017: *Hyvä elämä – turvallinen arki.* Valtioneuvoston periaatepäätös sisäisen turvallisuuden strategiasta, 5 October 2017.

Solevid, Maria, 2017: "Vi måste ta människors oro på allvar" in Ulrika Andersson, Jonas Ohlsson, Henrik Ekengren Oscarsson & Maria Oskarson (eds.) *Larmar och gör sig till.* Göteborg: Göteborgs universitet, SOM-institutet.

Stakston, Britt, 2019: "Samtiden präglas av en övertro på samtal med högerextremister" in *Dagens Nyheter,* 2 April 2019.

Streeck, Wolfgang, 2017: "The Return of the Repressed" in *New Left Review,* 104, 5–18, March–April.

Strömbäck, Jesper, 2016: "Trots varningsklockor, inga tecken på försvagad social sammanhållning" in Jonas Ohlsson, Henrik Ekengren Oscarsson & Maria Solevid (eds.) *Ekvilibrium.* Göteborg: Göteborgs universitet, SOM-institutet.

Strömbäck, Jesper, 2017: "Stabilitet i en föränderlig värld: medieanvändning och social sammanhållning" in Ulrika Andersson, Jonas Ohlsson, Henrik Ekengren Oscarsson & Maria Oskarson (eds.) *Larmar och gör sig till.* Göteborg: Göteborgs universitet, SOM-institutet.

Subotić, Jelena, 2016: "Narrative, Ontological Security, and Foreign Policy Change" in *Foreign Policy Analysis,* 12:4, 610–627.

Suomen Eduskunta, 2015: Keskustelualoite vihateoista ja rasismista Suomessa. PTK 50/2015 vp. Minutes of parliament session at https://www.eduskunta.fi/FI/vaski/Poytakirja/Documents/PTK_50+2015.pdf.

Suomen Eduskunta, 2016a: Valtioneuvoston selonteko sisäisestä turvallisuudesta. PTK 57/2016 vp. Minutes of parliament session at https://www.eduskunta.fi/FI/vaski/Poyta kirja/Documents/PTK_57+2016.pdf-.

Suomen Eduskunta, 2016b: Keskustelualoite ääriliikkeistä ja väkivallasta Suomessa. PTK 95/2016 vp. Minutes of parliament session at https://www.eduskunta.fi/FI/vaski/Poyta kirja/Documents/PTK_95+2016.pdf.

Sveriges Radio, 2014: "Godmorgon, världen! 'Finns det en åsiktskorridor?'" in *P1, Sveriges Radio*, 8 January 2014.

SVT, 2020: *Sverige möts*. https://kontakt.svt.se/guide/sverige-mots [Accessed 10 May 2020].

SVT Nyheter, 2020: "Hur länge sedan var det du pratade med någon som inte tycker som du?". https://www.svt.se/sverigemots/ [Accessed 15 February 2021].

Teodorescu, Alicia, 2017: "Stig fram, alla vuxna i rummet" in *Göteborgs-Postem*, 7 October 2017.

Tepora, Tuomas & Roselius, Aapo (ed.) 2018: *Rikki revitty maa: Suomen sisällissodan koke-mukset ja perintö*. Helsinki: Gaudeamus.

Truedson, Lars (ed.) 2017: *Misstron mot medier*. Stockholm: Institutet för medistudier.

Upola, Terhi, Ali-Hokka, Anne & Orispää, Olli, 2018: "Keskustelu on välttämätöntä, mutta yhteisymmärrys ei – ja 7 muuta asiaa, jotka Kuplat-sarja opetti" in *Yle.fi*, 27 May 2018. https://yle.fi/uutiset/3-10223341 [Accessed 10 May 2020].

Virkkula, Simopekka, 2017: "'Ihmiset ovat raivoissaan, ja minä ymmärrän sen'. Halla-aholainen maahanmuuttokriitikko ja punavihreä poliitikko katsoivat elokuvan vihapuhe-Suomesta" in *Aamulehti.fi*, 21 January 2017. www.aamulehti.fi/kulttuuri/ ihmiset-ovat-raivoissaan-ja-mina-ymmarran-sen-24215346 [Accessed 10 May 2020].

Werner, Jack, 2019: "Osäkert om drömmen om det öppna samtalet går att uppfylla" in *Dagens Nyheter*. https://www-dn-se.ezp.sub.su.se/nyheter/sverige/jack-werner-osakert-om-drommen-om-det-oppna-samtalet-gar-att-uppfylla/ [Accessed 10 May 2020].

Wolodarski, Peter, 2013: "Marschen från torget till den smala åsiktsgränden" in *Dagens Nyheter*, 15 December 2013.

YLE, 2015: "A2 Pakolais-ilta" in *Yle Areena*, 2 March 2016. https://areena.yle.fi/1-2449147 [Accessed 10 May 2020].

YLE, 2016: "A2 Turvattomuus-ilta" in *Yle Areena*, 6 October 2015. https://areena.yle.fi/1-3081799 [Accessed 10 May 2020].

YLE, 2018: "Kuplat" in *Yle Areena*. https://areena.yle.fi/1-4247394 [Accessed 10 May 2020].

11 Persistent paradoxes, turbulent times

Gender equality policies in the Nordics in the 2010s

Johanna Kantola

The Nordic countries are internationally known for their high levels of gender equality. 'Gender equality' has indeed become both a central component of the countries' national identities and even an export item, especially for Sweden, which has been seen to offer its good practices and policies to other countries. The Nordic model of welfare states is intrinsically connected to the issue of gender equality and the Nordic states have both promoted gender equality and benefited from it. The extensive public sector has offered jobs for women and care for their children, thus enabling women's participation in the labour market. The ideas about what gender equality consists of – the so-called Nordic discourse on gender equality – are firmly intertwined with the policies and institutional practices of the welfare states.[1] Ideologically, the discourse has promoted equality of outcome as opposed to more liberal notions of equality of opportunity. This sets the Nordic ideas about gender equality apart from many other European countries and the European Union (EU).

At the same time, gender scholars within Nordic countries have long worked to expose the remaining gender inequalities and the paradoxes of the Nordic model: high levels of violence against women, gender-segregated labour markets, gender pay gaps, and masculine domination in politics. Paradoxically, despite high levels of gender equality, Finland, Sweden and Denmark top European domestic violence rates.[2] Gender pay gaps are at a comparatively high level too, around 16 per cent in Finland in 2019, compared to 10.7 per cent in Sweden in 2018.[3] In politics, gendered practices devalue women's expertise in, for instance, economics and foreign policy. Women find it difficult to combine motherhood and a political career. Moreover, hate speech has made the positions of young women politicians particularly vulnerable.[4] Outright misogyny has been revealed, although not thoroughly discussed, in Finnish and Swedish politics by the #MeToo campaign against sexual harassment.[5] Gender scholars have worked together with the women's movement and femocrats within the state to develop gender policies and policy making tools to tackle gender inequalities.

Feminist scholars have turned their attention to the Nordic countries to analyse the effects of neoliberalism on gender equality and policies.[6] In the Nordic countries, neoliberalism has questioned some of the basic tenets of gender

DOI: 10.4324/9780429026690-11

equality policy including: the central role played by the welfare state in providing jobs and universal services; state institutions advancing gender equality and not outsourcing these jobs to projects and third sector actors; and the very definition of equality as a political value.[7] Each of these has been evaluated in terms of efficiency: markets, third sector and competition are easily deemed more efficient than state-based services and structures. With this trend, paralleling the debates on the crises of the welfare states, notions of 'equality' more generally, and 'gender equality' more specifically, have been challenged. With the rise of neoliberalism and New Public Management (NPM), 'equality of outcome', which the Nordic framework has been based on, appears old-fashioned, a drag on an otherwise dynamic economic system, and demanding too much focus on structures of inequality and placing too little emphasis on individual merit.[8]

The changes in the equalities framework have been accompanied by the widening of categories of inequality from gender and class to cover multiple inequalities including, most commonly, race and ethnicity, religion and belief, sexual orientation, age and disability. For gender equality, this signifies that gender as a category can no longer be considered in isolation from other bases of inequality. Feminist theory employs the concept of intersectionality[9] to highlight the ways different inequalities intersect, leading to unique forms of discrimination, for example, for ethnic minority women. The challenges posed to the Nordic discourse of gender equality by multiculturalism have been discussed in scholarly debates drawing attention to the extent to which it has mainly benefited majority women and men.[10]

The objective of this chapter is to explore a central paradox: how the model countries for gender equality fail to increase levels of gender equality. A persistent challenge has been that gender equality has been characterized by good policies on paper, which suffer from an implementation gap in practice.[11] In the 2010s, in Sweden, the impact of neoliberal discourse and policies, and, in Finland, the impact of the economic crisis and austerity politics, have been argued to be detrimental to gender equality policies.[12] This chapter explores how – when combined with the influence of populism, nationalism, and conservatism – the limitations and vulnerabilities of the Nordic model become visible.

The Nordic model for gender equality: does it exist or did it ever?

The Nordic model of women-friendly welfare states

Gender equality has been argued to be 'one of the most prominent hallmarks' of the Nordic welfare model and its distinctive welfare state character.[13] In feminist debates, the countries have been described as 'women-friendly welfare states', a term coined by Helga Maria Hernes (1987). The term sets Nordic feminist perspectives on the state apart from the more Anglo-American feminist theories about the state. A central dynamic of friendliness towards women was, according to Hernes, the interplay between a broad political mobilization of women 'from below' and responses 'from above' in terms of state feminism and institutionalization of gender equality. This interplay differed considerably, however, Sweden was the most institutionalized and Denmark was the most bottom-up-oriented gender model, whereas Norway and Finland have taken a middle position.[14] Another central feature was the fact that the male breadwinner model was abandoned, and Nordic women gained economic autonomy relatively early compared to women in other Western countries. It happened first in Finland in the 1950s, in Denmark and Sweden in the 1970s and in Norway in the 1980s.[15] Hence, the benchmark for women's employment at 60 per cent in 2010 in EU's Lisbon Strategy was already reached in the late 1970s and 1980s in the Nordic countries. Furthermore, Nordic women gained a voice, and the political representation of women was for many years ranked among the top five in the world.

In more recent research, the concept of the women-friendly welfare state has been theorized as a powerful discourse that silences issues such as domestic violence or sexuality and promotes certain subject positions for women and men.[16] As a discourse, the women-friendly welfare state has fostered a belief in decision-makers and citizens alike that the state is 'good': for instance, in case of serious societal problems such as domestic violence, it is believed to provide services to victims. However, this has not been the case in Finland where there has traditionally been a serious lack of services provided, and the country has been called a laggard and underperformer with respect to services and legal change in relation to violence against women.[17] The discourse on the women-friendly welfare state makes it harder to fight the problem as there is a belief that things are fine 'in the model country of gender equality' where gender equality has already been achieved. The concept of the women-friendly welfare state has also been studied as a particular normative notion based on Nordic values of equality that have been exported to the EU and its member states as well as to other parts of the world.[18]

The Nordic experience has exposed some paradoxes connected to the dominant vision of gender equality. In this vision, the key aim has been to achieve equality through integration of women in the labour force. The Nordic labour markets are highly gender-segregated into public female-dominated and private male-dominated sectors. A gender gap in wages and incomes that is closely related to this segregation and the division of care in the family has persisted. Despite many women having a high level of education, which has exceeded men's, the share of female managers is restricted. Another example comes from the jobs provided by the women-friendly welfare state to women. Paula Koskinen Sandberg argues that jobs in the government sector have deeply institutionalized lower pay and position for women.[19] The struggles around, for example, increasing nurses wages in Finland illustrate the difficulties of achieving higher pay levels for women in low-paid public sector jobs and in a corporatist system where wages are negotiated between male-dominated labour market organizations.[20]

Nordic models differ in many ways from other European and EU ways of promoting gender equality. The EU traditionally used anti-discrimination law to advance gender equality, for example, in relation to equal pay, social security and labour markets.[21] Unlike in the EU, in the Nordic countries, the tradition of promoting gender equality is in many ways connected to welfare state policies and corporatist procedures discussed previously.[22] Equality is understood as a social concept connected to social justice rather than to the liberal individualist framework. This means that a number of issues that have been elsewhere seen as inequalities that need to be outlawed with anti-discrimination measures (such as equal pay in the EU) have been treated with welfare policies or positive measures and discussed as labour market issues in corporatist working groups in Nordic countries. These ideas about gender equality and its promotion have been firmly intertwined with each country's institutions and policies. Gender equality there has been established as a labour market and social welfare issue rather than as an inalienable right to non-discrimination.[23]

In such a setting, anti-discrimination law was not seen as a primary tool for enhancing equality. As a result, gender equality policy has traditionally relied on positive measures.[24] Anti-discrimination law aims at creating a level playing field and equal opportunities by outlawing discriminatory practices. In cases of discrimination, however, it places the responsibility on the individual that has been discriminated against to pursue the case, for example, by taking it to court. Positive measures, by contrast, aim at correcting initial disadvantages and embody a different notion of gender equality. Instead of aiming at equal opportunities, positive measures aim at substantive equality and equality of outcome. Such notions of equality are based on the idea that it is appropriate to deviate from formal equality (equal opportunity) in order to make the position of the underrepresented group better.[25]

Concrete positive measures used in the Nordic countries include quotas, for example, for company boards, especially in Norway.[26] In addition, states have relied on gender mainstreaming and different responsibilities placed on employers and public authorities to promote gender equality in workplaces, in pay, or in education.[27] Positive measures then operate on the basis of a fundamentally different logic. They remove the responsibility from the individual and make it the employers' duty to change certain structures (e.g. working hours) that may put the underrepresented group at disadvantage (e.g. late meetings being difficult to attend due to childcare responsibilities). At the same time, gender action plans have been vulnerable to attempts to make states and governments more efficient. For example, gender action plans under conservative governments in Finland have been reduced in style and form to a narrow range of bullet points, and the political character of gender equality questions has disappeared.[28]

Despite these similarities, Nordic countries have distinct gender profiles in relation to the institutionalization of gender policy, women's movement organization, and ideological emphases placed on motherhood or liberty.[29] For instance, in Denmark, gender equality policies have been thinner than in other Nordic countries and liberalism has informed both the women's movement and state activities to a greater extent than in other Nordic countries.[30] In Norway, the ideology of motherhood has been prominent. In Finland too, the state-funded Home Care Allowance has resulted in mothers staying at home to a greater extent than in other Nordic countries with children under the age of three. In Sweden, the impact of feminism and the willingness to analyse gendered power structures, for instance, when implementing gender mainstreaming, has been stronger than in other Nordic countries.[31]

Shortcomings and blindspots

Notwithstanding the differences, the Nordic gender equality discourse has been argued to suffer from similar shortcomings. The consequences of the ideational constructions of gender equality and its institutionalizations have been extensively explored. It has been argued that the highly developed social policies for parents have in fact reproduced gender segregation and inequality in the family and the labour market, among other things, because more women than men tend to take parental and childcare leaves.[32] The emphasis placed on social rights and welfare policy has resulted in women's bodily rights, for example, in relation to violence against women, receiving less attention.[33]

While the idea of friendliness towards women of Nordic welfare states has been based on the premise of an idea of women's common and collective interests,[34] it has become evident that Nordic gender policies have been only directed at some women (and men) and may, in fact, increase inequalities between women. Postcolonial feminists have challenged the grand vision of women-friendly welfare states, arguing that this vision has been based on the situation of white, middle-class women.[35] Gender equality is at the centre of the debates on immigration and multiculturalism in these countries and helps to define who belongs to the welfare states.[36] In this process, the Nordic discourse on gender equality is constructed in opposition to these 'others'.[37] For example, in Denmark, there has been a turn towards discussing gender inequality as a cultural problem prominent among immigrant minorities as opposed to majority Danes among whom it has already been achieved.[38]

In this way, 'the passion of equality' has been questioned, also because the Nordic countries in international comparisons fare relatively worse in reducing inequalities between ethnic majorities and minorities, compared to their achievements in relation to class and gender.[39] Postcolonial critiques of Nordic welfare states and Nordic feminist practices and scholarship problematize the ways in which discourses on nationhood, belonging and welfare states construct categories such as immigrants.[40] They can, for example, be constructed as in need of special education about gender equality or as the likely perpetrators of violence.

In relation to outlawing discrimination on bases other than gender – race, ethnicity, disability, age, sexual orientation – the impact of the European Union's anti-discrimination law becomes significant. Since the Lisbon Treaty and new directives in the 2000s, EU anti-discrimination directives have outlawed discrimination on the basis of not only gender but also race, ethnicity, religion and belief, age and sexual orientation.[41] For example, in Finland, the need to transpose EU directives resulted in the country's first non-discrimination law which outlawed discrimination on the basis of these other categories of inequality and not just gender.[42]

Both European soft and hard laws have shaped national policies and discourses in the Nordic countries, and have been used in different ways by domestic actors. Overall, the EU directives have moved the countries towards stronger provisions against discrimination.[43] The EU frameworks have also changed the gender equality discourse in these countries. Some of the subtle trends that have been identified in scholarly debates in the gender equality discourse include becoming more technical, managerial and individual based,[44] focusing more on protecting motherhood[45] and moving away from the universality of welfare services because of EU-funded local workplace-specific gender equality projects.[46] These shifts are subtle and uneven, yet, may result in more fundamental changes in discourse and practices over time.

Current challenges to gender equality in Finland: neoliberalism, conservatism, nationalism

By way of example, the case of Finland illuminates some of the current challenges to the type of equality regime described previously. I recently studied the issue with Anna Elomäki exploring the impact of the right-conservative-populist government in power since 2015 and how it has significantly intensified austerity politics, weakened gender equality policy and harshened immigration policy. The Finnish political context and the government's policies are underpinned by three political projects: neoliberalism, conservatism and nationalism.[47] These gendered projects converge in public policies and discourses in a manner that poses particular challenges for gender equality and feminism. Much of the feminist literature on the relationships between these three projects has focused on the combined effect of neoliberalism and conservatism.[48] Notably, various policies in Finland draw on not only neoliberalism and conservatism but also nationalism to ensure their success. In other words, Finland recently faced a political moment where the three political projects of neoliberalism, conservatism and nationalism came together to form a 'triangle' informing public politics.[49] While the focus of this section is on Finland and the unique impact of the conservative-right-populist government 2015–2019 and its impact of gender equality policies, neoliberalism, conservatism and nationalism pose challenges to the other Nordic countries too, even if the effects and timings are likely to vary across the countries.

The figure of a triangle as an analytical tool illustrates the particular challenges that the convergence of neoliberalism, conservatism and nationalism poses to feminism.[50] When looking at the traditions of women and feminist mobilization, it is evident that Finland has a strong feminist tradition in areas where the women's movement has cooperated closely with the state (manifested in

patterns of state-based funding, practices of consultation and hearings on legislative and policy proposals, and close personal networks between actors).[51] Parts
of the women's movement have furthermore become increasingly professional
and specialized. Finland has an established set of women's organizations that
work on their specific niche issues: mainstream gender equality policy, minority women, sexual equality, or human rights. Each organization has specialized
in advancing certain forms of equality or challenging particular inequalities. In
such a context, austerity politics and increased visibility of conservative values
and anti-immigration stances created the new dynamics.[52]

Of the three political projects that became so visible, the detrimental impacts
of neoliberalism – marketization of public services, transferring of costs and
risk from the state to individuals and families; employment and social policies that give responsibility to individuals; and governance reforms that extend
private sector management practices to the public sector – on the Finnish
'women-friendly' welfare state have been extensively explored.[53] As elsewhere,
recent economic and financial crises have provided opportunities to advance
the neoliberal project.[54] The conservative-right-populist government of Juha
Sipilä adopted significant cuts in public services and benefits, including the
dismantling of the hallmark of the women-friendly welfare state, namely the
statutory right to public childcare for all children. It has also proposed to cor-
poratize and marketize public social and healthcare provisions and transfer
costs from employees to private employers in order to increase international
competitiveness.[55]

The long-standing influence of conservatism, which we defined narrowly as
a conservative stance on moral and ethical issues that involves the promotion
of conventional family structures and gender roles,[56] has meant that the Finnish welfare state has been weaker and less 'social-democratic' than its Nordic
counterparts. The influence of conservatism is visible in, among other things,
the Finnish care regime that provides financial incentives for parents to care
for their children at home as well as in the long-standing political neglect of
intimate partner violence.[57] The visibility of traditional views on gender and
family has in the past years increased in political and public speech, and they
now shape government's gender equality policies through the Centre Party and
The Finns. The 2015 government programme was the first in 20 years that did
not mention gender equality as the goal of the government, and gender equality policy has been narrowed with regard to the long-standing goal of more
equal division of care between women and men.[58] The higher status given to
family was manifested in that for the first time there was a designated government minister for family affairs, but no designated minister for gender equality
in 2015–2019. While the anti-abortion views of two of the three leaders of
the coalition parties did not lead to new restrictions in the area of reproductive
rights, the conservative agenda gained visibility through a citizen's initiative to
allow health care personnel to abstain from prescribing or performing abortions
due to reasons of consciousness.[59] Foreign Minister Timo Soini (The Finns/

The Blue Future) participated in an anti-abortion march in Canada causing a vote of confidence in the parliament but no resignation.[60]

The third political project informing gender equality policy today is nationalism, which can be defined as exclusionary politics of closed borders and racialized distinctions between 'us' and 'them' expressed in the growing support for far-right populist parties.[61] Anti-immigration, anti-multicultural and racist arguments have become more visible and acceptable in public speech since the populist Finns Party became the third largest party in the parliamentary elections of 2011, entered the government in 2015, and illustrated its consolidated position despite an internal split by becoming the second-largest party after the 2019 parliamentary elections.[62] While strict immigration policy has been characteristic of Finnish policy for decades, the policies were hardened since the Finns Party entered the government in 2015 and were able to set the political agenda and dominate the political discourse about immigration and multiculturalism in the face of the increasing numbers of refugees to Europe. The party worked to ensure Finland would not be an attractive country for refugees by reducing benefits, legislating stricter rules for family reunification[63] and shaping Finland's EU relationship by refusing to agree to the common compulsory refugee allocation policy and quota mechanism. The anti-immigration policies and the racist rhetoric have been gendered: Finnish women were to be protected from the violence of another culture's men.[64]

As evident from the Finnish case, gender plays a central role in all three political projects and each of them poses challenges for gender equality and feminism.[65] While neoliberal discourses and policies portray both women and men as rational economic actors and push women to the labour market, policies that dismantle the welfare state and re-privatize and informalize care rely on and intensify women's unpaid or poorly compensated work, increasing class-based and racialized inequalities among women.[66] Conservatism, in turn, can be seen as an explicitly anti-feminist force that relies on and promotes traditional views on gender and the family and resists changes in these areas.[67] Gender relations play a crucial role in all nationalist projects,[68] and racializing nationalist projects appropriate notions of gender equality and gendered violence for their own purposes and are closely connected to anti-feminism, misogyny and views that 'gender equality has gone too far'.[69]

Although neoliberalism, conservatism and nationalism are gendered in different ways and pose distinct challenges to gender equality and feminism, they may work against gender equality in mutually reinforcing ways. Feminist theorists have conceptualized the relationships between the three political projects mainly in pairs, focusing on the relationship between neoliberalism and conservatism.[70] One of the most well-known accounts is Wendy Brown's analysis of the convergence of the 'economic-political rationality' of neoliberalism and 'moral-political rationality' of conservatism.[71] In different national contexts, the coalition between neoliberalism and conservatism has been seen lead to doubly unfavourable conditions for the women's movement.[72] It has also been suggested that due to the convergence of neoliberalism and conservatism, it has become difficult for feminists to reject one without embracing another.[73] The relationship between conservatism and nationalism and its significance for feminism has been addressed mainly in research on right-wing populism, in which conservative views on gender and the family meet a harsh anti-immigration stance and racism.[74] The links between neoliberalism and nationalism have been explored in research on the connection of 'welfare chauvinism' targeting migrants to the neoliberal restructuring of the state,[75] but the significance of these links for gender equality and feminism remains to be analysed. Theoretical debates that would bring the three political projects together are scarce.[76]

In particular, traditional women's organizations have difficulties in addressing the joint impact of neoliberalism, conservatism and nationalism on gender equality.[77] Their close relationships to political parties that advance these political projects make voicing a strong critique impossible and lead to co-optation and silences that can be interpreted as support for these policies. However, at the same time, the political context shaped by the triangle of neoliberalism, conservatism and nationalism has also provided fertile ground for new feminist actors that do not shy away from directly opposing the three political projects and are also more interested in resisting the combined effects of neoliberalism, conservatism and nationalism.[78] Feminist actors who take the intersectional approach seriously are more likely than organizations focusing on women or gender equality to treat nationalism and racism as core feminist concerns and engage with the intersections of the three political projects.[79]

Conclusions

While there are differences between the Nordic countries, it is possible to discern a Nordic discourse on gender equality. This discourse has been traditionally based on a notion of gender equality that is advanced in public life with the help of welfare policies and positive measures. It has foregrounded gender as a binary relationship between women and men and paid less attention to tackling inequalities in relation to the other axis of difference and power such as race and ethnicity. The position of anti-discrimination law has been weaker in the Nordic countries, and has been strongly influenced by the European Union. The second part of the chapter explored the case of Finland and the ways in which feminism and gender equality policies have been shaped by the forces of neoliberalism, conservatism and nationalism. The challenges may be similar to other Nordic countries as well given the strong role played by radical-right populists and anti-feminist and anti-gender-equality groups across the region. The Nordic model faces challenges from multiple directions: neoliberalism questions the governance and bureaucratic structures of gender equality policies, the very trademark of the Nordic gender equality model; conservatism questions the universality of the model to a new extent; and nationalism constructs gender equality as a differentiating value (between majorities and minorities), not a value that unites. At the same time, however, different challenges may foster new forms of feminist activism that support development of Nordic gender equality policies and models.

Notes

1 Siim 2000, Borchorst et al. 2012.
2 Fundamental Rights Agency 2014, Hearn, Strid, Husu & Verloo 2016.
3 Elomäki, Kantola, Koskinen Sandberg & Ylöstalo 2019, Koskinen Sandberg 2018.
4 Erikson & Josefsson 2018, Kantola 2019.
5 Kantola & Koivunen 2019.
6 Hudson, Rönnblon & Teghtsoonian 2017.
7 E.g. Brunila 2009, Holli & Kantola 2007, Kantola, Nousiainen & Saari 2012.
8 Kantola & Squires 2010, 2012.
9 Crenshaw 1991.
10 Keskinen, Tuori, Irni & Mulinari 2009, Melby, Ravn & Carlsson Wetterberg 2009, Magnusson, Rönnblom & Silius 2008.
11 Holli & Kantola 2007.
12 Rönnblom & Alnbratt 2016, Elomäki, Kantola, Koskinen Sandberg & Ylöstalo 2018, Elomäki, Kantola, Koivunen and Ylöstalo 2019, Elomäki & Ylöstalo 2018, 2020.
13 Melby, Ravn & Carlsson Wetterberg 2009, 4.
14 Borchorst et al. 2012, Borchorst 1999.
15 Borchorst et al. 2012.
16 Kantola 2006.
17 Nousiainen & Pentikäinen 2017.
18 Borchorst & Siim 2008, 208, Towns 2002, Jezierska & Towns 2018.
19 Koskinen Sandberg 2018, see also Koskinen Sandberg, Törnroos & Kohvakka 2018.
20 Koskinen Sandberg & Saari 2019, Saari, Kantola & Koskinen Sandberg 2019.
21 Kantola 2010.
22 Skjeie & Teigen 2005.
23 Nousiainen 2008.
24 Nousiainen 2005.
25 Nousiainen & Pylkkänen 2001, 260.
26 Teigen 2015.
27 Nousiainen 2005.
28 Elomäki & Ylöstalo 2017.
29 Melby, Ravn & Carlsson Wetterberg 2009, 5.
30 Borchorst et al. 2012, Rolandsen Agustín & Sata 2013.
31 See Borchorst et al. 2012.
32 Borchorst & Siim 2002, 93.
33 Kantola 2006, Lindvert 2002.
34 Borchorst & Siim 2008, 209–210.
35 de los Reyes, Molina & Mulinari 2003.
36 Mulinari, Keskinen, Irni & Tuori 2009, 5.
37 Ibid.
38 Borchorst & Siim 2008, 215.
39 Borchorst et al. 2012.
40 Mulinari, Keskinen, Irni & Tuori 2009, 5, Norocel 2016, Keskinen, Norocel & Jørgensen 2016.
41 Kantola 2010.
42 Kantola & Nousiainen 2012, Borchorst et al. 2012.
43 The Commission had found the Danish transposition of the equal pay directive to be insufficient and the infringement procedure resulted in Denmark appearing before the European Court of Justice. This was an example of a clash between the Nordic model

of ensuring equal pay through collective agreements and the EU anti-discrimination model where the Court found that the Nordic model did not sufficiently ensure pay equity. The EU law also expanded the meaning of equal treatment and extended the rights of pregnant workers against dismissal and indirect discrimination in Denmark. Similar changes in equality legislation have taken place in Finland and Sweden after the countries became EU members in the 1990s (Holli & Kantola 2007, Nousiainen 2005).
44 Brunila 2009.
45 Kantola & Nousiainen 2012.
46 Eräranta & Kantola 2016.
47 Elomäki & Kantola 2018.
48 E.g. Brown 2006, Phipps 2014, Porter 2012.
49 Elomäki & Kantola 2018.
50 See ibid.
51 Holli 2003.
52 Elomäki & Kantola 2018.
53 E.g. Julkunen 2010, Heiskala & Kantola 2010, Kantola & Kananen 2013.
54 Cf. Walby 2015.
55 Elomäki & Kantola 2018.
56 Ibid.
57 Ibid.
58 Elomäki & Ylöstalo 2017, Elomäki, Kantola, Koskinen Sandberg & Ylöstalo 2019.
59 Elomäki & Kantola 2018.
60 Jauhola & Lyytikäinen 2020.
61 See Elomäki & Kantola 2018, Norocel 2013.
62 Kantola & Lombardo 2019, Keskinen, Norocel & Jørgensen 2016, Ylä-Anttila & Luhtakallio 2017.
63 Pellander 2015.
64 Keskinen 2012, 2013, Elomäki & Kantola 2018.
65 See Elomäki & Kantola 2018.
66 E.g. Bakker 2003, Brown 2015, Bargawi, Cozzi & Himmelweit 2017.
67 Verloo 2016.
68 Yuval-Davis 1997.
69 Keskinen 2012, 2013, Mulinari & Neergaard 2014, see Elomäki & Kantola 2018.
70 See Elomäki & Kantola 2018.
71 Brown 2006.
72 Knight & Rodgers 2012.
73 Phipps 2014, 12.
74 E.g. Köttig, Bitzan & Petö 2017.
75 E.g. Keskinen, Norocel & Jørgensen 2016.
76 Elomäki & Kantola 2018.
77 Ibid.
78 Elomäki, Kantolaa, Koivunen & Ylöstalo 2020.
79 Elomäki & Kantola 2018.

References

Bakker, Isabella, 2003: "Neo-Liberal Governance and the Privatization of Social Reproduction: Social Provisioning and Shifting Gender Orders" in Isabella Bakker & Stephen Gill (eds.) *Power, Production and Social Reproduction*. Basingstoke: Palgrave Macmillan, 66–82.

Bargawi, Hannah, Cozzi, Giuseppe & Himmelweit, Susan (eds.) 2017: *Economics and Austerity in Europe. Gendered Impacts and Sustainable Alternatives*. London: Routledge.

Borchorst, Anette, 1999: "Equal Status Institutions" in Christina Bergqvist, Anette Borchorst, Ann-Dorte Christensen, Viveca Ramstedt-Silén, Nina C. Raaum & Auður

Styrkasdottir (eds.) *Equal Democracies? Gender and Politics in the Nordic Countries.* Oslo: Scandinavian University Press, 167–189.

Borchorst, Anette, Freidenvall, Lenita, Kantola, Johanna, Reisel, Liza & Teigen, Mari, 2012: "Institutionalising Intersectionality in the Nordic Countries? Anti-Discrimination and Equality in Denmark, Finland, Norway and Sweden" in Andrea Krizsan, Hege Skjeie & Judith Squires (eds.) *Institutionalizing Intersectionality? The Changing Nature of European Equality Regimes.* Basingstoke: Palgrave Macmillan, 59–88.

Borchorst, Anette & Siim, Birte, 2002: "The Women-Friendly Welfare State Revisited" in *Nora: Nordic Journal of Women's Studies*, 10:2, 90–98.

Borchorst, Anette & Siim, Birte, 2008: "Woman-Friendly Policies and State Feminism: Theorizing Scandinavian Gender Equality" in *Feminist Theory*, 9:2, 207–224.

Brown, Wendy, 2006: "American Nightmare: Neoliberalism, Neoconservatism, and De-Democratization" in *Political Theory*, 34:6, 690–714.

Brown, Wendy, 2015: *Undoing the Demos. Neoliberalism's Stealth Revolution.* New York: Zone Books.

Brunila, Kristiina, 2009: *Parasta ennen. Tasa-arvotyön projektitapaistuminen.* Department of Education, Research Report 222. Helsinki: University of Helsinki.

Crenshaw, Kimberlé, 1991: "Mapping the Margins: Intersectionality, Identity Politics, and Violence Against Women of Color" in *Stanford Law Review*, 43:6, 1241–1299.

de los Reyes, Paulina, Molina, Irene & Mulinari, Diana, 2003: *Maktens (o)lika förklädnader. Kön, klass & etnicitet i det postkoloniala Sverige.* Stockholm: Atlas.

Elomäki, Anna & Kantola, Johanna, 2018: "Theorizing Feminist Struggles in the Triangle of Neoliberalism, Conservatism, and Nationalism" in *Social Politics*, 25:3, 337–360.

Elomäki, Anna, Kantola, Johanna, Koivunen, Anu & Ylöstalo, Hanna, 2019: "Affective Virtuosity: Challenges for Governance Feminism in the Context of the Economic Crisis" in *Gender, Work & Organization.* https://doi.org/10.1111/gwao.12313.

Elomäki, Anna, Kantola, Johanna, Koivunen Anu & Ylöstalo, Hanna, 2020: "Samettikolmiosta uuteen politisoitumiseen: muuttuva feministinen toimijuus" in Johanna Kantola, Paula Koskinen Sandberg & Hanna Ylöstalo (eds.) *Tasa-arvopolitiikan suunnanmuutos.* Helsinki: Gaudeamus.

Elomäki, Anna, Kantola, Johanna, Koskinen Sandberg, Paula & Ylöstalo, Hanna, 2019: "Tasa-arvopoliitikan toteuttaminen Suomessa 2010-luvulla" in *Tasa-arvovaltuutetun kertomus eduskunnalle 2018.* Tasa-arvojulkaisuja 2018:4. Helsinki: Ombudsman for Equality, 147–177.

Elomäki, Anna & Ylöstalo, Hanna, 2017: "Tasa-arvopolitiikan U-käännös?" in *Politiikasta.fi.* https://politiikasta.fi/tasa-arvopolitiikan-u-kaannos/ [Accessed 1 October 2019].

Elomäki, Anna & Ylöstalo, Hanna (eds.) 2018: *Gender Equality in the Government Budget – Gender Impact Assessment of the Budget and Gender Budgeting.* Publications of the Government's Analysis, Assessment and Research Activities 52/2018. Helsinki: Prime Minister's Office.

Elomäki, Anna & Ylöstalo, Hanna, 2020: "Talous on tasa-arvokysymys: taloudellistunut tasa-arvo ja sukupuolisokea talouspolitiikka" in Johanna Kantola, Paula Koskinen Sandberg & Hanna Ylöstalo (eds.) *Tasa-arvopolitiikan suunnanmuutos.* Helsinki: Gaudeamus.

Eräranta, Kirsi & Kantola, Johanna, 2016: "The Europeanization of Nordic Gender Equality: A Foucauldian Analysis of Reconciling Work and Family" in *Gender, Work & Organization*, 23:4, 414–430.

Erikson, Josefina & Josefsson, Cecilia, 2018: "The Legislature as a Gendered Workplace: Exploring Members of Parliament's Experiences of Working in the Swedish Parliament" in *International Political Science Review.* Online first. https://doi.org/10.1177/01925121 17735952.

Fundamental Rights Agency, 2014: *Violence Against Women: An EU-Wide Survey*. Luxembourg: Publications Office of the European Union. https://fra.europa.eu/sites/default/files/fra_uploads/fra-2014-vaw-survey-main-results-apr14_en.pdf [Accessed 1 October 2019].

Hearn, Jeff, Strid, Sofia, Husu, Liisa & Verloo, Mieke, 2016: "Interrogating Violence Against Women and State Violence Policy: Gendered Intersectionalities and the Quality of Policy in The Netherlands, Sweden and the UK" in *Current Sociology*, 64:4, 551–567.

Heiskala, Risto & Kantola, Anu, 2010: "Vallan uudet ideat: hyvinvointivaltion huomasta valmentajavaltion valvontaan" in Petteri Pietikäinen (ed.) *Valta Suomessa*. Helsinki: Gaudeamus, 124–148.

Hernes, Helga M., 1987: *Welfare State and Woman Power: Essays in State Feminism*. Oslo: Norwegian University Press.

Holli, Anne M., 2003: *Discourse and Politics of Gender Equality in Late Twentieth Century Finland*. Helsinki: University of Helsinki.

Holli, Anne M. & Kantola, Johanna, 2007: "State Feminism Finnish Style: Strong Policies Clash with Implementation Problems" in Joyce Outshoorn & Johanna Kantola (eds.) *Changing State Feminism*. Basingstoke: Palgrave Macmillan, 82–102.

Hudson, Christine, Rönnblon, Malin & Teghtsoonian, Katherine (eds.) 2017: *Gender, Governance and Feminist Post-structuralist Analysis: Missing in Action?* London: Routledge.

Jauhola, Marjaana & Lyytikäinen, Minna, 2020: "Kutistettu feminismi? Suomen ulkosuhteiden tasa-arvopolitiikan muutokset ja pysyvyydet kylmän sodan YK-feminismistä 2010-luvun ulkopolitiikan tolkkutasa-arvoon" in Johanna Kantola, Paula Koskinen Sandberg & Hanna Ylöstalo (eds.) *Tasa-arvopolitiikan suunnanmuutos*. Helsinki: Gaudeamus.

Jezierska, Katarzyna & Towns, Ann, 2018: "Taming Feminism? The Place of Gender Equality in the 'Progressive Sweden' Brand" in *Place Branding and Public Diplomacy*, 14:1, 55–63.

Julkunen, Raija, 2010: *Sukupuolen järjestykset ja tasa-arvon paradoksit*. Tampere: Vastapaino.

Kantola, Anu & Kananen, Johannes, 2013: "Seize the Moment: Financial Crisis and the Making of the Finnish Competition State" in *New Political Economy*, 18:6, 811–826.

Kantola, Johanna, 2006: *Feminists Theorize the State*. Basingstoke and New York: Palgrave Macmillan.

Kantola, Johanna, 2010: *Gender and the European Union*. Basingstoke and New York: Palgrave Macmillan.

Kantola, Johanna, 2019: "Women's Organizations of Political Parties: Formal Possibilities, Informal Challenges and Discursive Controversies" in *NORA – Nordic Journal of Feminist and Gender Research*, 27:1, 4–21.

Kantola, Johanna & Koivunen, Anu, 2019: *Too Much, Too Little? Comparing #Metoo Campaigns in Finnish and Swedish Politics and media*. Paper presented at the European Conference on Politics and Gender, University of Amsterdam, the Netherlands, 4–6 July 2019.

Kantola, Johanna & Lombardo, Emanuela, 2019: "Populism and Feminist Politics: The Cases of Finland and Spain" in *European Journal of Political Research (EJPR)*, 29, 1–21.

Kantola, Johanna & Nousiainen, Kevät, 2012: "Euroopan unionin tasa-arvopolitiikka: velvoittavaa lainsäädäntöä ja pehmeää sääntelyä" in Johanna Kantola, Kevät Nousiainen & Milja Saari (eds.) *Tasa-arvo toisin nähtynä: oikeuden ja politiikan näkökulmia tasa-arvoon ja yhdenvertaisuuteen*. Helsinki: Gaudeamus, 124–142.

Kantola, Johanna, Nousiainen, Kevät & Saari, Milja, 2012: "Johdanto: Tasa-arvosta ja sen lukemisesta toisin" in Johanna Kantola, Kevät Nousiainen & Milja Saari (eds.) *Tasa-arvo toisin nähtynä: oikeuden ja politiikan näkökulmia tasa-arvoon ja yhdenvertaisuuteen*. Helsinki: Gaudeamus, 7–30.

Kantola, Johanna & Squires, Judith, 2010: "The New Politics of Equality" in Colin Hay (ed.) *New Directions in Political Science*. Basingstoke and New York: Palgrave Macmillan, 88–108.

Kantola, Johanna & Squires, Judith, 2012: "From State Feminism to Market Feminism" in *International Political Science Review*, 13:3, 382–400.

Keskinen, Suvi, 2012: "Limits to Speech? The Racialized Politics of Gendered Violence in Denmark and Finland" in *Journal of Intercultural Studies*, 33:3, 261–274.

Keskinen, Suvi, 2013: "Antifeminism and White Identity Politics. Political Antagonisms in Radical Right-Wing Populist and Anti-Immigration Rhetoric in Finland" in *Nordic Journal of Migration Research*, 3:4, 225–232.

Keskinen, Suvi, Norocel, Ov Cristian & Jørgensen, Martin Bak, 2016: "The Politics and Policies of Welfare Chauvinism Under the Economic Crisis" in *Critical Social Policy*, 36:3, 321–329.

Keskinen, Suvi, Tuori, Salla, Irni, Sari & Mulinari, Diana (eds.) 2009: *Complying with Colonialism Gender, Race and Ethnicity in the Nordic Region*. Farnham: Ashgate.

Knight, Melanie & Rodgers, Kathleen, 2012: "The Government is Operationalizing Neo-Liberalism: Women's Organizations, Status of Women, and the Struggle for Progressive Social Change in Canada" in *NORA – Nordic Journal of Feminist and Gender Research*, 20:4, 266–282.

Koskinen Sandberg, Paula, 2018: "The Corporatist Regime, Welfare State Employment, and Gender Pay Inequity" in *NORA – Nordic Journal of Feminist and Gender Research*, 26:1, 36–52.

Koskinen Sandberg, Paula & Saari, Milja, 2019: "Sisters (can't) Unite! Wages as Macro-Political and the Gendered Power Orders of Corporatism" in *Gender, Work & Organization*, 26:5, 633–649.

Koskinen Sandberg, Paula, Törnroos, Maria & Kohvakka, Roosa, 2018: "The Institutionalised Undervaluation of Women's Work: The Case of Local Government Sector Collective Agreements" in *Work, Employment and Society*, 32:4, 707–727.

Köttig, Michaela, Bitzan, Renate & Petö, Andrea (eds.) 2017: *Gender and Far Right Politics in Europe*. Basingstoke: Palgrave Macmillan.

Lindvert, Jessica, 2002: "A World Apart. Swedish and Australian Gender Equality Policy" in *NORA*, 10:2, 99–107.

Magnusson, Eva, Rönnblom, Malin & Silius, Harriet (eds.) 2008: *Critical Studies of Gender Equalities. Nordic Dislocations, Dilemmas and Contradictions*. Stockholm: Makadam.

Melby, Kari, Ravn, Anna-Birte & Carlsson Wetterberg, Christina (eds.) 2009: *Gender Equality and Welfare Politics in Scandinavia: The Limits of Ambition?* Bristol: Policy Press.

Mulinari, Diana, Keskinen, Suvi, Irni, Sari & Tuori, Salla, 2009: "Introduction: Postcolonialism and the Nordic Models of Welfare and Gender" in Suvi Keskinen, Salla Tuori, Sari Irni & Diana Mulinari (eds.) *Complying with Colonialism: Gender, Race and Ethnicity in the Nordic Region*. London: Routledge, 1–18.

Mulinari, Diana & Neergaard, Anders, 2014: "We are Sweden Democrats Because We Care for Others: Exploring Racisms in the Swedish Extreme Right" in *European Journal of Women's Studies*, 21:1, 43–56.

Norocel, Ov Cristian, 2013: *Our People a Tight-Knit Family Under the Same Protective Roof: A Critical Study of Gendered Conceptual Metaphors at Work in Radical Right Populism*. Helsinki: University of Helsinki.

Norocel, Ov Cristian, 2016: "Populist Radical Right Protectors of the Folkhem: Welfare Chauvinism in Sweden" in *Critical Social Policy*, 36:6, 371–390.

Nousiainen, Kevät, 2005: "Tasa-arvon monet kasvot. Kansainvälisistä vaikutuksista Suomen tasa-arvo-oikeudessa" in *Lakimies*, 7–8:2015, 1188–1209.

Nousiainen, Kevät, 2008: "Utility-Based Equality and Disparate Diversities" in Dagmar Schiek & Victoria Chege (eds.) *European Union Anti-Discrimination Law*. London: Routledge, 187–214.

Nousiainen, Kevät & Pentikäinen, Merja, 2017: "Naisiin kohdistuva väkivalta ihmisoikeuskysymyksenä: Suomi alisuorittajana" in Johanna Niemi, Heini Kainulainen & Päivi Honkatukia (eds.) *Sukupuolistunut väkivalta: Oikeudellinen ja sosiaalinen ongelma*. Tampere: Vastapaino, 51–67.

Nousiainen, Kevät & Pylkkänen, Anu, 2001: *Sukupuoli ja oikeuden yhdenvertaisuus*. Helsinki: University of Helsinki.

Pellander, Saara, 2015: "'An Acceptable Marriage': Marriage, Migration and Moral Gatekeeping in Finland" in *Journal of Family Issues*, 36:11, 1472–1489.

Phipps, Allison, 2014: *Politics of the Body: Gender in a Neoliberal and Neoconservative Age*. Cambridge: Polity Press.

Porter, Ann, 2012: "Neoconservatism, Neoliberalism and Social Policy in Canada. Challenges for Feminism" in *Canadian Women's Studies*, 29:3, 19–31.

Rolandsen Agustín, Lise & Sata, Robert, 2013: "Gendered Identity Constructions in Political Discourse: The Cases of Denmark and Hungary" in Monika Mokre & Birte Siim (eds.) *Negotiating Gender and Diversity in an Emergent European Public Sphere*. Basingstoke: Palgrave Macmillan, 60–77.

Rönnblom, Malin & Alnbratt, Kerstin, 2016: *Feminism som byråkrati: jämmställdhetsintegrering som strategi*. Stockholm: Leopard Förlag.

Saari, Milja, Kantola, Johanna & Koskinen Sandberg, Paula, 2019: "Implementing Equal Pay Policy: Clash Between Gender Equality and Corporatism" in *Social Politics*, 1–25, June 2019.

Siim, Birte, 2000: *Gender and Citizenship: Politics and Agency in France, Britain, and Denmark*. New York: Cambridge University Press.

Skjeie, Hege & Teigen, Mari, 2005: "Political Constructions of Gender Equality: Travelling towards . . . a Gender Balanced Society?" in *NORA Nordic Journal of Women's Studies*, 13:3, 187–197.

Teigen, Mari, 2015: *Gender Quotas for Corporate Boards in Norway*. EUI Department of Law Research Paper No. 2015/22. SSRN. https://ssrn.com/abstract=2617172 or http://dx.doi.org/10.2139/ssrn.2617172.

Towns, Anne, 2002: "Paradoxes of Gender (In)Equality: Something is Rotten in the Gender Equal State of Sweden" in *Cooperation and Conflict*, 37:2, 157–179.

Verloo, Mieke, 2016: *Should We (Re)Consider Conservatism to be an Anti-Feminist Force?* Unpublished manuscript.

Walby, Sylvia, 2015: *Crisis*. Cambridge: Polity Press.

Ylä-Anttila, Tuukka & Luhtakallio, Eeva, 2017: "Contesting Gender Equality Politics in Finland: The Finns Party Effect" in Michaela Köttig, Renate Bitzan & Andrea Petö (eds.) *Gender and Far Right Politics in Europe*. Basingstoke: Palgrave Macmillan, 29–48.

Yuval-Davis, Nira, 1997: *Gender and Nation*. London: Sage Publications.

12 Adapting the Nordic welfare state model to the challenges of automation

Heikki Hiilamo

The inclusive Nordic welfare model has facilitated economic growth, stable business environments and excellent living conditions as demonstrated by a number of scholars.[1] The Nordic 'happy democracies' have been characterised by consensual decision-making procedures, corporatism, relatively high voter turnout, wide representation of various social groups, active membership in social organisations and remarkable levels of both institutional and social trust. These qualities have contributed to the development of exceptionally strong public institutions, which in turn are justifiably connected to remarkable social outcomes in terms of well-being. However, as all investment prospectuses for private financial investors tend to emphasise, past performance is no guarantee of future results. The Nordic model was born under the lucky stars of regulated financial markets. It seems to have survived the earlier challenges of economic globalisation, but what will happen in the future and what kind of changes are to be expected if the model is to live up to its promise of producing equitable outcomes? From the start, a key feature of the inclusive Nordic model has been a high labour force participation rate. During the last 25 years the countries have shied away from the target of full employment but still aim to sustain a high rate of employment. Will it be possible to sustain this goal in the future?

Ever since the seminal study by C. B. Frey and M. A. Osbourne,[2] there has been a lively debate on the future of work (see further discussion in the chapter by Holmén). The primary issue discussed in these debates is the expected impact of technological change, which includes broad and vague concepts such as automation, robotisation, ever-increasing computing power, Big Data, the penetration of the Internet, the Internet-of-Things, online platforms and artificial intelligence. Irrespective of the term used, one school of thought claims that machines will displace human labour – not just blue-collar tasks but white-collar ones as well – which will consequently result in labour market disruptions, while another school emphasises job polarisation in terms of both wages and employment vulnerability between routine middle-skilled workers and non-routine low-skilled and high-skilled workers. The debate has focused mainly on the role of technology, while other factors, such as societal institutions, have gained less attention. At present, the question of how to find meaningful employment for those at the margins of the labour market has urgent

DOI: 10.4324/9780429026690-12

relevance throughout the Western world. As globalisation and technology are feared to eliminate more jobs, an increasing number of people may be unable to make ends meet with earnings from employment.

According to Pulkka, the expected effects of technological changes on future labour markets can be studied with two possible trajectories. With reference to effects of previous technology-induced disruptions, the 'this time is different' scenario suggests that progression in digital technologies and artificial intelligence is exponential and stable. Therefore, it is difficult to foresee the dynamics of the new demand for labour, harder for current workers to adjust to it with education and almost impossible for educational institutions to provide future workers with the type of skills needed. The scenario implies that without a major overhaul in policies, the digital economy will cause mass unemployment in the short and long term. The biggest losers will be people with low education, but the highly-educated are also harmed.[3]

The opposing 'this time is no different' scenario maintains that in wake of technological changes people have always been able to re-educate themselves for new jobs and that technological change has always created new jobs. This Neo-Schumpeterian scenario acknowledges the fact that while technological change has destructive effects on labour markets, it also has positive effects. Technology changes people's lifestyles and creates a demand for jobs that do not exist today or that currently play a very minor role. However, even this view comes with the prediction that, depending on time lag effects, automation will lead to more evolution of job tasks and short-term unemployment.[4]

For both scenarios, the time lag effect between the displacement of tasks and the creation of new tasks (reinstatement effects) due to automation is an important factor. Daron Acemoglu and Pascual Restrepo highlight the fact that the degree of labour market disruption depends on new tasks and new skills:

> New tasks tend to require new skills. But to the extent that the workforce does not possess those skills, the adjustment process will be hampered. Even more ominously, if the educational system is not up to providing those skills (and if we are not even aware of the types of new skills that will be required so as to enable investments in them), the adjustment will be greatly impeded.[5]

Another factor that has an effect on inequality deals with changes in skill premiums and the associated inequality in wages and employment security. Pulkka maintains that even in the best-case scenario, the expected effects of technological changes will increase uncertainty in the labour market, while in the worst case they may induce disruption to the paid employment model.[6]

From the social justice point of view of John Rawls, it can be argued that the situation of the worst-off in a society is a powerful indicator of how successful the entire society is. When it comes to two vulnerable groups, children and the elderly, the Nordic countries have exhibited very low levels of poverty. These achievements are closely related to extensive investments in the Nordic countries to ensure that all children have equal rights to participate in education, health care and so on, and that they should be entitled to the necessary nutrition and housing resources so they can take full advantage of these rights. As small and open economies, the Nordic countries are forced to adopt technology as capital investments to better compete in the global markets. A high rate of employment is needed to collect taxes for these public investments. Highly developed public institutions demand a high level of taxes. Therefore, the question of technologically induced unemployment is crucial for the fiscal sustainability of the Nordic model.[7]

The eradication of poverty is not merely a matter of expenditures and compensation. Rather, as illustrated by Jon Kvist et al., it is primarily a question of investing in human capital especially among children and the youth. Children and the youth will utilise the human capital when they enter the labour market. The unique feature of the Nordic model is that it capitalises on the promotion of human capital accumulation among the less privileged. That has also boosted intergenerational mobility, which allows all talents to be utilised for the benefit of the societies and their people.[8]

This chapter studies the agility of the Nordic welfare and labour market model to adapt to the expected challenges of technological change and the specific focus areas that ensure equality of labour market outcomes in the wake of automatisation. We pay attention to both challenges and solutions adopted in the Nordic countries. The focal point of the analysis is on three dimensions of the Nordic model: namely social trust, human capital investment and labour markets. In connection to human capital investment, there is a separate review of young people's situation (the NEET – Not in Education, Employment or Training – debate). The chapter on labour markets includes a review on the universal basic income debate. The discussion is based on a review of literature on the Nordic welfare state model and the budding literature in the field of technological change and the welfare state.

Social trust

A convincing body of literature demonstrates that the level of trust in a society has consequences for economic performance as well as for individual well-being. The fact that Nordic countries display a high degree of trust in all dimensions has deep historical roots. The state bureaucracies have functioned well since King Gustaf Vasa (1521–1560), founder of the Swedish Kingdom, paid special attention to the administration of his country. Swedish statesman Axel Oxenstierna (1583–1654) went to great lengths to develop the state bureaucracy in the Swedish Kingdom.

In contrast to many other countries, the state and the municipalities in Scandinavia grew to be strong and powerful enough not to be harnessed as mere vehicles of some particular interest. One indication of this is that in Scandinavia the word 'state' is often used synonymously with 'society'. The population records of the Swedish Kingdom kept mainly for military conscriptions created a basis for effective taxation, which in turn was a crucial precondition for the independence of the state vis-à-vis other societal actors, and later for the construction of the welfare state.[9]

Robert Putnam has identified two dimensions of social capital: bridging or inclusive, and bonding or exclusive social capital. These two dimensions create different kinds of solidarity. The bridging form of social capital generates broader identities (a broad usness) and brings larger sections of society together by unifying them, whereas bonding social capital pertains to specific, group-based solidarity. The bonding form of social capital generates closer ties. However, because of its in-group solidarity, it may create strong out-group antagonism. Welfare state functions are more than simply distribution: who gets what and how much. The institutional set-ups of welfare state policy programmes unify and divide people and social groups.[10]

Throughout its history, social policy has had bridging and bonding functions. In the Nordic countries, the emphasis has been on the bridging side – the basic principle in social policy schemes has been universalism, as expressed through people's insurances and the public education system. The policy goal of full employment and the solidarity enforced through a collective bargaining system have emphasised the bridging function of social capital.[11] However, the balance may shift towards the bonding side of social capital if technological change increases differences in productivity across labour markets and if these differences are no longer equalised either through a collective bargaining system or by social policy programs.

An important part of the Nordic model is the established and well-functioning collective bargaining system. The role of social partners, employer federations and trade unions reflects a high degree of institutional trust, which has been crucial in the construction of social policy programmes. There has been a cross-class alliance behind many of the core welfare reforms and both the employee and employer organisations participated in these mutual pacts. The collective bargaining system has promoted solidarity through broad-based wage agreements where low-productivity and female-dominated sectors have gained at the expense of male-dominated export industry sectors.[12]

Labour union membership has declined in Nordic countries with new forms of contracted work and other types of non-standard employment contracts. It is quite likely that technological change will bring about and promote new forms of employment such as micro-jobs with very short durations, self-employment and outsourcing. That may, in turn, weaken the role of labour unions and reduce their influence in policy-making. The downside is that the weakest members of the labour force might not be able to collectively defend their interests. That may not only reduce institutional trust endowed in a collective bargaining system but also have a negative effect more generally on social trust.

Social trust is also important for the development of remedies against possible disruptions in the labour market. If we implement, for example, universal basic income as a safeguard against the risks of automation and give government grants with no strings attached to the people, it should be a sign of and be based on trust. In turn, the recipients' trust in society is reinforced by the fact that society is prepared to entrust them to use the money for good purposes. The relationship between society and the recipients is thus based on reciprocal trust.

Human capital investment

Today, perhaps more than ever before, a nation's economic success is dependent on its human capital and innovations. The Nordic social investment strategy recognises the inputs or social investment policies and the outputs or the returns of social investment policies. The endeavour to establish universal access to education was a prominent feature in the conception of the education systems of the Nordic countries and grassroots level educational systems were harnessed to accomplish the task. Comprehensive schools were directed to provide the same basic education for all.[13]

With the emergence of the knowledge-based economy, the focal points of public policies are cognitive and non-cognitive skills developed in early childhood according to James Heckman and Dimitriy V. Masterov. In early childhood, publicly provided child day care and preschool education make up an important part of the social investment, as succeeding policies rest on the cognitive skills learned in these formative years. Early childhood education and care (ECEC) involves elements of both physical care and education (socialisation as well as cognitive stimulation). Though the comprehensiveness and levels vary, all Western European countries have direct income transfers to families with children, but few other countries have as extensive ECEC policies for families with children as the Nordic countries do, as illustrated by Hiilamo and Kangas. Sweden and Denmark have the highest share of children (from birth to two years old) in public day care. The share is the lowest in Finland despite the fact that there is a day care guarantee. The reason is a cash-for-care programme (CFC) called the 'child home care allowance'.[14]

Cash-for-care programmes are relatively low, flat-rate benefits paid to parents after paid parental leave. The benefits do not fully compensate for wage losses; hence they are fundamentally different from the paid parental leave payments. These benefits may impede access to the labour market for mothers with small children and hamper their ability to adapt to changes in the labour market. The first CFC was enacted in Finland in 1985 in order to offer alternative support to families who did not take advantage of ECEC services while their youngest child was under the age of three. The scheme is an important part of Finnish care policies. More than 50 per cent of eligible mothers receive CFC. Mothers with lower education levels are overrepresented among the recipients. According to Guðný Björk Eydal et al., a similar scheme was enacted in Norway in 1998, but participation has gradually decreased. In Sweden, the idea of CFC has been highly contentious politically. In Sweden, a CFC scheme has been enacted twice, in 1994–1995 and 2008–2016, but in 2016 a new centre-left government decided to abolish the legislation. In Denmark, it is possible to receive CFC, but it is used by very few parents, since the Danish care policies emphasise ECEC services for children from the age of one year. In Iceland, CFC has not been legislated.[15]

The dynamic nature of the social investment strategy entails that skills acquired in one stage of life should provide the foundation for the formation of further skills or their use in the next stage of life. Early cognitive skills establish the foundation for learning throughout a person's life. This is ever more important with the view of expected need to adopt new skills and tasks in the future. The cognitive and formal qualifications acquired during childhood and youth are intended to meet the skill demands of the labour market, where returns are also given a monetary form in terms of revenue to the exchequer and various insurance and saving schemes. Even now, the CFC system poses a considerable risk to Nordic mothers lacking higher education who are stuck long-term with a low-level benefit without contact to labour markets. There is evidence that choosing CFC instead of ECEC will lead to poorer educational outcomes for Finnish children and for Norwegian children.[16] This risk will be aggravated if technological change increases uncertainty in the labour markets.

The reforms in Nordic school systems were accomplished by involving schools in the realisation of social goals such as equal opportunity and community fellowship. The Nordic vision of child education is that children from less privileged backgrounds should be enabled to receive an education on par with children from more privileged backgrounds. As Eva Österbacka shows, the educational system is crucial for explaining to what degree the parental background is inherited. Students' performance in the Nordic countries is less dependent upon family background than in most other countries.[17] Maintaining educational equality is a challenging task given the important role of private schools in Denmark and the effects of the Swedish liberalisations of the 1990s, which facilitated the foundation of private schools and encouraged students to actively choose schools, thereby concentrating students from educated families to the schools with the best reputations. In contrast, the private school system plays a minor role in Finland and Norway. Technological change may require more fiscal inputs as well as policy reforms in the future to guarantee equal opportunity in education.

The NEET debate

The quest for social investment can be also expressed by a shift from decommodification to recommodification, as Natalie Morel et al. point out. According to K. Albæk et al., the shift is particularly important for young people, as research indicates that unemployment has a 'scarring effect' and affects future labour market opportunities. For technical reasons, Nordic youth unemployment figures include large numbers of students who, besides studying, are also looking for work. Youth unemployment rates are much higher in Finland and Sweden than they are in Norway and Denmark, a difference which may be largely explained by how pupils in the school-based vocational training systems in Sweden and Finland are classified as outside the labour force, or as unemployed if they are looking for a job, whilst apprentices in the apprenticeship-based vocational training systems in Norway and Denmark are classified as employed. For this reason, NEET rates, that is young people between the ages of 18 and 24 who are not employed, or in education or training programmes, can be posited as a more relevant indicator of youth disengagement.[18]

Nearly all young people start upper-secondary educations in the Nordic countries in academic or vocational tracks. According to the OECD,[19] a significant proportion of Nordic students do not complete upper-secondary education, and large proportions of these young people are in NEET situations for certain periods of time. The situation is clearly worst in Finland. In all Nordic countries besides Iceland, boys are far more likely to experience NEET status than girls. Young people, and especially young men, in vocational tracks are overrepresented among those who do not complete their three- or four-year courses within five years. The worryingly high non-completion rates are often attributed to the fact that young people have not acquired basic skills in reading, writing and mathematics in primary education. This problem is expected to worsen with digitalisation if new policies are not implemented.

The discourse on NEET young people in the Nordic countries is closely tied to the welfare state orientation. As the OECD shows, low birth rates and ageing populations are shifting the dependency ratios of young and older adults to people of working age across the Nordic countries. As a consequence, the long-term sustainability of the welfare state is under pressure and the importance of integrating young people into the labour markets should be emphasised. The consensus is that young people with education should be employed as quickly as possible and that those without education should start toward one as soon as possible – provided they are able to do so. Against this backdrop, young people who are neither working nor participating in education or training are perceived as a problem, as neither contributing to the welfare state in the present nor gaining qualifications and experience to contribute in the future.[20]

The NEET young people are a heterogeneous group with a variety of subgroups such as young people with low levels of education, young people whose parents have low levels of education, and those with an immigrant background. The NEET young people face a heightened risk of falling outside the labour market and 'society' the longer their NEET status lasts. This implies that increased likelihood of future social exclusion, rather than the ongoing situation, is the most important problem for NEET young people. However, it is important to note that the future-orientation and probabilistic conceptualisations in this type of youth research do not necessarily correspond well with the experiences of the people it concerns. In any case, there is an urgent need to develop policies to reduce the number of long-term NEET young people. This emphasis will be heightened should technological change increase unemployment more among less educated youth as a number of scholars have predicted.[21]

Labour markets

In the beginning of the 1990s, Denmark implemented a series of labour market reforms denoting a shift from passive to active labour market policies. These policies were later coined as 'flexicurity' and gave Denmark a reputation of being a forerunner among all the OECD countries in tackling unemployment among those at the margins of the labour market. While departing from the original ideas of the Nordic model, the Danish reforms tightened the eligibility for unemployment benefits, decreased benefit periods, and introduced workfare elements into unemployment insurances and other social policies. The reforms were legitimised by emphasising reciprocity between the citizens and society. This was called a 'right and duty principle'. The reasoning was that individuals had a right to income support as long as they were willing to work and actively searched for jobs. In return, society was obliged to assist job-seekers in improving their job prospects. The reform labour market regulation was dismantled making it easier to 'fire and hire', which became the trademark of the Danish model that gained international recognition. Other Nordic countries have followed suit, but to a lesser degree.[22]

In terms of labour market institutions, the Nordic countries are classified among the so-called coordinated market economy countries as opposed to liberal market economy countries.[23] This is the model in which production is more coordinated than in the liberal market model: employers and labour unions are both represented in collective bargaining organisations and education provides vocational and skills-based training rather than general education, and has guaranteed historically more stable employment careers. Nordic labour market institutions encourage long-term employment through comprehensive employment protection legislation. With the exception of Denmark, the Nordic labour market institutions with a high degree of inertia might not allow easy and quick adoption of policies to tackle major changes.[24]

According to M. R. Busemeyer, in the wake of technological change, the types of skills workers possess may determine their range of exit options as much as their general education levels. M. Estevez-Abe et al. claim that workers in the Nordic coordinated market regimes may be less mobile across different occupations relative to workers in liberal market regimes. For these reasons technological change would arguably have a substantial impact on workers' employment prospects and economic security in the Nordic countries where workers have vocational and skills-based training with the least cross-occupational mobility, at least in the short-term since the learning and updating of skills takes time.[25]

As part of the project to ensure full employment and comprehensive utilisation of talents, the Nordic welfare state model has certainly helped women to enter the labour market. The policies also appear to have lowered the income differentials between males and females. However, gender relations are perhaps not as equal as they seem at first glance.[26] The other side of the coin is that Nordic women are predominantly working in the welfare sector, which leads to a high degree of occupational segregation by gender. This occupational segregation has a triple effect upon gender equality. Firstly, women may be stuck low-paying public-sector occupations. Secondly, their representation in high-paying occupations may be lower than in countries with smaller public sectors. Thirdly, women are overrepresented in part-time jobs that may be more easily replaced when technological change takes place. Were technological change to hit the public service sector hard, it would harm gender equality and increase the gender pay gap. However, on average, females have higher educational attainment than males. Currently, public-sector workers are more likely to be cushioned from the displacement effects of technological change than private sector workers, but the situation might change if the public service outsourcing trend continues.[27]

Critics of the Nordic model claim that providing generous benefits destroys incentives to work. Also, within the Nordic area, there are vociferous political calls for income inequality in order to increase the incentives for work and thereby enhance economic growth. Empirical findings suggest it is very hard to empirically justify social inequalities by referring to their beneficial effects on employment and economic growth.[28] However, it is still an open question if earning-related unemployment benefits with high replacement rates, typical in Nordic countries, lock in unemployed workers who previously worked in sunset industries.

The deep economic crisis in the 1990s showed that the universal and advanced Nordic welfare states were able to absorb macro-economic shocks and stabilise living conditions when needed. Despite skyrocketing unemployment and rising income differences, differences in disposable incomes and poverty did not change that dramatically. Imagine what could happen in another welfare state if within a three year period unemployment rose from 4 to 18 per cent and the GDP fell by 13 per cent as was the case in Finland between 1991 and 1993.[29] With the previously proven antidotes, the Nordic labour markets rebounded quite well after the global economic crises in 2008. The scenario could be different if technological change induced a continuous decline in paid employment.

Migration also needs to be considered in analysing the effect of technological change on the Nordic model. Migrants, especially women, have generally lower labour market participation rates, in part, due to the skill composition of migrants entering advanced West European economies. Much of the recent active labour market policies in the Nordic countries have aimed at integrating such groups into the labour market.[30]

Increasing ethnic diversity does not constitute a threat to the Nordic welfare state as such, but given the high level of unemployment among immigrants, the in-group and out-group distinction has already started to play a greater role (most notably in Denmark). As shown by W. van Oorschot, in all European countries people perceive immigrants as less deserving than, for example, the unemployed.[31] The nationalist-populist parties using anti-immigration banderols are receiving a substantial share of votes in the Nordic countries by claiming that the universal, generous benefits will attract people from other countries interested in such benefits. In Finland, unemployment protection for migrants was weakened in 2016.

Ideally, there should be no wedge between the well-off payers and the worse-off beneficiaries in the Nordic model. As Nelson highlights, there would be no room for 'welfare backlash', since everybody contributes to and everybody benefits from the system. However, the in-group and out-group distinction and related political debates might become even more destructive if the technological change increases unemployment among less educated populations who are more likely to vote for populist parties.[32]

The rise of populist parties has coincided with decreased support for Social Democratic parties to whose political ambitions the Nordic model is sometimes attributed to. The Nordic policies are generally not the result of particular political movements, but rather endorsed by a wide spectrum within the political field.[33] However, party-based political division on migration issues might undermine universalism, which is one of the most important trademarks of the Nordic welfare state. In principle, social and health benefits are for all. They are neither targeted to the needs of some specific vulnerable groups, nor are they exclusive benefits for privileged occupational groups or immigrant populations. At the core of universalism is a sense of commonality; it is an expression of human rights.

The pension policies in the Nordic countries have aimed to increase participation of aged workers, for example, through built-in incentives to delay labour market exit and part-time pension schemes. In the wake of automation, these policies may prove insufficient if older workers are also required to quickly learn new skills and adapt to new modes of work.

Basic income debate

Societal disruptions create windows of opportunity. After the economic collapse of 2008, new radical ideas were emerging and were considered more realistic because the context had changed suddenly and completely. Universal basic income as a solution to expected uncertainties in the labour market has gained traction in a number of countries. Also, politicians and business elites have taken an interest in basic income. As a result, a number of countries have embarked on experiments with basic income. Between 2017 and 2018, the Finnish state ran an experiment with basic income. There are ongoing, planned and interrupted basic income experiments in also in Kenya, the Netherlands, Canada, Scotland, Uganda, and the United States.[34]

In the 1970s, the concept of basic income gathered interest from legislators and governments in the United States and Canada resulting in local experiments.[35] The four negative income tax experiments in five US states between

1968 and 1980 and in the Canadian province of Manitoba between 1974 and 1979 were deemed a success in terms of informing the decision-makers on the effects of experimental interventions but disappointing for the basic income advocates. In the 1970s and 1980s, basic income was debated in Sweden as a response to ideas put forward by scholars such as Milton Friedman and André Gorz as well as experiments conducted in the United States and Canada. Later, both Swedish and Danish debates focused on freedom from work and criticised the full employment ideology. However, among the Nordic countries, only Finland has shown more than academic interest in the topic.[36]

Since the mid-1990s, Finnish public discourse promoted the idea of a short form of workfare coined as 'activation' with the catch phrase 'work is the best social security'. The policies emphasised unemployed persons' skills and motivation and they justify activation through reciprocity, making participation in activation measures a norm and a moral responsibility. In 2001, the Rehabilitative Work Act was introduced as an effort to re-integrate the long-term unemployed into the labour market and to improve their life management skills through forced employment.[37]

The Finnish basic income experiment was based on a completely different ideology. In this experiment, a randomly selected group of two thousand unemployed Finns were paid €560 per month for a study period of two years regardless of employment status, a much different system than Finland and neighbouring countries had been used to. The preliminary results released in 2019 by the Ministry of Social Affairs and Health indicate no positive employment effects in the experiment group. The final results of the experiment released in 2020 pointed to the same direction. Early government responses signal that basic income will not become mainstream in reforming social security in Finland.[38]

Workfare policies otherwise applied in Finland as well as in other Nordic and Western countries focus on conditionality. Should there be conditions for benefits or can we trust people and just give them money? In exchange for access to benefits, there are conditions as well as social services such as training programmes, job-seeking assistance, or other care services. There is a fear that if there are no conditions, people will just run away and turn their backs on society. Social workers will be left with no way of providing support in their professional capacities. The new set of policies to support those in the margins of the labour market needs to find a balance between employment promotion services and income guarantee programmes.

Conclusions

The sustainability of the Nordic model requires that the Nordic countries quickly adopt new technology to compete in global markets. Highly developed public institutions demand a high rate of employment and a reasonably high level of taxes. The question of technologically induced unemployment is of paramount interest for the fiscal sustainability of the Nordic model.

Social trust is undeniably an important element in the development of remedies against possible disruptions in the labour market. This means that there is a two-way connection between successful employment outcomes and strong public institutions. A high rate of employment with a considerably high rate of taxation is needed to support and develop public institutions, while strong public institutions with emphasis on early-life social investments are needed to support employment outcomes.

With new forms of contracted work and other types of non-standard employment contracts, such as micro-jobs, labour union membership has declined in the Nordic countries. That may not only weaken the role of labour unions in policy-making but also reduce institutional trust endowed in collective bargaining. If any country were to implement, for example, universal basic income as a safeguard against the risks of automation, it should be a sign of social trust in the individual.

Ensuring gender equality in the labour market in the wake of automation calls for education and employment policies that would reduce occupational segregation by gender. There is also an ever more important argument for a stronger role of the state in guaranteeing employment among those who are vulnerable to employment shocks created by technological change. Possible areas for supported employment include education and care where human labour is more difficult to replace with machines. There is also an urgent need to develop policies to reduce the number of long-term NEET young people.

The comprehensive Nordic welfare state policies are responsible for the equal social outcomes in the Nordic countries. Generally they have been endorsed by a large spectrum of the political field. However, party-based political division on migration issues and emergency of discriminatory policies against migrants may undermine universalism, which is one of the most important trademarks of the Nordic welfare state.

Notes

1 Acemoglu & Robinson 2012, Andersen et al. 2007, Hiilamo, Merikukka & Haataja 2018, Kvist, Fritzell, Hvinden & Kangas 2012.
2 Frey & Osborne 2013, 2017.
3 Pulkka 2018.
4 Arntz, Gregory & Zierahn 2016.
5 Acemoglu & Restrepo 2018, 13.
6 Pulkka 2018.
7 Katzenstein 1985.
8 Kvist, Fritzell, Hvinden & Kangas 2012.
9 Fukuyama 1995, Hiilamo et al. 2013, 16.
10 Putnam 2000.
11 Flora 1984.
12 Swenson 2002.
13 Denmark still has folkeskole, though.
14 Hiilamo & Kangas 2009.

15 Hiilamo & Kangas 2009, Giuliani & Duvander 2017, Eydal, Rostgaard & Hiilamo 2019.
16 Karhula, Erola & Kilpi-Jakonen 2017, Hiilamo, Merikukka & Haataja 2018, Kosonen & Huttunen 2018. On Norwegian children, see Havnes & Mogstad 2011.
17 Österbacka 2004. See also Telhaug, Medias & Aasen, Petter 2006.
18 Bäckman et al. 2011, Holte, Swart & Hiilamo 2018.
19 OECD 2017.
20 Holte, Swart & Hiilamo 2018.
21 Albæk et al. 2015, Halvorsen, Hansen & Tägström 2012, Frey & Osborne 2013, 2017, Autor 2015, Arntz, Gregory & Zierahn 2016.
22 Hiilamo & Komp 2018, Oorschot 2006.
23 See e.g. Soskice 1999.
24 Soskice 1999.
25 Estevez-Abe, Iversen & Soskice 2001, Busemeyer 2014.
26 Hiilamo & Kangas 2009.
27 Mandel & Semyenov 2006, Datta-Gupta, Smith & Verner 2008.
28 Heinrich 2003, Kenworthy 2004.
29 Kiander & Vartia 2011.
30 Hiilamo et al. 2013.
31 Oorschot 2006.
32 Nelson 2003.
33 Hiilamo & Kangas 2009.
34 McFarland 2017.
35 See Hum & Simpson 2001.
36 Perkiö 2019.
37 Hiilamo & Komp 2018.
38 De Wispeleare, Halmetoja & Pulkka 2018.

References

Acemoglu, Daron & Restrepo, Pascual, 2018: "The Race between Man and Machine: Implications of Technology for Growth, Factor Shares, and Employment" in *American Economic Review*, 108:6, 1488–1542.

Acemoglu, Daron & Robinson, James, 2012: *Why Nations Fail: The Origins of Power, Prosperity and Poverty*. London: Profile Books.

Albæk, Karsten, Asplund, Rita, Barth, Erling, Lindahl, Lena & Simson von, Kristine, 2015: "Ungdomsarbeidsløshet i Norden [Youth Unemployment in Nordic Europe]. in *Søkelys på arbeidslivet*, 31:1–2, 78–90.

Andersen, Torben, Holmström, Bengt, Honkapohja, Seppo, Korkman, Sixten, Söderström, Hans Tson & Vartiainen, Juhana, 2007: *The Nordic Model: Embracing Globalization and Sharing Risks*. Helsinki: The Research Institute of the Finnish Economy (ETLA).

Arntz, Michael, Gregory, Thomas & Zierahn, Ulrich, 2016: *The Risk of Automation for Jobs in OECD Countries: A Comparative Analysis*. Working Papers No. 189. Paris: OECD Social, Employment and Migration, OECD Publishing.

Autor, David, 2015: "Why are There Still So Many Jobs? The History and Future of Workplace Automation" in *Journal of Economic Perspectives*, 29:3, 3–30.

Bäckman, Olof, Jakobsen, Vibeke, Lorentzen, Thomas, Österbacka Eva & Dahl, Espen, 2011: *Dropping Out in Scandinavia: Social Exclusion and Labour Market Attachment among Upper Secondary School Dropouts in Denmark, Finland, Norway and Sweden*. Working Paper 2011:8. Stockholm: Institute for Future Studies.

Busemeyer, Marius, 2014: *Skills and Inequality: Partisan Politics and the Political Economy of Education Reforms in Western Welfare States.* Cambridge: Cambridge University Press.

Datta-Gupta, Nabanita, Smith, Nina & Verner, Mette, 2008: "The Impact of Nordic Countries' Family Friendly Policies on Employment, Wages & Children" in *Review of the Economics of the Household,* 6:1, 65–89.

De Wispeleare, Jürgen, Halmetoja, Antti & Pulkka, Ville-Veikko, 2018: "The Finnish Basic Income Experiment – Correcting the Narrative" in *Social Europe,* 8 November 2018. www.socialeurope.eu/the-finnish-basic-income-experiment-correcting-the-narrative.

Estevez-Abe, Margarita, Iversen, Torben & Soskice, David, 2001: "Social Protection and the Formation of Skills: A Reinterpretation of the Welfare State: Varieties of Capitalism: The Institutional Foundations of Comparative Advantage" in David Soskice & Peter Hall (eds.) *Varieties of Capitalism: The Institutional Foundations of Comparative Advantage.* Oxford: Oxford University Press, 145–183.

Eydal, Guðný Björk, Rostgaard, Tine & Hiilamo, Heikki, 2019: "Family Policies in the Nordic Countries: Aiming at Equality" in Guðný Björk Eydal & Tine Rostgaard (eds.) *Handbook of Family Policy.* Cheltenham: Edward Elgar Publishing, 195–208.

Flora, Peter (ed.) 1984: *Growth to Limits* (vol. 1). Berlin: de Gruyter.

Frey, Carl & Osborne, Michael, 2013: "The Future of Employment: How Susceptible are Jobs to Computerisation?" 17 September 2013. Archived by Archive.org.

Frey, Carl & Osborne, Michael, 2017: "The Future of Employment: How Susceptible are Jobs to Computerisation?" in *Technological Forecasting and Social Change,* 114:C, 254–280.

Fukuyama, Francis, 1995: *Trust: The Social Virtues and the Creation of Prosperity.* London: Penguin Books.

Giuliani, Giuliani & Duvander, Ann-Zofie, 2017: "Cash-for-Care Policy in Sweden: An Appraisal of Its Consequences on Female Employment" in *International Journal of Social Welfare,* 26:1, 49–62.

Halvorsen, Björn, Hansen, Ole-Johnny & Tägström, Jenny, 2012: *Unge på Kanten: Om inkludering av utsatte ungdommer* [*Young People on the Edge: Labour Market Inclusion of Vulnerable Youths*]. Nord 2012:005. Copenhagen: Nordic Council of Ministers.

Havnes, Tarjei & Mogstad, Magne, 2011: "No Child Left Behind: Subsidized Child Care and Children's Long-Run Outcomes" in *American Economic Journal: Economic Policy,* 3:2, 97–129.

Heinrich, Georges, 2003: "More is Not Necessarily Better: An Empirical Analysis of the Inequality – Growth Tradeoff Using the Luxembourg Income Study" in *Luxembourg Income Study.* Working Papers 344. Luxembourg: LIS.

Hiilamo, Heikki & Kangas, Olli, 2009: "Trap for Women or Freedom to Choose? The Struggle Over Cash for Child Care Schemes in Finland and Sweden" in *Journal of Social Policy,* 38:3, 457–475.

Hiilamo, Heikki, Kangas, Olli, Fritzell, Johan, Kvist, Jon & Palme, Joakim, 2013: *Recipe for a Better Life: Experiences from the Nordic Countries.* Helsinki: CMI Martti Ahtisaari Centre.

Hiilamo, Heikki & Komp, Kathrin, 2018: "The Case for a Participation Income: Acknowledging and Valuing the Diversity of Social Participation" in *The Political Quarterly,* 89:2, 256–261. https://doi.org/10.1111/1467-923X.12511.

Hiilamo, Heikki, Merikukka, Marko & Haataja, Anita, 2018: "Long-Term Educational Outcomes of Child Care Arrangements in Finland" in *SAGE Open,* 8:2. https://doi.org/10.1177/2158244018774823.

Holte, Bjørn Hallstein, Swart, Ignatius & Hiilamo, Heikki, 2018: "The NEET Concept in Comparative Youth Research: The Nordic Countries and South Africa" in *Journal of Youth Studies,* 22:2, 256–272. https://doi.org/10.1080/13676261.2018.1496406.

Hum, Derek & Simpson, Wayne, 2001: "A Guaranteed Annual Income: From Income to the Millennium" in *Policy Options*, 22:1, 78–82.

Karhula, Aleksi, Erola, Jani & Kilpi-Jakonen, Elina, 2017: "Home Sweet Home? Long-Term Educational Out-Comes of Childcare Arrangements in Finland" in Hans-Peter Blossfeld, Nevena Kulic, Jan Skopek & Moris Triventi (eds.) *Childcare, Early Education and Social Inequality: A Cross-National Perspective*. Cheltenham: Edward Elgar Publishing, 268–285.

Katzenstein, Peter, 1985: *Small States in World Markets: Industrial Policy in Europe*. Ithaca, NY: Cornell University Press.

Kenworthy, Lee, 2004: "Welfare States, Real Income and Poverty" in *Luxembourg Income Study*. Working Papers 370. Luxembourg: LIS.

Kiander, Jaakko & Vartia, Pertti, 2011: "Lessons from the Crisis in Finland and Sweden in the 1990s" in *Empirica*, 38:1, 53–69.

Kosonen, Tuomas & Huttunen, Kristiina, 2018: *Kotihoidon tuen vaikutus lapsiin*. Tutkimuksia 115. Helsinki: Palkansaajien tutkimuslaitos.

Kvist, Jon, Fritzell, Johan, Hvinden, Björn & Kangas, Olli (eds.) 2012: *Changing Social Equality: The Nordic Welfare Model in the 21st Century*. Bristol: Policy Press.

Mandel, Hadas & Semyenov, Moshe, 2006: "A Welfare State Paradox: State Interventions and Women's Employment Opportunities in 22 Countries" in *American Journal of Sociology*, 111:6, 1910–1949.

McFarland, Kate, 2017: *Current Basic Income Experiments (and Those So Called): An Overview*. Updated 19 October 2017. https://basicincome.org/news/2017/10/overview-of-current-basic-income-related-experiments-october-2017/ [Accessed 10 October 2018].

Nelson, Kenneth, 2003: *Fighting Poverty: Comparative Studies on Social Insurance, Means-Tested Benefits and Income Redistribution*. Stockholm: Swedish Institute for Social Research.

OECD, 2017: *Education at a Glance 2017*. OECD Indicators. Paris: OECD Publishing.

Oorschot, Wim, van, 2006: "Making the Difference in Social Europe: Deservingness Perceptions among Citizens of European Welfare States" in *Journal of European Social Policy*, 16:1, 23–42. https://doi.org/10.1177/0958928706059829.

Österbacka, Eva, 2004: *It Runs in the Family: Empirical Analyses of Family Background and Economic Status*. Åbo: Åbo Akademi University Press.

Perkiö, Johanna, 2019: "From Rights to Activation: The Evolution of the Idea of Basic Income in the Finnish Political Debate, 1980–2016" in *Journal of Social Policy* [published online ahead of print], 1–17. https://doi.org/10.1017/S0047279418000867.

Pulkka, Ville-Veikko, 2018: "This Time May Be a Little Different: Exploring the Finnish View on the Future of Work" in *International Journal of Sociology and Social Policy*, 39:1–2, 22–37. https://doi.org/10.1108/IJSSP-05-2018-0070.

Putnam, Robert, 2000: *Bowling Alone: The Collapse and Revival of American Community*. New York: Simon & Schuster.

Soskice, David, 1999: "Divergent Production Regimes: Coordinated and Uncoordinated Market Economies in the 1980s and 1990s" in Herbert Kitschelt, Peter Lange, Gary Marks & John D. Stephens (eds.) *Continuity and Change in Contemporary Capitalism*. Cambridge Studies in Comparative Politics. Cambridge: Cambridge University Press, 101–134.

Swenson, Peter, 2002: *Capitalist Against Markets: The Making of Labor Markets and Welfare States in the United States and Sweden*. Oxford: Oxford University Press.

Telhaug, Alfred, Medias, Asbjörn & Aasen, Petter, 2006: "The Nordic Model in Education: Education as Part of the Political System in the Last 50 Years" in *Scandinavian Journal of Educational Research*, 50:3, 245–283.

13 Education 4.0.

Nordic long-term planning and educational policies in the fourth industrial revolution

Janne Holmén

In the last two centuries, the world has experienced rapid technological development, often described as a series of industrial revolutions. These revolutions have not only increased productivity but also disrupted older industries and caused unemployment among their former employees. One of the main strategies for avoiding polarization between workers displaced from older industries and the beneficiaries of change has been education: primarily trying to adapt the skill levels of workers to the new demands of the economy. For a long time, these attempts seemed successful. In the early 1970s, on the cusp of the third industrial revolution, advanced economies still enjoyed full employment, despite centuries of labor-saving technological progress. However, the third industrial revolution, characterized by the creation of an information society, has deviated from the former in respect that unemployment and employment in low-salary jobs have remained high, despite decades of attempts to alleviate the situation through educational and other means.

In the 2010s, many observers believe that the information society has evolved to such an extent that we are at a qualitative tipping point; it is time to talk about a fourth industrial revolution. Although the exact nature and even existence of the fourth industrial revolution are subjects of discussions, it is generally characterized by increased automation through robotics and artificial intelligence (AI). This would further reduce the demand for human labor in manual jobs and in white-collar jobs previously untouched by automation. In addition, the rapidly decreasing costs of renewable energy production are believed to have a disruptive influence on the fossil fuel industry. Concerns are raised that this might lead to mass unemployment on a scale not experienced before and cause polarization between a few highly skilled individuals, who are essential to the new economy and who cannot be replaced by robots, and everyone else.

The phrase 'industrial revolution' was coined in 1799 in France as an attempt to describe the country's efforts to catch up with England's industrialization.[1] Thus, the concept did not originate among economic historians describing technological and economic changes that had already taken place but was invented by actors intent on bringing about change. Also, in the case of the fourth industrial revolution, reform-oriented actors are the pioneers in the use of the concept. In a revolution, old truths are invalidated and the path towards

DOI: 10.4324/9780429026690-13

the future can be remapped. The idea of an impending, inevitable revolution is therefore useful for reformers seeking to legitimize their descriptions of current problems and proposals for future solutions.

According to a study conducted by the OECD in 2013, Sweden and Finland were the two countries in the world where employees have experienced the greatest technological and organizational changes in the workplace, while Norway was number six.[2] In addition, a traditional part of the Nordic model has been to use education to reduce inequality. Thus, it is particularly fruitful to study strategies for combating the polarizing effects of technological changes in these three countries: the technological pressure for change is imminent and the motivation to find a solution can be expected to be comparatively high. Adding to the general challenge that technological development provides to the Nordic model, Norway, Sweden, and Finland all face particular threats, which are paradoxically imbedded in the specific nature of each nation's success. Swedes fear that their long period of strong economic development is threatened by the poor basic skills of school leavers. Finland has struggled economically for a decade, and claims are made that its position as an educational model country makes necessary school reforms difficult. Meanwhile, in Norway, it is feared that wealth from the petroleum industry has hampered innovation and education.

The aim of this chapter is to analyze how government planning in Sweden, Finland, and Norway perceives the challenges caused by rapid technological and societal change, and its recommendations for how the educational system should adapt to these challenges. Long-term forecasts and plans for economic and social development will be investigated to determine whether they predict a future in which technological advancement will continue at the current pace, or whether they foresee an imminent dramatic increase in the pace of innovation and technological advancement. The role long-term plans prescribe for education in meeting these scenarios will also be explored. In addition, it is investigated how the conclusions from the long-term forecasts affect plans for the education system and curricula directly regulating the present school system.

Optimists and pessimists

The hopes connected to technological development, as well as the fears that it will cause mass unemployment, are based on the belief that productivity will rise as a consequence of labor-saving innovations. However, Erik Brynjolfsson, Daniel Rock, and Chad Syverson have pointed out a paradox in this regard. While technology optimists, such as technologists and venture capitalists, foresee imminent productivity gains from AI, robotics, and other emerging technologies, pessimists – economists, sociologists, statisticians, and government officials – notice that measured productivity growth is actually declining. Brynjolfsson, Rock, and Syverson claim that both optimists and pessimists may be right: for example, while AI is a general-purpose technology (GPT) that has great potential to raise productivity, it takes time and additional investments to reach that point. Since the increased amount of time and resources spent on AI innovation has not yet resulted in any significant output, productivity seems to be falling. A similar decline in productivity has been observed during periods of investment in earlier GPTs, such as portable power (electricity and the combustion engine) in the 1910s and information and communication technology (ICT) in the early 1990s, after which productivity accelerated from 1915 to 1924 and from 1995 to 2004.[3]

The discussion regarding skill-biased technological change is rooted firmly within the pessimist paradigm: it is an academic discussion among economists based on forward projections of historical data. On the other hand, the discourse on the fourth industrial revolution is rooted in an optimist paradigm, propagated by technologists who predict an imminent technological and social transformation. In effect, proponents of the fourth industrial revolution are also using a historical argument to support their view. However, rather than extrapolating from the recent trajectory of the development curve, they look at historical inflection points in the curve – the first three industrial revolutions – and predict that we are now approaching yet another such event, which might be more rapid and disruptive than the previous ones.

Wolfgang Streeck bases his prediction that the current interregnum will continue indefinitely on the absence of a practically possible vision of a progressive future.[4] Among technology optimists, progressive visions do undoubtedly exist. However, their practicality remains to be proven.

Skill-biased technological change and education

A common explanation for the rise of income inequalities since the 1970s is skill-biased technological change. According to this theory, some technologies are so demanding of skill that only the most skilled individuals benefit from them, thereby elevating their incomes and leaving the rest of the workforce behind. However, the topic is hotly contested. Among the controversial issues are the questions of why earlier technological changes have not caused the same effect, how the phenomenon is related to globalization, and whether it can be observed outside the United States, which has been the object of most research. Another central question is whether there is a deterministic relationship between current technological change and inequality, or if the outcomes can be affected by, for example, educational policies.

In recent decades, the number of workers employed in high- and low-wage jobs has increased, while it has decreased in middling jobs. David Autor, Laura Katz, and Melissa Kearney claim that computerization has replaced middling routine tasks but has raised the productivity of low-wage manual work as well as of high-wage abstract work. As a result, wages for abstract work are elevated, while wages for manual work either rise through increased productivity or sink due to increased competition from displaced routine workers relocating to manual tasks.[5]

According to Daron Acemoglu, the last 200 years of US and European history suggest that unemployment and low wages caused by technological change are temporary. However, he stresses that this time around it might be different. If earlier technological changes increased the demand for labor and increased wages, and the present combination of technology and abundant labor supply does not, we may today face technology-driven unemployment despite the historical record.[6]

Claudia Goldin and Lawrence Katz claim that skill-biased technological change cannot explain the growing polarization of the last decades, since skill-biased technological change has occurred at a fairly continuous rate since the late 19th century, a rate that was only slightly elevated during the years 1979–1999. Instead, they argue that the widening gaps are attributable to a reverse in the trend of increased education that took place in the 1970s. Their interpretation is that although skill-biased technological change increased the demand for skilled workers from the late 19th century until the 1970s, the supply of educated workers increased even faster, reducing the wage premium for education and thereby curbing income inequality. Since 1980, the demand for skilled workers has increased faster than the supply, which has been hampered by, for example, rising costs of college education in the United States. As a result, wages for skilled workers have gone up and income inequality increased.[7]

According to Goldin and Katz, widespread secondary education contributed to enhanced economic growth and income equality in the United States from the late 19th century. They even suggest that 'it was mass secondary school education that checked the more extreme forms of socialism later embraced by Europe'.[8] Thus, the United States experienced less polarization than Europe in the early 20th century because of its uniquely advanced and egalitarian educational policies, while in the 21st century it has lagged behind countries such as Sweden, Finland, and Norway in educational and thereby also economic and social equality.

However, job polarization is present also in the Nordic countries. From 1993 to 2006, Norway and Sweden experienced classical polarization with an increase in high- and low-wage jobs and a decrease in middling jobs, while Finland experienced a downgrade with an increase in low-wage jobs and a decrease in both middling and high-wage jobs.[9]

The fourth industrial revolution and education

One of the earliest iterations of the fourth industrial revolution was the German Industrie 4.0, launched in 2011 by the federal government. It was hoped that technologies such as the Internet and improvements in robotics would allow for production that is tailor-made to the customers' individual preferences.[10] In contrast to earlier factories that have produced large quantities of identical products, Industrie 4.0 tracks each individual product at every step, implementing adaptations according to the specifications of the consumer.

The most visible advocate of the idea that we are approaching a fourth industrial revolution is Klaus Schwab, executive chairman of the World Economic Forum (WEF). According to the WEF, the fourth industrial revolution 'is characterized by a fusion of technologies that is blurring the lines between the physical, digital, and biological spheres'.[11] The WEF made the fourth industrial revolution widely known through its 2016 world forum and has proposed strategies for closing the inequality gap in the fourth industrial revolution, acknowledging the importance of education.[12]

Michael Peters argues that in order to adapt to the fourth industrial revolution, education must become an open ecosystem by utilizing new technology. For example, massive open online courses (MOOCs) could mitigate the adverse effects of rising college fees, which hinder people from acquiring skills needed in the transformed, knowledge-intensive labor market.[13] Similarly, Carl Benedikt Frey and Michael Osborne claim that MOOCs can mitigate constraints set up by economy, geography, or lack of time. According to them, traditional education with rigid programs spanning a specific period of time represents an outdated factory-based education that emerged during the 19th-century industrial revolution.[14]

Also Erik Brynjolfsson and Andrew McAfee see improved education, such as MOOCs, as a way of combating the 'spread' of incomes that technological change can produce, but they do not believe that technology will solve the problem by itself. On the contrary, since some highly motivated self-starters take part in university courses through MOOCs at the ages of 12–14, originally small knowledge gaps are enlarged. They claim that digitization of education will only reduce the spread if serious efforts are made in that direction.[15]

Forecasting the future

In Finland, Sweden, and Norway, long-term governmental forecasting generally recognizes that technological change will transform society and that the schools need to adapt. However, in these three countries there are also important differences in the descriptions of how, and to what extent, these changes will affect society and its educational system.

Norwegian planners foresee that the country's wealth based on hydrocarbon fuels will decrease. They also fear that the oil incomes have caused imbalances in several important sectors of Norwegian society. *Produktivitetskommisjonen* notes in its final report of 2016 that productivity growth had dropped alarmingly since 2005. Petroleum revenues had fed the growth of the service sector, where productivity remained low. The commission blames the resource-based economy for the low efficiency and completion rates in the Norwegian education system, and the low innovation level in the business sector. It concludes that the general level of education is the most important factor for productivity and predicts that future industries will increasingly be knowledge-based. Therefore, it is problematic that the number of masters and doctoral students in Norway are low, especially in the sciences. According to the commission, there is not a single world-class university in Norway, while its research system is 'subject to extensive political skewing towards broad social objectives'.[16]

The technologies associated with the fourth industrial revolution are seen as a solution to these problems. However, compared to Sweden and, particularly, Finland, Norwegian planners put relatively little emphasis on the need for becoming a technological leader and exporter of high-tech industrial products. Instead, they consider it of great importance that Norway is able to benefit from innovations originating elsewhere in order to raise productivity in its large service sector.[17] Focusing on use rather than invention of technology has, according to technology historian David Edgerton, made sense historically, since countries that have mainly copied innovations made elsewhere, such as Italy, have managed to achieve similar growth figures as centers of innovation, such as Britain.[18]

Although Swedish *Långtidsutredningen* discusses the future impact of nano-, bio-, and information technology, fields into which Sweden has invested heavily, the report envisions a relatively undramatic development. It foresees that the industrial restructuring that has been going on for decades will continue at the current pace. In addition, the report considers Sweden well adapted for the challenges to come because of its high-functioning systems of higher and adult education. However, the comprehensive schools' ability to provide coming generations with basic skills is a concern.[19] The report also notices a significant difference in labor participation between native and foreign-born residents. Since the report concludes that the gap can be explained entirely by differences in education and skills, it recommends raising the educational level of immigrants.[20]

Referring to economic research on skill-biased technological change, *Långtidsutredningen* believes that with education the Swedish labor market can upgrade instead of polarize. This is already happening among women, and in order for men to follow, they might need to be educated in occupations traditionally filled by women.[21] *Digitaliseringskommissionen* predicted more disruption, quoting estimates that 35–53 percent of jobs will be lost to digitalization within two decades. Since digitalization is skill-biased, it benefits those with high education over those with low. Routine work would be replaced, causing a middle job squeeze, which will increase competition among manual workers. This can cause a rift between people with different educational levels, a development that society counteracts by, for example, life-long learning and a competence insurance that enables individuals to reeducate in the middle of their careers.[22]

Digitaliseringskommissionen's report also contains a radical vision of Sweden in 2030, written by the consultancy firm Exponential Holding AB. There, teachers are transformed into tutors, as students learn to search for relevant information online and collaborate digitally with peers across national borders. Teaching has become optimized as schools have improved their ability to collect and interpret data. By emphasizing interdisciplinary thinking and entrepreneurial skills in schools, humans are prepared for niches where they can still compete with computers in the labor market.[23]

Technology's role for raising productivity in the public sector receives little attention in Sweden. *Långtidsutredningen* discusses the public sector at length, but its suggestions for handling increasing stress on public welfare services are limited to redistribution of existing productive capacity through raised retirement age, raised taxes, or changed priorities between public commitments.[24]

It is in Finland that we find the most dramatic visions about technology-driven transformation of society and the most revolutionary ideas about education. The 2015 report *Finland – The Silicon Valley of Industrial Internet* claimed that Finland could follow one of three development paths. As 'the Silicon Valley of industrial internet', Finland would gain 48,000 jobs by 2023. However, this was only possible if the executive management and boards of companies as well as the public sector commit to this goal. This development path was described as the best possible future, where the industrial internet is the 'New Nokia'. If Finland did not achieve this but still managed to become an 'agile applier' of the industrial internet, 16,000 new jobs would be created by 2019. However, if Finland instead became a 'sluggish follower', 16,000 jobs would be lost by 2019.[25]

The report suggested 15 measures that would help Finland become the 'Silicon Valley of industrial internet'. They included improved adult education at different organizational levels, reformed university programs emphasizing phenomenon-based education and software skills, utilizing digital learning materials and online courses, learning from best practices between companies, and tax breaks for individuals seeking to educate themselves at their own initiative. In addition, it suggested that 5 percent of public procurements should be earmarked for innovative solutions. This would improve productivity in the public sector and support tech companies.[26] The report *Suomi osaamisen kasvu-uralle* claimed that since the labor force in Finland is not growing, it is vital to utilize digitalization and technology in the service sector in order to maintain social and health-care services.[27]

The emphasis on Finnish companies learning from each other, rather than competing against each other as in a liberal market model, is not surprising considering that Finland displays the highest degree of corporatist enterprise cooperation among the Nordic countries.[28]

In 2013/2014, the report *100 Opportunities for Finland and the World* launched a devastating attack on the present Finnish educational system. Among its drawbacks were inefficient centralization to physical school buildings, half a billion yearly trips to school, and internalization of the 'out-dated teaching content' of teachers. This led to an increasing deficit of know-how despite educational investments, which was mirrored throughout the economy. However, the report contained a vision of how technology could help alleviate these problems:

The lectures of the best experts are attended independently online, the exercises are performed on the computer or with the help of remote controllable robots and simulators, and the instructor supervises the performance and directs it, if required. Gaming is applied to teaching. Discussions and peer learning take place in shared projects online or by meeting in person. Virtual glasses and remote controlled robots are used in on-the-job learning. The robots give examples of the work to be performed, and with their help the instructor can supervise and guide the learner without being physically present. Know-how is proven and evaluated independently from the teaching, and in rapidly changing areas the proof of know-how is temporary.[29]

Unfortunately, '[p]olitical decision-making, interests of trade unions, and habitual values and reverences' slowed down necessary change.[30]

A follow-up report in 2018 reiterated that one of the greatest threats against a future-oriented learning process was the teaching profession's aversion to change and lack of knowledge. The great power of the teachers and university professors and their organizations was slowing down change.[31]

The ferocity of the report reflects that it is taking on a formidable adversary, the strong Finnish teaching profession. Other reports support an alternative vision of the future of Finnish education, which values the competence of the nation's teachers and portrays it as an asset that Finland can market and sell internationally. So far, Finnish educational exports have focused on traditional teacher competencies rather than technology. However, also reports that show strong support for Finnish teachers stress the need for technological innovation. There, Finnish teachers are not described as reactionary but as 'generators of change'.[32]

Signs of problem have been visible in Finnish higher education for a while but have only recently been taken seriously in government reports. In 2015, a report from the Ministry of Education and culture mentioned that entry rates for tertiary education had declined from 77 percent to 63 percent from 2005 to 2012, making Finland drop from sixth to tenth place among OECD countries. This development was apparently not considered to be of pressing concern, since it was not addressed in the final recommendations of the report.[33]

In the Ministry of Education's Visio2030 report of 2017, the fact that the share of 25- to 34-year-olds with higher education (41 percent) had shrunk beyond the OECD average was indeed considered problematic, although the problem was attributed to slow throughput rather than low entry rates. Since Finland's public spending as a share of GDP for higher education is the highest among OECD countries, the system was described as inefficient. The report aimed to combine know-how with equality and efficiency, and claimed that small nations need to focus their resources on niches where they can be internationally competitive. By 2030, higher education should be available for all and at least 50 per-cent of 25- to 34-year-olds would have a higher education. The vision also embraced flexible and individual educational tracks and a renewal of education through digitalization.[34] The report did not attempt to resolve the apparent contradiction between an individualized, flexible, student-centered education and the perceived need for a national focus.

Planning education and adapting curricula

Educational planning in Sweden, Norway, and Finland highlights the need for the school system to adapt to technological development. The Finnish report *Uusi oppiminen* (2013) was ambivalent towards the country's success in the PISA tests.[35] It should not be a source of contentment but 'obliges us to develop teaching by investing in new environments and models for learning'. The success proved that Finland had high-quality teacher education, but it was still necessary to renew pedagogical practices and integrate technology in everyday education. Such a development could in time form the foundation of a significant educational export. Finland might educate the teachers and children of the world, the report claimed.[36]

The Swedish educational strategy (2017) for growth and equality claims that technology and digitalization will change society and the labor market. The school must adapt by acquiring technical infrastructure and raising the teachers' digital competence. For example, programming should become an ingredient of many subjects in comprehensive schools.[37]

The Norwegian *Fremtidens skole* claims that digital competencies are crucial for future innovation and technological development in the private and public sectors. Technological development and complex problem-solving demand creativity and inventiveness, which will be of great importance to Norway's economic development and competitiveness.[38]

The guidelines in recent national curricula on how to prepare students for the future labor market are strikingly similar. The current Finnish curriculum for the comprehensive school (2014) emphasize digital aids and competencies. The general part mentions seven competencies, of which 'digital competencies' are number five and 'work life competencies and entrepreneurship' number six. Innovation is mentioned as part of competency one, 'ability to think and learn'. In the subject-specific part of the curriculum, innovation is only mentioned in connection to traditional handicrafts, *sloyd*, where it occurs no less than seven times.[39] Apparently, proponents of *sloyd*, which disappeared from US schools in the early 1900s but still lives on in the Nordic countries, have embraced innovation in order to legitimize the subject's future existence. However, the Finnish comprehensive school curriculum is dominated by digitalization, which is mentioned in connection with all subjects except physical education, 162 times in total.

At the time of writing, the Swedish curricula for the comprehensive schools and upper secondary schools date from 2011. However, as of July 1, 2018, these curricula were revised to include digital competencies. The revisions concerned the general aims of education as well as the particular goals of individual subjects such as mathematics, history, languages, and technology. The word 'digital' was inserted 13 times in the general curriculum for the upper secondary school, seven in a single paragraph. This paragraph, which stresses the importance of entrepreneurship and innovation for the students' future in the labor market, was significantly expanded. While digitalization was not mentioned at all in the original paragraph, the revision made digitalization its main theme.[40] Thereby, the curricula clearly states that the key to future employment is digital competencies.

In Norway, a major revision of national curricula is currently pursued. The general goals of education were revised in 2017, but, unlike Sweden and Finland, none of them are directly related to the demands of the labor market. However, the core elements of each subject are developed by work groups, which should include persons having experience with digital tools, entrepreneurship, and innovation.[41] The new curricula were gradually introduced from August 2020.

Thus, in all three countries, students are expected to find future employment by mastering entrepreneurship, innovation, and, primarily, digitalization. The focus on digitalization in the late 2010s turned out to be timely, as the corona virus outbreak in 2020 led the three countries to temporarily replace traditional schooling with distance education.

Conclusions

The term 'the fourth industrial revolution' is found only in sources dating from after its breakthrough at the 2016 WEF. It was used by Norway's minister of finance in 2016 and in the Finnish Visio2030 report of 2017.[42] It is associated with a belief in an imminent radical shift in technological development, and this technology optimism is prominent also in earlier Finnish reports, especially *100 Opportunities for Finland and the World*. The Swedish *Långtidsutredningen*, which sees future development as a continuation of present trends at the current pace, does not use the concept but is instead referring to skill-biased technological change. Technology-pessimist circles also dominate the Norwegian *Produktivitetskommisjonen*. Optimists and pessimists alike are trying to predict the future, but with different research methods and narrative traditions. While the pessimists write in academic style and rely on mathematics and statistical extrapolation from current trends, the optimists write in management-literature style and produce lists of innovations that they claim are on the brink of causing a revolution. Although *100 Opportunities for Finland and the World* (2013/2014) is unusually long with a hundred items, it is similar to WEF's list of 23 technologies from 2016 or Citibank's six from 2015.[43] In Sweden, Stefan Fölster at the market-oriented think tank Reforminstitutet has written two technology optimist books that include lists of technologies.[44] *Digitaliseringskommissionen* partly based its assumption of 35–53 percent job loss in two decades on Fölster's research.[45] Although technology optimism is an international discourse with similar manifestations all over the world, Finland stands out in the degree of influence that optimists assert over government long-term planning.

This might be explained in part by the institutional framework of government planning. Traditionally, in all three Nordic countries public planning was done by government-appointed committees that published reports in official series.[46] This practice still exists in Sweden and Norway, while in Finland the committee report system was abandoned in 2002. The continuity is especially apparent in Sweden, where *Långtidsutredningen* (2015) is the twentieth report by that name since 1948. Such deep institutional roots lend a historical perspective to forecasting, which might contribute to a more gradual image of future development. In Finland, since no central committee report series exist, smaller reports are written by ministries, or, as *100 Opportunities for Finland and the World*, by the Committee for the Future, appointed directly by parliament. The rupture with the traditional committee system might have made it easier for new groups to assert influence over the planning process.

A decade of economic recession in Finland has made successive governments suggest a number of reforms intended to improve Finland's economic competitiveness. However, they have met strong resistance from certain professions, civil servants, the academic community, and labor unions. Traditionally, these groups were represented in the committees responsible for long-term planning. By circumventing broad interest groups and putting planning in the hands of a small group of technology optimists, hopes are that a faster planning process not bogged down by vested interests can be achieved. However, the inclusion of interest groups in committees meant that when a report was finally published they were more likely to support the proposed reforms, since they had been able to influence them. Today, the most extreme technology optimist visions of the Finnish school are destined to meet fierce resistance from the teaching profession.

In Norway, technological development is seen as a way to counteract structural problems caused by the resource-based economy. Hopes are tied to raising productivity in the service sector, which has swelled due to petroleum revenues. Thus, Norway put more emphasis on adapting and utilizing technology than on developing and selling it. Use of technology in the public sector is discussed in Finland, but as a means of stimulating tech companies or overcoming labor shortages, while the idea is not discussed at all in Swedish reports.

The main focus in Sweden and Finland is on developing and exporting high-tech products. All three countries encourage the use of technology in education, modes of learning that stimulate creativity and adaptability, as well as life-long learning. These ideas are not new and have circulated for at least half a century.

However, there are also important differences between the countries' description of educational challenges. While Norway fears that its system of higher education lacks international competitiveness, Swedish reports are content with the system of higher education but are concerned with the basic skills of non-graduates, which have been highlighted by poor results in international comparisons. The erosion of basic skills is perceived as a threat to the positive economic development that Sweden has experienced for decades. Finland's comprehensive school system is renowned for a good and egalitarian distribution of skills, but since Finland, in spite of its well-functioning traditional education system, has experienced a long recession, good basic skills cannot be prescribed as a recipe for future success. This has opened the field for visions about a high-tech revolution of the Finnish educational system, where no educational traditions or institutions are taken for granted. Perhaps it is not surprising that hopes of a future revolutionary transformation are highest in societies where current economic development is least satisfactory. The problems in Finland's system of higher education have only recently caught the attention of government reports.

While technological change is mainly seen as an opportunity in Finland and Norway, in Sweden the threat of skill-biased technological change is discussed more thoroughly. However, it is believed that Sweden can avoid skill-biased polarization and instead achieve upgrading, for example by raising the educational level of immigrants and reeducating males for traditionally female work.

The school system has been described as modeled on the factory of the first industrial revolution: a mass production facility for uniform knowledge transmission. In theory, a school modeled on the tailor-made manufacturing of the fourth industrial revolution should be able to achieve the individualized learning that has been long dreamt of among educationalists. However, although such a fundamental transformation of the school organization is envisioned by some long-term future forecasts, especially in Finland, it is absent from direct educational planning. Recent curricula are focused on transmitting digital competencies through the old educational structure rather than on using digitalization to reform it.

Notes

1 Crouzet 1996, 45.
2 OECD 2013, 51.
3 Brynjolfsson, Rock & Syversson 2017, 33.
4 Streeck 2016, 35 f.
5 Autor, Katz & Kearney 2006, 2008.
6 Acemoglu 2015.
7 Goldin & Katz 2008, 119–121.
8 Ibid., 87.
9 Goos, Manning & Salomons 2009, 61.
10 Federal Ministry of Economic Affairs and Energy homepage, 'Industrie 4.0'.
11 Schwab 2017, WEF Homepage, 'The fourth industrial revolution: what it means and how to respond'.
12 WEF Homepage, 'Ways to close the inequality gap in the fourth industrial revolution'.
13 Peters 2017, 4f.
14 Frey & Osborne 2015, 90f.
15 Brynjolfsson & McAfee 2016 (2014), 208–214.
16 NOU 2016:3, 6.
17 Jensen 2016, NOU 2015:1, 9, *Nasjonal kompetansepolitisk strategi 2017–2021*, 2017, 12, NOU 2016:3, 6.
18 Edgerton 2008 (2006).
19 SOU 2015:104, 85, 195, 201f, 213f, 312f.
20 Ibid., 201f.
21 Ibid., 174–184, 236f.
22 SOU 2016:89, 104–107.
23 Ibid., 171–175.

254   *Janne Holmén*

24 SOU 2015:104, 295–298.
25 The 'agile applier' is described as an 'agile developer' in the figure on page 20 in the English version of the report. However, in the Finnish original *ketterä soveltaja* is used in both places, and it is best translated as agile applier. Ailisto, Mäntylä & Seppälä (eds.) 2015, 20f.
26 Ailisto, Mäntylä & Seppälä (eds.) 2015, 26–30.
27 Opetus ja kulttuuriministeriö 2015:14, 12f.
28 Martin & Thelen 2007, 13.
29 Linturi, Kuusi & Ahlqvist 2014, 28f.
30 Linturi, Kuusi & Ahlqvist 2013, 27f, 2014, 28f (Quote).
31 Linturi & Kuusi 2018, 150, 2019, 175.
32 *Uusi oppiminen* 2013, 3f, Raatikainen & Tarvainen 2013, quote on 87, Tiihonen & Hietanen (eds.), 2014, 7, *Koulutusvienti kartalle* 2015, 30, Opetus ja kulttuuriministeriö 2016, 7.
33 Opetus ja kulttuuriministeriö 2015:11, 9, 73.
34 Opetus ja kulttuuriministeriö 2017, 13ff, 19, 22.
35 The PISA test is an international student assessment conducted by the OECD.
36 *Uusi oppiminen*2013, 3f 'velvoittaa meitä kehittämään kouluopetusta investoimalla uusiin oppimisympäristöihin ja oppimismalleihin', 6.
37 SOU 2017:35, 96f.
38 NOU 2015:8, 26, 31.
39 Gflgu 2014, 21–23.
40 Gy11 2018, 3.
41 Utdanningsdirektoratet, Kjerneelementer.
42 Jensen 2016, Opetus ja kulttuuriministeriö 2017, 7.
43 Schwab 2017, Frey & Osborne 2015, 23–56.
44 Fölster 2016, Sanandaji & Fölster 2016, Reforminstitutet homepage.
45 SOU 2016:89, 104.
46 Statens offentliga utredningar (SOU) in Sweden, Norges offentlige utredninger (NOU) in Norway, and until 2002 Valtion komiteamietinnöt in Finland.

References

Acemoglu, Daron, 2015: "Localised and Biased Technologies: Atkinson and Stiglitz's New View, Induced Innovations, and Directed Technological Change" in *The Economic Journal*, 125:583, 443–463.
Ailisto, Heikki, Mäntylä, Martti & Seppälä, Timo (eds.) 2015: *Finland – The Silicon Valley of Industrial Internet*. Publications of the Government's analysis, Assessment and Research Activities, 10/2015.
Autor, David H., Katz, Lawrence F. & Kearney, Melissa, 2006: "The Polarization of the U.S. Labor Market" in *American Economic Review*, 96:2.
Autor, David H., Katz, Lawrence F. & Kearney, Melissa, 2008: "Trends in U.S. Wage Inequality: Revising the Revisionists" in *The Review of Economics and Statistics*, 90:2.
Brynjolfsson, Erik & McAfee, Andrew, 2016 (2014): *The Second Machine Age. Work, Progress, and Prosperity in a Time of Brilliant Technologies*. New York: Norton.
Brynjolfsson, Erik, Rock, Daniel & Syversson, Chad, 2017: *Artificial Intelligence and the Modern Productivity Paradox: A Clash of Expectations and Statistics*. The National Bureau of Economic Research, Working Paper No. 24001. www.nber.org/papers/w24001 [Accessed 30 November 2018].
Crouzet, Francois, 1996: "France" in Mikuláš Teich & Roy Porter (eds.) *The Industrial Revolution in National Context: Europe and the USA*. Cambridge: Cambridge University Press, 36–63.

Edgerton, David, 2008 (2006): *The Shock of the Old. Technology and Global History Since 1900.* London: Profile Books.

Federal Ministry of Economic Affairs and Energy Homepage, 2018: *Industrie 4.0.* www. bmwi.de/Redaktion/EN/Dossier/industrie-40.html [Accessed 30 November 2018].

Fölster, Stefan, 2016: *Robotrevolutionen. Sverige i den nya maskinåldern.* Johanneshov: MTM.

Frey, Carl Benedikt & Osborne, Michael, 2015: *Technology at Work: The Future of Innovation and Employment.* Oxford: Citigroup/Oxford Martin School. www.oxfordmartin.ox.ac. uk/downloads/reports/Citi_GPS_Technology_Work.pdf [Accessed 30 November 2018].

Gflgu, 2014: "Grunderna för läroplanen för den grundläggande utbildningen 2014" in *Utbildningsstyrelsen.* www.oph.fi/lp2016/grunderna_for_laroplanen [Accessed 15 January 2018].

Goldin, Claudia & Katz, Lawrence F., 2008: *The Race between Education and Technology.* Cambridge, MA: Harvard University Press.

Goos, Marten, Mannings, Alan & Salomons, Anna, 2009: "Job Polarization in Europe" in *The American Economic Review,* 99:2, 58–63.

Gy11 (with revisions 2018): *Läroplan – Gymnasieskolan.* www.skolverket.se/polopoly_ fs/1.261821!/lgy11.pdf [Accessed 11 January 2018].

Jensen, Siv, 2016: "Den fjerde industrielle revolusjon – muligheter til å bedre ressursut-nyttelsen" in *Innlegg på IKT-Norges konferanse,* 12 April 2016. www.regjeringen.no/no/ aktuelt/den-fjerde-industrielle-revolusjon – muligheter-til-a-bedre-ressursutnyttelsen/ id2483283/ [Accessed 30 November 2018].

Koulutusvienti kartalle, 2015: Koulutusviennin asiantuntijaryhmän raportti Eduskunnan tule-vaisuusvaliokunnan vienninedistämismatkalta Latinalaiseen Amerikkaan 11.-19 Octo-ber 2015, Eduskunnan tulevaisuusvaliokunnan julkaisu 3/2016.

Linturi, Risto & Kuusi, Osmo, 2018: *Suomen sata uutta mahdollisuutta 2018–2037. Yhteiskun-nan toimintamallit uudistava radikaali teknologia.* Eduskunnan tulevaisuusvaliokunnan julkaisu 1/2018.

Linturi, Risto & Kuusi, Osmo, 2019: *Societal Transformation 2018–2037. 100 Anticipated Rad-ical Technologies, 20 Regimes, Case Finland.* Eduskunnan tulevaisuusvaliokunnan julkaisu 10/2018.

Linturi, Risto, Kuusi, Osmo & Ahlqvist, Toni, 2013: *Suomen sata uutta mahdollisuutta. Radi-kaalit teknologiset ratkaisut.* Eduskunnan tulevaisuusvaliokunnan julkaisu 6/2013.

Linturi, Risto, Kuusi, Osmo & Ahlqvist, Toni, 2014: *100 Opportunities for Finland and the World. Radical Technology Inquirer (RTI) for Anticipation/ Evaluation of Technological Break-throughs.* Publication of the Committee for the Future 11/2014.

Martin, Cathie Jo & Thelen, Kathleen, 2007: "The State and Coordinated Capitalism: Con-tributions of the Public Sector to Social Solidarity in Postindustrial Societies" in *World Politics,* 60:1, 1–36.

Nasjonal kompetansepolitisk strategi 2017–2021, 2017: www.regjeringen.no/no/dokumenter/ nks/id2527271/ [Accessed 30 November 2018].

NOU, 2015:1: *Produktivitet – grunnlag for vekst og velferd.* Produktivitetskommisjonens første rapport.

NOU, 2015:8: *Fremtidens skole. Fornyelse av fag og kompetanser.* Utredning fra et utvalg opp-nevnt ved kongelig resolusjon, 21 June 2013. Avgitt til Kunnskapsdepartementet, 15 June 2015.

NOU, 2016:3: *Ved et vendepunkt: Fra ressursøkonomi til kunnskapsøkonomi.* Produktivitetskom-misjonens andre rapport.

OECD, 2013: *OECD Skills Outlook 2013: First Results from the Survey of Adult Skills.* OECD Publishing. http://dx.doi.org/10.1787/9789264204256-en [Accessed 30 November 2018].

Opetus ja kulttuuriministeriö, 2015:11: *Towards a Future Proof System for Higher Education and Research in Finland*. Publications of the Ministry on Education and Culture, Finland.

Opetus ja kulttuuriministeriö, 2015:14: *Suomi osaamisen kasvu-uralle. Ehdotus tutkintotavoitteista 2020-luvulle*. Opetus- ja kulttuuriministeriön työryhmämuistioita ja selvityksiä.

Opetus ja kulttuuriministeriö, 2016: *Uusi peruskoulu – ohjelma. Oppijalähtöisyys, osaavat opettajat ja yhteisöllinen toimintakulttuuri*. http://minedu.fi/documents/1410845/4583171/Uusi+peruskoulu+-ohjelma+%289.9.2016%29 [Accessed 30 November 2018].

Opetus ja kulttuuriministeriö, 2017: *Korkeakoulutus ja tutkimus 2030-luvulle. Taustamuistio korkeakoulutuksen ja tutkimuksen 2030 visiotyölle*. http://minedu.fi/documents/1410845/4177242/visio2030-taustamuistio.pdf/b370e5ec-66d3-44cb-acb9-7ac4318c49c7 [Accessed 30 November 2018].

Peters, Michael A., 2017: "Technological Unemployment: Educating for the Fourth Industrial Revolution" in *Educational Philosophy and Theory*, 49:1, 1–6.

Raatikainen, Tiina & Tarvainen, Eliisa, 2013: "Kolutusvienti ja opettajan kansainväinen ura" in *Uusi oppiminen*. Eduskunnan tulevaisuusvaliokunnan julkaisu 8/2013.

Reforminstitutet Homepage. www.reforminstitutet.se/en/om-reforminstitutet/ [Accessed 23 November 2017].

Sanandaji, Nima & Fölster, Stefan, 2016: *Framtidens Jobb*. Stockholm: 8tto/Volante.

Schwab, Klaus, 2017: *The Fourth Industrial Revolution*. London: Portfolio Penguin.

SOU, 2015:104: *Långtidsutredningen 2015*. Stockholm: Huvudbetänkande.

SOU, 2016:89: *För digitalisering i tiden*. Stockholm: Slutbetänkande av digitaliseringskommissionen.

SOU, 2017:35: *Samling för skolan. Nationell strategi för kunskap och likvärdighet*. Stockholm: Slutbetänkande av 2015 års skolkommission.

Streeck, Wolfgang, 2016: *How will Capitalism End? Essays on a Failing System*. London: Verso.

Tiihonen, Paula & Hietanen Olli (eds.) 2014: *An Enabling State – Experimenting Finland*. Publication of the Committee for the Future, Finland 10/2014.

Utdanningsdirektoratet, Kjerneelementer. www.udir.no/laring-og-trivsel/lareplanverket/fagfornyelsen/kjerneelementgruppene/ [Accessed 11 January 2018].

Uusi oppiminen. Eduskunnan tulevaisuusvaliokunnan julkaisu 8/2013.

WEF Homepage. *The Fourth Industrial Revolution: What it Means and How to Respond*. www.weforum.org/agenda/2016/01/the-fourth-industrial-revolution-what-it-means-and-how-to-respond/ [Accessed 30 November 2018].

WEF Homepage. *Ways to Close the Inequality Gap in the Fourth Industrial Revolution*. www.weforum.org/agenda/2017/01/4-ways-to-close-the-inequality-gap-in-the-fourth-industrial-revolution [Accessed 30 November 2018].

Index

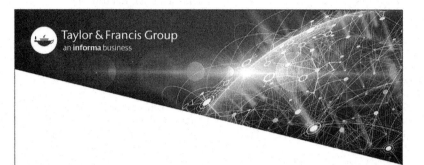